THE PENTATEUCH

THE ANCHOR BIBLE REFERENCE LIBRARY is designed to be a third major component of the Anchor Bible group, which includes the Anchor Bible commentaries on the books of the Old Testament, the New Testament, and the Apocrypha, and the Anchor Bible Dictionary. While the Anchor Bible commentaries and the Anchor Bible Dictionary are structurally defined by their subject matter, the Anchor Bible Reference Library will serve as a supplement on the cutting edge of the most recent scholarship. The new series will be open-ended; its scope and reach are nothing less than the biblical world in its totality, and its methods and techniques the most up-to-date available or devisable. Separate volumes will deal with one or more of the following topics relating to the Bible: anthropology, archaeology, ecology, economy, geography, history, languages and literatures, philosophy, religion(s), theology.

As with the Anchor Bible commentaries and the Anchor Bible Dictionary, the philosophy underlying the Anchor Bible Reference Library finds expression in the following: the approach is scholarly, the perspective is balanced and fair-minded, the methods are scientific, and the goal is to inform and enlighten. Contributors are chosen on the basis of their scholarly skills and achievements, and they come from a variety of religious backgrounds and communities. The books in the Anchor Bible Reference Library are intended for the broadest possible readership, ranging from world-class scholars, whose qualifications match those of the authors, to general readers, who may not have special training or skill in studying the Bible but are as enthusiastic as any dedicated professional in expanding their knowledge of the Bible and its world.

David Noel Freedman
GENERAL EDITOR

THE ANCHOR BIBLE REFERENCE LIBRARY

THE PENTATEUCH

AN INTRODUCTION TO THE FIRST FIVE BOOKS OF THE BIBLE

JOSEPH BLENKINSOPP

Doubleday

NEW YORK LONDON TORONTO SYDNEY AUCKLAND

The Anchor Bible Reference Library

Published by Doubleday
a division of Random House, Inc.
1540 Broadway, New York, New York 10036

The Anchor Bible Reference Library,
Doubleday, and the portrayal of an anchor
with the letters ABRL are trademarks of Doubleday,
a division of Random House, Inc.

Book design by Patrice Fodero

The Pentateuch was originally published
as an Anchor Bible Reference Library hardcover
by Doubleday in 1992.

Book design by Patrice Fodero

The Library of Congress has cataloged the 1992
Anchor Bible Reference Library hardcover edition as follows:

Blenkinsopp, Joseph
    The Pentateuch : an introduction to the first five books of the
Bible / by Joseph Blenkinsopp.
        p.   cm. — (The Anchor Bible reference library)
    Includes bibliographical references and index.
    1. Bible.   O.T.   Pentateuch—Introductions.   I. Title.
II. Series.
BS1225.2.B544   1992
222′.1061—dc20   91-22988
                                                          CIP

ISBN 0-385-49788-1
Copyright © 1992 by Joseph Blenkinsopp
All Rights Reserved
Printed in the United States of America
First Anchor Bible Reference Library paperback edition: February 2000.

10 9 8 7 6 5 4 3 2 1

CONTENTS

FOREWORD

The final decade of the century would seem to be a good time to assess what has been achieved in the study of the Pentateuch and to speculate on the direction research is likely to take in the future. For whatever reasons, perhaps only illusory ones, the final years of a century seem to mark the end of one phase and the beginning of something new. With respect to our topic, for example, the first critical introduction to the Old Testament, that of Johann Gottfried Eichhorn, appeared in 1783, and was followed shortly afterward by the epoch-making work of de Wette. Exactly a century later, in 1883, Wellhausen published his *Prolegomena,* which expounded the documentary hypothesis in its classical form, thus laying the foundations for another century of critical inquiry. Now, in the final decade of the twentieth century, the question facing us is whether that hypothesis can survive and, if so, in what form. While there is no dominating presence in the field of Hebrew Bible studies comparable to Wellhausen, the combined efforts of scholars in the seventies and eighties, especially in the German and English language areas, has given fresh impetus to the study of the Pentateuch which promises to set it on a new course. It is this uncertain, but in several respects promising, situation which I attempt to document in the following chapters.

We need to recall at the outset that the critical study of the Bible is one

aspect of the intellectual history of the modern world since the Enlightenment, and is therefore affected, as are other aspects, by currents of
thought, intellectual fashions, and assumptions, sometimes tacit, that make
up the contemporary *Zeitgeist.* With benefit of hindsight, we can now measure the extent to which eighteenth-century rationalism, nineteenth-century Romanticism, the Hegelian philosophy of history, and other major
trends predisposed our predecessors in the field to reach certain conclusions about the religious history of Israel and early Judaism and even
influenced the exegesis of specific texts. The cultural and intellectual
forces bearing on the work of our contemporaries are rather less apparent,
but certainly no less real. What we do notice, however, is that a strong
reaction has set in against certain assumptions shared by almost all scholars who have worked on these texts previously, down to the last significant
phase in the middle decades of the century associated with the German
scholars Gerhard von Rad and Martin Noth. We are speaking of the tendency to accord a privileged status to origins and the earliest stages of
development, to concentrate exclusively on diachronic analysis and the
development of ideas, and therefore to put a premium on the identification and chronological ordering of sources. Many of our colleagues today
have become disillusioned with all of this, and are advocating alternative
approaches. In addition, and with specific reference to the Pentateuch, the
documentary construct itself has begun to show enough cracks and strains
to place its survival in doubt. We cannot yet speak of a paradigm shift,
since no convincing and comprehensive alternative is in sight, but at a
century's distance from Wellhausen we are clearly at an important turning
point in the study of the Pentateuch.

A major challenge, not just to the documentary hypothesis but to the
historical-critical method which generated it, derives from those biblical
scholars who have been influenced by new (or in some cases not so new)
theories of literary criticism. In literary theory the turning away from the
historical-critical approach dates back to the early decades of this century
with the emergence of what came to be known as the New Criticism.
Concentration on the text itself, without reference to the circumstances of
its production, its authorial intention, assuming this could be known, or
the information which might be extracted from it, also characterized the
formalist, structuralist, and deconstructionist schools of literary theory,
and their influence on the interpretation of both Old and New Testament
has been increasingly in evidence over the last several years. While results
to date have been rather less than overwhelming, we have had some interesting new readings of individual texts and have come to appreciate more
the purely literary and aesthetic qualities of the Hebrew Bible, and especially its narrative component.

We would have to add, however, that the new literary approach to biblical texts has some built-in limitations which make it impossible for us to speak of the emergence of a new paradigm. At the most obvious level, the fact that these are ancient texts from a very different time and culture, written according to quite different literary conventions, in a different language, and often heavily edited, cannot simply be set aside. The interpreter should not have to pretend that the text is a literary unity when there are fairly obvious indications to the contrary. Then again, there is much in the Hebrew Bible that resists this kind of synchronic, nonreferential reading; suffice it to think of the laws which are of such central and irreducible importance in the Pentateuch. A more general problem, however, is the following. While there will always be a sense in which biblical texts, like all texts, are "infinitely interpretable"—a phrase of Martin Buber's—emphasis on plurality of meanings can also mean that the essential point of reference is no longer in the text but in the individual interpreter—that, in other words, the text is subordinated to the self-understanding of the reader and the hermeneutical distance between text and reader has been abolished. The consequent privatization of meaning is particularly unfortunate when we are dealing with canonical texts which have come to play a sustaining role in communities of memory and faith.

For reasons both practical and theoretical, therefore, I assume in the present study that the diachronic and synchronic readings of biblical texts are both legitimate and both necessary. I have therefore paid attention to the formation of the Pentateuch, following the tradition of historical-critical inquiry since the late eighteenth century, while trying to emphasize its structure and internal organization and those of its major components and individual texts. The present study is not in any sense a commentary on the Pentateuch. Issues are raised and, where possible, solutions are presented with respect to some of the more important texts, but for further elucidation the reader is referred to the commentaries and other works listed in the notes and bibliography.

To avoid any possible misunderstanding at the outset, I should add that this is in no sense a theology of the Pentateuch, always assuming that the Pentateuch is an entity capable of generating a theology. It is unfortunate that during the heyday of historical-critical study, throughout the nineteenth and the early twentieth centuries, theological interpretation lagged behind the critical analysis of texts, and the gap appears to have widened with the collapse of the Biblical Theology Movement following World War II and the rise to greater prominence of conservative theological opinion hostile to the historical-critical reading of biblical texts. I can only state my conviction that historical-critical and literary study is not only consistent with theological meanings but a necessary preliminary for elaborating a truly contemporary theology, Christian or Jewish, which accords to these texts a privileged status of some kind. The present volume limits

THE PENTATEUCH

CHAPTER 1

Two Centuries of Pentateuchal

Scholarship

The Beginnings of Critical Inquiry

The view long traditional in both Judaism and Christianity is that Moses authored the entire Pentateuch. Here and there in the Pentateuch Moses is said to have written certain things, including laws (Ex 24:4) and the vow to extirpate the Amalekites (Ex 17:14), but nowhere is it affirmed that the Pentateuch was authored by Moses, or indeed by anyone else. One would therefore think that what calls for an explanation is not why most people stopped believing in the dogma of Mosaic authorship, but rather why anyone believed it in the first place. One explanation is to be found in the concern for authorship and book production that first emerged in late antiquity. The Wisdom of Ben Sira (Ecclesiasticus), written in the early second century B.C., is the first Jewish book in anything like the modern sense of the term that has come down to us, and one in which the author for the first time identifies himself (Sir 50:29). From about the same time polemical requirements led Jewish apologists to compare Moses favorably, as lawgiver and compiler of the national epos, with his Greek counterparts. The same point is made forcibly and tendentiously by Josephus where he names Moses as author of five books containing the laws and

1

traditional history (*Apion* 1:37–40). Given the frequent occurrence in the Pentateuch of such phrases as "the book of the law of Moses," the attribution to Moses of the laws, and eventually of the narrative in which the laws are embedded, is understandable. And where Mosaic authorship continues to be maintained, the belief that inspiration must be channeled through specific named individuals has certainly played a part.

The close association between Moses and the law, first clearly and consistently attested in Deuteronomy and commonplace during the Second Temple period, goes far to explain how the entire work came to be attributed to him. Just as it became standard procedure to assign sapiential compositions (Proverbs, Ecclesiastes, Song of Songs) to Solomon and liturgical hymns to David, so laws, wherever and whenever enacted and promulgated, came to be attributed to Moses and endowed with the authority of his name. In this respect the Pentateuch as a whole, and Deuteronomy in particular, are among the earliest examples of Jewish pseudepigraphy, a genre abundantly attested from the last two centuries before the Common Era.

If it seems clear to the critical reader today that the thesis of Mosaic authorship cannot survive even a cursory reading of the Pentateuch, this was certainly not always the case. When in the twelfth century the Spanish scholar Abraham Ibn Ezra chose, in his commentary on Deuteronomy, to voice his misgivings, he felt obliged to do so in a kind of code:

> Beyond Jordan . . . if so be you understand the mystery of the twelve . . . moreover Moses wrote the law . . . the Canaanite was then in the land . . . it shall be revealed on the mountain of God . . . then also behold his bed, his iron bed . . . then you shall know the truth.

One scholar who had no difficulty cracking the code was Spinoza who, in the eighth chapter of his *Tractatus Theologico-politicus,* published in 1670, listed the biblical verses alluded to, verses which according to Ibn Ezra may not have been written by Moses. (The passages in question are Deut 1:1; 3:11; 27:1–8; 31:9; Gen 12:5; 22:14). To these Spinoza added arguments of his own, leading to the conclusion that "it is thus clearer than the sun at noonday that the Pentateuch was not written by Moses but by someone who lived long after Moses." A couple of decades earlier, in Chapter 33 of *Leviathan,* Thomas Hobbes had used a similar line of argument leading to the same conclusion: "It is therefore sufficiently evident that the five books of Moses were written after his time, though how long after it be not so manifest."

Both Hobbes and Spinoza were, at the time of writing, beyond the reach of official religious censure, but this was not the case with other critical inquirers into biblical matters. The French Oratorian priest Richard Simon, a contemporary of Spinoza and one of the pioneers in the critical study of the Pentateuch, discovered the need for prudence the hard way after publishing his *Histoire Critique du Vieux Testament* in 1678. Simon acknowledged the role of Moses in the production of the Pentateuch, merely adding the suggestion that the work owed its final form to scribes active up to the time of Ezra. The outcome, nevertheless, was that his book followed Spinoza's on the Roman Catholic Index, most of the 1,300 copies printed were destroyed, and he himself was, in effect, banished to a remote parish in Normandy, the French hierarchy's equivalent of Devil's Island. Some copies survived, however, and one was translated into German a century later by Johann Salomo Semler, and in that form contributed significantly to research on the formation of the Pentateuch that was then getting under way in German universities. The book was also translated into English, but was received no more favorably in England than it had been in France.

The occurrence in the Pentateuch of different divine names—Elohim and Yahweh (Jehovah in its older form)—was first exploited as a means of distinguishing between parallel sources in a book published in 1711 by Henning Bernhard Witter, pastor of the Lutheran church in Hildesheim. Far from making the bestseller lists, Witter's monograph went completely unnoticed and was rescued from oblivion only in 1925, by the French scholar Adolphe Lods. Witter avoided possible censure by speaking of sources used by Moses in compiling the Pentateuch. Independently of Witter, as it seems, Jean Astruc, physician at the court of Louis XV and an amateur Old Testament scholar, published in Brussels in 1753 a study in which he singled out in Genesis an Elohistic and Jehovistic source, together with other material independent of both of these. These sources he designated simply A, B, and C. Astruc was not interested in challenging the dogma of Mosaic authorship. On the contrary, his aim was to defend it against those who, like Spinoza, rejected it out of hand. What he proposed was the rather odd idea that Moses had arranged these early sources synoptically, rather like a synopsis of the gospels, but that the pages got mixed up in the course of transmission. This theory of distinct and parallel sources—or *mémoires,* as Astruc called them—was taken over, amplified, and fine-tuned by Johann Gottfried Eichhorn, professor at Göttingen University and author of the first critical Old Testament introduction (1780–83). Eichhorn also assigned an authorial role to Moses, at least with respect to Exodus-Deuteronomy, but did so in his own way. As a child of the Enlightenment, he argued that Moses began his career as an Egyptian savant and only subsequently went on to found the Israelite nation. Later, however, after de Wette published his famous treatise on Deuteronomy, Eichhorn abandoned the idea of Mosaic authorship altogether.

It is important to bear in mind that the criterion of divine names was, from the beginning, quite limited in application. Initially it was applied only to Genesis and the first two chapters of Exodus—in other words, down to the point in the narrative at which the divine name YHWH was revealed to Moses (Ex 3:13–15, with a parallel version in Ex 6:2–3). It was thought that after this point there was no further need for the Elohist source to avoid using the name YHWH. Assuming a reasonable level of consistency in the narrative, and a desire to avoid anachronism on the part of the Elohist writer, this argument makes reasonably good sense. But it has since been pointed out by several critics of the theory that the incidence of divine names is not nearly as consistent as the hypothesis requires, that in particular the Garden of Eden story combines both in a single designation (YHWH Elohim), and that the alteration of names is patient of other explanations (Whybray 1987, 63–72). We shall have ample opportunity to confirm these misgivings in the course of our study.

During this first period of critical inquiry there were also those who, while rejecting the traditional belief, remained unconvinced by the arguments for parallel sources. One alternative was to suggest a plurality of quite disparate sources which, when eventually put together long after the time of Moses, eventuated in the Pentateuch. The first to propose this fragment hypothesis, as it came to be called, was the Scottish Roman Catholic priest Alexander Geddes (1737–1802). Geddes was one of the few British biblical scholars at that time who took the trouble to learn German and keep up with developments in German academic circles. Like Simon before him, he incurred ecclesiastical censure for his pains, in addition to widespread vituperation from conservative churchmen of other denominations. His work had little effect in Britain, but its most important conclusions were taken over by Johann Severin Vater, professor at the University of Halle from 1800, to be further developed, with important modifications, in the writings of Wilhelm de Wette during the first decade of the next century (Fuller 1984; Rogerson 1984, 154–57).

The Nineteenth Century from de Wette to Wellhausen

The situation at the beginning of the nineteenth century was, then, that practically all Old Testament scholars outside of the ecclesiastical mainstream rejected the idea that Moses had authored the Pentateuch in its entirety. Some were prepared to concede that he compiled laws, others that he may have left behind an account of Israel's vicissitudes in the wilderness. Perhaps, too, the bulk of Deuteronomy could be traced back to him—with the obvious exception of the last eight verses narrating his death and burial, which even the traditional Jewish opinion assigned to a later hand (b. BB 15a). But similar concessions could not be made with respect to the narrative of events preceding the age of Moses. Contradictions of fact, repetitions, parallelism in terminology and in the way specific events are narrated, notable differences in ethos and emphasis—all seemed to call for a quite different explanation. The more conservative solution was to assume that Moses had made use of sources to take the story back to creation. But increasingly the opinion prevailed that this part of the narrative resulted from a later combination of either a multiplicity of sources or two continuous narrative strands. Those convinced that the incidence of divine names provided the key to source division postulated an earlier Elohistic (E) source and a later Jehovistic (J) source, their chronological order dictated primarily by the tradition according to which the name YHWH was first revealed in the Mosaic age. In 1798 Karl David Ilgen refined this source division by distinguishing between an earlier Elohistic author and a later one. Ilgen had the idea that he was reconstructing the Jerusalem temple archives, which must have been destroyed or dispersed when the city was sacked by the Babylonians in 587 B.C. He was very likely correct about the existence of such archives, but it is unlikely that we shall ever know what they contained.

All agree that the work of Wilhelm Martin Leberecht de Wette (1780–1849) marks a decisively new phase in the investigation of the Pentateuch. De Wette demonstrated convincingly that the Books of Chronicles present a totally different picture of the religion of Israel under the monarchy from that of Samuel-Kings. More specifically, they assume that a complete legal system governing cultic matters (sacrifice, priests, Levites, etc.) had been established by Moses and was fully operational from the beginning of the monarchy, the point at which the history in Chronicles begins. Since this is not at all what we find in the earlier historical books, he concluded that the religious institutions as described in Chronicles must be a retrojection of the situation obtaining at the time of writing in the late Persian or early Hellenistic period. It therefore seemed reasonable to conclude that the legal material in the Pentateuch, or at least the ritual legislation, dates from a time after the monarchy had passed from the scene. De Wette went on to argue that the early narrative traditions in the Pentateuch, though of great religious value to the reader sensitive to their appeal, cannot be used as historical source material. They represent rather Israel's mythic view of its origins, its place in the world, and its destiny.

In his dissertation of 1805 de Wette identified the law book discovered in the temple during the reign of Josiah, last great king of Judah, with an early version of Deuteronomy. While he was not the first to notice correspondences between the legislation in Deuteronomy and the reform measures recorded as following on the discovery (2 Kings 22–23), he drew conclusions from this observation that set the study of the Pentateuch on a new course. Dating the Deuteronomic law book to the seventh century served as a pivotal point, since it permitted a distinction between earlier legislation and practice not in accord with it and later enactments that presupposed it. De Wette concluded that in its final form Deuteronomy was the most recent of the literary complexes in the Pentateuch. He rounded out the picture by postulating an early annalistic strand and a later theocratic one, both pre-Deuteronomic, which were eventually conflated and expanded by a prophetic source. These corresponded roughly to the J, P, and E of the classical documentary hypothesis, though eventually arranged in a different order (Kraus 1956, 160–75; Rogerson 1984, 28–49).

It is worth noting that Old Testament scholars were applying the same principles and methods of historical and source analysis to the Pentateuch as classical scholars were applying, already during de Wette's lifetime, to the Homeric poems. A decade before de Wette's dissertation appeared, Friedrich August Wolf published his *Prolegomena to Homer,* in which he sought to demonstrate the composite nature of the epics. Yet de Wette took a quite different approach to the reading of biblical texts from that of the rationalist critics of the late eighteenth and early nineteenth centuries. He never abandoned the idea that critical exegesis must be in the service of the Christian church and the Christian life. The primary concern must always be with the *religious* meaning of the texts, to grasp which historical-critical analysis was indispensable. They must therefore be read with sympathy and a sense of connaturality born of the reader's own religious experience. In this respect de Wette reflected the influence of the intuitive approach to literature of Johann Gottfried Herder, whose *Vom Geist der Hebräischen Poesie* (*On the Spirit of Hebrew Poetry,* 1783) invited the reader to enter empathically into the spiritual and emotional world of the biblical authors. De Wette's contacts with Friedrich Schleiermacher, his colleague for a short time at the newly founded University of Berlin, strengthened this experiential and intuitive exegesis of texts.

De Wette's enthusiasm for the literary remains of early Israel was not matched by his attitude to the religion of post-exilic Judaism. The degenerative view of religious development throughout the biblical period, which would appear very clearly in Wellhausen's *Prolegomena* of 1883, is already detectable in Herder's characterization of post-exilic religion as pharisaical and slavishly legalistic. Along similar lines, de Wette spoke of Second Temple Judaism as a hybrid intellectual system lacking that essential quality of *Gefühl* (feeling, soul) which alone gives life. It was, he said, "ein Chaos welches eine neue Schöpfung erwartet" ("a chaos calling for a new creation").[1] His friend and colleague Schleiermacher went further by calling into question the link between the Old and New Testaments. A century later Adolf Harnack, in his study of the second century Gnostic Marcion, would make the same point more trenchantly: whatever may have been the theological exigencies and perceptions of the first or the sixteenth century, there was no longer any need for the Christian church to burden itself with the Jewish Scriptures.

Throughout the nineteenth century Old Testament scholars focused their energies on identifying, dating, and describing sources—either a limited number of continuous narratives or a much larger assemblage of smaller units. Much less attention was paid to the editorial process by means of which these sources were incorporated into one comprehensive narrative structure. Questions that may seem obvious to us were rarely asked: Why were contradictions and inconsistencies between one source and another not resolved in the editorial process? Why were earlier versions of events, re-narrated in later sources, not simply omitted? One way of avoiding the implication that the final editor did not know his business was to postulate a single narrative base or *Grundschrift* that was then expanded by a gradual process of supplementation. While some forms of the fragment hypothesis came close to this option, the deficiency was made good only with the appearance of Heinrich Ewald's *History of Israel* in the 1840s. Ewald, professor at the University of Göttingen until he was dismissed in 1867 for refusing to take the Prussian oath of loyalty, argued that an Elohist document which also contained the laws in Exodus 20–23 was filled out with excerpts from a Jehovistic source by an editor active during the late Judean monarchy. The final product was a narrative covering the first six books of the Bible (therefore a Hexateuch) that Ewald called "The Great Book of Origins." It reached its final form by a process of editorial amplification covering several centuries, a process that Ewald boldly laid out in great detail (Kraus 1956, 182–90).

A further step was taken a few years later by Hermann Hupfeld, professor successively at Marburg and Halle, in an important monograph on the sources of Genesis. Following the lead of Ilgen more than half a century earlier, Hupfeld distinguished between an earlier Elohist strand and a later one, with the important difference that the former corresponded to what subsequently became known as the Priestly source (P). Together with an even later Jehovistic document (J), these came to form the substance of Genesis as we have it. The final and decisive move toward the classical position of Wellhausen, with the sources in the chronological order JEDP, was made by Edouard Reuss of the University of Strasbourg. Reuss pointed out that the pre-exilic prophets betray no familiarity with the Mosaic legal system, and that the ritual law in particular, closely related as it is to Ezekiel, could not have originated earlier than the exilic period (6th century B.C.). Reuss presented these ideas in lectures as early as 1833 but did not publish them. It was left to his student and friend Karl Heinrich Graf to demonstrate by detailed argument some thirty years later that Hupfeld's first Elohist source, containing narrative and law of the

Priestly kind, was the latest rather than the earliest literary component of the Pentateuch (Kraus 1956, 222–29). The same conclusion was reached independently by the Dutch scholar Abraham Kuenen in a monograph on the history of Israel published in 1869. It was this discovery that provided the essential *point d'appui* for Wellhausen's historical reconstruction of the religion of Israel in the *Prolegomena* of 1883.

With benefit of hindsight, we can now see clearly the motivation for the enormous amount of energy expended during this entire period on the identification and dating of sources. Few of the scholars we have mentioned had any great interest in the purely literary and aesthetic aspects of the texts they submitted to such minute scrutiny. What inspired their work was rather the goal of reconstructing the historical development of religious ideas and institutions in Israel, and for this the placing of sources in chronological sequence was an essential preliminary. In any age, not excluding our own, it is difficult to see clearly and acknowledge the constraints and limitations—social, cultural, psychological—within which scholars go about their work. Old Testament scholarship is, after all, one facet of the intellectual history of the modern world and as such is influenced by the presuppositions, often tacit, of the age in which it is carried on. From our privileged perspective in time we can note, more clearly than those then active in the field, the extent to which this entire enterprise was dominated by the concept of development, and especially the development of ideas. We observe, for example, how ideas of cultural primitivism, prevalent in the Romantic movement of the late eighteenth and early nineteenth centuries, were brought to bear, by Herder and de Wette, among others, on the religion of early Israel as reflected in sources deemed to come from that time. More recent ethnological fieldwork, and theoretical studies based on it, have placed a large question mark against the alleged spontaneity and freedom from ritual constraints of so-called "primitive" societies, quite apart from the question of whether early Israel qualifies as such a society. Even Wellhausen, writing toward the end of the nineteenth century, shared this romantic view of early Israelite religion and lamented the process of *Denaturierung* (denaturing) that brought it to an end.

The historical development was construed differently, but no less subjectively, by those who fell under the allure of Hegel's philosophy. The influence of Hegel on nineteenth-century biblical scholarship has no doubt been exaggerated, but its impact was certainly felt. We see it clearly in such works as George's *The Older Jewish Festivals* (1835), preeminently in Vatke's *Biblical Theology* published in the same year, and residually in Wellhausen who tells us, on the first page of the *Prolegomena,* that he learned the most and the best from Vatke (Kraus 1956, 179–82; Perlitt 1965). One could, with a little goodwill, construe the pre-exilic period according to the Hegelian dialectic of a primitive nature religion and its antithesis in the ethical individuality of the prophets. But greater problems arise when we try to integrate post-exilic Judaism into the system as a stage in the progress of the Absolute Spirit toward its embodiment in the Christian reality. The failure of nineteenth-century scholarship to give a satisfactory account of post-exilic Judaism reveals more clearly than anything else, it seems to me, the artificial nature of the theories of development according to which the history of Israel was being construed.

The practice, common to much nineteenth-century scholarship, of extracting religious ideas from sources, and hypothetical sources at that, was also not free of difficulty. Constructing a "religion of Israel" on the basis of these ideas begs the question to what extent, if at all, the ideas of the writers and compilers corresponded to what people in ancient Israel were actually doing and thinking in the religious sphere. This problem is, of course, still with us. Even a tentative reconstruction of the religion of Israel in any given period requires that we take account of much more than the ideology of those individuals or collectivities—prophetic, Deuteronomic, priestly, Levitical, scribal, or whatever—to whom the texts are attributed. There is also the fact that the Old Testament itself is only a part of the literary output of ancient Israel—selected, arranged, and edited according to a very specific religious and ideological point of view.

In attempting to reconstruct the religious history of Israel, the scholars whose work we have been discussing had little to go on apart from the Old Testament texts themselves. The first archaeological excavations in Mesopotamia—those of Paul-Emile Botta at Khorsabad and Austen Henry Layard at Nimrud and Nineveh—took place in the 1840s, and Major Henry Creswicke Rawlinson took the first step in deciphering Akkadian cuneiform, with the help of the trilingual Bisitun inscription of Darius I, in 1849. But it was not until George Smith published his *Chaldean Account of Genesis* in 1876, based on the eleventh tablet of the Gilgamesh epic discovered at Nineveh, that these discoveries began to have an impact on Old Testament studies and on the public in general. Palestinian archaeology had an even later debut, the first more or less scientific exploration being that of the Egyptologist Sir Flinders Petrie at Tell Hesi in 1890. For most of the nineteenth century, therefore, Old Testament scholars had to work more or less exclusively with the biblical text without benefit of controls today considered essential.

JULIUS WELLHAUSEN

In the broad range of his interests and accomplishments, Julius Wellhausen (1844–1918) represents a kind of scholarship that is practically extinct today. In addition to his text-critical and philological works, he also wrote commentaries on the gospels and was one of the pioneers in pre-Islamic Arabic studies. But his principal achievement was to synthesize and refine the work of predecessors, from de Wette to Graf, in a historical sketch of the religious history of Israel which, in a certain sense, has dictated the agenda of Old Testament studies to the present day. While Wellhausen had very definite and very critical ideas about religious phenomena which he took no trouble to disguise, it is important to note that he wrote as a historian, not as a theologian. An instinct of honesty not shared by all his contemporaries led him to resign his first appointment in the theological faculty of Greifswald when it became clear to him that he should not be training candidates for ecclesiastical ministry, and thereafter he pursued his scholarly career in other faculties at other universities—successively Halle, Marburg, and Göttingen.

In keeping with the revised Reuss-Graf-Kuenen dating, the basic premise of Wellhausen's historical reconstruction was that the Mosaic law stands at the beginning not of Israel but of Judaism. The source criticism on which this conclusion was based was laid out in impressive detail in articles published in 1876 and 1877 and republished in book form twelve years later under the title *Die Composition des Hexateuchs und der historischen Bücher des Alten Testaments (The Composition of the Hexateuch and the Historical Books of the Old Testament)*. The principal conclusions may be summarized as follows. The earliest sources J and E, not always clearly distinguishable on the basis of the respective divine names, were combined into a coherent narrative by a Jehovistic editor. A distinct source to which Wellhausen assigned the siglum Q (standing for *quattuor*, four, with reference to the four covenants Wellhausen claimed to find in the narrative from creation to Sinai) provided the basic chronological structure for the Priestly material that was fitted into it. In its final form this P material included the ritual law contained in the so-called Holiness Code (Leviticus 17–26) which itself was dependent on Ezekiel. P, therefore, forms the latest stage in the editorial history of the Pentateuch or Hexateuch, apart from some very late retouchings in the Deuteronomic style. Deuteronomy itself came into existence independently of the other sources. A first edition appeared in connection with the Josian reform in 622 B.C. and was subsequently expanded with narrative, homiletic, and legal material. Since the narrative in Deuteronomy betrays familiarity with JE but not with P, the book must have been combined with the earlier sources before it was combined with P. The correct sequence, therefore, is JEDP, and the end result was the publication of the Pentateuch in its final form at the time of Ezra in the fifth century B.C.

The motivation for this detailed source-critical work, no longer in such great favor today, is that it provided the essential basis for reconstructing the religious history of Israel. This was the task Wellhausen set himself in his *History of Israel,* the first of two projected volumes published in 1878, his *Prolegomena zur Geschichte Israels* of 1883 (translated into English in 1885 under the title *Prolegomena to the History of Ancient Israel*), and, covering much the same ground, the article "Israel" in the ninth edition of the *Encyclopaedia Britannica* (1881, 396–431). In the *Prolegomena* Wellhausen examined the principal religious institutions of Israel in their historical development, dealing successively with place of worship, sacrifice, festivals, priests and Levites, and the endowment of the clergy. Under each of these headings he claimed to find evidence for progressive institutional control eventuating in the comprehensive legal and ritual system of the post-exilic theocracy. These findings were then confirmed by a survey of the historical books including the narrative in the Hexateuch. From all of this Wellhausen concluded that the legal-ritual system attributed to Moses in the Pentateuch stands at the end rather than at the beginning of the historical process, and therefore constitutes the Magna Carta not of Israel but of post-exilic Judaism.

As closely argued and brilliantly original as it is, Wellhausen's historical reconstruction is very much a product of the intellectual milieu of the late nineteenth century. While certainly not Hegelian in its main lines (as is often claimed), it is dominated by the kind of generalization characteristic of the Hegelian philosophy of history. Ideas have an almost hypostatic character; witness, for example, his statement that "the idea as idea is older than the idea as history" (*Prolegomena,* 36). We also note the urge to explain the historical process by periodization, following a very common tendency in nineteenth-century Old Testament scholarship, no doubt influenced by Hegel, to tripartite organization (e.g., nature religion, propheticism, Judaism). In Wellhausen's work, then, JE corresponds to the period of nature religion, of worship arising spontaneously from the circumstances of daily life and of festivals firmly attached to the agrarian calendar. The Deuteronomic centralization of worship put an end to this spontaneity and at the same time sealed the fate of prophecy by its insistence on a written law:

> With the appearance of the law came to an end the old freedom, not only in the sphere of worship, now restricted to Jerusalem, but in the sphere of the religious spirit as well. There was now in existence an authority as objective as could be; and this was the end of prophecy (*Prolegomena,* p 402).

By the time of the Priestly Code the process of "denaturing" was complete, religion was dominated by the clerical caste which remade the past in its own image, thereby judaizing it, and Israel was transformed from a people to an ecclesiastical community.

While there can be no doubt about Wellhausen's aversion to Judaism and the prevalence of antisemitism in academic circles at that time, it becomes clear as we read to the end of the *Prolegomena* that his animus is directed more at the propensity of religious institutions in general to stifle the free and spontaneous expressions of the human spirit. For that reason the Christian church also comes in for censure in that, according to Well-hausen, it modeled itself on Judaism rather than on the teachings of Jesus. Wellhausen's Jesus proclaimed a "natural morality" (his term) and threw off the stranglehold of the legal-ritual system, but his teaching was betrayed by the Church in the same way that Judaism, while preserving the message of the great prophets, ended by neglecting it.

To the End of World War II

The four-source documentary hypothesis in the form proposed by Wellhausen quickly established itself as the critical orthodoxy and was reproduced, with considerable variations, in a great number of introductions to the Old Testament and monographic works. Dissenters were not lacking, but until recently dissent did not present a serious challenge, and a century after Wellhausen no alternative paradigm has as yet threatened to replace it. Following a predictable pattern, observable long before Well-hausen, opposition continued to come from conservative churchmen. In the mid-nineteenth century E. W. Hengstenberg, professor at the University of Berlin from 1828 to 1869, wielded considerable influence as the representative of conservative reaction to the new criticism and arbiter of academic politics. E. B. Pusey, holder of the Regius Professorship of Hebrew at Oxford for over half a century until his death in 1882, played a somewhat similar role in England. The conservative temper of most churchmen in the English-speaking world assured the proponents of the new ideas a less than enthusiastic reception. So, for example, John William Colenso, Bishop of Natal and author of a detailed analysis of the Pentateuch incorporating the latest German scholarship, was deposed from his bishopric in 1869. William Robertson Smith, noted Semiticist and the earliest champion of Wellhausen in the United Kingdom (he also translated most of the *Prolegomena*), was removed from his chair in Aberdeen in 1881. Notwithstanding these setbacks, the documentary hypothesis, in one form or another, obtained a firm foothold in academic circles in Britain and, to a lesser extent, in the United States also.

Given the prejudicial view of Judaism that seemed inseparable from it, the historical-critical study of the Pentateuch naturally won few recruits among Jewish scholars in the nineteenth century. It was also understandable that the scientific study of Judaism *(Wissenschaft des Judentums),* when it got under way in the early decades of that century, abandoned research on the Hebrew Bible to Christian scholars, concentrating instead on other aspects and epochs of Jewish history. The point was made forcibly, if with some exaggeration, in Solomon Schechter's characterization of the "higher criticism" as "the higher antisemitism." In the period with which we are concerned, however, several Jewish scholars took direct issue with the position of Wellhausen. Yehezhel Kaufmann and those who followed his lead attacked the dating of the sources, especially P, though without challenging the basic methods used by historical critics (Kaufmann 1960, 175–200; Hurwitz 1974). There were others, however—conspicuously Umberto Cassuto and Moshe Hirsch Segal—who rejected the hypothesis in toto (Cassuto 1961; Segal 1967). Only in the period after World War II, with the emergence of Jewish biblical scholarship in the United States and Israel, do we find any real convergence between Christian and Jewish scholarship on the Pentateuch and the Hebrew Bible in general.

With some few distinguished exceptions—including Richard Simon, Jean Astruc, and Alexander Geddes, mentioned earlier—Roman Catholic scholarship had taken little part in the earlier phase of the historical-critical study of the Bible. The situation was not improved by the violent conservative reaction to the Modernist Movement during the pontificate of Pius X in the first decade of the twentieth century, a reaction also directed against critical biblical scholarship in general.[2] A decree of the Biblical Commission of 1906 reaffirmed the Mosaic authorship of the Pentateuch, though it conceded that Moses may have used sources and need not have committed everything to writing with his own hand. In the course of time more liberal counsels prevailed, but the net result was that Roman Catholic scholars entered the critical mainstream only in the period after World War II, at about the same time that Jewish biblical scholarship was beginning to make an impact. For the fundamentalist churches in the English-speaking world and elsewhere, Mosaic authorship has, of course, remained a basic article of faith.

Apart from widening the gap between the Church and the academy, rejection of the historical-critical method has had little effect in the long run. It neither promoted nor significantly hindered further inquiry into its implications. More detailed investigation of the criteria used to identify the four sources threatened, however, to subvert the documentary hypothesis from within. A more rigorous application of these criteria—lexicographical, stylistic, thematic—led several documentary critics to posit sources within the sources. With benefit of hindsight we see that this was not so surprising, since the Priestly source, the critical one for Wellhausen, had emerged from an originally undifferentiated Elohist source (E). The Yahwist source (J), by most documentarians considered the earliest, proved to be especially vulnerable to this kind of fragmentation. Rudolph Smend (1912) divided it into parallel strands named simply J^1 and J^2, and several others followed his lead, adding their own variations (e.g., Simpson 1948). Otto Eissfeldt identified a more primitive strand in J to which he assigned the siglum L for *Laienquelle* (lay source) (Eissfeldt 1966, 191–94). Along much the same lines Julius Morgenstern came up with a Kenite source (K), Robert Pfeiffer with an Edomite strand (S for Seir = Edom), and Georg Fohrer with a nomadic source (N), all identified as components of J.[3] Something of the same fate awaited E, always something of a ghostly *Doppelgänger* to J, which Otto Procksch (1906) divided into E^1 and E^2. There were also those who wanted to eliminate E altogether, notably Paul Volz and Wilhelm Rudolph (1933). Wellhausen himself had argued for a double redaction of Deuteronomy (D), and since then the composite nature of this book has been generally acknowledged. The Priestly source (P), finally, was found to contain at least two strands, designated by Gerhard von Rad P^a and P^b (von Rad 1934), and by others in different ways.

The problem inherent in these procedures is fairly obvious. If the demand for absolute consistency is pressed, the sources tend to collapse and disintegrate into a multiplicity of components or strands. While this demand has not always been pushed to its logical, not to say lunatic, limits, the possibility has always been present. At the beginning of the century we have the chastening experience of Bruno Baentsch, who identified seven Ps, each with a primary and sometimes a secondary redaction, necessitating a veritable alphabet soup of algebraic signs.[4] If, on the other hand, variations and inconsistencies are admitted within one and the same composition, a situation entirely normal in literary works ancient and modern, it would be a short step to questioning the need for distinct sources or documents identified by features peculiar to each. This need not happen, of course, but work on the sources since Wellhausen has shown that the hypothesis is more vulnerable than the documentarians of the nineteenth century imagined.

During the latter part of the nineteenth century few Old Testament scholars evinced any great interest in the possibility of a comparative approach to the biblical texts. Wellhausen himself made no effort to exploit what was then available from the ancient Near East. This was not the case with Hermann Gunkel (1852–1932), whose commentary on Genesis, the first edition of which appeared in 1901, marked a new departure in a direction that was eventually to lead away from the reigning hypothesis. Gunkel did not question the existence of sources, but his interest lay rather in their prehistory, rooted, as he believed, in the nonliterate culture of Israel before the rise of the monarchy. Gunkel was much influenced by the History of Religions School, represented at that time preeminently by Max Müller, a movement which gave great importance to the comparative study of religious texts. He was also familiar with the pioneering work in genre studies of Eduard Norden (1898) and Ferdinand Brunetière (1890). By close attention to the literary and aesthetic features of the individual narrative units in Genesis, he believed it possible to establish their respective types, or *Gattungen,* and identify the social situations which generated them. A basic postulate was that these narratives reached their present form by a process of oral composition and oral transmission. The weight was therefore shifted from large-scale documents (J and E) to smaller units, from texts to traditions, and from individual authors to the anonymous products of a preliterate society.

Following the lead of the Danish folklorist Axel Olrik, Gunkel characterized the narrative material in Genesis as *saga.* Use of this term has given rise to much discussion and confusion since, strictly speaking, in English usage the term refers to medieval Icelandic prose narratives which may or may not have incorporated oral traditions. Olrik, however, whose much-quoted paper "Epic Laws of Folk Narrative" influenced the third edition of Gunkel's *Genesis* (1910), used the German term *Sage* in a quite general way to include myth, legend, and the like. In this respect he was simply following accepted usage in German. A century earlier the Grimm brothers had followed up their *Kinder- und Hausmärchen* (1812–15) with *Deutsche Sagen* (1816–18), a collection of stories which, unlike folk tales, were at least ostensibly related to historical individuals and events. Gunkel's use of the term for the Genesis narratives was therefore not as inappropriate as is generally thought, at least with respect to the stories about Abraham, Isaac, and Jacob.

One problem left unsolved by Gunkel is the rather fundamental one of how to determine the oral basis of a literary work. Gunkel operated partly by intuition and partly by making certain assumptions about the nature of early Israelite society. On this latter point he seems to have been misled by the analogy with European and especially Germanic antiquity. The social setting of the storyteller entertaining his audience around the fire on a winter night is perfectly fitting for the peasant culture of the Black Forest, but rather less so for early Israel. There is also the need to distinguish between narrative formed as a result of oral composition and transmission and a literary work incorporating oral traditions. The Kalevala epic of Finland is full of oral folklore material, yet it is a literary work composed by Elias Lönrot in the 1830s and 1840s. Failure to keep in mind this distinction has bedeviled discussion of oral tradition in the Old Testament context since Gunkel's time.

Gunkel did not challenge the documentarians, whose contributions he

acknowledged and made use of in his Genesis commentary, but the new
approaches introduced by him, known as form criticism *(Formgeschichte,*
literally "the history of forms") and the history of traditions *(Traditionsgeschichte)* were eventually to elicit questions which the documentarians
would find difficult to answer. His emphasis on oral tradition is reflected in
the work of Gerhard von Rad, one of the most prominent Old Testament
scholars of this century, whose essay "The Form-Critical Problem of the
Hexateuch" (1938) was to prove very influential. Starting from the conviction that the standard source criticism had reached a dead end, von Rad
proposed to begin with the final form of the Hexateuch (Genesis through
Joshua), which he regarded as a massively expanded version of an originally brief and simple credal statement. This "historical credo" is found in
its clearest and most pristine form in Deut 26:5–9, the liturgical form of
words pronounced by the Israelite farmer at the offering of the firstfruits
in the sanctuary. It is also reflected in similar texts in the Hexateuch (Deut
6:20–24; Josh 24:2–13) and, freely adapted, in certain psalms which re-
hearse the saving deeds wrought by YHWH on behalf of his people (Pss
78; 105; 135; 136). He noted that this "Hexateuch in a nutshell," as he
called it, deals with the entry of the ancestors into Egypt, the exodus and
occupation of the land, but says nothing about the giving of the law at
Sinai. He went on to argue that this omission can be explained only on the
supposition that Sinai belongs to an entirely separate stream of tradition.
This led to the conclusion that the exodus-occupation tradition originated
in the festival of Weeks (Shavuoth) at Gilgal during the time of the
Judges, while the Sinai tradition had its origins in the festival of
Tabernacles (Sukkoth) at Shechem in the Central Highlands. These distinct traditions, he concluded, came together for the first time in the work
of the Yahwist writer (J) during the time of the United Monarchy, and it
was the same writer who added the primeval history (Genesis 1–11) as a
preface to the story bounded by the promise to Abraham and the occupation of the land.

Von Rad therefore believed, with Gunkel, that the answers sought by
the source critics are to be found in the earliest period, before any of the
sources were put together. But unlike Gunkel he located the social origin
of the narrative in the amphictyonic cult of early Israel, and specifically in
the time-hallowed form of words accompanying certain acts of worship.
With the taking over of this "canonical" language by the Yahwist, cultic
recital was transformed into literature, the catalyst for the transformation
being what von Rad called "the Solomonic enlightenment." Von Rad acknowledged the contribution of the later sources, but the pattern laid
down by the controlling genius of the Yahwist remained essentially unaltered.

Von Rad was not the first to propose a cultic origin for the traditions of ancient Israel. Some years earlier the Norwegian scholar Sigmund Mowinckel had argued that the decalogue originated as part of a great New Year Festival in the period before the monarchy (Mowinckel 1927, 120–45), and another Scandinavian scholar, Johannes Pedersen, interpreted Exodus 1–15 as the deposit of cultic recital for Passover (Pedersen 1934). Along somewhat the same lines the German scholar Albrecht Alt argued that the apodictic laws, especially the "thou shalt not" type in which the deity addresses the community directly, must have originated in a cultic setting (Alt 1934). Narrative obviously can have a place in cult, but unfortunately none of these scholars felt it necessary to explain precisely how cult can generate narrative. It has also become apparent that von Rad's alluring hypothesis was based on some rather dubious assumptions. Most scholars would now agree that the style and wording of Deut 26:5–9 —the "wandering Aramean" passage—suggest a Deuteronomic composition rather than an ancient liturgical formulation. Not all have been persuaded by the thesis that the exodus-occupation and Sinai traditions developed from geographically and calendrically distinct liturgies, and the portrait of the Yahwist (J) as a product of the Solomonic *Aufklärung* remains very much in the realm of speculation.

Closely linked with the name of von Rad is that of Martin Noth, for whom the cult of the tribal federation in the pre-state period was also of decisive importance. Noth was primarily a historian, but his contribution to the study of the Pentateuch was scarcely less significant than that of von Rad. In his *Uberlieferungsgeschichtliche Studien* of 1943 (the first part of which has appeared in English under the title *The Deuteronomistic History;* see Noth 1981) he argued that Deuteronomy, with the exception of some parts of Chapters 31–34, was composed as an introduction to the Former Prophets, i.e., Joshua through 2 Kings. It is therefore to be distinguished from the first four books of the Bible containing the history of universal and Israelite origins. Five years later he published *Uberlieferungsgeschichte des Pentateuch* (trans., *A History of Pentateuchal Traditions,* Englewood Cliffs, N.J., 1972) which, in spite of the title, assumes a Tetrateuch rather than a Pentateuch. While his stated aim in this work was to give a comprehensive account of the formation of the Tetrateuch, much the greater part of the book deals with its prehistory before the emergence of the monarchy. It is also rather curious that neither von Rad, who worked with a Hexateuch, nor Noth, who worked with a Tetrateuch, thought it necessary to account for the fact that what we have is neither a Hexateuch nor a Tetrateuch but a Pentateuch.

As the title of his later work suggests, Noth set out to reconstruct the origin and development of the traditions which went into the making of the biblical narrative of Israelite origins. As he saw it, these traditions were generally limited in scope and tied to particular localities, generally sanctuaries. In the course of time they coalesced into five major themes identified as guidance out of Egypt, guidance into the arable land, promise to the ancestors, guidance in the wilderness, and the revelation at Sinai. They may have been written down at an early stage—Noth was uncertain but spoke of a *Grundschrift*—but in any case they represent a deposit of very early oral tradition. The social situation in which these traditions coalesced and achieved fixity was the tribal federation and its cult, a situation which Noth believed was analogous with that of the ancient Greek amphictyonies. At this point, therefore, we are fairly close to von Rad's "little credo" and his theory of cultic origins in general.

From what has been said so far, it will be seen that the main difference between the approach of these two scholars is that for Noth the essential content, themes, and sequence of the history were laid down before any of the documents was written. He even makes the remarkable claim that "the emergence of the total Pentateuch . . . is no longer of great importance traditio-historically. For what is involved here is a *purely literary work* [my emphasis], one that has contributed neither new tradition material nor substantive viewpoints to the reworking or interpretation of the materials."[5] In other words, he accepts the documents J, E, and P, which he attributes to individual authors; but with few exceptions—the addition of the early history of humanity by J, genealogical linkage by P—they added nothing essential to what was already there.

I pointed out a moment ago that Noth was primarily a historian, and it is fairly clear that the principal aim of his traditio-historical labors was to lay the foundation for a historical reconstruction of the earliest phase of Israelite history. Since form-critical and traditio-historical investigations offer the possibility of getting behind later editorial constructs, it is obvious that they have important implications for the historian. Suffice it to recall how the form-critical studies on the gospels of Dibelius and Bultmann, both at one time students of Gunkel, have influenced the study of the historical Jesus and of earliest Christianity. Noth's conclusions with respect to the historicity of Moses matched those of Bultmann with respect to Jesus. He argued that the only secure datum is the burial tradition located on the east bank of the Jordan, but omitted to explain how Moses came to play such a dominant role in the tradition as it developed toward its mature formulation in the Pentateuch.

Some of the methodological problems inherent in the approach of von Rad, Noth, and others who worked along similar lines have already been noted. There is the question how worship, which can certainly act as a vehicle for a narrative tradition, can also generate it. There is the problem of deciding whether a written text originated in oral tradition and, if so, how old that tradition is. Noth adopted the principle that the shorter the account the more likely it is to be ancient, but comparative studies have shown that this is by no means always the case. And even where it can be shown that oral material has been incorporated into a written work, what we have is still a literary work which merits study according to the canons of literary criticism. It would, finally, be astonishing if the historical experience of Israel over at least half a millennium made as little impression on the Pentateuchal narrative as Noth seemed to imply.

More radical theories of oral tradition, especially those advocated by Scandinavian scholars, have provoked even greater skepticism. Drawing on the work of the Uppsala scholars H. S. Nyberg and Harris Birkeland, Ivan Engnell argued for an alternative to the documentary hypothesis according to which the ancient traditions contained in the Pentateuch were transmitted orally down into the post-exilic period, at which time they were finally committed to writing in a comprehensive P-edited document (Engnell, 1960, 1969). The Pentateuch in its final form is certainly a product of the post-exilic period, but Engnell failed to demonstrate how the traditions in question could plausibly have been transmitted over a period of at least five or six centuries exclusively in oral form. The extensive literary corpus from Late Bronze Age Ugarit (Ras Shamra) demonstrates at least the possibility that substantial literary works could have been produced in the early period of Israelite history. In this respect, at least, the thesis of a verse epic underlying early Israelite prose narrative, proposed with the Ugaritic texts in mind by William Foxwell Albright and Frank Moore Cross, makes better sense.[6] The only question is whether the thematic and prosodic evidence supports this conclusion, on which point the verdict has been generally negative. In any case there is much in the Pentateuch that is not patient of this explanation, so that we are left with a literary work which at most incorporated and modified some segments of early epic material.

RECENT DEVELOPMENTS: THE DOCUMENTARY HYPOTHESIS IN CRISIS

Many of the scholars whose work we have been discussing remained active for several years after the end of World War II, when normal scholarly activity could be resumed. For at least two decades, in fact, it was more or less business as usual in Old Testament studies. Practically all introductions which appeared during those years continued to expound the documentary hypothesis as the consensus opinion and the received wisdom. Of these the most influential remains that of Otto Eissfeldt, the third edition of which, published in 1964, was practically identical with the original publication thirty years earlier. The same impression was given by the surveys that appeared from time to time—those of the British scholars H. H. Rowley (1950), C. R. North (1951), R. E. Clements (1979), and the

French scholar Henri Cazelles (1966, 1968). One notes in particular the pervasive influence of von Rad's portrait of the Yahwist as the great theologian of the early monarchy, especially in the context of the Biblical Theology Movement which flourished in the twenty years or so following the war, especially in the United States. Theologies of the individual sources began to appear, especially of J and P. (For reasons that should now be obvious, E had a much lower profile; as Cazelles wryly remarked, "ce malheureux élohiste n'a pas de chance"). Dissident voices were still heard—for example, Umberto Cassuto's *The Documentary Hypothesis,* first published in 1941, was translated into English and reprinted often in the postwar years—but they failed to disturb the general scholarly consensus.

A question which still needs to be asked is whether the history of traditions approach pioneered by Hermann Gunkel is in the last analysis reconcilable with the hypothesis of distinct documents. We have seen that von Rad and Noth worked with both traditions and documents, but it is significant that the latter, while accepting the existence of the documents, assigned a very minor role to them. Ivan Engnell, on the other hand, published his traditio-critical Introduction to the Old Testament in 1945 in which he denied the existence of pre-exilic sources altogether, retaining only a comprehensive post-exilic P work alongside the Deuteronomistic corpus. Other Scandinavian scholars (e.g., Nielsen, 1954) adopted similar positions, as we have seen. It would appear possible, theoretically, to trace the history of the tradition within each of the sources, but the problem would then be to reconcile the results with the individual blocks of traditional material, e.g., von Rad's exodus-occupation and Sinai traditions and Noth's five major themes.

Other problems arise in connection with the dating of the sources. In one prominent strand of English-language scholarship, especially in the United States, there seems to be a correlation between theologically conservative opinion and a predilection for higher dating. The trend is particularly in evidence in what has been called the Albright school, now in its third or even fourth generation. W. F. Albright himself held that the Pentateuch was substantially complete by 522 B.C. at the latest (Albright 1957, 345–47). David Noel Freedman, who studied with Albright, has opted more cautiously for the fifth or possibly the sixth century, the final stage being the separation of the narrative down to the death of Moses from the later epoch. The earliest sources, from the tenth to the eighth centuries B.C., were edited together during the reign of Hezekiah after the Assyrian conquest of the Northern Kingdom. Deuteronomy and the first edition of the Deuteronomic History (hereafter Dtr) were dated by him to the seventh century, and the Primary History resulted from the combination of JE, D, and Dtr. The P source, spanning the history from creation to the occupation of the land, was put together in the early exilic period and was incorporated into the Primary History no later than the mid-sixth century. Freedman is inclined to accept the traditional view, also favored by Wellhausen, that the Pentateuch achieved canonical status as a result of the activity of Ezra (Freedman 1962, 1963, 1987).

Attempts to establish the great antiquity of the religious traditions of Israel on nonliterary grounds also had implications for the dating of the sources in which they came to expression. This is especially the case with the covenant, the great antiquity of which, as idea and institution, was argued by George Mendenhall of the University of Michigan, using the analogy of Hittite suzerainty treaties dating from the fourteenth and thirteenth centuries B.C. (Mendenhall, 1955). A similar conclusion was reached, apparently independently, by Klaus Baltzer in his study of the covenant formulary in its historical development (Baltzer, 1971 [1964]). The Hittite treaty analogy enjoyed a considerable vogue for a while, but in recent years its weak points have been increasingly exposed. At the same time, a close analysis of passages dealing with the covenant relationship, and especially the Sinai pericope in Exodus 19–34, suggested a quite different conclusion, that the covenant in its mature theological formulation was a creation of the Deuteronomists, and therefore no earlier than the seventh century B.C. The issue continues to be debated (and will be examined in greater detail in Chapter 6), but it can at least be said that a very early date for passages in which the covenant idea is expressed can no longer be taken for granted.

The thesis of the Deuteronomic, and therefore late origin of the covenant idea, first presented systematically by the German scholar Lothar Perlitt (1969), raises serious issues for the dating of the sources. For if Perlitt is correct in arguing that the Sinai covenant pericope in Exodus 19–34 is essentially a Deuteronomic composition, rather than a narrative based on a combination of J and E, his thesis would pose a direct threat at one crucial point to the postulate of one or more continuous narrative sources from the early period of Israel's history. But quite apart from this debatable issue, the arguments for an early dating of J and E, and especially for dating J to the first century of the Israelite monarchy, have never been particularly effective over the entire span of the narrative. Eissfeldt's appeal to "enthusiastic acceptance of agricultural life and national-political power and cultus" as a characteristic of this early J source (*The Old Testament. An Introduction*, 200) may apply to *some* passages, but is wide of the mark if referred to Genesis 1–11, which speaks of the curse on the soil, exile, and the vanity of human pretensions in general. These and other features of this first narrative section have continued to provoke questions about the accepted dating. As early as 1939 Julius Morgenstern, impressed by the universalistic perspective of the J matter in Genesis 1–11, proposed a post-exilic date, though he did not trouble to argue the point in detail (Morgenstern 1939, 93). In a study of Genesis 2–3 published in 1962 the Spanish scholar Luis Alonso-Schökel drew attention to the use of mythological and sapiential language of a kind paralleled in later books of the Old Testament. When taken with the total absence of allusion to the Garden of Eden story in pre-exilic texts, these features suggested to him the conclusion that a later, post-prophetic date would be more appropriate (Alonso-Schökel 1962, 315). Similar lexicographical and thematic arguments for a late date for Genesis 2–3 were compiled by George Mendenhall (1974), but it was left to the Canadian scholar Frederick V. Winnett, in his presidential address to the Society of Biblical Literature (Winnett 1965, 1–19), to work out more thoroughly the hypothesis of a post-exilic J throughout Genesis. He proposed, however, that this late source was based on an earlier J supplemented by E and then incorporated into the final Priestly redaction at the end of the fifth century B.C.[7]

Winnett's views were further developed by Norman E. Wagner, one of his students, who also rejected the idea basic to classical theory that the successive narrative blocks of the Pentateuch had been arranged in a continuous narrative from early times. What he proposed was a vertical rather than horizontal division of the narrative material. The early history of humanity, the stories about the ancestors, the exodus narrative, and the rest each underwent an independent process of formation up to the point in the post-exilic period when a Judean, Yahwistic compiler provided the editorial linkage. Wagner illustrated the problem being addressed by pointing out that while the E stratum of the Joseph story points to an origin in the north of the country, the material attributed to E in the Abraham and Isaac narratives is located in the region of Beersheba in the Negev (Wagner 1967). Proceeding along much the same lines, another student of Winnett's, John Van Seters, reads the Abraham story as a response to the exilic situation, thus enabling him to align the promises to the ancestors with the optimistic message of Second Isaiah. Van Seters understands his exilic J to be an author rather than a deposit of oral tradition. In general agreement with T. L. Thompson, whose 1974 study *The Historicity of the Patriarchal Narratives* set out to refute the widely accepted second-millennium setting for the Abraham cycle, Van Seters takes Abraham to be a fictional creation in the service of theology, rather like the biblical Job. But in spite of these major innovations, he continues to endorse the kind of literary and source criticism employed by the documentarians.[8]

We mention here in passing a rather different attempt to outflank the documentarians, that of the Jewish scholar Samuel Sandmel (Sandmel 1961, 105–22). His proposal was that the Pentateuch reached its present form by a process of accretion and the application of procedures of a kind attested in the haggadic midrash. Old stories were continually retold from the perspective of a later time and thus, as he put it, were neutralized by addition rather than simply expunged. Thus the threefold narrative of the endangered ancestress (Genesis 12, 20, and 26) and the twofold account of Hagar and her son (Genesis 16 and 21) can be explained by the tendency of the biblical authors to modify and embellish without having to assign them to different sources. Sandmel is doubtless correct in supposing that there are literary procedures in the Bible analogous to midrash, but, as Whybray has pointed out, the Hebrew Bible taken as a whole is not comparable with commentary on it, and the haggadic procedures cannot by themselves explain the planned structure of the Pentateuchal narrative as a whole (Whybray 1987, 222).

A more recent attempt to oust the Yahwist from his (or, if one follows Harold Bloom, her) niche at the court of Solomon or his son Rehoboam is that of Hans Heinrich Schmid, whose monograph *Der sogennante Jahwist* (1976) extended the investigation into the other books of the Pentateuch. Impressed by the extent to which passages attributed to J by the documentarians betray prophetic and Deuteronomic features (e.g., the call of Moses in Exodus 3–4, reminiscent of prophetic commissionings), Schmid argued that the first consecutive narrative of founding events was put together by members of the Deuteronomic circle. This was achieved, thought Schmid, by combining the existing larger units of tradition into a consecutive history held together thematically by the promise of land, nationhood, and blessing. As the title of his book *(The So-called Yahwist)* suggests, the J of the classical documentarians, now assimilated to the Deuteronomists (D), no longer exists as such. Schmid drew attention to the analogy between the formation of this large-scale work, dated to the seventh century B.C., and the creation of the Deuteronomistic History (Dtr) out of diverse source material. If he is right, and of course not all agree that he is, the entire history from creation to the fall of the Judean kingdom would essentially be a Deuteronomistic composition.

About the same time, another defector from the documentary hypothesis, the Heidelberg professor Rolf Rendtorff, was independently reaching similar conclusions. By the late sixties Rendtorff was convinced that the standard source criticism of the Pentateuch was incompatible with the traditio-historical method exemplified by the work of von Rad, his predecessor in the chair at Heidelberg (Rendtorff 1969). The problem with the work of von Rad and Noth as Rendtorff saw it was that their allegiance to Wellhausen prevented them from carrying their traditio-historical method to its logical conclusions. He argued that in proceeding from the smallest units to the larger complexes of tradition and thence to the final form of the work, there is no place for hypothetical literary sources, sources which in any cases are nowhere referred to in the biblical corpus itself. Rendtorff made his public break with the consensus in a paper read at the Edinburgh meeting of the International Society for Old Testament Studies in 1974 and published the following year (Rendtorff 1975). The detailed arguments were subsequently presented in his *Uberlieferungsgeschichte des Pentateuch (Tradition History of the Pentateuch)* and *Das Alte Testament: Eine Einführung* (1983, 166–74; trans., *The Old Testament: An Introduction,* 1986, 157–64).

Rendtorff's main contention, similar to a point made by Wagner, is that the larger units or building blocks of the Pentateuchal narrative attained their present form independently of each other and were combined editorially only at a late stage. There are therefore no continuous pre-exilic narrative sources corresponding to the J and E of the documentarians. Genesis 1–11 has a literary character quite different from that of Genesis 12–50 and has no intrinsic or necessary connection with it. The Moses exodus story likewise does not presuppose the stories of the ancestors, and the same can be said for the remaining narrative blocks. Editorial linkage was first effected by a D redactor, primarily by extending the promise of land, nationhood, and divine guidance and blessing to the entire corpus by means of strategically placed cross-references (e.g., Gen 50:24; Ex 33:1–3). Rendtorff also accepts a post-exilic Priestly editorial strand, but on a much reduced scale, and only as far as Ex 6:2–9, recording Moses' commission to speak to Israel in the name of YHWH.

Rendtorff has undoubtedly put together an interesting case, one which has already given rise to a considerable amount of debate and discussion.[9] The basic issue raised by him seems to focus on the relation between the more or less distinct themes of the narrative blocks (Genesis 1–11, Genesis 12–50, etc.) and the overall narrative logic of the Pentateuch or Hexateuch, oriented as it is to the emergence of Israel as a twelve-tribal entity. The question is, are the blocks as distinct and discrete as Rendtorff supposes? Does not the exodus story call for an explanation of the people of Israel's presence in Egypt, how they got there, and what they did when they left? The essential cohesion of the Pentateuchal story could also be established in ways other than by the promise theme—for example, by a comprehensive chronological grid or proleptic allusion to cultic sites (e.g., Shechem, Bethel, Beersheba) frequented by the Israelites after the settlement in the land. Other debatable issues may be briefly mentioned. (1) In view of the indications pointing to the incorporation of Deuteronomy into the P-edited narrative (discussed in Chapter 7), is not the Pentateuch in its final form a Priestly rather than a Deuteronomic work? (2) Can the passages cited by Rendtorff as linking the story of the ancestors with later events, generally no more than a verse or two, be shown to be both editorial and Deuteronomic? (3) Whatever may be said about Genesis—certainly different in character from the other four books—are the later narrative sections (exodus, wilderness, occupation of the land) so different from one another that they could not have formed a continuous narrative at a relatively early date, and at any rate earlier than Deuteronomy?[10]

SOME PROVISIONAL CONCLUSIONS

While it is still too early to assess adequately the long-term impact of these studies of the last two decades, they have at least produced a situation in which the documentary hypothesis, in the form proposed by Wellhausen, can no longer be taken for granted. It may be helpful to summarize the main areas of uncertainty in what can be no more than an interim report.

(1) There is no longer a consensus on the existence of identifiable, continuous narrative sources covering the entire range of the Pentateuch from the pre-exilic period. There was debate long before this most recent period on the precise extent of such sources, and specifically, on whether J and E continued beyond the occupation of the land. Questions had also been raised about a fair number of passages which seemed resistant to the usual procedures, e.g., the war of the nine kings in Genesis 14 and the dialogue between Abraham and YHWH over the fate of Sodom in Gen 18:22–33. The Joseph story presented a special problem since its literary character (generally identified as *Novelle*) is so clearly different from the preceding ancestral stories. There were those who, while content with an early date, rejected the standard JE source division and defended its substantial unity (Coats 1973; Donner 1976). Others accepted source division but dated the sources or strata to a later period (Redford 1970; H. - C. Schmitt 1980). Different again was the explanation of R. N. Whybray (1968), who read it as a sapiential composition from long after the time of Solomon, and that of A. Meinhold (1978), who aligned it with Esther as a diaspora *Novelle*. Since the Joseph story forms the narrative link between the ancestors and the sojourn in Egypt, the question of its date and provenance would inevitably have consequences for the development of the tradition and its literary expression.

(2) Criticism of the standard paradigm has taken aim at the J source, and it is difficult to see how the hypothesis could survive its displacement to a much later date, *a fortiori,* its complete elimination. On this issue the positions of John Van Seters and Hans Heinrich Schmid, while by no means generally accepted, have won some adherents. By way of example, we may mention the study of H. Vorländer (1978), who argued for an

exilic or early post-exilic Jehovistic work, principally on the basis of the almost complete absence in pre-exilic texts outside the Tetrateuch of allusion to the narrative content of J and E. He concluded that the Babylonian exile in the sixth century B.C. seems to provide the most plausible setting for the development of a genuine historiographical tradition and for the introduction of such mythic themes as are found in Genesis 1–11. Vorländer's work illustrates very well the problems inherent in establishing a plausible social and cultural setting for these ancient texts. Von Rad's "Solomonic enlightenment" seemed to be the right option at one time, but relatively few would endorse it today. The Babylonian exile is also arguable, but it remains only one of several possibilities.

(3)   The tendency to lower dating, strongly in evidence in recent writing, is not without its problems. To an uncomfortable extent it has to rely on an *argumentum e silentio* or, as Whybray put it, on the principle that what is not positively known to be early must be late (Whybray 1987, 108). It also puts those who deny the existence of early sources under obligation to fill the vacuum left in the pre-exilic period by their displacement, in other words, to provide an alternative account of the development of the tradition in either oral or written form or both. Few of the proponents of late dating have as yet addressed this issue.

(4)   Much less attention has been paid in recent years to the other documents postulated by the hypothesis. We have seen that E has long been problematic, and there is no longer much enthusiasm for retaining it. Deuteronomy stands apart, of course, but several of the authors surveyed have pursued clues to D editing in the first four books, a matter that will concern us at a later point. The old issue of the origin of Deuteronomy and the related question of its dating are still debated, and seem likely to be forever debatable. P has stood up best to scrutiny, because of its more distinctive vocabulary, style, and ideology. An origin in the Babylonian diaspora is still favored by most, though the followers of Yehezkel Kaufmann date it earlier and some others (e.g., Vink 1969) date it later. Debate continues as to whether P stands for a distinct narrative source or a stage in the redaction of an existing narrative corpus; and there are also different ways of explaining the relation of the P narrative to the extensive corpus of cultic and ritual legislation.

(5)   This brings us to the final point. The reader will have noticed that the discussion so far has focused almost exclusively on narrative. Over the last two centuries relatively little attention has been paid to the legal material, in spite of its preponderant bulk and importance. Pending a more thorough account of the development of the legal tradition in a later chapter, it will suffice at this point to say that the bracketing of laws with the early narrative sources, especially the so-called covenant law book (Exo-

dus 20–23) with E and the so-called ritual decalogue (Ex 34:11–26) with J, has never been successfully demonstrated. The entire issue of the relation between law and narrative still remains to be clarified.

So far we have been dealing with problems arising from within the confines of the historical-critical method, and therefore posed in their own terms by its practitioners. In recent years, however, the method itself has come under attack from literary critics applying their own experience in reading texts to a reading of the Hebrew Bible. This has led to a call for a new approach to reading biblical texts by those who deplore what Robert Alter refers to as the excavative techniques of critical biblical scholarship (Alter 1981, 13). It is certainly the case that very few of the scholars mentioned in this chapter showed much interest in or appreciation for the aesthetic aspects of the texts which they spent their lives studying. There were, of course, exceptions; one thinks of Bishop Robert Lowth's lectures *On the Sacred Poetry of the Hebrews* (1753), of Johann Gottfried Herder some years later, and of Hermann Gunkel in more recent times. It should also be said that the study of literary types or *Gattungen* has obvious affinities with genre study, an important aspect of literary criticism in the broadest sense, even though the motivation for biblical scholars was historical and sociological rather than literary. At any rate, the very few essays of a literary kind published in the late nineteenth and early twentieth centuries, essays like R. G. Moulton's *The Literary Study of the Bible* (1899), concentrated heavily on identifying and describing genres—epic, lyric, proverbial, and the like.

The emergence of the New Criticism, pioneered by I. A. Richards, William Empson, and others in the twenties and thirties, marked a decisive break with the historical, philological, and referential approach to literature dominant throughout the nineteenth and early twentieth centuries. The New Criticism operated on the assumption that the text is a closed system, and as such should be interpreted apart from either the historical or other realia to which it refers or the circumstances of its production and reception. In other words, the text has a life of its own independent of its origins and even of its author's intention, assuming it could be known. This approach, therefore, stood in direct antithesis to the emphasis on original meanings in historical-critical studies of biblical texts. Most of the more recent critical theories—Russian formalism, French structuralism, deconstructionism—share the same nonreferential, text-immanent approach while carrying their own ideological freight. Perhaps the only exception is Marxist literary theory, which somewhat ironically shares the same concern for historical and sociological situations generative of texts as biblical scholarship in the modern period (Eagleton 1976).

It was inevitable that sooner or later text-immanent methods would be practiced on biblical texts, and it is no surprise that their arrival coincided with a growing disillusionment with the "excavative" techniques documented in this chapter. This is not the place to review the considerable output of recent years, but it would be safe to say that the results to date have not been overwhelming. It is also no surprise that the best results have come from those professional literary critics with an informed interest in the Bible and a knowledge of Hebrew, conditions which of course reduce the pool considerably.[11] What has come to be known as "canonical criticism," represented preeminently by Brevard S. Childs of Yale University, has something in common with the New Criticism, though its concerns are theological rather than literary. The basic point seems to be that the appropriate object of theological reflection is the biblical text in its final form rather than hypothetically reconstructed earlier stages of formation (Childs 1979). This is not the place to evaluate this approach at the level of detail which it merits. The discussion of the canonical form of the Pentateuch in Chapter Two will reveal some overlap with Childs' position, but also a considerable amount of disagreement.

What should be affirmed at the present juncture is the need for coexistence between different interpretative systems with their quite different but not necessarily incompatible agendas. We need an edict of toleration to discourage the tendency of new theories to proscribe their predecessors. This might, for example, encourage us to recover the insights of the patristic writers or the great Jewish exegetes of the Middle Ages. It would leave us free to look for the aesthetic aspects of the "text in itself" without feeling obliged to condemn the quite different project of the historical-critical practitioner. It is simply false to affirm, as Northrop Frye does, that historical criticism is of a kind for which "disintegrating the text became an end in itself" (Frye 1982, xvii). It was not always done well, but its goal, access to the religious experience of Israel in the different stages of its development, was quite different from that of literary criticism in the broader sense. There are aspects of religious experience and levels of meaning in biblical texts accessible only by using a historical-critical approach to them. Returning finally to the Pentateuch, it is true that the documentary hypothesis has increasingly been shown to be flawed, and will survive, if at all, only in a greatly modified form, but that does not mean that we should ignore the results of the last two centuries of investigation. Our task is to find better ways of understanding how the Pentateuch came to be without writing off the real advances of our predecessors. This is the task we aim to pursue in the following chapters.

NOTES

1. W. M. L. de Wette, *Biblische Dogmatik Alten und Neuen Testaments* (Berlin, 1913, 3rd ed.), 139.

2. A lively account of this chapter of history is narrated by Gerald P. Fogarty, S. J., *American Catholic Biblical Scholarship. A History from the Early Republic to Vatican II* (New York, 1989).

3. J. Morgenstern, "The Oldest Document of the Hexateuch," *HUCA* 4(1927) 1–138; R. Pfeiffer, *Introduction to the Old Testament* (New York, 1948, 2nd ed.), 159–67; E. Sellin and G. Fohrer, *Introduction to the Old Testament* (Nashville & New York, 1968), 159–65.

4. Reference in C. North, "Pentateuchal Criticism," in H. H. Rowley (ed.), *The Old Testament and Modern Study. A Generation of Discovery and Research* (Oxford, 1951), 56.

5. M. Noth, *A History of Pentateuchal Traditions* (Englewood Cliffs, N.J., 1972), 248.

6. W. F. Albright, *From the Stone Age to Christianity* (Garden City, N.Y., 1957, 2nd ed.), 249–50; F. Moore Cross, Jr., *Canaanite Myth and Hebrew Epic. Essays in the History of the Religion of Israel* (Cambridge, Mass., 1973), ix.

7. Winnett had already proposed the view that the first full-scale narrative was no earlier than the sixth century B.C. in his *The Mosaic Tradition* (Toronto, 1949).

8. For Van Seters' more important publications on this subject, see the bibliography (262 ff.).

9. The issues raised by Schmid and Rendtorff are discussed by a panel of English-language scholars in *JSOT* 3 (1977), 2–60. German reactions include E. Zenger, "Wo steht die Pentateuchforschung heute?," *BZ* 24 (1980), 101–16 and A. H. J. Gunneweg, "Anmerkungen und Anfragen zur neueren Pentateuch-forschung," *ThRu* 50 (1985), 107–31. Gunneweg also criticizes the work of Hermann Vorländer and Swedish scholar Sven Tengström's *Die Hexateucherzählung: Eine literaturgeschichtliche Studie* (Lund, 1976), in which he argues for a continuous narrative *Grundschrift* from Genesis 12 to Joshua 24. One could also consult reviews of Rendtorff's monograph by F. Langlamet in *RB* 84 (1977), 609–22, E. Otto in *VuF* 22 (1977), 82–97, and W. McKane in *VT* 28 (1978), 371–82. Rendtorff's student Erhard Blum has extended the thesis of the independent formation of the main narrative blocks to the narrative cycles about individual ancestors, a view by no means original; see his *Die Composition der Vätergeschichte* (Neukirchen, 1983). Along similar lines, Frank Crüsemann's "Die Eigenständichkeit der Urgeschichte. Ein Beitrag zur Diskussion um den Jahwisten" in J. Jeremias and L. Perlitt (ed.), *Die Botschaft und die Boten. Festschrift für Hans Walther Wolff zum 70. Geburtstag* (Neukirchen, 1981), 11–29, rejects the idea that Genesis 1–11 was composed as a preface to the ancestral stories. He argues that both blocks were quite distinct until linked editorially by means of Gen 11:27–32 (not Gen 12:1–3). Also worthy of note is the study of Martin Rose, Professor of Old Testament at the

University of Neuchatel, entitled *Deuteronomist und Jahwist. Untersuchungen zu den Berührungspunkten beider Literaturwerke* (Zurich, 1981). Following the lead of H. H. Schmid, he proposes that the J passages constitute a late D stratum reflecting the somber effect of the disasters of the sixth century B.C. There is therefore no consecutive narrative of national origins prior to the work of the Deuteronomists. See also his more recent article "La Croissance du Corpus Historiographique de la Bible—Une Proposition," *RTP* 118 (1986), 217–36.

10. A point well made by George W. Coats, *JSOT* 3 (1977), 30–32, based on his own work on the wilderness traditions and the unifying factor of the life of Moses. We shall return to this point later.

11. I have in mind particularly the perceptive reading of biblical texts by Robert Alter in *The Art of Biblical Narrative* (New York, 1981). Harold Bloom's commentary on the J source, which he attributes to a lady of the court and probably also of the blood royal during the reign of Rehoboam, is based on the new and very free translation of David Rosenberg (see Harold Bloom and David Rosenberg, *The Book of J* (New York, 1990).

CHAPTER 2

THE BASIC FEATURES OF

THE PENTATEUCH:

STRUCTURE AND CHRONOLOGY

STORY LINE

Though the basic meaning of *tôrāh* is "instruction" or "law," the Pentateuch or Torah is first and foremost a narrative. The sequence of events
may be summarized as follows. God (Elohim) created the world and everything in it in six days and rested on the seventh. The earth, however,
was uncultivated, and there was no rainwater and no one to put it to use.
God (now YHWH Elohim) therefore formed a man and set him in the
garden of Eden, giving him access to everything in it with the exception of
a certain tree. Since the animals, also formed out of the earth, did not
provide suitable companionship for the man, YHWH Elohim made out of
the man's body a woman whom he joyfully acknowledged as a suitable
companion. But a snake skillful in speech persuaded her, and through her
the man, to eat fruit from the tree from which they were forbidden to eat,
resulting in their expulsion from Eden. Children were born, one son killed
the other, and the initial evil flowered throughout the wider society, leading to the destruction of all life in a great deluge with the exception of
Noah, his immediate family, and the species taken with him into the ark. A

31

new order was established, but another aberration within Noah's family tainted the new humanity, and with the confusion of tongues at Babel the nations were dispersed over the earth.

In the tenth generation after the deluge, Abram (later Abraham) was called by God to emigrate from Mesopotamia to Canaan with the promise that from him would spring a great nation. After various difficulties Abraham and his wife Sarah bore children in old age; first Ishmael, through Sarah's proxy Hagar, then Isaac. After surviving an attempted ritual sacrifice, the latter obtained a Mesopotamian wife, Rebekah, who in her turn bore him two sons, Esau and Jacob, later renamed Israel. Conflict between these two sons, beginning, remarkably, in the womb, led to the securing of the birthright and blessing by Jacob, the younger. At the cost of a twenty-year exile in Mesopotamia as a hired hand of his uncle Laban, Jacob won two wives, Leah and Rachel, who with the help of proxy-wives gave him twelve sons and a daughter. Upon his return to Canaan there occurred a reconciliation of sorts with Esau and a last meeting with Isaac before the latter's death.

In the course of time Joseph, second youngest of the sons and Jacob's favorite, aroused the jealousy of his brothers, who conspired to kill him. The plot miscarried; Joseph survived, and after traders had carried him as a slave to Egypt he rose to the highest position in the service of the Pharaoh. The rest of Jacob's family were meanwhile compelled by famine to emigrate to Egypt, where eventually a reconciliation took place and they were permitted to settle. The original seventy settlers grew into a numerous and powerful people until a new Pharaoh ascended the throne and, for reasons that are not entirely clear, launched a genocidal campaign against them.

One of these Israelites in Egypt, son of Levite parents, survived under remarkable circumstances—the massacre of Hebrew infants ordered by the tyrant—and was brought up in the palace as an Egyptian. Chancing one day to see an Egyptian beating a Hebrew worker, Moses killed the Egyptian and buried the body in the sand. Word of the homicide nevertheless spread, and he was forced to flee for his life to Midian, where he married Zipporah, daughter of the priest of Midian, and fathered the first of two sons named Gershom. While guarding his father-in-law's sheep in the wilderness, he had an extraordinary experience in which a deity revealed himself as YHWH, God of the Hebrews, and sent him on a mission to lead his oppressed people out of bondage. With the help of his brother Aaron, Moses eventually succeeded in this mission, but only after the Egyptians experienced a series of disasters culminating in the death of the firstborn children. After celebrating a spring festival, the Israelites headed out into the wilderness and the pursuing Egyptians were providentially destroyed as they attempted to follow them across a body of water.

The Israelite horde, reported to be 600,000 strong, not counting women and children, continued to plot an erratic course which led them, after several crises and setbacks, to a mountain in the Sinai. There Moses received a revelation from YHWH: first, ten commandments which were promulgated at once, then a collection of laws communicated to Moses alone. There followed a covenant ceremony and the revelation to Moses of the plan for a mobile sanctuary, together with detailed specifications for how worship was to be conducted in it. During Moses' absence on the mountain, however, an act of apostasy led to the breaking and rewriting of the law tablets and the issuing of further statutes. The cult was then set up as prescribed, the priesthood was inaugurated, and after the lapse of about a year, the Israelites were able to proceed on their way.

After further difficulties, including an abortive attempt to invade Canaan, they arrived in Moab, on the east bank of the Jordan. The hostility of the Moabite king was deflected by an inspired seer hired to curse them, and those who succumbed to the allure of orgiastic rites practiced in the region were summarily dispatched. More statutes were issued, and preparations were made for occupying the land on the west bank of the Jordan. On the last day of his life Moses reminded the people of the providential events that had transpired and the obligations thereby incurred. His valedictory address included a new collection of laws and norms for living in the land about to be occupied. Joshua was installed as Moses' successor, whereupon Moses died at the age of 120 and was buried in an unmarked grave.

ANOMALIES

This, then, is the story within which resides the meaning the reader of the Pentateuch is invited to decode. It is this text in its narrative integrity, and not this or that source, which in the last analysis is the object of interpretation. If, however, we compare the Pentateuch with other literary works, either ancient or modern, of comparable length, we cannot help noticing some obvious anomalies. Consider, for example, the narrative tempo of the work. According to the chronological scheme of the Pentateuch itself, the events recorded cover 2,706 years, yet the Israelite stopover at Sinai, the description of which occupies about one-fifth of the length, lasted only one year. About the same space is allotted to one day, the last day in the life of Moses. (See Deut 1:3 for the date.) The reason is, of course, that more than one-third of the entire narrative is taken up with laws, a feature which accounts for the designation *Torah* in Jewish tradition, but anomalous nonetheless.

In *The Art of Biblical Narrative* Robert Alter distinguishes between event, defined as a significant junction in the narrative continuum, and summary, that which serves either to link events or to introduce material unsuitable for concrete rendering as event (Alter 1981, 63). If we apply Alter's distinction to our text we find that summary—for the most part in the form of genealogy, list, and law—occupies about one-third more space than the narration of events. We may also note that one indication of the distinctive character of Genesis is its more normal profile as narrative in that only about 14 percent of the book consists in summary. Other features of the narrative which led earlier readers to identify juxtaposed sources—repetitions, digressions, inconcinnities of different kinds—are perhaps no more than we might expect in an ancient work. Similar features occur in Herodotus and other early Greek historians, and they too incorporated sources, sometimes on a large scale and generally without attribution.

To speak of the narrative integrity of the Pentateuch obliges us to consider its relation to the continuing narrative in the Former Prophets (Joshua through 2 Kings), a narrative covering the period from the occupation of Canaan to the Babylonian exile, that is, to a point around the middle of the sixth century B.C. If we ignore the tripartite division of the Hebrew Bible and the division of each part into books, we have before us a consecutive history from creation to exile. This we may describe as a national history with a long introduction connecting the history of the nation with its own prehistory and the early history of humanity. This long historiographical work, to which David Noel Freedman has given the name "the Primary History" *(IDB* 3:712 and *passim*), runs more or less parallel with the later work consisting in Chronicles with Ezra-Nehemiah, which is therefore the Secondary History. The main differences between these histories are that the latter covers the period to the reign of David by means of genealogy, and that it extends beyond the Primary History to the founding of a new commonwealth after the return from exile.

The issue of narrative integrity is therefore complicated by the fact that the first nine books of the Bible (Genesis through Kings) form one connected historical continuum. The point will be made more clearly if we consider the following features of the Pentateuchal narrative which point beyond its conclusion.

(1) Omission of the conquest of Canaan leaves a prominent motif in Genesis, the promise of land, up in the air. On the other hand, the conquest itself, once successfully completed, is seen as the honoring of an ancient commitment often repeated. The point is made very clearly in Josh 21:43–45, which rounds off the story of the occupation and reads like the finale to it.

YHWH gave Israel all the land he had sworn an oath to their ancestors to give them; so they took possession of it and settled in it. YHWH gave them secure occupancy in keeping with all his sworn commitments to their ancestors. Not one of all their enemies could resist them; YHWH delivered all their enemies into their power. Not one of all the good promises made by YHWH to the house of Israel went unfulfilled; all came to pass.

If, therefore, we confine ourselves to the narrative horizon of the Pentateuch, we would have to speak not of promise fulfillment but of promise deferred (see, e.g., Clines 1978).

(2)   In passages dealing with the sanctuary and worship we detect a pattern extending beyond the limits of the Pentateuch. The creation account in Genesis 1 anticipates the establishment of worship in its seven-day structure, the sabbath rest of God, and the creation of the heavenly bodies on the fourth day to determine the liturgical calendar. According to the same learned priestly-scribal tradition, the Sinai revelation consists in precise stipulations for the setting up and operation of the wilderness sanctuary, which sanctuary is then established in the promised land after the conquest (Joshua 18–19). Reading further, we find that the building of Solomon's temple is dated 480 years after the exodus (1 Kings 6:1) and is thereby fitted into a chronological schema beginning with creation. Of this schema more will be said later in the chapter.

(3)   A major theme, repeated often throughout the history of the monarchy, is the threat of disaster, and especially exile, in consequence of disobeying the divinely revealed commandments. Now it seems that this theme is anticipated in the first episode recorded after the creation (Genesis 2–3), the only difference being that it is given a universal reference consistent with its place at the beginnings of human history. The Man is placed in a desirable environment, he is given a command, he disobeys it, and in consequence he is exiled, but not without some hope for the future. It may also be no coincidence that the story of human origins, like the Primary History, ends in Mesopotamia with the forward movement of history stalled for the time being.

There is therefore little doubt that Pentateuch and Former Prophets may be and at some stage of the tradition were intended to be read as one consecutive history. But it is also true that the Pentateuch, ending as it does with the death of Moses outside the land, came to be seen as a coherent narrative in its own right, with its own distinctive structure and meaning.

Many attempts continue to be made in explanation of these narrative ambiguities. Working within the broad lines of the documentary hypothesis, David Noel Freedman extended the Deuteronomistic History (Dtr) backward, resulting in a narrative continuum from creation to exile, though the compiler added nothing essential to the JEP record of the early phase to the death of Moses. In its final form this history was complete by the mid-sixth century B.C., and from it the Pentateuch was divided off in the following century in response to the needs of the post-exilic community (Freedman 1962, 1963, 1975a, 1975b, 1987). Freedman, therefore, combines a fairly standard form of the documentary hypothesis with Noth's Dtr inclusive of Deuteronomy. It will be recalled that Noth found practically no trace of the D source in the first four books (i.e., the Tetrateuch), so that according to him the Pentateuch was formed by the simple expedient of detaching Deuteronomy from Dtr and attaching it to Genesis-Numbers. This relatively simple proposal has, however, been challenged by those who claim to find evidence of the Deuteronomic hand in the first four books of the Bible. While we will be dealing with this matter in some detail in subsequent chapters, it may be helpful to give some idea of the variety of opinion before going any further.

Until recently, Noth's thesis of a clear-cut distinction between the first four books of the Pentateuch and the fifth had been challenged only sporadically, e.g., by the German scholar Werner Fuss, who identified a D compositional strand in the account of Moses' commissioning, the carrying out of his mission, the miracle at the sea, and the journey to Sinai (Fuss 1972). The thesis of a late J proposed by Van Seters, Schmid, and a few others does not necessarily have implications for D editorial activity in Genesis, Exodus, and Numbers. But we have seen that Schmid attributes to D much of the material conventionally assigned to J, especially the connecting links in the narrative and passages containing theological interpretation. The Sinai pericope, for example, is essentially a D composition according to Schmid. Martin Rose takes the same route, redescribing the J material as the final D stratum, embodying a more reflective and somber approach to human capabilities in the religious sphere. He therefore reverses the usual order of dependence by claiming that the historical reminiscence, generally in the homiletic mode, in Deuteronomy and Dtr provided the basis for the more straightforward third-person narrative in Exodus and Numbers (Rose 1981, 1986). More recently still, William Johnstone of the University of Aberdeen has argued for a major D redactional stratum throughout the Sinai pericope in Exodus 19–40 and, more specifically, in the Exodus version of the decalogue (Johnstone 1987, 1988).

As noted in Chapter 1, Rendtorff advances the more limited claim that a D redactor was responsible for editorial linkage between the ancestral narratives and the exodus–Sinai-occupation complex. But it seems that he too is moving in the direction of a D redaction of the entire narrative from Genesis to Kings. So, for example, he invites us to compare the following recapitulatory statements:

> So Joseph died, and all his brethren, and all that generation. . . . and a new king arose over Egypt who did not know Joseph (Ex 1:6, 8).

> So Joshua ben-Nun, the servant of YHWH, died at the age of one hundred and ten years . . . likewise all that generation were gathered to their fathers, and another generation arose after them that did not know YHWH (Judg 2:8, 10).

The implication seems to be that the D compiler has left his mark on the history of events both before and after the time of Moses. This would go beyond the claim that the Genesis-Numbers narrative serves as an introduction to Dtr (Rendtorff 1977, 166–69), a conclusion at which other scholars also arrived.

THE PENTATEUCH AS AN ANCIENT HISTORIOGRAPHICAL WORK

While this issue of the narrative integrity of the Pentateuch, and the related question of its relation to the historical work following it, continue to be discussed on the basis of internal indications, the debate took a new and interesting turn when the possibility of comparison with other works from antiquity was raised. As long as the documentary hypothesis held sway, there was little motivation to ask this question, and to the best of my knowledge no one did ask it. But now the suggestion has been made (in Van Seters 1983 and Whybray 1987) that the Pentateuch may be profitably compared with early Greek historiographical works, especially Herodotus and his near-contemporaries Hecataeus of Miletus and Hellanicus of Lesbos. Van Seters is primarily concerned with Dtr and J, the latter dated by him to the time of the Babylonian exile, but he also allows that the Pentateuch itself is a historical work comparable to Dtr (Whybray 1983, 229–32). The same point is made more forcibly by Whybray, who sets out to demonstrate that the Pentateuch is not the end product of a long process of redaction but the work of one controlling genius, an author in the true sense of the word who incorporated sources, none necessarily very ancient, in much the same way as Herodotus.

The attraction of this comparison is at least enhanced by the fact that

Herodotus wrote around the middle of the fifth century B.C., a date often proposed for the Pentateuch in its final form. It is argued that both works juxtapose narrative units, many of them transcribed from sources without attribution, connecting them loosely with such phrases as "after these things," "about that time," and the like. Both also have a significant fictional component. Speeches and conversations are put into the mouths of characters, a perfectly normal procedure in ancient historiography, and incidents of a moralistic or entertaining nature fill out the narrative scheme. Whybray suggests, for example, that the stories about the ancestors in Genesis may as well have been modeled on the fictional Job as the reverse (Whybray 1983, 238–41). Folktale motifs are freely adopted; the account of the infancy of Moses in Exodus 1–2, for example, is quite comparable with that of Cyrus in Herodotus (1:68). When speaking of the distant past, both works record such legendary elements as the great age and size of the ancestors and exhibitions of their preternatural strength.

Van Seters and Whybray reject the common assumption that different styles necessarily mean different sources. Both Herodotus and the author-redactor of the Pentateuch incorporate sources, of course, but they also know how to adapt style to subject matter. Digressions, some quite lengthy, characterize both works; for example, almost all of the second book of the *History* digresses from the narrative line to give ethnographic information about Egypt. Both works also evince a predilection for genealogy, though it is conceded that Herodotus lacks the overall genealogical scheme that is such a prominent feature of the Pentateuch. Numbers are either of the stereotypical kind or greatly exaggerated; compare, for example, the 600,000 Israelite adult males who marched out of Egypt (Ex 12:37) with the 700,000-strong invasion army of Xerxes (Her 4:87). In these and similar respects, it is claimed, the Pentateuch is not essentially different from other historiographical works from antiquity.

While it is clear from the prologue to the *History* (1:1–5) that the primary concern of the author was with the causes and course of the great war with Persia, the work focuses no less than the Pentateuch on the "great nation" theme. In both works this theme is developed biographically, through the rendering of the lives and characters of individuals, exemplary or otherwise. Both Van Seters and Whybray anticipate the objection that unlike Herodotus, the Pentateuch is controlled throughout by assumptions about divine causality and divine-human interaction. Herodotus is certainly not so explicitly theological, but it is maintained that the twinned themes of human pride and retribution, hubris and nemesis, are rarely far below the surface and are often explicitly stated. From these considerations the conclusion is drawn that the Pentateuch is a historical work, incorporating sources none of which is necessarily very ancient or comprehensive in scope, the production of an author of great literary skill, a "controlling genius" (Whybray 1987, 235) who was probably a contemporary or near-contemporary of Herodotus.

What are we to make of this interesting solution to an old problem? Taken singly, the parallels stated are intriguing and sometimes striking; but they must be weighed against the differences, which are much more in evidence. One of the most basic of these is that the *History* is a work attributed explicitly to its author, who introduces himself in the opening sentence. It is narrated throughout in the first person and bears the stamp of its author, who maintains a conversational relationship with his readers, offering his own opinions, judgments, and reservations about what he records. It is true that the theological dimension is not lacking in Herodotus, but the tone is nevertheless clearly secular. No one would think of describing the *History* as sacred literature. Herodotus records marvelous events. Sometimes he simply reports, as in the story about Aristeas of Proconnesus seen walking around long after his death (4:14–15); at other times he reports only to dismiss, as with reports of lycanthropy among the Neuri (4:105). He passes on bits of gossip and has an eye and ear for ethnological curiosities and a tendency to provide his own often bizarre explanations—as, for example, why baldness is rare among Egyptians (3:12) or why longevity is common among Ethiopians (3:114). There are also erotic episodes, some narrated in considerable detail; an early example is that of Caudales, ruler of Sardis, obliging his wife to appear naked before Gyges (1:8–12). Consider, finally, the detailed description of military events leading to the decisive defeat of Xerxes, a description occupying three of the nine books of the *History*. There is nothing remotely resembling this in the Pentateuch.

The prominence in the Pentateuch of moral instruction and of laws, comprising about a third of the total length, also sets it apart from the Greek historiographical tradition. Indications not just of sources but of major editorial restructurings as, for example, the incorporation of Deuteronomy into the Priestly history, must also be taken into account. Van Seters allows that his J historical work was further edited by P, which complicates the question of final authorship. In these respects, then, the Pentateuch looks rather different from the work of a known and named author like Herodotus who stamps his own authorial mark on the source material adopted.

Another feature of the Pentateuch that sets it apart from Herodotus is the link between the national history and universal history recorded in the first eleven chapters of Genesis. This feature does not appear in Herodotus, but it does appear in the work of Hecataeus of Miletus, one of the historians or logographers to whom Herodotus alludes (2:143; 5:36, 125–26; 6:137). The surviving fragments of Hecataeus suggest the author's intention of connecting contemporary history with incidents and themes from the heroic past (e.g., the Argonauts) and with remote antiquity, in this instance the epoch of Deucalion, survivor of the deluge, and his three sons. (Jacoby 1957, 1–47; Pearson 1939, 25–139; Van Seters 1983, 10–15, 43–44.) Another near-contemporary of Herodotus, Hellanicus of Lesbos, also wrote historiographical and ethnographic works in which genealogy, etymology, etiology, and eponymous heroes played an important role. His history of Attica, referred to by Thucydides (1:97), traced the line of Athenian kings back to the deluge and attempted to construct a precise chronology measured in generations of forty years. This resulted in 1,020 years from the deluge to the first Olympiad, which interestingly enough is almost identical with the biblical interval between the deluge and the exodus (1,010 years: 365 from the deluge to the migration of Abraham, 215 from that point to entry into Egypt, 430 for the time spent in Egypt, according to Ex 12:40).

In other works of Hellanicus the great families of his day were provided with genealogies going back into mythical times, indeed to the time of the gods and the creation of the first human being. As in Genesis 1–11, this earliest epoch is marked by the great divide of the deluge. The three grandsons of Deucalion, counterpart of the Mesopotamian Utnapishtim (or Ziusudra or Atrahasis) and the biblical Noah, survived the deluge after the ark came to rest on Mount Parnassus. They went on to found cities and beget the Dorians, Ionians, and Aeolians, the three great branches of the Greek peoples. (Jacoby 1957, 104–52; Pearson 1939, 132–225; Van Seters 1983, 22–23, 27–28.)

The writings of Hecataeus and Hellanicus, together with those of other early Greek logographers, have survived only in fragments, the order and, in some cases, the authenticity of which cannot always be firmly established. Attempts to fill in the gaps and discern the overall structure will therefore be somewhat speculative. It does seem possible, nevertheless, to discern the profile of a national history linked with the pre-deluge and post-deluge worlds by means of genealogies, mythical eponymous heroes, stories of gods and giants, and the like (Van Seters 1988). In these respects parallelism with the Mesopotamian mythical tradition is evident, and the biblical history has similar features. How is this to be explained? Van Seters (1983, 53–54) suggests that the cities of the Phoenician littoral, with which the Greeks had contacts long before the time of Herodotus, served as a cultural link between Greece and Israel. The suggestion is plausible but unfortunately cannot be verified, since no comparable historiographical material has come down to us from pre-Hellenistic Phoenicia. As important as they are in other respects, the texts from Ras Shamra-Ugarit provide none, and the fragments of the *Phoenician History* of Philo of Byblos, from the late first century A.D., cannot be used with confidence to fill the gap (Barr, 1974; Oden, 1978).

From these considerations I would think it reasonable to draw the conclusion that taken by itself, the Pentateuch is not comparable to any of the works discussed. As Whybray himself puts it (Whybray 1987, 241), it exists historically in a kind of limbo, and structurally also it is sui generis. If, however, the Pentateuch is taken together with Dtr, which follows, we at once detect the pattern of a national history traced back to the origins of humanity, a pattern which emerged in the Near East and the Levant and remained standard long after the biblical period. In the Hellenistic age both the *Babyloniaka* of Berossus and the *Aigyptiaka* of his younger contemporary Manetho exhibit this feature (Drews 1975, Lambert 1976, Burstein 1978, Adler 1983). The former is a history of Babylonia written in indifferent Greek for the Seleucid king Antiochus I. It takes the history down into the Persian period and connects it with the archaic age, beginning with creation and the emergence of civilization in the Euphrates basin. Knowledge of creation was revealed to Oannes, first of the seven *apkallu,* and the earliest epoch has ten kings before and ten after the deluge, which is described in some detail. The postdiluvian kings connect with the historical period of the Medes, Assyrians, and Babylonians, leading to a somewhat detailed treatment of the reign of Nebuchadnezzar II and his successors in the Neo-Babylonian empire. A final section deals with the Persian kings from Cyrus to Artaxerxes II. Along similar lines, Manetho composed a history of Egypt ending at about the same time as the *Babyloniaka,* i.e., with the reign of Nectanebo (ca. 341 B.C.). While it contains no theogony or cosmogony, it traces a line from the time of the gods to that of the demigods and spirits of the dead (i.e., mythical rulers), and thence to the thirty dynasties known to history. Both works may be read as a nationalistic or nativist reaction to the cosmopolitan Hellenism propagated by the Diadochoi.

In composing his history, Berossus drew on the mythic-historiographical tradition of Mesopotamia, and specifically on such well known texts as the creation myth *enuma elish, atraḥasis,* and the king lists, which provided a point of departure and conceptual framework for a universal history.[1] But the mythic and archaic element was combined with the chronicles of rulers which can lay claim to being in some degree genuinely historical. Most of the Mesopotamian royal inscriptions dealing with the *res gestae* of rulers are of limited historical scope. Some of the Neo-Assyrian and Neo-Babylonian chronicles, however, take in a fairly long period of time. The *Chronicles of the Early Kings* covers about eight centuries beginning with Sargon of Akkad, the so-called *Synchronistic History* begins in the fifteenth century and ends in the eighth, and the *Eclectic Chronicle* takes us from the Kassite period to the Neo-Babylonian. (For a convenient summary, see Van Seters 1983, 60–92.) Yet none of these evinces any interest in universal history. As far as Mesopotamia is concerned, we have to wait until the Hellenistic period for anything like this to emerge; the first extant example is the history of Berossus.

If our reading of Hecataeus and Hellanicus is correct, the Greeks seem to have anticipated Berossus by some two centuries in adapting this form of universal history to their own situation, in dependence on a basic Mesopotamian pattern. Dependence on Mesopotamian thought, apparent centuries earlier in Hesiod (Lambert and Walcot 1965, Walcot 1966, West 1988), leads us naturally to recall the many points of contact with Mesopotamian culture in the Pentateuch. It seems reasonable to conclude that in the first nine books of the Hebrew Bible, Israel anticipated the Greeks in producing a national history traced back to creation and the mythic origins of humanity.

In this *limited* sense, then, the Pentateuch is an incomplete and truncated work. It remains to be determined how it came into existence and achieved the authoritative status it enjoyed, a status superior to Prophets and Writings in Judaism, and a uniquely authoritative status in the Samaritan community. This is a complex and as yet unsolved problem to which we will have to return later.

DIVISIONS AND STRUCTURE

The familiar chapter divisions of the Hebrew Bible, introduced into the Vulgate by Stephen Langton, Archbishop of Canterbury (1150–1228), began to appear in Hebrew MSS in the later Middle Ages. Verse division was already in place in the Talmudic period, but verses were referred to not by number but by identifying quotes, often just a single word, known as *simānîm* (signs). Verse numbering is generally credited to the French reformer Robert Estienne, who allegedly divided the Greek New Testament into verses during a coach journey from Paris to Geneva in 1550. Three years later he extended the system to his French translation of the entire Bible, and thereafter it came into common use. (We may suspect that the need for quick access to biblical ammunition in the theological controversies of that time provided the required motivation.) The Masoretic Bible was divided into sections for the purpose of liturgical reading rather than on the basis of purely literary criteria, though of course attention was paid to sense and context. Different liturgical praxis in the land of Israel and Babylonia required different lectionaries. In Palestine, Torah was read over a span of three to three and a half years, to which corresponded slightly more than 150 sections, or *sĕdārîm*. In Babylonian communities, however, the reading was completed in a year, necessitating only about fifty-four longer sections, or *pārāšôt*. These sections were then subdivided into short paragraphs, or *pisqôt*, separated by a space of at least

three letters. These appear already in the Qumran biblical texts. According-
ing to an early tradition, they were introduced to give Moses time for
reflection between each subsection (Sifra 1:1).

Much more important for grasping the basic structural features of the
Pentateuch is the division into five books. It is well known that titles in use
in most modern translations derive from the Old Greek or Septuagint
version (LXX), whereas in the Hebrew Bible, in keeping with the common
practice in antiquity, the title is simply the first word or words of the book
(e.g., *Bĕrē'šît* for *Genesis*). Practically no attention has been paid to the
fivefold division of the Pentateuch, no doubt because it was assumed to be
merely a matter of book production, of how much could fit on a scroll, and
therefore without exegetical significance. I hope to show, nevertheless,
that this structural feature deserves a closer look. That it was already in
place by the end of the first century A.D. is apparent from a passage in
Josephus which though well known deserves to be quoted in full (the
translation of *Apion* 1:37–41 is that of Henry St. John Thackeray in the
Loeb Classical Library):

> It therefore naturally, or rather necessarily, follows (seeing that with us it
> is not open to everybody to write the records, and that there is no discrep-
> ancy in what is written; seeing that, on the contrary, the prophets alone
> had this privilege, obtaining their knowledge of the most remote and an-
> cient history through the inspiration which they owed to God, and commit-
> ting to writing a clear account of the events of their own time, just as they
> occurred)—it follows, I say, that we do not possess myriads of inconsistent
> books, conflicting with each other. Our books, those which are justly ac-
> credited, are but two and twenty, and contain the record of all time.
>
> Of these, five are the books of Moses, comprising the laws and the
> traditional history from the birth of man down to the death of the lawgiver.
> This period falls only a little short of three thousand years. From the death
> of Moses until Artaxerxes, who succeeded Xerxes as king of Persia, the
> prophets subsequent to Moses wrote the history of the events of their own
> times in thirteen books. The remaining four books contain hymns to God
> and precepts for the conduct of human life.
>
> From Artaxerxes to our own time the complete history has been writ-
> ten, but has not been deemed worthy of equal credit with the earlier
> records, because of the failure of the exact succession of the prophets.

Josephus does not name the five books containing "the laws and the traditional history," nor does 2 Esdras (the Ezra Apocalypse), written some-

what earlier, in which we hear of Ezra rewriting, with the help of five scribes and fortified by a fiery liquid, the twenty-four sacred books lost in the destruction of the temple (2 Ezra 14:45). But it is at least clear that the total of twenty-four, slightly higher than that of Josephus, can be explained only on the assumption of a multiple-book Torah.[2]

The New Testament often speaks of "the law and the prophets" (e.g., Mt 5:17; Lk 16:16; Acts 13:15; Rom 3:21), yet never refers to the fivefold division of the Law. But it has often been pointed out that the first gospel contains five discourses of Jesus, each concluding with the same kind of formulaic statement (Mt 7:28; 11:1; 13:53; 19:1; 26:1). Since the author is at pains to present Jesus as a second Moses, this structural feature would seem to be modeled on a fivefold Torah. None of the five books is mentioned by name in the New Testament, however; the first occurrence in Christian writings seems to be the reference to Deuteronomy in the Epistle to Barnabas (10:2), generally dated ca. 130 A.D. There may be an indirect allusion in Matthew which opens with the superscription *biblos geneseōs,* referring back to either Gen 2:4 or 5:1 in LXX. The fourth gospel, on the other hand, opens with the first words of Genesis corresponding to its title in Hebrew.

Writing several decades before the composition of the gospels, Philo of Alexandria informs us that the first of the five books in which the holy laws are written bears the name and inscription of Genesis, a name given to it by Moses himself (*De Aeternitate Mundi* 19; cf. *De Opificio Mundi* 12 and *De Posteritate Caini* 127). Elsewhere (in *De Plantatione* 26) he has occasion to quote the opening verse of Leviticus, referring to the book by name. At several points he also quotes from Deuteronomy which, however, he calls *The Protreptics,* a not inappropriate title.[3] The date can be pushed back further on the basis of indications in the Qumran scrolls, some admittedly of uncertain interpretation. Allusion to "the books of the law" in the Damascus Document (CD VII), for example, suggests a plurality of books. A Qumran fragment of what seems to be a liturgical text may also bear on this issue and refer to books in a fivefold arrangement. The editor, Père Barthélemy, translates the relevant phrase *kwl [s]prym ḥwmšym* as "all the books of the Pentateuch" or, as he prefers to read, "all the books of the Psalter."[4] It would be surprising to find Psalms divided into five books so early, but even if the allusion is to Psalms, it would still imply the prior existence of a fivefold Torah. For this arrangement of Psalms is meant to suggest that they are to be recited as a meditation on and an aid to observance of Torah, as the keynote Psalm 1 suggests. This reading of the fragment is, in any case, not entirely secure, so too much weight should not be placed on it.[5]

The Letter of Aristeas also speaks of "the scrolls of the law of the Jews" (par. 30) and "the books" (46, 176, etc.) with reference to the Pentateuch, and earlier still, Aristobulus (frag. 3:2) has an allusion to all the books of the law at the time of Ptolemy Philadelphus. 1 Enoch is also divided into five books, each indicated by an Ethiopic number in one of the major MSS. While the date of these numbers cannot be determined, the fivefold division seems to be dictated by the contents. It therefore may have been suggested by the fivefold division of Torah, called "the five fifths of the law" (*ḥămišāh ḥumšē hattôrāh*) in Jewish tradition.

Jesus ben Sira's encomium of the great figures of Israel's past, written toward the beginning of the second century B.C., covers the biblical books from Genesis to Nehemiah in the form of one continuous narrative. The same continuity appears in other paraphrases of biblical books during the later Second Temple period—in Jubilees, Demetrius, Artapanus, and Pseudo-Philo—which of course does not exclude the possibility that the fivefold Pentateuch was known at that time. Ben Sira, however, seems to have been familiar with a text in which the Latter Prophets were arranged in the way familiar to us today: Isaiah, Jeremiah, Ezekiel, and the Twelve (Sir 48:20–49:10).[6] This would suggest, *a fortiori,* that Torah was divided into five books by the beginning of the second century B.C. A final observation concerns the LXX use of the term *deuteronomion touto* to translate the Hebrew *mišnēh hattôrāh hazzo't* ("a copy of this law") at Deut 17:18 (cf. also Josh 8:32). This can hardly be a simple mistake, since in that case the translator would have written *deuteron nomon* or something of the sort. It therefore suggests that the title of the fifth book of Moses was already in circulation at that time.

The question may now be posed whether the division of the narrative into five books is a purely formal feature, dictated by the practical consideration of scroll length, or whether it should be considered in some way exegetically significant. Since we do not know the circumstances in which any of the biblical books, including the Pentateuch, were first written, we cannot assume that the Pentateuchal narrative existed in continuous form and was then, for whatever reasons, broken up into five sections. It is conceivable that Genesis and Deuteronomy existed at one time as independent texts, though perhaps not exactly in their present forms, but this cannot be assumed for the other three, which do not give the impression of self-contained compositions. Leviticus and the first part of Numbers (to 10:28) continue the narrative of the Sinai event begun in Exodus. The ordination of priests in Leviticus 8 follows logically from the prescriptions for that ritual in Exodus 29. So, whatever the original situation, some breakdown of the material in the second, third, and fourth books must have been required at some point.

The most obvious explanation is that division of the material was dictated by the length of scroll considered convenient for either private or public liturgical use.[7] Theoretically, a parchment scroll could be of almost any length. We hear, for example, of a scroll 150 ft. long containing the entire *Iliad* and *Odyssey*. The Temple Scroll, longest of those discovered at Qumran, was originally at least 8.75 m. in length, and the great Isaiah scroll (1QIsa[a]) somewhat shorter at 7.35 m. Fragments containing verses from Genesis, Exodus, and Numbers were found in the Wadi Murabba'at, probably from one and the same scroll, which the editors thought may have contained the entire Pentateuch.[8] Assuming a layout comparable with that of 1QIsa[a], such a scroll must have been in excess of 33 m., which would not have made for easy handling. While there is no reason to doubt that the entire Pentateuch could have been put on one scroll—a practice which continues in synagogues to this day—a scroll of this length would have been more for display purposes or very occasional use. Convenient handling may therefore have dictated a division into several scrolls of more manageable length.

Whatever the reason for the division, we can hardly assume that it was done in a purely mechanical way according to length. Exodus and Numbers, the second and fourth of the five, are almost exactly equal in length (16,713 and 16,413 words respectively) while Leviticus, the middle book, is by far the shortest (11,950 words), not much more than half the length of Genesis. There is also nothing inevitable about the cutoff points. Genesis could have ended appropriately with the summary list of seventy Israelites (Gen 46:8–27) since the remaining narrative deals with events in Egypt. We have seen that the cultic ordinances in Exodus 25–31 and 35–40 spill over into Leviticus and Numbers, while Numbers itself concludes with laws promulgated in the same location as those of Deuteronomy (Num 36:13; cf. Deut 1:1–5).

To illustrate the point that in antiquity the structuring of a work was an important vector of meaning in its own right, we might look at the arrangement of Latter Prophets. Bringing together the twelve "minor prophets" (the term is misleading but in common use) made practical sense since they could fit on a roll of comparable length to those of the three longer prophetic books (14,355 words as against 16,933 for Isaiah, 21,835 for Jeremiah, and 18,730 for Ezekiel). But this will not explain why the last of the twelve, opening with the same formulaic expression as the two sections preceding it ("oracle—word of YHWH": Zech 9:1; 12:1; Mal 1:1), has been made into a separate book with a fictitious attribution (cf. *mal'ākî*, my messenger, Mal 3:1). It looks as if a deliberate attempt was made to come up with a total of twelve; and this conclusion is confirmed and explained by the final paragraph of the prophetic collection which promises the reconciliation, meaning the reunion and reconstitution, of dispersed twelve-tribal Israel by means of an eschatological prophetic figure (Mal 3:23–24; cf. the paraphrase of this passage in Sir 48:10). This permits the suggestion that the 3 + 12 arrangement of Latter Prophets is intended to recall the three patriarchs and the twelve sons of Jacob-Israel or, in other words, the totality of reconstituted Israel as the object of eschatological faith. Duodecimal symbolism is familiar from Qumran and the New Testament; but it is also attested much earlier, for example, in the first part of Chronicles (1 Chron 1–9) and in Ezra-Nehemiah.[9] I am suggesting, therefore, that numerical symbolism of this kind dictated the final form of the prophetic collection and in doing so insinuated a certain perspective from which it was to be read.

It would therefore not be remarkable if the division of Torah into five books, rather than, say, four or six, was the outcome of a similar decision rather than being merely a matter of convenience. The fivefold arrangement highlights Leviticus as the central panel of the pentad, containing as it does the prescriptions identifying the reconstituted Israel of the Second Commonwealth as a holy community distinct from the nations of the world. If this is so, the structure of the foundational narrative, now severed from the history of events subsequent to the death of Moses, encodes an essential clue to its meaning. In the next chapter we shall be looking at the similar configuration of the two *toledot* series in Genesis, also arranged in pentads, which directs attention to the central panel of each of them as a point of particular exegetical density.

TIME FRAME

Read along its temporal axis, the Pentateuchal narrative reveals a distinctive feature in the frequent occurrence of precise dates. It will not be difficult to demonstrate that, as precise as they may be, these chronological markers are undoubtedly fictive. We shall see that even in the historical period, that of the monarchy, whatever data may have been available have been fitted into a preconceived chronological schema. A great deal of effort has been expended on the attempt to decode the chronological system or systems used by the biblical authors, in spite of which no clear consensus has emerged. The subject has proved to be particularly addictive for the apocalyptically and esoterically minded, as much in the ancient world as in the modern one. It has been suggested, for example, that Eusebius deliberately scrambled the chronology of the antediluvian period in order to nullify calculations of the date of the Second Coming by contemporary millennarian enthusiasts (Adler 1983, 433–34).

The task of decoding has also been greatly complicated by the different figures of the Septuagint and the Samaritan Pentateuch, not to mention the Book of Jubilees and Josephus. On this matter, too, there have been many attempts to explain the differences in terms of competing systems. While there have been those who defended the priority of the LXX schema (e.g., Bork 1929), or have argued that a common source underlies all three (e.g., Jepsen 1929, Klein 1974), most have concluded that the system of the Masoretic text is basic (e.g., Bousset 1900, Murtonen 1955, Larsson 1983). In any case, each system must first be examined within its own terms of reference. Without attempting to be in any sense exhaustive, we may set out the pivotal dates of MT as follows, with the cumulative total of years dating from creation (A.M. = *anno mundi,* from the year of creation):

Reference	Event	A.M.
Gen 1:26–27	Creation of Adam	1
Gen 5:3	Birth of Seth	130
Gen 5:28	Birth of Noah	1056
Gen 5:32	Birth of Shem	1556
Gen 7:6, 11	Beginning of deluge	1656
Gen 8:13	Drying of the earth	1657
Gen 11:10	Birth of Arpachshad to Shem	1658[10]
Gen 11:24	Birth of Terah	1876
Gen 11:26	Birth of Abram	1946
Gen 12:4	Migration of Abram	2021
Gen 47:9	Jacob and sons in Egypt	2236
Ex 12:40–41	Exodus from Egypt	2666
Ex 40:1–2, 17	Setting up of the tabernacle[11]	2667
Num 10:11	Departure from Egypt	2667
Deut 1:3; 34:7	Death of Moses; entry into Canaan	2706
1 Kings 6:1	Beginning of construction of Solomon's temple	3146

It is tolerably clear that a comprehensive and coherent scheme of some kind underlies this chronological sequence. The span of 2,666 years from creation to exodus is two thirds of 4,000, which may have been understood, perhaps on the basis of astronomical calculations, to constitute a world epoch or "great year."[12] It is also striking that the 430 years of the sojourn in Egypt—one of several estimates[13]—match exactly the period of the monarchy calculating from the fourth year of Solomon, when he began to build the temple, and taking the lengths of reigns as they are in Former Prophets without overlaps or other adjustments. If, then, we allow fifty years for the exile or, more precisely, from the destruction of the first temple to the decision to build the second, the cycle of 4,000 years ends, in terms of absolute chronology, with the rededication of the temple by the Maccabees in 164 B.C. Unless this is just a remarkable coincidence, it indicates a very late date for the insertion of the chronological data, or at least for the final revision of an existing schema.[14]

I do not think it would be helpful to give an inventory of alternatives to this 4,000-year cycle, some extremely complex, and others both complex and bizarre. We may limit ourselves to noting those that follow the lead of early rereadings of the biblical text. In one of the vision narratives in 2 Esdras, the woman barren for thirty years who appears to the seer is explained with reference to the 3,000 years preceding the building of Solomon's temple (2 Esd 10:44–46). Many years ago D. W. Bousset (*ZAW* 20 [1900] 136–47) took this event to be pivotal in the chronology and the midpoint of the course of human history (in which case the end should have come during the 1980s). Guided by Daniel, the Book of Jubilees, and 1 Enoch (91:11–17; 93:1–10), others proposed a septennial system, the basic unit being a "week" of 490 years followed by a great jubilee year (e.g., Koch 1983; see also Wiesenberg 1961). Others again fell back on the Mesopotamian sexagesimal system. Berossus, for example, has 432,000 years before the deluge, broken down into 120 *sars,* each 3,600 years in length (Drews 1975, Adler 1983). Not all of these suggestions are necessarily incompatible one with the other, especially if, as some maintain, the biblical authors used more than one system.[15]

It is at least clear from the chronological notation in 1 Kings 6:1, of a kind very rare in Former Prophets, that the building of Solomon's temple was regarded as a decisive turning point in the historical continuum abundantly marked in the Pentateuch. The 430 years following encompass the period from the construction to the destruction of that temple. The addition of fifty years for the exile brings that number up to the 480 years between exodus and first temple, ending at the point when, according to Ezra 1, a start was made on the second temple. That the period of exile was computed in learned clerical circles at fifty years—seven times seven followed by the jubilee—is apparent from Lev 26:34–36 and 2 Chron 36:21, which interpret the exile as the sabbatical rest of the land. The same calculation explains the dating of Ezekiel's vision of the new temple in the twenty-fifth year of the exile, that is, halfway to the jubilee year of liberation (Ezek 40:1). The same vision also transfers the numerical symbolism from the temporal to the spatial axis, since the measurements of the temple and surrounding enclosure are in multiples of five with a predominance of twenty-five. Thus, the entire sacred enclosure, the temenos, measures 25,000 square cubits (Ezek 48:20).[16] It results, therefore, that we have three major turning points—exodus, first temple, and second temple —separated by periods of identical length, namely, 480 years.

Before leaving Ezekiel, we recall that the prophet was commanded to lie on his left side for 390 days and on his right for 40 days to symbolize the punishment of Israel and Judah, respectively (Ezek 4:5–6). Here too, therefore, we come up with the same total as the sojourn in Egypt and the time of the kingdoms, both periods marked, according to Ezekiel, by religious infidelity. The determination of time derives very probably from a later glossator, and it seems to imply a calculation of the time of duress in store for the people of the two former kingdoms. Assuming a point of departure in the first deportation (598/597 B.C.), the end of Judah's exile would be foreseen for 558/557 B.C. If the starting point for the Northern Kingdom is the fall of Samaria in 722 B.C., the punishment would be due to end with the advent of Alexander the Great in 332 B.C., a surprisingly late date which may explain why LXX altered 390 years to 190 years. The 390 years of Ezekiel shows up again in the Damascus Document (CD 1:5–6) as a time of wrath calculated from the conquest of Judah by Nebuchadnezzar. There follows a period of twenty years' groping, after which a "Teacher of Righteousness" is raised up. This would bring us to 176 B.C., the accession year of Antiochus III, who launched the first "final solution of the Jewish problem."

Whatever we make of these numerological speculations, they illustrate the belief that the course of events in the past determines the future and provides the essential clue, if one could but crack the code, to the divine plan for humanity. It is one way, perhaps no longer our way, of saying that in spite of appearances to the contrary, God controls the course of events which therefore have a direction and a goal.

The relation between sacred time and sacred place is also apparent in the care taken to give the exact date for the setting up of the wilderness sanctuary and its cult, the specifications for which were revealed to Moses in a vision analogous to that of Ezekiel (Ex 24:15a–18b; 40:1–2, 17). The date in question falls on the first day of the year following the exodus, perhaps dictated by the conclusion of the deluge on the first day of the first month of the second year. According to the Priestly perspective, the setting up of the sanctuary was the climax of the wilderness experience, leading to the final goal of its establishment in the promised land (Josh 18:1). The same idea will recur in the "Song at the Sea" where the wilderness journey has its terminus at the holy mountain on which the sanctuary is to be raised (Ex 15:17–18).

Some Provisional Conclusions

Now that the documentary hypothesis is under attack at several key points, with no alternative as yet close to winning general acceptance (see the provisional conclusions to Chapter 1), any attempt to explain the formation of the Pentateuch must be tentative. Our discussion of the Pentateuch's internal structure and organization, its principal divisions, and its chronology should, however, throw some light on the final and no doubt most important stage in this process of formation. The principal conclusions are as follows:

(1)   That the Pentateuchal narrative originally formed part of an ambitious national history may be deduced from the themes which feature in it, the chronological schema which points to a terminus outside of it, and the foreshadowing of later events in its early chapters. This history, including as it did the early history of humanity and the story of Israel's ancestors, is in many respects unique while at the same time being structurally comparable to other historiographical essays from antiquity.

(2)   The chronological markers cannot be lifted cleanly out of the narrative, and therefore were not added to it after its completion. As we shall see in Chapters 3 and 4, they are part and parcel of the *toledot* structure in Genesis, including the story of the deluge, the chronology of which is integrated into the narrative. The determination of time spent in Egypt (Ex 12:40–41) and the building of Solomon's temple (1 Kings 6:1) are also integral to the narrative structure. If we allow for a revision of the chronology to bring it into line with the rededication of the temple by the Maccabees in 164 B.C., the overall schema seems to focus on the building of the Second Temple and the reestablishment of the cult after the return from exile. This in its turn suggests that the creation of the Pentateuch as a distinct corpus, the redaction of the laws as the civic constitution of the temple community of Judah under Persian rule, and the reestablishment of the temple and its cult are related aspects of the emergence and consolidation of the Judaism of the Second Commonwealth.

(3)   The decision to create a distinct literary corpus ending with the death of Moses implies the designation of the Mosaic age as a constitutive and normative narrative to the exclusion of what follows. While the language of canonicity is of course of much later origin (the word "canon" being first used in this sense by Athanasius in the middle of the fourth century A.D.), the canonical nature of this new literary creation can be seen as much in what it excludes as in what it includes. Exclusion of the history subsequent to Moses suggests that that history was seen to be for the most part a record of failure. There also appears to be a conscious effort to neutralize the ambiguous and problematic aspects of prophecy while incorporating the ethical teaching of the great prophets. The statement toward the end of the Pentateuch that since the death of Moses there has arisen in Israel no prophet like him (Deut 34:10) suggests a concern to define the Mosaic revelation as qualitatively different from the sporadic and potentially disruptive revelations claimed by prophets. Pointing in the

same direction is the redefinition of prophecy as Mosaic in the Pentateuch itself (Deut 18:15–22).

(4)   Closure with the death of Moses also permits a reading of the Pentateuch as a biography of Moses with a long introduction. The prestige of Moses, not much in evidence in pre-exilic writings outside the Pentateuch, is clearly related to the importance of the laws as the constitution of the newly founded commonwealth after the return from exile—hence the anomaly referred to earlier in the chapter, that all the laws, no matter when promulgated, must be backdated to this normative epoch. And, finally, the fivefold arrangement of the Pentateuch, with Leviticus as the central panel, reflects the great importance of the ritual law in this later period.

NOTES

1. The Sumerian king lists may at one time have contained an account of the deluge; see J. Van Seters, *In Search of History, Historiography in the Ancient World and the Origins of Biblical History* (New Haven & London, 1983), 72.

2. Professor David Noel Freedman suggests that the number 24 may be connected in some way with the division of the *Iliad* and *Odyssey* into twenty-four books each and the Greek epic tradition in general.

3. In *De Fuga et Inventione* 170, however, he assigns Lev 25:11 to this composition, an understandable lapse if he was quoting from memory. *The Testament of Moses* (1:5), contemporary with or a little earlier than Philo, also mentions Deuteronomy by name.

4. D. Barthélemy and J. T. Milik, *Discoveries in the Judaean Desert* (= DJD) I (Oxford, 1955), 132–33.

5. The first letter of *sprym* is missing and the second is unclear due to a tear in the fragment. The presence of two other numerals, *šlyšyt* and *ʾrbʿt*, in a fragment of six lines also gives one pause.

6. Cf. the parchment roll of the Twelve from Wadi Murabbaʿat, dated between the two revolts (DJD II, 181–205).

7. Menahem Haran has given close attention to scroll production; see his "Book-Scrolls in Israel in Pre-Exilic Times," *JJS* 33 (1982) 161–73, and "Book-Scrolls at the Beginning of the Second Temple Period. The Transition from Papyrus to Skins," *HUCA* 54 (1983) 111–33. He argues that skins came into use as a writing surface in the early Second Temple period as a result of the increased length of biblical books, the adoption of scribal rules, and the process of canonization beginning with Deuteronomy. He also argues that the books of the Pentateuch were written on separate scrolls from the beginning, since all could not fit on

one roll. See also his more recent article "Book-Size and the Device of Catch-Lines in the Biblical Canon," *JJS* 36 (1985) 1–2.

8. *DJD* II (Oxford, 1961), 75–78.

9. See Ezra 2:2 = Neh 7:7; Neh 5:17; 8:3–14, 24, 35. This may be one indication that the author saw the reconstitution of the community as fulfilling prophecy; see Klaus Koch, "Ezra and the Origins of Judaism," *JSS* 19 (1974) 173–97; J. G. McConville, "Ezra-Nehemiah and the fulfilment of prophecy," *VT* 36 (1986) 205–22.

10. Or A.M. 1656, if "two years after the flood" (Gen 11:10) is a gloss.

11. On the first day of the first month; hence creation, the emergence of the postdiluvian world (Gen 8:13), and setting up of the sanctuary all take place on New Year's Day.

12. An idea often repeated; see, for example, J. Wellhausen, *Prolegomena*, 308–9; G. von Rad, *Genesis. A Commentary*, 67; M. D. Johnson, *The Purpose of the Biblical Genealogies* (Cambridge, 2nd ed., 1988), 31–32; A. Murtonen, "On the Chronology of the Old Testament," *StTh* 8 (1955) 133–37. Archbishop Ussher's well-known fixing of the date of creation at 4004 B.C.–in his *Annales Veteris et Novi Testamenti* published in the mid-seventeenth century–was achieved by working backward from the birth of Christ.

13. Neither the 430 years of Ex 12:40–41 nor the 400 (ten generations) of Gen 15:13 tallies with the chronology of Moses: 120 years life span of which 80 correspond to the oppression in Egypt and 40 to the time in the wilderness. See S. von Kreuzer, "430 Jahre, 400 Jahre oder 4 Generationen—zu den Zeitangaben über den Agyptenaufenthalt der 'Israeliten'," *ZAW* 98 (1986) 199–210.

14. See A. Murtonen, "On the Chronology of the Old Testament," 137; G. Larsson, "The Chronology of the Pentateuch: A Comparison of the MT and LXX," *JBL* 102 (1983) 401–9; "The Documentary Hypothesis and the Chronological Structure of the Old Testament," *ZAW* 97 (1985) 316–33. Larsson follows K. Stenring, *The Enclosed Garden* (Stockholm, 1966), in postulating the use of three calendars to preserve secrecy, one of which came into use only in the third century B.C.

15. See Stenring and Larsson (note 14). A. Jepsen, "Zur Chronologie des Priesterkodex," *ZAW* 47 (1929) 251–55, maintained that an older P chronological system based on the date of the construction of Solomon's temple was revised after the completion of Zerubbabel's temple.

16. On which see W. Zimmerli, *Ezekiel 2* (Philadelphia, 1983), 344, who, however, holds that the starting point of the calculations is the 7×7 years plus one of the Jubilee.

C H A P T E R   3

Human Origins
(Gen 1:1–11:26)

The Historiographical Pattern

The impulse to trace the course of history backward to human origins arose not only from a natural curiosity about the remote past, but also from a need to validate the present social and political order. The basic idea was that normative value is to be found only in the past, and the more remote the better. This is certainly true of Mesopotamia, in which the idea of historical progress is conspicuously absent. Everything necessary for society, including political and religious institutions, the social order, and even the basic technologies, had been present from the beginning. The task of each successive generation, therefore, was to sustain and, where necessary, restore the primeval order of things. What B. A. van Groningen (1953, p. 61) says about ancient Greece—he is speaking of the function of genealogies—could be applied, *mutatis mutandis,* to the Near East as a whole:

So we meet everywhere this ardent desire to establish a genealogical connection. At the base of it lies the conviction that the solidarity created by the ancestors in the past in every separate clan and in every larger group is of decisive importance for those who live now. These interrelations explain the present; they give meaning and value to the things of today. Here too the past forcibly engrosses the thought and the imagination. Here too it possesses normative strength. If the Greeks ask what the present reality is, what it must be and how it should be, they look backward to find the answer. This answer depends on that which they see or take for granted in the past.

For ancient Mesopotamia the basic mythic-historiographical pattern is set out in the *Atraḥasis* text, about two-thirds of which is now readable as a result of collating fragments dating from the seventeenth to the sixth century B.C. (Lambert and Millard 1969; Oden 1981). The sequence of events is as follows. After the begetting of the gods, those of the lower order, the Igigi, go on strike and refuse to continue their onerous service to the high gods. The solution to this problem is found to lie in the creation of humans, initially seven male and seven female, by Belet-ili, mistress of the gods, assisted by Enki. Their task is to take over cultic work, thus solving the problem that had arisen in the divine sphere. In due course, however, the noise and tumult of humanity on the overcrowded earth[1] led to the decision by the gods to reduce the population by a series of disasters at intervals of 1,200 years. When these Malthusian measures failed in their effect, the decision was taken to destroy the human race by a deluge. Enki, however, forewarned the sage Atrahasis, instructing him to build a boat, take on animals and birds, and ride out the deluge, which then began and lasted seven days and nights. Atrahasis survived and offered sacrifice on the purified earth, and the mother goddess produced a lapis object to remind her that this must not happen again. The conclusion is unclear, but it appears that humanity was reorganized to avoid a recurrence of the disaster.

It will be seen that the decisive structural feature of this story, the peripaty, is the deluge brought about by a decision of the gods. It occupies the same position in the king lists, here too as the great divide in a history beginning with the origins of human civilization ("when kingship was lowered from heaven") and traced down to the first dynasty of Ur. It is true that there is no account of the deluge in the extant versions of the lists, though there may have been at an earlier stage, and it reappears in the Berossus version from the Seleucid period to which we referred in the Chapter 2.[2] The Sumerian deluge tablet from the British Museum, of which about one-third has been restored, is also part of a larger history, though the course of that history remains obscure.[3] The situation is different in *Gilgamesh,* the canonical form of which was discovered in Ashurba-nipal's library in Nineveh (seventh century B.C.), in which the story of the deluge has been fitted into a new context, as is the case in Genesis.

The pattern is essentially the same in the *Babyloniaka* of Berossus from the Hellenistic period. Berossus also gives great value to the remote past as normative, and to the all-sufficient divine revelations communicated to humanity at that time by the seven primeval sages. Berossus, however, has no theogony and no rebellion in heaven. After the creation of the first (hermaphroditic) humans by the god Bel, there follows a period of 432,000 years ($36{,}000 \times 12$) covering ten reigns, the last that of Xisouthros (corresponding to the Sumerian Ziusudra), survivor of the deluge, which is described at length. Ten more reigns follow the deluge, carrying the story down into the historical period of the great kingdoms (Drews 1975; Lambert 1976; Burstein 1978; Adler 1983).

Variations of the same pattern and many of the same themes occur in early Greek myth, to the extent that dependence on Mesopotamian thought is no longer in doubt. This is acknowledged to be the case with Hesiod (eighth century B.C.), whose *Theogony* is the earliest surviving attempt to synthesize the myths of divine and human origins (Walcot 1956, 1966; Lambert and Walcot 1965). The theme of history as progressive degeneration is also stated clearly and schematically by means of the four ages represented by metals (gold, silver, bronze, iron) in Hesiod's *Works and Days.* According to this early mythic tradition, the birth of the gods is followed by the appearance of giants issuing from the marriage of earth *(gē)* and heaven *(ouranos),* reminiscent of Gen 6:1–4, then of heroes including the first inventors *(prōtoi heuretai),* reminiscent of the Cain line (Gen 4:17–22). This, then, leads into the historical period. The Trojan War stands somewhere near the junction of the mythic and the historical. It is interesting to note that, following the *Atraḫasis* pattern, it functions in the old epic tradition as the final solution of Zeus to the problem of overpopulation (Kikawada and Quinn 1985, pp. 37–38, 48). This would seem to confirm the Malthusian interpretation of the deluge in the much earlier Mesopotamian work.

Something was said in the previous chapter about the early Greek logographers who further systematized the work of Hesiod. It is only at this later point in time, the sixth and fifth centuries B.C., that we begin to hear of the deluge as the great divide in the early history of humanity. As in Genesis, the main thrust seems to be to forge a link between the primeval age and existing nations, families, and individuals. In the late sixth century Hecataeus of Miletus wrote an ethnographic and genealogical work in which he traced contemporary races and clans back to Heracles and the heroic age. About a century later (the dates are not known precisely) Hellanicus of Lesbos divided his *Deucalioneia* into the early history of humanity beginning with Phoroneus, the first man, and the history of the deluge and the post-deluge world. After the ark came to rest on Mount Parnassus, Deucalion became the progenitor of a new humanity and his three sons the eponymous ancestors of the Dorians, Ionians, and Aeolians, the three branches of the Greek people.

The conclusion seems to be warranted that the first eleven chapters of Genesis stand within the same historiographical tradition, comprising in effect Israel's own version of human origins. It remains for us to determine, by a closer scrutiny of its several parts, where it stands within that tradition and what its distinctive features are.

THE PATTERN REPRODUCED IN GENESIS

Even a fairly casual reading of these first eleven chapters will confirm that the *Atraḫasis* pattern is reproduced, with modifications, to a quite remarkable degree. There is no theogony, which is hardly surprising in an officially monotheistic society, though we may be hearing a faint echo of it in the *toledot* (generations) of the heaven and earth (2:4a). The creation of the world is therefore followed by human instead of divine rebellion, bringing on punishment consisting in progressive exile—from Eden, the arable land (*'ădāmāh*) and, climactically, the world itself at the deluge. At the conclusion of the deluge, which is also an act of cleansing and the removal of blood-guilt, the deity gives a pledge of nonrecurrence by means of the rainbow (cf. the lapis object), and there follows a new world order in which the three sons of the survivor are progenitors of the peoples inhabiting the purified earth. Also prominent is the theme of history as progressive degeneration, as in *Atraḫasis* and Hesiod, and the origin of different technologies including agriculture, city building, and metallurgy.

It is equally apparent that in Genesis 1–11 the deluge is structurally the decisive event. While the situation obtaining after this point is in some important respects different, the narrative signals, more clearly than in the parallel versions, the correspondence between the before and the after. The deluge itself is described as an act of uncreation, the undoing of the creative process described at the beginning, resulting in a return to the watery chaos from which the world order emerged in the first place. The blessing on the first man is repeated (9:1), as is the command to reproduce and fill the earth (9:1, 7), perhaps a counter to the punishment resulting from overpopulation in the Mesopotamian version. Permission to eat meat (9:3–5) recalls the primordial dispositions about food (1:29–30). The drunkenness of Noah, occasioning the sin of Ham/Canaan (9:20–27), runs parallel to the primal sin in Eden. The one is an act of eating, the other of drinking; both have to do with plants, the one unspecified, the other the vine; both, therefore, come about in relation to the natural environment. Both have an unmistakable though muted reference to the abuse of the sexual function involving nakedness; and to the snake in Eden corresponds Canaan, both of whom are put under the curse. We are therefore invited to interpret each in the light of the other, an invitation taken up, somewhat surprisingly, by few exegetes.

The extensive use of genealogies and lists aligns Genesis 1–11 with both the Mesopotamian king lists and the early Greek historians. As in Berossus, who lists ten kings before the deluge and ten after, Genesis has ten antediluvian and ten postdiluvian ancestors arranged in linear genealogies (5:1–32; 11:10–26), one of the clearest indications that the biblical narrative is a fairly late variant of a tradition attested from the early second millennium—the Nippur flood tablet—to the Hellenistic period. A distinctive feature of Genesis 1–11, however, is that these lists are incorporated into a larger narrative structure covering the entire span of the primeval history. Our first task, therefore, is to take a closer look at this structure.

THE *TOLEDOT* SERIES

One of the most distinctive features of Genesis is the series of *toledot* (generations) organized in two pentads covering (1) the early history of humanity, and (2) the prehistory of the Israelite people.[4] This feature is one of several indications that Genesis reached its present form as the result of a process in several respects quite different from that of the other four books of the Pentateuch (cf. Rendtorff 1977, pp. 20–28). *Toledot,* always in the plural, means "generations" or "genealogy." The more usual word for "generation" is *dôr,* though *toledot* has a quite different connotation from *dôrôt,* plural of *dôr,* in its reference to a sequence or series as a whole; hence the meaning "history" in Modern Hebrew, for which there is no adequate equivalent in Biblical Hebrew. While *toledot* presupposes a basic genealogical structure, it does not exclude narrative development; in fact, some of the later *toledot* are composed almost entirely of narrative. It is also important to bear in mind that genealogical material, the numerative as opposed to the purely narrative element (Westermann 1984, 3), carries its own distinctive "message." Narrative expansions of genealogies or lists of rulers, more often than not fairly limited in extent, are well attested. In the Sumerian king list we hear of En-men-barage-si, who carried away as spoil the weapon of Elam, of Etana, who was taken up into heaven, of Mes-kiag-gasher, who went into the sea and came out toward the mountains, and of En-me-kar, who built the city of Uruk (ANET, pp. 265–66). The capacity of genealogies to generate narrative expansion is, as we shall see, well attested in Genesis.

The presence of such significant structures in an ancient narrative like Genesis 1–11 is hardly surprising, and similar features have in fact been identified by commentators in different parts of the book. These often involve ring composition or chiasm, sometimes with a fivefold structure, as, for example, in the deluge story (McEvenue 1971, 31), the tower of Babel (Radday 1972, 12–23; Sasson 1980, 211–19), the ten trials of Abraham in Gen 11:27–22:24 (Cassuto 1964, 294–95) and the Jacob cycle (Fishbane 1979, 40–62). If we agree that in ancient compositions structure is a particularly significant vector of meaning, we may suggest that the fivefold arrangement of the *toledot* series is no more fortuitous than the fivefold division of the Pentateuch. It draws our attention at once to the deluge as the central panel of the first series, in keeping with the structurally decisive situation of this event in other ancient accounts of origins. We shall see in due course that the same position is occupied by the Jacob narrative in the second pentad, and both exceed in length those that precede and follow.

The first *toledot* series is arranged as follows:

1.	2:4a	Heaven and earth	2:4b–4:26 (or 1:1–4:26)
2.	5:1	Adam	5:1–6:8
3.	6:9	*Noah*	6:9–9:29
4.	10:1	Noah's three sons	10:1–11:9
5.	11:10	Shem	11:10–26

In any narrative it is possible to identify different levels of meaning, different structures and lines of force, and this especially in narratives like those of Genesis which were not written by one author at one time. We shall now go on to examine each of these five sections in turn, working under the assumption that this particular structural feature provides an important clue to meaning at one level. The emphasis will therefore be on structure; for detailed information on specific exegetical issues the reader may wish to consult the commentaries.

I. HEAVEN AND EARTH (GEN 1:1–4:26)

This is the first of the ten *toledot* in Genesis, all identical with the
exception of Gen 5:1, "this is *the book of* the generations of Adam" *(zeh
sēper tôlĕdôt 'ādām)*. It is also the most problematic, since it is unclear
whether it refers back to the creation account in 1:1–2:3, and therefore is
located exceptionally in the final position, or whether it refers forward to
2:4b–4:26. The latter option is often taken (e.g., Scharbert 1970, 46; Cross
1973, 302; Cohn 1983, 4), but it is not without its problems. The addition of
the phrase "when they were created" *(bĕhibbarĕ'ām)* with the same verb
as in 1:1 points backward rather than forward, and the Eden story does not
deal with heaven and earth but only earth, and one bit of it in particular.
As a part of the series, we would also expect it to cover the period before
the first human generation (5:1), and Westermann (1984, 16–17, 26–28)
may be justified in detecting in this first of the series a hint of the theogony
with which many other origin narratives open. On the other hand, the
book of the generations of Adam (5:1) gives the impression of being the
first in the series, as it is in the Chronicler's history (1 Chron 1:1), which
raises the possibility that 1:1–4:26 may have been tacked on to a *toledot*
book beginning with Adam in Chapter 5. My own suggestion is that the
formula has been placed deliberately at 2:4a both to make way for the
solemn exordium of Gen 1:1 and to effect the transition between the origin of heaven and earth and what happened subsequently on earth, the
point of transition being unobtrusively effected by the verbal inversion—
heaven and earth, earth and heaven (2:4a, b).

The Creation of Heaven and Earth (1:1–2:3)

According to the documentary critics this is the first paragraph of the P
source. With very few exceptions (especially Mowinckel 1937, who added
a contribution from E), these critics have read the early history of humanity as a conflation of an early J and a late P source, their respective contributions being more or less as follows:

	J	Combined	P
Creation of the world			1:1–2:4a
Garden of Eden	2:4b–3:24		
Cain and Abel	4:1–16		
The Cain line	4:17–26		
The Adam line (10)			5:1–32
Divine-human unions	6:1–4		

Decision to bring flood	6:5–8		
Flood		6:9–9:19	
Sin of Ham/Canaan	9:20–27		
Noah after the flood			9:28–29
"Table of nations"		10:1–32	
City and tower of Babel	11:1–9		
The Shem line (10)			11:10–26

We have seen that the existence of a continuous J source of early date (10th or 9th century B.C.), beginning here, has been repeatedly questioned in recent years. P has been more resistant to revision, no doubt on account of its highly characteristic and formulaic language. As we proceed we shall accumulate evidence for a literary prehistory of Genesis 1–11 quite different from that of the classical documentary theory. The immediate task, however, is to grasp the major structural features of this first section. On a whole range of other exegetical issues, the subject of a vast and rapidly expanding literature, the reader is referred to the commentaries, the most comprehensive of which in recent years is that of Claus Westermann (1984, 74–177).

The most distinctive and obvious of these structural features is the arrangement in seven days, six of which are occupied with the work of creation arranged in parallel triads as follows:

I	(3–5)	Light Separation of light and darkness	IV	(14–19)	Sun, moon, stars Separation of day and night
II	(6–8)	Firmament Separation of lower and upper water	V	(20–23)	Water and air creatures
IIIA	(9–10)	Dry land Separation of water and dry land	VIA	(24–28)	Land creatures humans
IIIB	(11–13)	Vegetation	VIB	(29–31)	vegetation as food

VII (2:1–3) The sabbath of God

The following points should be noted:

(1) The works of creation, eight in all, have been fitted into six days, resulting in a double assignment on the third and sixth days.

(2) The seven days represent the liturgical week, the day beginning in the evening, and the week crowned by Sabbath. Sabbath was instituted at

Sinai (Ex 20:8–11), though anticipated in observance at an earlier stage in the wilderness (Ex 16:22–30). That it also crowns the work of constructing the wilderness sanctuary (Ex 31:12–17) is one of several indications of a parallelism between world-building and sanctuary-building. The point is being made that Sabbath is rooted in the created order of things.

(3)   The work of separation is confined to the first four days, a cosmic counterpart to the distinction between "clean" and "unclean" in the ritual law. A subtle pointer in the same direction is the insistence, repeated seven times, that the living creatures were created according to their kinds, that is, their proper distinctions.

(4)   The formula "God saw that it was good" occurs five times, the last occurrence couched in a more solemn form. The divine naming of created things ceases after the appearance of the earth. Henceforth, naming is to be part of the human task of "subduing and dominating," that is, replicating on earth the order established by God in the cosmos as a whole.

(5)   The arrangement in parallel triads is certainly not accidental. The heavenly bodies correspond to light, the denizens of water and air to the firmament, and land animals and human beings to dry land, their natural habitat. Correspondence between the last pair (IIIB and VIB) makes the point that both animals and humans were created herbivores. It is a kingdom of peace with no shedding of blood. Permission to kill for food given after the deluge (9:3–5) indicates, therefore, a lower order of performance, not part of the original creation. The state of peaceful coexistence has been lost.

(6)   The seven-day structure also directs attention to the creation of the heavenly bodies on the fourth day, the midpoint of the creation week. Apart from providing light, their function is to serve as signs, festivals, days, and years or, in other words, to fix the liturgical calendar. The reckoning of sacred time from this point has a logic of its own. It follows the creation of undifferentiated light on the first day, the firmament as the backdrop for the heavenly bodies on the second, and the earth from which they are observed and their movements calculated on the third. The correlation between sacred time and sacred space is carried forward by a carefully worked out chronological schema which, as we have seen, assigns special importance to the setting up of the sanctuary at Sinai and, in due course, in the promised land. The interconnectedness of these points on P's historical continuum is indicated by verbal and thematic parallels: the spirit of God is an active agent in creation and the construction of the sanctuary (Ex 31:3), both conclude with Sabbath, and the sanctuary is erected on the first day of the first month, corresponding to the New Year's Day of creation (Blenkinsopp 1976; Fishbane 1979, 11–13). This

symbolic connection between cosmos and temple, creation and worship, is of course not peculiar to Israel. Just as the P narrator traces a line from creation to the construction of the sanctuary and the establishment of the cult, so in *enuma elish* the creation of the world concludes with the building of a temple for the praise of the creator–deity. We may add that the author of Job also depicts the world as a temple, the laying of the foundation stone of which is accompanied by a joyful liturgy:

> Where were you [God asks Job] when I established the earth?
> Tell me, if you are so clever!
> Who fixed its measurements? — Surely you know!
> Or who stretched the measuring line upon it?
> On what were its bases sunk?
> Or who laid the cornerstone,
> When the morning stars sang together,
> And all the sons of God exulted for joy? (Job 38:4–7)

The Eden Narrative (2:4b–3:24)

Following immediately on the systematic presentation of creation in 1:1–2:3, the Eden narrative carries the message that the emergence of evil is subsequent to the creation of the world and humanity. In this respect the biblical perspective is quite different from the Mesopotamian view of origins, according to which violence and strife are, so to speak, built into the fabric of the created order. The Eden narrative therefore transfers the rebellion theme from the divine realm to the human one. It may therefore be read as generated by reflection on the creation account in Genesis 1, though of course this possibility could not be entertained as long as it was assumed that Gen 2:4b–3:24 antedated that account by several centuries.

The Eden story follows a fairly clear narrative logic, presenting few difficulties of the kind usually solved by appealing to editorial additions and manipulations. One minor problem surfaces, however, in the author's description of the physical environment, the scenario (2:4b–14). We hear of a source of water gushing out like a hydrant (if this is the meaning of the obscure Hebrew word 'ēd 2:6) which could not be put to use, presumably for irrigation, before the appearance on the scene of a work force. But somewhat later the author speaks of a river rising in Eden and dividing into four tributaries that supply water to much of the eastern world in which Eden is situated (2:10–14). The many commentators who have bracketed this passage as a later addition may be correct, especially since the placing of the man in the garden is repeated immediately after it, a resumptive technique often indicative of an insertion (2:8, 15). In that case the four-branched river may have been intended as a clarification of the '*ēd,* in keeping with which we hear that the man's function is to till the ground, thus fulfilling the need referred to earlier (2:15 cf. 2:5).

Commentators have also found the mention of two special trees problematic, since familiar mythic structures and the corresponding iconography demand one tree only. Initially only the tree of life is said to be in the middle of the garden (2:9), which is as it should be, but later the woman places the tree of the knowledge of good and bad there also in reply to the snake's leading question (3:3). It is this tree from which they are forbidden to eat, and from which nevertheless they do eat, impressed by its capacity to confer a wisdom in some respects proper to divinity (3:6, 22). The final statement of YHWH Elohim (3:22), and the description of the ensuing expulsion (3:24), could be interpreted to imply that they had not yet eaten of the tree of life, though not forbidden to do so. But it is also possible, indeed more probable, that the immunity from death which it conferred required periodic partaking of its fruit, as seems to be the case in the *Gilgamesh* poem. Once denied access to the tree of life, they were therefore doomed sooner or later to die. Whatever the correct solution, these special trees represent two stages intermediate between the human and divine spheres. The tree of the knowledge of good and evil represents a wisdom which, though ostensibly godlike, leads to the miseries of the human condition and eventually to death. The tree of life stands for immunity from death which, paradoxically, is put beyond human reach by striving for a wisdom which is full of deadly ambiguity. If this is a correct reading, the two trees are a requirement of the narrative logic of the story, and it becomes unnecessary to postulate the somewhat inept intervention of a later editor.

According to the standard documentarian view, Gen 2:4b–3:24 is the first episode in a continuous J narrative from the early monarchy, perhaps as early as the United Monarchy (10th century B.C.). This dating rests exclusively on a certain understanding of the character of the work itself, principally its "enthusiastic acceptance of agricultural life and of national-political power and cultus" (Eissfeldt 1966, 200; a nearly identical assessment is in Fohrer 1968, 149, 151). But we have already noted that, whatever may be the case with passages attributed to J elsewhere in the Pentateuch or Hexateuch, this is not an appropriate characterization of this passage, or indeed of any of the other J passages in Genesis 1–11 which emphasize the curse on the soil, banishment, exile, and the divine repudiation of human pretensions in general and in the political sphere in particular. In addition, the criterion of divine names is not satisfied here, where the deity is referred to as YHWH Elohim, except in the conversation between the snake and the woman where both speak of Elohim (3:1–5).

It is also worth noting that the Eden story is nowhere referred to in any pre-exilic text, that is, at any time prior to the Neo-Babylonian period. Beginning at that time, however, we begin to hear of it with some frequency (Ezek 28:13; 31:9, 16, 18; 36:35; Isa 51:3; Joel 2:3). Of special interest is the parallel version in Ezekiel's lament over the king of Tyre (Ezek 28:11–19), a version reproducing the same narrative structure and featuring most of the motifs of the Genesis account. The king is in Eden, the garden of God; there is the guardian cherub; iniquity comes about through the corruption of wisdom, leading to expulsion. Peculiar to Ezekiel is the perfect beauty and wisdom and the royal status of the garden's occupant. Precious stones are mentioned in both versions, but only Ezekiel places the garden on the mountain of God, the mythic world center.

A date considerably later than the United Monarchy is also suggested, though not positively established, by an examination of the vocabulary of Gen 2:4b–3:24, including:

(i) words elsewhere attested exclusively or primarily in exilic or post-exilic texts: 'ēd (source of water) Gen 2:6 cf. Job 36:27; neḥmād (pleasant) Gen 2:9; 3:6; cf. Ps 19:11; Prov 21:20; tāpar (sew) Gen 3:7; cf. Ezek 13:18; Job 16:15; Eccl (Qoh) 3:7; 'ēbāh (enmity) Gen 3:15; cf. Num 35:21–22 (P); Ezek 25:15; 35:5; 2 Chron 32:15; šûp (bruise?) Gen 3:15; cf. Ps 139:11; Job 9:17; 'eṣeb (labor) Gen 3:16; cf. Ps 127:2; Prov 5:10; 10:22; 14:23; 15:1; tĕšûqāh (longing) Gen 3:16; cf. Song 7:11.

(ii) words especially characteristic of late wisdom: 'ărûm (crafty) Gen 3:1; cf. Prov 12:16 and passim; Job 5:15; 15:5;[5] lĕhaśkîl (to confer wisdom) Gen 3:6; cf. Prov 13:12 etc.; Job 33:20.

This list is certainly not exhaustive,[6] but even more significant is the prominence in the narrative of themes and topoi characteristic of the wisdom writings. These include the tree of life, identified in Prov 13:12 as a desire fulfilled (ta'ăwāh bā'āh), the same term as in Gen 3:6 (cf. also Prov 3:18; 11:30; 15:4); eating as a euphemism for sexual activity (cf. Prov 6:30; 30:20); and the naming of the animals by the man, which is reminiscent of Solomon's onomastic wisdom (cf. 1 Kings 4:33). This too is only a sampling, but it suggests that our passage is to be aligned with the sapiential tradition at a relatively mature stage of its development. Comparison with certain passages in Ezekiel, Proverbs 1–9, and Job (e.g., the allusion to the first man in Job 15:7–8) suggests further that this tradition now considers it appropriate to incorporate mythic representations in a highly sophisticated way for its own purposes—what Plato called "philosophizing by means of myth." It would be possible to argue, for example, that just as Genesis 1–11 as a whole corresponds to the structure of the Atraḥasis myth, so the garden of Eden story has incorporated many of the themes of the great *Gilgamesh* poem.[7] We shall have occasion to test the hypothesis of a late date when we look at the other passages in Genesis 1–11 attributed by the documentarians to the J source.

A related issue concerns the purpose and function of the Eden story in the context of the larger narrative which it introduces. To begin with, we detect a significant parallelism between Gen 2:4b–3:24 and the course of the Primary History as dictated by the prophetic-Deuteronomic presuppositions of its author or authors. Like Israel, the man is placed in a favorable environment, at which point of the narrative the verb employed *(wayyanniḥēhû,* Gen 2:15) recalls the standard Deuteronomic term for secure possession of the land *(měnûḥāh,* e.g. Deut 12:9; 25:19; 1 Kings 8:56). Permanency in that environment is, however, contingent on obeying a commandment, and death is threatened as punishment for disobedience. But what follows, at both the micro- and macro-narrative levels, is not death but banishment and exile. Behind the figure of the seductive serpent we also detect the cults practiced by the native inhabitants of the land, and behind the words he utters the promises which they hold out for their practitioners. The role of the woman also has its counterpart in the Deuteronomic concern with women as the occasion for adopting these cults (e.g., Deut 7:3–4), the parade example, of course, being Solomon (1 Kgs 11:1–8). One would therefore think that the pattern of events in the history has generated a reflective recapitulation, recasting the national experience in universal terms by the learned use of familiar mythic themes and structures, and placing it at the beginning as a foreshadowing of what was to follow.

We cannot leave this subject without commenting on the thematic parallels between Gen 2:4b–3:24 and the so-called Succession History in 2 Sam 11–20 and 1 Kings 1–2.[8] Beginning with David's adultery, a crime on which David himself passes the death sentence (2 Sam 12:5), though it is not carried out, there is recorded a series of offenses all involving in some way the abuse of the sexual function: Amnon's rape of Tamar (2 Sam 13), Absalom's usurpation of his father's harem (2 Sam 16:20–23), and Adonijah's attempt to possess Abishag (1 Kgs 2:15–17). Two of these episodes involve the intervention of an ostensibly wise agent whose intervention leads, however, to disastrous consequences. Jonadab, described as a very wise man (2 Sam 13:3), uses his "wisdom" to bring about Amnon's evil design, leading to the latter's death; Ahithophel, the sage counselor, performs a similar service for Absalom (2 Sam 16:20–23), with consequences no less fatal for both. The case of the wise woman of Tekoa is somewhat different (2 Samuel 14), but even here we observe how her mission on behalf of the exiled Absalom leads eventually to his defeat and death. It is also worth noting that the same woman's fiction of the two brothers, one of whom murders the other, is himself threatened with death and is saved from the consequences of his act by direct intervention of the king (2 Sam 14:5–11), is structurally exactly parallel to the Cain and Abel story.[9]

Both the Eden story and the Succession Narrative, therefore, exhibit the same deterrent attitude to a kind of wisdom which not only promises more than it can deliver but also leads away from the traditional religious resources, resulting in disaster and death. The Succession History has been widely regarded as a masterpiece of Hebrew prose from the reign of Solomon, and therefore roughly contemporary with the J source. Recently, however, Van Seters has challenged the consensus, arguing on literary grounds that this narrative is a later addition to Dtr. (Van Seters 1983, 277–91). Much earlier R. N. Whybray, while not challenging the early date, made a strong case for assigning it to the genre of wisdom literature rather than historiography (Whybray 1968). The issue clearly needs further scrutiny, but if Van Seters is right about the date of composition, and Whybray about its literary character, we would have further support for a later dating of the Eden story, read as a sapiential reflection in narrative form on the historical experience of Israel.

The Cain and Seth Lines (4:1–26)

Most commentators treat the story of the fratricide (4:1–16), the partially segmented genealogy of Cain (4:17–24), and the Adam-Seth-Enosh line (4:25–26) separately, but it is also possible to read the entire chapter as one segmented Adamic genealogy with narrative developments. Easily the longest of these is the account of the fratricide (2b–16). Much briefer notices are attached to Cain-Enoch (17), Lemech (20–24), Seth (25), and Enosh (26). We noted earlier that this kind of narrative development from genealogy is a well-attested phenomenon, the only remarkable feature here being the unusual length of the first passage indicated. The skeletal genealogical structure is as follows:

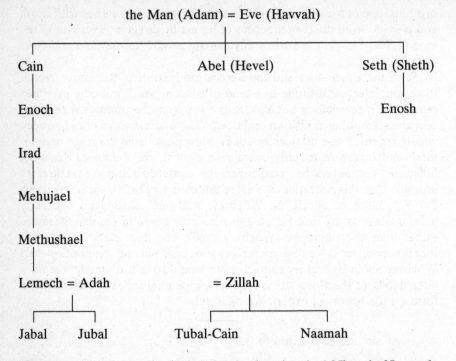

The three sons of the Man (Adam for the first time in 4:25) and of Lemech prepare us for the three sons of Noah, progenitors of the new humanity after the deluge, and recall the three sons of Deucalion, ancestors of the Greek-speaking peoples. Since the birth of Seth is recorded after the history of the seven-generation Cain family, it might seem that the YHWH cult was introduced after a dark period when the "true religion" was unknown. This would imply that the chapter ends on an upbeat note. But such a reading would go directly against the thrust of the antediluvian history as a whole. We would also have to suppose that the compiler failed to notice that YHWH is mentioned by name throughout the Cain story, and that Eve invokes that name at the birth of her first child. We conclude, then, that the compiler brought together different genealogical traditions and dealt with the two surviving lines in birth order without regard to strict chronological sequence.

The relation of this genealogical material to the Adam *toledot* in the following chapter calls for comment. Five of the names (Adam, Seth, Enosh, Enoch, Lemech) are identical, and four appear to be variants (Kenan–Cain, Mahalalel–Mehujael, Jared–Irad, Methuselah–Methushael). Most commentators conclude that the ten-member P genealogy has drawn on the more fragmentary data in Chapter 4 to provide comprehensive genealogical coverage of the antediluvian period. This, however, leaves us

with the problem of explaining the variants in the Adam *toledot,* and it has
been pointed out that a ten-member genealogy is the norm, ten generations representing the optimum length for a genealogy (Finkelstein 1966,
Malamat 1968, Miller 1974). It seems therefore more likely that both chapters have drawn, more or less independently, on a common source which is
represented more fully in the P material.

The narrative of 4:1–16 has generally been assumed to have a long
prehistory which commentators have worked hard to reconstruct. The sociological explanation of the fratricide, in particular, has a long and distinguished pedigree that can be traced through Gunkel, Robertson Smith,
Stade, and Wellhausen to Ewald and no doubt beyond. (See the sensible
remarks of Skinner 1930 [1910] 111–15). As interesting as these speculations may be, the main task of the interpreter is to grasp the logic and
structure of the story itself and its place in the larger narrative context.
First, then, is its relation to the preceding episode; for even if the story of
the fratricide originated as an alternative primeval event (e.g., Westermann 1984, 311), which is by no means certain, it now follows the Garden
of Eden episode. All indications are that the two passages belong together,
in the sense that what happens in the garden determines what takes place
after the expulsion. They are united in the first place by the *'ādām-
'ădāmāh* motif. Bearing in mind the occupation of Cain's father, a tiller of
the soil (2:15), one already sees an ominous note in the description of this
son as *'obēd 'ădāmāh,* a tiller of the ground which has been cursed (3:17).
The alert reader is therefore already prepared for trouble, and when it
comes, it ends with the repetition of the curse and a further expulsion, this
time from the arable land (3:24; 4:11; both with the verb *grš*). So much for
"enthusiastic acceptance of agricultural life" (Eissfeldt 1960, 200). The
pattern of wrongdoing, punishment, expulsion, and mitigation of the penalty is therefore replicated outside of Eden, and the primal disorder begins
to spread throughout the descendants of the first couple.

The passages also have enough in common stylistically to leave little
doubt that they derive from the same source. Both use symbolic names—
Adam, Eve (Havvah), Cain, Abel (Hevel)—and it is worth noting that this
last term, meaning "breath," "vanity," occurs frequently in sapiential
compositions, especially, of course, Qoheleth. Both also feature personifi-
cations—the talking snake and sin as a *robēṣ,* a beast of prey or demon
crouching at the door (4:7).[10] Westermann's suspicion that such a personification is unlikely at the early date assigned to J is understandable (Westermann 1984, 300), but if the date of composition is much later the problem does not arise. We might then compare it with the personification of
wisdom and her opposite number or shadow in Proverbs 1–9. Another
common feature is the use of dialogue, and we note that the interroga-
tion of the man in the garden and his son in the open country follows the

same pattern: where are you? where is your brother? The warning issued to Cain also recalls the words spoken to the woman in the garden, and there are no grounds, textual or otherwise, for recourse to editorial intervention:

> 'el 'îšēk těšûqātēk wěhû' yimšol-bāk
> (to your husband will be your longing, and he will master you, 3:16)
> 'ēlekā těšûqātô wě'attāh timšol-bô
> (towards you is its longing, but you can master it, 4:7)

There are other instances, e.g., "the face of the earth" (2:6 and 4:14) and "east of Eden" (3:8 and 4:16) which, taken together, leave little doubt that we are dealing with one continuous narrative by one and the same author.

The threefold segmentation of the Adamic line in this section soon becomes twofold, thus setting up a contrast between the descendants of Cain and those of Seth. In the seven-member Cain line only the beginning and the end are emphasized, which seems to be a common feature of genealogies in traditional societies. The principals are presented as the originators of different technologies, corresponding to the *prōtoi heuretai* of early Greek mythographers; and we may note how prominent are new beginnings in Genesis 1–11 in general (4:26; 6:1; 9:20; 10:8; 11:6). Agriculture and animal husbandry are already in place (see 4:2), but Cain, surprisingly in view of his previously announced destiny as a *na vanadnik,* also founds a city (4:17).[11] This feat will be duplicated by Nimrod (10:11) and the people from the east who settle in the Mesopotamian plain (11:1–9). The beginnings of cattle rearing, the playing of musical instruments, and metalworking are then attributed to Jabal, Jubal, and Tubal-cain, respectively (4:20–22). In view of the increasing tempo of violence over the course of these seven generations, expressed vividly in Lemech's savage paean of vendetta (4:23–24 cf. 4:15), it is difficult to avoid the conclusion that technological progress is being linked with moral degeneration, as in Hesiod's *Works and Days.* This, again, is consistent with a certain understanding of the "message" of the Eden narrative.

The brief allusion to the Seth line does not require appeal to editorial intervention (as Westermann 1984, 338). The contrast between the technological advance and moral regression in the Cain line and the one "invention" of the Sethites, the introduction of the YHWH cult, is clearly deliberate. At this point the narrative breaks off and the first of the *toledot* series comes to an end.

Conclusion

This first section is structurally the most problematic due to the location of the superscript (2:3a). I suggested that it has been displaced from its usual initial position by the solemn opening of the creation account, and the Eden narrative has been added to effect the transition from the creation of the world to the early history of the earth and of humanity. The transition is indicated by the inversion of the words "heaven and earth" at the point of juncture (2:4), and perhaps also by the designation YHWH Elohim in the Eden narrative, combining as it does the divine names of the preceding and subsequent sections. The view adopted here is that in Gen 2:4a–4:26 one of Israel's later sages set out to give us a more reflective account of the first flowering of evil in early humanity. He may also have been motivated to present, at the very outset, the pattern which would be reproduced in the history of Israel to which these early chapters serve as prologue.

II. HUMANITY BEFORE THE DELUGE; THE ADAM LINE (5:1–6:8)

This second section of the first pentad consists in a ten-member linear genealogy, segmented only at the end with the three sons of Noah (5:1–32), and a reflective comment on the growth of evil in antediluvian society, continuing a theme broached in the first section (6:1–8).

The relation of the *toledot* series to the P source has been under inconclusive discussion for a long time, a situation entirely normal in Old Testament scholarship. The view that the *toledot* structure is the work of a later interpolator or glossator had its advocates in the early decades of the century (e.g., Eichrodt 1916), but is rarely heard today (see Budde 1914, 1916; Eissfeldt 1958, 1961). There is, in fact, no reason to separate the titles from the genealogical material that provides the structural framework of Genesis. More difficult to dispose of is the opinion that a distinct *toledot* book somewhat along the lines of 1 Chronicles 1–9 was incorporated into the P narrative (von Rad 1934, 33–40; 1961, 68). The fact that the *toledot* series does not extend throughout the entire P narrative might be taken to support this opinion, and the reference back to the creation account made at the beginning of this second section (5:1b–2), in which *ʾādām* occurs as a collective noun with the verb in the plural, might suggest an expansion of the genealogy to link it with the P creation account. The question cannot easily be decided, and in any case the *toledot* series is well enough integrated into this early section of the history to be considered an essential part of it.

The Adam Line (5:1–32)

The ten-member genealogy from Adam to Noah inclusively runs parallel with the ten postdiluvian ancestors in 11:10–26, both together providing a comprehensive outline of the early history of humanity. This genealogical schema is still often compared to, or even thought to be modeled on, the Sumerian king lists, though the formal and functional differences are more apparent than the similarities (Lambert 1965, Hartman 1972, Hess 1989). A closer analog would be the first chapter of the history of Berossus, beginning with creation and listing ten names before and ten after the deluge, an account of which is included. The formulaic pattern on which the genealogy in Genesis 5 is built includes the following information: age of the ancestor at the birth of a son, extent of his life span after this point, births of other sons and daughters, total life span, death. David Clines has acutely observed here a tension between the abundant life implicit in the divine blessing and command ("God blessed them and said to them, 'Be fruitful, multiply, and fill the earth,' " Gen 1:28) and the steady recurrence of death as a result of sin (Clines 1978, 66–68). To this we may add the more mundane observation that the pivotal position of the birth of a son facilitates the construction of the overall chronological system, for without it one would not be able to calculate the time elapsed between the creation of the first man and the deluge.

The formulaic evenness of the genealogy is disturbed only at the beginning, at the end, and in the numerically significant seventh position. The brief passage immediately after the title (5:1b–2) links the genealogy with creation, and with the creation of humanity in particular; and the repetition of the phrase "in his likeness, after his image" in the following verse (5:3) makes the point that the divine image is transmitted from the first man to his descendants. Unlike the title, which refers to Adam as an individual, the brief insertion that follows it speaks of humanity in general as 'ādām, as in the creation account of Genesis 1. It is rounded off elegantly with an inclusion ("on the day when he created them") and adds the name-giving which, in a sense, makes the genealogy possible.

The significant seventh position is occupied by Enoch (5:21–24), whose life span of 365 years, by far the shortest, has obvious links with the solar calendar. A connection with Enmeduranki, king of Sippar, city of the sun god Shamash, has often been suggested, and in view of later developments of the Enoch tradition this king's fame as founder of the guild of priest-diviners is obviously of interest. It is also noteworthy that Evedoranchos, presumably the equivalent of Enmeduranki, is seventh in the antediluvian list of Berossus, and that he too was taken up by the gods. What we are to make of these connections is by no means clear. Exegetically more significant is the fact that in the context of the genealogy Enoch's "walking with

God" implies a negative verdict on his contemporaries, an implication even more apparent where the same phrase is used of Noah, a man blameless in his generation (Gen 6:9). The greatly reduced life span also has the advantage of removing Enoch from the scene well before the deluge in which his son Methuselah appears to have perished. (According to the MT chronology Enoch died in A.M. 987 and Methuselah in A.M. 1656, the year of the deluge). We shall go on to see that this notice about Enoch provides an important clue for the interpretation of the genealogy as a whole.

The formula has been modified toward the end of the genealogy in order to introduce an explanation of the name Noah (5:29) and supply the names of his three sons (5:32). The name etiology, the subject of endless discussion, may be translated literally as follows:

This one will comfort us *(yĕnaḥămēnû)* from our work
and from the toil *('iṣṣabôn)* of our hands, from the
ground *('ădāmāh)* which YHWH has cursed.

If, as Freedman suggested *(ZAW* 64[1952] 190–94), the verbal stem is *nwḥ*, with the sense of resting, we would have a good fit with the name, though the point would remain somewhat elusive. The more obvious option of *nḥm*, on the other hand, would do very well if the name were Nahum or something of the sort, but would not naturally suggest the name Noah. The reference, therefore, must remain uncertain, though it is generally taken to refer to the cultivation of the vine initiated by Noah, a passage conventionally assigned to J (9:20–21). That the name etiology itself is from the hand of J has never been doubted: it uses the divine name YHWH, refers back to the curse on the *'ădāmāh* (3:17 J), and features the same rare word for toil *('iṣṣabôn)* as appears there (3:16, 17). From the documentary point of view, however, the problem then is that we have a J insert into an undoubtedly P context. While it might be argued that this is an editorial intrusion in the style of J from someone who wished to make a connection with 3:17 (as Westermann 1984, 359–400), a simpler explanation is that it is one of several indications in Genesis 1–11 that the material assigned to J by the documentarians represents a compositional stage later than the material assigned to P.

Something was said earlier about the problematic relation between the Cainite and Sethite lines in 4:17–26 and the ten-member Adam line in 5:1–32. No matter how this relationship is explained,[12] it is at least clear that the Adam genealogy conveys a distinctive message of its own. While nothing is said explicitly about the progressive spread of evil, the positioning of Seth and Enosh before Cain (Kenan) and his line, together with the pointed remarks about Enoch, conveys the message of a progressive moral

degeneration reaching the point of no return in the critical seventh generation.[13] Whether the same can be deduced from the life span of the
Adamites is less clear. Certainly they are higher than the average life
expectancy of the postdiluvians, but within the antediluvian genealogy
itself, leaving aside the special cases of Enoch and Noah, only four have a
shorter life span than their immediate predecessors, and the longest, those
of Jared and Methuselah, both exceed that of Adam by a considerable
margin. The only clear indication, therefore, would be the greatly reduced
age of Lemech, father of Noah. All such speculations remain quite uncertain, however, since they are based on the assumption of the originality of
the MT numbers over against those of LXX and the Samaritan Pentateuch. In addition, all these fictive numbers are determined by the chronological schema into which they have been fitted and about which we still
know very little.

The Spread of Evil in the Antediluvian World (6:1–8)

The passage immediately following the genealogy comprises an explanation in mythical terms of the prevalence of arbitrary power in the antediluvian world (1–4) followed by a reflective comment on this situation (5–8).
It is generally read as the J introduction to the deluge, though in the
context of the *toledot* structure its links are with what precedes rather than
with what follows. The connection is made explicitly in the opening
phrase, "when humanity was beginning to multiply on the surface of the
ground, and daughters were born to them," for that is precisely what the
genealogy, which also mentions daughters, is about. We can therefore set
aside the identification of the "sons of God" and "daughters of men" with
Cainites and Sethites respectively, an identification still occasionally argued. It seems, rather, as if the author of Gen 6:1–8 set out to "decode"
the meaning of the genealogy in the light of later developments, across the
great divide of the deluge.

There can be no doubt that the telegrammatically brief notice about
divine–human marriages comes from the same hand, or at least the same
milieu, as the preceding J narratives. The divine name YHWH is employed and there is the same interest in beginnings, the allusion to the
insidious abuse of the sexual faculty, and the unembarrassed use of mythical categories. It relates a further attempt to break through the barrier
separating the divine and human spheres, following the frustrated attempt
of the man and woman in Eden to achieve divine status (3:22).

The theme of marriage between divine beings and human women was
not unknown in ancient Mesopotamia but seems to have been especially
popular in the West, to judge by Homer, Hesiod, and *The Catalogue of
Women*. Van Seters has argued for an important Western component in

Genesis 1–11, and for dependence of his exilic J source on *The Catalogue of Women*, probably mediated by Phoenicians. Intriguing as it is, this hypothesis labors under all kinds of problems. The best estimate of the date of *The Catalogue* would make it either contemporary with or slightly later than the J of Van Seters, and we would have to assume not only that a copy of *The Catalogue* was in Phoenician hands shortly after its composition, but also that it had been translated into a Semitic language—unless, of course, J could read Greek.[14] The theme itself is, in any case, of much greater antiquity, in whatever form it was known to the biblical writer. Its popularity also continued down into late antiquity, and it was well represented in Enoch and the Book of Jubilees. It has even served as a familiar theme in science fiction writing as, for example, in *The Midwich Cuckoos* of John Wyndham.

The outcome of this titan promiscuity is stated in 6:4, but unfortunately the garbled state of the text makes it difficult to know what is going on. Literally translated, it runs as follows:

> The *nephilim* were on the earth in those days [and also later] when the sons of god consorted with the daughters of men who bore them children. These are the heroes of ancient times, men of renown.
>
> (The phrase in parenthesis, *wĕgam 'aḥărē-kēn,* is a gloss introduced to explain how descendants of the *nephilim* were still around long after the deluge; for in Num 13:33 the Israelite reconnaissance party reported sighting giants descended from the *nephilim,* who, of course, should have perished in the deluge.)

It is not clear whether the *nephilim* were on the scene before this act of superhuman hubris or were rather the outcome of it, and therefore identical with the heroes mentioned *(gibbôrîm)*. A derivation from the verbal stem *npl* (= fall) gives the meaning "fallen ones" and therefore brings to mind the familiar theme of rebellion in heaven and the casting down of the insurgent divine beings. The Hurrian Kumarbi myth, though not a parallel to Gen 6:1–4 *(pace* Speiser 1964, 45–46), is of this kind, as is the Greek myth about the Titans, and an echo of a Canaanite version can be heard in an Isaian poem about the fall from heaven of Daystar, son of Dawn (Isa 14:12–20).[15] Close to if not identical with the *nephilim* are the *gibbôrîm,* the first of whom was Nimrod, founder of the first Mesopotamian empire (Gen 10:8–11). We are therefore invited to think of the *gibbôrîm* as potentates, aspirants to absolute and arbitrary political power. Their eventual reduction to impotence in Sheol is graphically described by Ezekiel in a satirical poem on the Egyptian Pharaoh (Ezek 32:20–32), a poem in which they are described as *gibbôrîm nopĕlîm* [*or nĕpēlîm*] *mē'ô lām*[16] ("potentates fallen [or *nephilim*] from of old", v 27), language reminiscent of Gen 6:4.

The author, therefore, is carrying over the theme of Genesis 2–3 into the political sphere and will take this further in alluding to the rise of the Mesopotamian city states (10:8–11) and satirizing the cult and culture of Babylon (11:1–9). A related theme comes to expression in the description of these antediluvian *gibbôrîm* as "men of renown," literally "men of name." To make a name for themselves was the goal of the founders of Babylon (11:4), and this in contrast to Abraham (12:2), significantly of the line of Shem, the man whose name is Name (Jenkins 1978).

YHWH's declaration that his spirit will not remain[17] in humanity forever in that it is flesh (6:3) does not make a good fit with the context, and perhaps is out of place. But it seems that the deity is once again blocking the aspiration to pass beyond the confines of the human into the divine sphere, and specifically by the indefinite prolongation of physical existence. And if, as has been suggested, the declaration refers more directly to the preceding genealogy, the 120 years would connote a greatly reduced life span rather than a period of grace lasting three generations. That several of the later ancestors lived longer (e.g., Abraham, 175 years) does not rule out this interpretation. The writer may have been thinking only of the antediluvians, or he may have thought of 120 years as the maximum and ideal life span, one which in Israel would be attained by only Moses (Deut 34:7) and elsewhere, if we are to believe Herodotus, by only the long-lived Ethiopians and one or two other extraordinary individuals (Her 1:163; 3:23, on which see Kraeling 1947, 201).

The final passage in the second *toledot* (6:5–8) alludes again, by way of inclusion, to the creation of humanity (cf. 5:1–2) and, at the same time, serves as a transition to the central panel of the pentad by recording YHWH's decision to destroy. It is cast in the same reflective, sapiential mode as the earlier passages assigned to J, and its vocabulary betrays the same origin (e.g., *mē'al pĕnē hā- -'ădāmāh,* from off the face of the ground, cf. 4:14; *yit'aṣṣēb,* grieve, cf. 3:16, 17; 5:29). The profound sense of the ineradicable human tendency to evil, repeated in similar fashion after the deluge (8:21), is reminiscent of later prophecy (e.g., Jer 17:9–10) and the more somber reflections of the sages (e.g., Job 14:1–6). We might note, too, that allusion to "the impulse of the thoughts of his heart" *(yēṣer maḥšĕbôt libbô)* occurs elsewhere only in Chronicles, certainly post-exilic (see 1 Chron 28:9; 29:18). It will lead in due course to the rabbinic teaching on the *yēṣer hārā',* the evil impulse, a teaching based in good measure on this somber reflection which brings the story of the antediluvian world to a close.

III. NOAH AND THE DELUGE (6:9–9:29)

This third and central panel of the series is by far the longest and structurally the most important. The biblical story of the deluge is a fairly late version of a familiar narrative tradition attested from the time of the Sumerians to the Hellenistic period. It is a moot point whether an ancient Near Eastern version ever existed as an independent written narrative. In the major extant versions, *Atraḥasis, Gilgamesh,* the Hebrew Bible, and Berossus, it derives its meaning from a larger narrative complex of which it is a part.

From the early days of historical-critical investigation the story of the deluge has been one of the principal testing grounds for source analysis. Gunkel himself praised the documentary analysis of Genesis 6–9 as a masterly application of critical method (Gunkel 1964 [6th ed] 137). But even here there has been disagreement, and in recent years there has been a steady output of studies aimed at demonstrating the unity of the narrative.[18] It may therefore be necessary to affirm that it is possible to admire its literary qualities without denying the evidence for the conflation of sources. If it is accepted that the story of the deluge exhibits skillful construction—a narrative flow corresponding to the rise and subsidence of the floodwater leading to the turning point at which God remembers—there seems to be no good reason for denying credit to a redactor working with existing material. Source criticism and literary criticism, in the broader sense, are not incompatible, and it may be added that commentary that sets out to disprove the use of sources has not produced the best results to date.

The arguments which have led most scholars to postulate a combination of sources are fairly straightforward and have never been refuted. There are inconsistencies with respect to what was brought into the ark, the chronology, and perhaps also the manner in which the deluge was brought about. We hear of one pair, male and female, of each species (6:19–20; 7:14–16), but also of seven pairs of clean and one pair of unclean animals (7:2–3, 8–9). We are told that the flood lasted forty days (7:4, 12, 17; 8:6), or sixty-one, counting every day until the ground dried out (8:6–12), but we also hear of a duration of one hundred and fifty days (7:24; 8:3), a figure compatible with the five months from the beginning to the grounding of the ark on Ararat (8:4).[19] While the description of the disaster as a downpour of rain (7:4, 12; 8:2) is not necessarily incompatible with the more mythological language of the bursting forth of the fountains of the great deep (7:11; 8:2), it is more natural to think of the latter as providing a quite distinct perspective, especially if read in the larger context of Genesis 1–11.[20]

We have often been reminded that repetition is not in itself an indication of the composite nature of a narrative (e.g., by Alter 1981, 88–113), and with this we may readily agree. But the situation is rather different when we encounter parallel versions of episodes in which the parallels consistently exhibit distinctive characteristics. So, for example, Noah is told to board the ark with family members and specifically designated livestock. He does so, and then the command is repeated with the same people and differently designated livestock, and he does so again (6:18b–21, 22; 7:1–5). In such cases it is unreasonable to exclude editorial activity carried out according to canons somewhat different from those we would follow today.

Our reading of the Genesis narrative to this point has confirmed the essential correctness of the conventional source division, with the important difference that the parts assigned to J, rather than serving as the narrative basis for P, have the appearance of later expansion and commentary. The reader is invited to test this reading of the material in this central section of the first *toledot* pentad. If it is correct, P cannot be the final redactor, an assumption which (*pace* Cross 1973, 305 and *passim*) is improbable even on the hypothesis of an early J and a late P. Why, for example, would a final P redactor have left in the distinction between clean and unclean and the sacrifice after leaving the ark when, *ex hypothesi*, they were omitted from the P strand as anachronistic in the first place? We shall see that the material assigned to P constitutes a fairly complete and coherent story, and that what is left over after subtracting P does not. If a final redactor is postulated, an entirely reasonable supposition, he was presumably responsible for the arrangement of the material, may have added resumptive verses here and there to maintain narrative continuity, and perhaps also injected the occasional comment.[21] We shall now test these assumptions by a brief comment on the narrative divided into its constitutive paragraphs.

Title and Introduction (6:9–10)

The superscription and the notice about the three sons place the long narrative following in the context of the overall genealogical framework, the formulaic language of which is taken up again in the conclusion to this section (9:28–29). Mention of the sons, listed earlier (5:32), is also an example of a resumptive verse following an insertion (i.e., 6:1–8) the purpose of which is to maintain narrative continuity and provide a link with the next *toledot* beginning in 10:1. In the description of the protagonist as "a righteous man, perfect in his generations," it seems likely that "perfect" (*tāmîm*) has been added as a further qualification of "righteous" (*ṣaddîq*).

That Noah, like Enoch before him, "walked with God" obliges us to draw the same conclusions for the generation of the deluge as for that of Enoch.

The Deluge as Divine Punishment (6:11–13)

This opening paragraph illustrates the stylistic feature of composing narrative in short paragraphs rounded off in the manner of a palistrophe or ring composition. What is thereby emphasized, with great economy of language, is the condition of the earth *(hā'āreṣ,* repeated six times), the prevailing corruption (verbal stem *šḥt,* four times) and its expression in violence *(ḥāmās,* twice). While there is nothing specifically priestly about this language, its occurrence in Ezekiel, occasionally in dense concentration,[22] is one of several indications that the prophetic understanding of Israel's history as leading inexorably to disaster and exile, and especially as it comes to expression in Ezekiel, forms the subtext to P's deluge narrative.

The P version of human origins has no explicit account of what happened to bring about the deluge. We recall that *Atraḥasis* (1:352–59) speaks of the noise and tumult of an overcrowded earth, while *Gilgamesh* (11:14) states laconically that the hearts of the gods prompted them to do it. This opening statement in 6:11–13 simply draws out the implications of Noah's righteousness in contrast to those of his generations *(dorotāw,* plural, perhaps including the generations since Enoch). "God saw the earth, and behold, it was corrupt" recalls, not without pathos, God's survey of his original creation in Gen 1:31, a creation not yet disfigured by corruption and violence.

Instructions for Building the Ark (6:14–18a)

Translation of this passage is not as straightforward as it might appear, since it contains a high concentration of words rarely or not at all attested elsewhere. Thus *tēbāh* (ark) occurs only here and in the story of Moses' deliverance (Ex 2:3, 5); *qinnîm* (rooms; literally, nests) has a certain quaintness, but may be an erroneous reading for *qānîm* (reeds, rushes), as suggested by Edward Ullendorf *(VT* 4[1954] 95–96); *koper* (pitch or bitumen) is a hapax legomenon, but the Akkadian equivalent *kūprū* occurs at the same place in the *Gilgamesh version;* for *goper* (wood) pitch pine, teak, and cypress have been suggested, but its identity is uncertain, and it may have been chosen as much for assonance with *kāpartā . . . bakkoper* as for its quality as building material; *ṣohar* (roof? sun roof?), finally, is also hapax, and its precise meaning is unknown.

We note here also how the author creates a tight narrative weave: with eight commands briefly stated, a fivefold repetition of the verb "to make," and an emphasis on dimensions by placing them at the center of this short *pisqah*. These dimensions $(300 \times 50 \times 30)$ are, of course, fictive and pre-sumably significant in some way no longer understood. We might compare them with the perfect cube in *Gilgamesh* in which Utnapishtim rides out the deluge (11:24, 28–31). The instructions conclude with the repetition of the decision to destroy, recalling the language used earlier (6:12–13). There is also an advance announcement of the post-deluge covenant, illustrating once again the concern to bind the stages of the narrative into a unity.

Command to Board the Ark (6:18b–7:5)

Conflation of sources is apparent here for the first time. In the basic P account (6:18b–22) the members of Noah's family are listed (they will be again later in 7:7, 13; 8:15, 18), but the supplementary narrative speaks only of his household (7:1–5). The reason seems to be that P wishes to specify the minimum necessary for the expansion of humanity after the deluge in accordance with the divine blessing and command (Gen 1:28; 9:1). It is much the same with the animals, the listing of which follows closely the creation narrative: the minimum required, a male and female of each species (6:19–20; 7:9, 15–16), is all that need be mentioned, whereas the supplement needs to distinguish between clean and unclean in view of the sacrifice which is to follow. Besides, P is very clear that the purity laws and sacrifice were in force only from Sinai. The provision of food is a concern only for the basic P account, which speaks of food that *may be eaten,* reminding the reader that both people and animals are still vegetarian.

We note once again that the supplement, identical with the strand conventionally attributed to J, does not add up to a complete and independent narrative. The ark is introduced without explanation and with no account of its manufacture and function. At a later point there is no account of the disembarking; it passes directly from Noah looking out of the ark to the sacrifice on dry land. We take it that the base narrative was supplemented both to provide important correctives—the distinction between clean and unclean and the sacrifice—and to include interesting narrative material of unimpeachable antiquity, the sending out of the birds.

The command to board the vessel seems to have been featured in all versions of the deluge story, though unfortunately there is a gap at this point in the Sumerian tablet. *Atraḥasis* speaks of the hero's family and specifies birds and cattle, even clean animals (3:2, 32). The deluge is also announced for the seventh night (3:1, 37). Provisions are varied and plentiful in *Gilgamesh* (11:44–45, 70–75), while Berossus mentions only food and drink for Xisouthros and his family and friends. There are also significant similarities in the description of the catastrophe. We detect, finally, a note of bitter irony in the sending of rain (7:4), since, according to the same putative J source, the absence of rain had been a major problem at the very beginning of human history (Gen 2:5).

Embarkation (7:6–16)

The base narrative continues with the execution of the order to embark. The most salient feature of this passage is the repetition of the movement of people and animals into the ark, following the resumptive v 13 that repeats in almost identical terms the information given in v 7. Also repeated is what might be called the execution formula ("as God had commanded him"), which serves here and elsewhere in P as an *excipit* (vv 9, 15). Repetition functions as a form of emphasis, an application of the redundancy principle conveying to the alert reader the significance of this moment when the future of all humanity hung in the balance. The documentary explanation is that most of vv 7–10 represents the J version, but the situation is not so clear-cut at this point. We can say that there are, at a minimum, four supplements: the distinction between clean and unclean (8), the seven days preceding the deluge (10), the forty days' rainstorm (12), and the notice that YHWH shut Noah in (16). This last creates a severe problem for the standard source analysis: it has always been assigned to the early J source, yet it is intelligible only in the context of the surrounding P narrative. If, moreover, it is assumed to be part of a continuous J narrative, it would come too late, since the flood is already well under way (vv 10, 12). Its purpose is rather to explain, in the manner of midrash, how the ark could have stayed watertight (it is covered inside and outside with pitch) *after* Noah et al. had gone aboard.

Repetitions of the kind attested here are rarely simple restatements. There is usually some additional information, some slight forward movement of the narrative, to which the repetition itself draws attention. So, in this paragraph, we find a more precise chronological indication, of a kind first attested in Ezekiel, for the beginning of the catastrophe. From this, and from the final date in 8:14, we learn that the deluge lasted exactly one solar year. Mention of the fountains of the *tĕhôm rabbāh* (cf. Isa 51:10; Amos 7:4; Ps 78:15) and the windows of heaven also provide a fuller explanation of the "flood of waters" mentioned at the beginning. The three sons are also named, and this too in anticipation of the next phase of the history.

The Deluge Itself, Its Duration and Effects (7:17–24)

Compared with the Mesopotamian versions, the description of the actual deluge is quite restricted. Emphasis is placed rather on what leads up to and follows it—the solemn entry into the ark, which reads rather like a procession, and the establishment of a new order on the purified earth. Here too, in the description of the event, repetition provides the clue to what is most important—namely, the universality of destruction. The climax of the narrative coincides with the rising of the floodwater, indicated by a different cadence, a kind of recitative similar to the creation of humanity in Genesis 1:27:

> wayyibrā' 'ĕlohîm 'et-hā'ādām bĕṣalmô
> bĕṣelem 'ĕlohîm bārā' 'otô
> zākār ûnĕqēbāh bārā' 'otām

At the climactic point of the flood story we also note the folding in of the narrative on itself, the overlapping sequencing of the movement, the repetition of key words (mayim, "water," five times; the verbal stem gbr, "prevail," four times; 'al hā'āreṣ, "on the earth," three times) and their skillful juxtaposition:

> wayyigbĕrû hammayim wayyirbû mĕ'od 'al hā'āreṣ . . .
> wĕhammayim gābĕrû mĕ'od mĕ'od 'al-hā'āreṣ . . .
> ḥămēš 'eśrēh 'ammāh milma'lāh gābĕrû hammayim . . .
> wayyigbĕrû hammayim 'al-hā'āreṣ ḥămišîm
> ûmĕ'at yôm

At this point, with the water standing fifteen cubits over the highest mountain, the narrative has exhausted its forward movement, and we are prepared for the peripety, the turning point which follows.

Subsidence of the Floodwater (8:1–5)

That God's remembering Noah and his fellow passengers marks the turning point is generally acknowledged. (See, for example, the outline in Anderson 1978, 38). It is also agreed that the basic P narrative continues here, with the only expansion the allusion to rainfall in v 2. The theme of God remembering occurs elsewhere in P in connection with exile either in the past (Ex 2:24; 6:5) or in the future (Lev 26:42–45). That the P account of the deluge may be read as a response to the situation of exile is quite plausible, and has often been suggested.[23] Inundation is a natural metaphor for subjugation and defeat, and can be found in the Lament over the Destruction of Ur from the first half of the second millennium B.C. (ANET 455–63; Jacobsen 1981, 527) and occasionally in biblical texts (Ps 124:4–5; Jonah 2:2–3). It is also worth noting that outside of Genesis the name Noah occurs only in Ezek 14:12–20 and Isa 54:9–10, both from the exilic period. The Isaian text is particularly interesting, since it alludes to the covenant of Noah in a context dealing with the end of destitution and exile. We shall see in due course that an exilic context is also appropriate for the central panel of the second *toledot* series, focusing as it does on the exile of Jacob in Mesopotamia and his eventual return to the homeland.

The wind *(rûaḥ)* blowing over the earth and the fountains of the deep *(těhôm)* recall, and are no doubt meant to recall, the original creation. The inference is that the deluge is an act of uncreation, undoing the work of separation by returning everything to the primeval, watery chaos from which the created order first arose. By the same token, the new order established after the subsidence of the water is a new creation, an inference which will be drawn out even further in the conclusion to the P deluge narrative.

The Birds (8:6–12)

The reconnaissance mission of the birds has been spliced into the orderly chronological P account of the last stage of the event: the water began to subside after 150 days (8:1–3); the ark came to rest on Ararat on the seventeenth day of the seventh month (8:40); the water continued to subside until the tenth month, on the first day of which the tops of the mountains were visible (8:5); by the first day of the first month of the following year the water had disappeared (8:13); and on the twenty-seventh day of the following month the earth was dry (8:14). The insertion could be explained simply in terms of narrative interest and the desire to find room for a well-established motif (as in *Gilgamesh* 11:145–54). It could also function to explain, again in the manner of midrash, how Noah knew when it was time to disembark. For the conclusion of the episode we have to wait until 8:13, Noah's removal of the cover or awning and the confirmation that the ground was indeed dry.

Several commentators have decided that the first reconnaissance by the raven is intrusive, since it disturbs the symmetry of the three expeditions by the same bird at seven-day intervals. They also note that an explanation is offered only when the dove is launched for the first time. It is, of course, possible that an editor was influenced by the *Gilgamesh* version in which a raven, a dove, and a swallow are sent out in sequence. But it is also possible that when the raven did not report back for debriefing, Noah decided that a more cooperative emissary was called for. In any case, the function of the episode in the narrative as a whole is not affected.

Noah Leaves the Ark and Sacrifices (8:13–22)

The P account continues with the subsidence of the water and the gradual return from chaos to cosmos. With the drying of the earth on New Year's Day, there begins a new epoch for humanity. As the narrative now reads, the later date of v 14 (the twenty-seventh day of the second month) would represent a further stage, and commentators therefore have been at pains to distinguish between the two verbs used for the drying process (*ḥrb* in v 13, *ybš* in v 14). But it is also possible that v 14 is a correction of the previous statement based on a different chronology. At this point the voice of God is heard for the first time since the command to enter the ark (6:18–21), which means that the deluge is the time of the silence of God. This last phase is presented in the customary P form of command (15–17) and execution (18–19). The repetition of the creation command to be fertile and increase on the earth (v 17 cf. 1:22, 28) will be followed in due course by the blessing and the establishment of a new order (9:1–7).

The sequence of the P story is interrupted by the sacrifice which corresponds to a regular feature of this narrative tradition (e.g., *Gilgamesh* 11:159–61). The internal monologue or soliloquy of YHWH, matching the reflections preceding the catastrophe, and clearly from the same source, seems to suggest that YHWH had now come to terms with the ingrained and ineradicable evil in the human heart and, in consequence, will never again inflict annihilating judgment on humankind and on the earth on which it lives. The supplementary author is here providing his own psychologically more realistic version of the decision not to destroy again by means of a flood (9:15). With the solemn pronouncement "I will never again consider the ground accursed on account of humanity" (8:21) there is brought to an end a situation which had obtained since the first phase of human history in Eden (3:17), and this despite the fact that the effects of the first man's alienation from the soil—toiling for a living, enduring thorns and thistles—persist after the deluge (Rendtorff 1961, 69–78). In addition, the following verse serves as a kind of countervailing blessing, with its assurance that for as long as the earth lasts

> Seed time and harvest time
> Time of cold and time of heat
> Summer and winter
> Day and night
> Shall never cease.

The New Order in the Postdiluvian World (9:1–19)

The P deluge story ends with the establishment of a new world order communicated in two discourses of God (1–7, 8–17), both clearly marked by the stylistic device of inclusion. They are rounded off with a notice about the three sons of Noah (18–19) which serves as an inclusion for the deluge story as a whole (cf. 6:10) while at the same time preparing for the following *toledot*.

The new order consists, basically, in a return to the original creation with the divine blessing and command, a central motif of the P narrative as a whole (see, e.g., Brueggemann 1972, 397–413). It is not, however, an integral restoration. The permission to eat meat, and therefore to kill, indicates a lower order of existence and the loss of a primordial harmony, a situation parallel to the pattern in Hesiod's *Works and Days*. It is now apparent that the violence that precipitated the deluge can be controlled but not extirpated, a point made in more sapiential and reflective form in the supplementary narrative (8:21). The concession itself, however, carries two qualifications (3–4). The first forbids eating meat from which the blood has not been drained, the basis for the *těrēpāh* law in Deut 12:15–18 and Lev 17:10–16. The second goes beyond the killing of animals for food to state a general principle in what is for P a typically triadic form, with threefold repetition of key words:

> For your lifeblood I will require a reckoning:
> Of every animal I will require it
> Of every human being
> Of every man's brother I will require a reckoning for the life of a
> human being.

This last sentence then leads, by association, to the enunciation of a legal principle, a sentence of law, in gnomic style and chiastic form:

> *šopēk dam hā'ādām*
> *bā'ādām dāmô yiššāpēk*
> (He who sheds the blood of a man,
> By a man his blood shall be shed)

These dispositions for the protection of human life are validated with reference to creation in the image of God (1:26–27; 5:1–3). They provided the starting point for the so-called Noachide laws, originally seven in number, which for the rabbis constituted a fundamental torah for all humanity.[24]

The second discourse announces a covenant the substance of which is a guarantee that destruction by deluge will never recur. It is perhaps worth noting that the preceding dispositions are not covenant stipulations on the fulfillment of which the promise depends. The commitment of God addressed to both human and animal creation is unilateral and unconditional and therefore valid in perpetuity. It is a *bĕrît ʿōlām,* an everlasting covenant (9:16; also Gen 17:7, 13; Ex 31:16), meaning that it is not like ordinary covenants that must be renewed from time to time. All that is required is that God remember it, and that is what he does, according to the P narrator. Assurance is given by the sign of the rainbow, a motif taken from an older narrative tradition about the end of the flood. It is therefore not, as Wellhausen, Gunkel, and many others have suggested, the equivalent of burying the hatchet, a signifying of the end of hostilities with God hanging his war bow in the clouds.

The Noachide covenant is part of a larger structure encoded in the P narrative, the originality of which has not received sufficient recognition. Reading the covenant back into the early days of humanity, long before Israel appeared on the scene, introduces a universalistic perspective notably absent from the Deuteronomic traditions. It is therefore humanity as a whole and not Israel which is first brought into direct relationship with God as the recipient of promises, commitments, and (in the Noachide laws) a torah. As for Israel, the pivotal point of contact is moved backward in P to the time of the ancestors. This point is the Abrahamic covenant, the sign of which is circumcision (Genesis 17). Sabbath too is a perpetual covenant and sign (Ex 31:12–17), but neither circumcision nor sabbath observance is presented as a stipulation written into a bilateral agreement between God and Israel. The unconditional nature of this commitment of God, first to the world, then to Israel, would seem to be a response to the disasters of the early sixth century B.C. (the collapse of the state, the fall of Jerusalem, and the ensuing exile), in which respect it bears comparison with an important strand in the teaching of the exilic prophet Ezekiel (see especially Chapter 20).

Noah the Vintner (9:20–29)

This last paragraph of the Noah *toledot* is, like Gen 6:5–8, transitional; it has to do as much with the sons as with the father. It is clearly not part of the essential P story since the sons are unmarried and Ham, not Japhet, is the youngest. It is equally clear that it comes from the author of the Eden narrative, with which it is closely parallel. The sin occurs in connection with the natural environment (the *ʾădāmāh*) and specifically with a plant; there is a sexual connotation involving nakedness and clothing; Ham (or Canaan) is the functional counterpart of the snake; each narrative ends with a curse the outcome of which is an actual state of affairs: the condition of life for men, women, and snakes, and the subjection of the Canaanites, respectively. The structural correspondence is mutually illuminating, providing an exegetical resource not always exploited.

What exactly was done to merit the curse is a question endlessly discussed, the prize for ingenuity going to the proponents of the incest theory, according to which "seeing the nakedness of the father" implies violation of his sexual rights by intercourse with his wife. In other words, Ham witnesses "the primal scene," his father's ineffectual attempt at intercourse, and boldly takes his place, with the result that Canaan is born of this incestuous union. (Kikawada and Quinn 1985, 101–3). The theory is ingenious but overlooks the fact that the father alone is mentioned, it is he who is uncovered, and something is done to him. It is also a dubious procedure to extrapolate from the technical sense of 'erwat 'ab (the nakedness of the father) in Lev 18:8. Other explanations, only slightly less ingenious, are surveyed in the commentaries. For our purpose it will be sufficient to find here an allusion to the moral and specifically sexual depravity of the indigenous population and their cults as viewed from outside.

The oracle with which the brief story ends speaks of the subordination of the Canaanites, the supremacy of the descendants of Shem, and a hoped-for symbiotic relationship between them and the descendants of Japhet. This need not refer to a political situation in the earliest period of Israel's history (Speiser 1964, 62–63), or even earlier (Gunkel 1964, 81). Whenever the story is thought to have originated, these eponyms could be referred to different situations by different generations of readers. Recall, for example, that Ezra-Nehemiah alludes anachronistically to the indigenous element in the Persian province of Judah as Canaanites and deplores their "abominations" (Ezra 9:1, 11; Neh 9:24). It would also have been possible for Japhet to stand for the inhabitants of the Palestinian littoral in the same period, though that is not attested. At a much later date, some of the church fathers even interpreted the Japhet oracle as a prediction of the triumph of Christianity over Judaism!

The final chronological notice (9:28–29) serves as an inclusion to the *toledot* as a whole (cf. 5:32) and completes the pattern according to which the Adam-Noah line is laid out: when Noah was 500 years old he became the father of Shem, Ham, and Japhet; when the flood came the sons were about 100 years old; after the flood Noah lived 350 years more; thus all the days of Noah were 950 years, and he died (9:29).

IV. DESCENDANTS OF NOAH (10:1–11:9)

This fourth section of the history falls into the pattern, familiar to readers of the early Greek mythographers and historians, of a threefold division of postdiluvian humanity. The standard documentary view has it that the basic structure is provided by P, to whom are assigned the titles and conclusions of each section, short lists of descendants arranged conventionally in two generations with a predilection for the number seven, and the finale to the section as a whole in 10:32. It has further been assumed that a redactor has added J material to this P basis, material identifiable by its narrative quality (e.g., 10:8–12) or by the use of a different formula ("Cush became the father of Nimrod"). There are no additions to the Japhet list, for these inhabitants of Asia Minor, Armenia, and the Aegean were unknown in Israel at the time when J was assumed to have been written, i.e., in the ninth or tenth century B.C. As in the previous sections, however, the only question is whether this J material is as early as most documentary critics have assumed it to be.

What is, at any rate, clear is that each of these narrative strands has its own distinctive point of view. In keeping with its universalistic perspective, P wishes to show how this great array of nations is the result of the creation blessing and command to fill the earth. In addition to expanding the lists, in keeping with the broader cultural and historical perspective of its time, "J" wishes to demonstrate how the drive for power and status exercises its corrupting influence here as previously. Hence the allusion to another false start with the creation of the first empire in the land of Shinar (10:8–12), an allusion skillfully worked out in narrative form in the account of the frustration of that attempt in the same region (11:1–9).

Title and Japhet List (10:1–5)

The title introduces the fourth *toledot,* that of the three sons of Noah (cf. 5:32; 6:10; 7:13; 9:19). Their descendants, however, are listed in inverse order with a view to ending with Shem and thus setting up the final *toledot.* There appears to be no good reason for assigning the second half of 10:1 ("sons were born to them after the flood") to J, especially since the phrase "after the flood" occurs by way of inclusion in the final paragraph, i.e., in 10:32 (*pace* Westermann 1984, 498). The descendants will form a macrocosm of seventy peoples corresponding to the microcosm of Israel, also originally seventy in number (Gen 46:27; Ex 1:5). The concern, evident in the P strand, to survey the nations from a fixed point within Israel—an invisible point of reference in the list—may well have been a response to the diaspora situation reflected at other points of the P work.

The descendants of Japhet, whose name is probably related to that of the titan Iapetos, son of Uranus and Gaia and father of Atlas, Prometheus, and Epimetheus, are arranged in a list of seven "sons" and seven "grandsons." Most of them can be identified with ethnic groups settled in Asia Minor, Armenia, and the Aegean region. Ten of them are mentioned in

Ezekiel from the early exilic period. The list has not been expanded, either because it was not thought necessary or because of a lack of interest in this most distant branch of postdiluvian humanity. The notice linking the population of a coastal region with these peoples (10:5a) may, however, have been added. If the region in question is the Palestinian littoral, it may refer to the Greek-speaking outposts which were well established there by the Persian period.

Hamitic List (10:6–20)

This list of places and peoples, mostly to the south, is organized according to the four ethnic groups of Ethiopians (Nubians), Egyptians, Libyans, and Canaanites. Ethiopia and Egypt each have seven "sons," consisting in places for the former and ethnic groups for the latter, many so far unidentified. For Libya (Put, as in Ezek 27:10; 30:5; 38:5) no descendants are listed, perhaps for lack of knowledge or interest. Canaan has eleven, a composite group including the inhabitants of Phoenician cities and autochthonous Canaanite peoples. The Egyptian list is often assigned to J on the basis of the formula used ("X became the father of Y") and the plural form of ethnic names. This is possible, though we need not assume absolute uniformity even for P. The same conclusion has been proposed for the Canaanite list, which includes a brief description of boundaries (10:15–19). In view of the decline of Tyre after the thirteen-year siege by the Babylonians (ca. 586–573 B.C.) and the subsequent ascendancy of Sidon during the Persian period, it is interesting that the latter city is the first named in this Canaanite list.

The most substantial and certainly the most interesting expansion of the Hamitic list is the report about Nimrod (8–12), which may be translated as follows:

Cush begot Nimrod; he was the first to be a potentate on the earth. He was a champion hunter on account of YHWH; whence the saying goes, "Like Nimrod, a champion hunter on account of YHWH."[25] The main part of his kingdom was Babylon, Erech, Akkad, and Calneh in the land of Shinar. From that land he set out for Assyria and built Nineveh (and Rehoboth-Ir, Calah and Resen between Nineveh and Calah). Nineveh was the capital city.

[The phrase in parentheses has probably been added, in which case *hāʿîr haggĕdōlāh* refers to Nineveh rather than Calah; cf. Jonah 1:2 and 3:2–3.]

No one doubts that this bit of narrative has been added to the list, and there is good reason for believing that it belongs with the same supplementary material identified at several points already. It provides another example of the interest in beginnings (with the verb *hhl,* as in 4:6; 6:1; 9:20; 11:6), and Nimrod follows the example of Cain, who also built a city (4:17). He is also one of the *gibborîm* who walked the earth in ancient times (6:4). It is no longer possible to know who the writer had in mind, though several candidates, divine (Marduk, Ninurta), divine-human (Gilgamesh), and human (Tukulti-ninurta I) have been proposed. The attached proverb may well have been suggested by the hunting scenes which figure so prominently in Assyrian iconography, as any visitor to the Assyrian rooms in the British Museum will know. In the narrative context, at any rate, this Nimrod represents another stage in the spread of violence and hubris in the post-deluge world, a point that will be made more explicitly in the Tower of Babel story attached to the list (11:1–9) which, as we shall see, takes off from this brief report of the first empire in the land of Shinar.

The Shem List (10:21–32)

In this third branch of the human family P lists only five peoples and four descendants of Aram (10:22–23). Elamites, Assyrians, and Arameans are well known. Arpachshad is sometimes identified with Babylon, but the name appears to be Hurrian, and Arrapḫa (Kirkuk?) is a better candidate. Lud, elsewhere standing for Lydia, is unidentified. On the four Aramean place names we are completely in the dark. The partially segmented genealogy of Arpachshad (24–29) appears to have been added to the list. For four generations it follows the same order as in the final *toledot* (11:10–19), but adds a cadet Arab line with Joktan and his thirteen "sons." Not all these names can be identified, but those that can are located in the south of the great Arabian peninsula. This part of the list is often associated with Solomon's commercial interests in Arabia, which of course would fit the standard dating of the J source. But it could just as easily be placed in the Neo-Babylonian or Achemenid period, that is, during the time of Kedarite expansion and trade relations with the western states attested in later prophetic texts.

The City and Tower of Babel (11:1–9)

This admirably constructed little story must be read in conjunction with the preceding list. Its purpose is to explain the geographical dispersion of the peoples listed and the differentiation of languages among them, a feature mentioned explicitly in the list (10:5, 20, 31). There is therefore no contradiction with the listing of peoples each with its own language. But it is much more than a rather artless etiology, for in offering this explanation it presents the situation as a further stage in the breakdown of harmony in human relations. At the same time it serves as a counter to the optimism of the Priestly view that sees this proliferation of peoples on all sides as the outcome of the creation blessing and command. The author of the supplement does not deny this, but he introduces a more somber and disillusioned note of a kind heard more than once in these early chapters. More specifically, as hinted earlier, it represents a further narrative development of the report about Nimrod and the empire founded by him in Shinar (Mesopotamia).

The literary skill of the author of the Tower of Babel story, the same author encountered often in the preceding chapters of Genesis, has been the subject of considerable commentary in recent years (Kikawada 1974, 19–32; Fokkelman 1975, 11–45; Sasson 1980, 211–19). It is a perfectly balanced narrative that turns on the pivot or *Schwerpunkt* of its central statement in v 5—YHWH came down to see the city and the tower which the humans had built. This verse is preceded and followed by two citations, consisting in internal monologue, from the builders and YHWH respectively (3–4 and 6–7), but it is noteworthy that the parties never address each other; there is no communication. A human proposal is simply countered by a divine proposal. These quotations are, in their turn, enveloped by a statement about settling down at the beginning and uprooting at the end (1–2, 8–9), the latter repeating the key terms used in the former. The entire story is suffused with irony and in fact reveals itself at the end as a satirical play on the name Babylon: not gate of (to) the gods *(bab-ili)* but the place of confusion *(bll)*.

While none of these episodes in Genesis 1–11 provides absolutely clear information on the time and circumstances of composition, this little story may plausibly be read as satire directed against the Neo-Babylonian empire, comparable in intent if not in form, therefore, to certain passages in Second Isaiah (Isa 44:9–20; 46:1–2, 5–7; 47:1–15). Outside of Genesis, Shinar as the name for the southern Mesopotamian region occurs only in exilic or post-exilic texts (Isa 11:11; Zech 5:11; Dan 1:2), and the plain *(biq'āh)* in which the builders settled recalls the scene of Ezekiel's vision in the Babylonian diaspora (Ezek 3:22–23). If, as is generally thought, the tower is to be identified with the Etemenanki ziggurat shrine in Babylon dedicated to the god Marduk, the satire would be taking aim at the imperial cult as legitimating the political aspirations of the city, which is precisely what we find in Second Isaiah's polemic against the cult and culture of Babylon. This would not necessarily make the author of Gen 11:1–9 a contemporary of Second Isaiah, since the memory of the oppressive empire long survived the fall of Babylon in 539 B.C. It would, however, suggest a *terminus a quo* consistent with other indications pointing to a later date for the J material in Genesis 1–11.

V. HUMANITY AFTER THE DELUGE: THE SHEM LINE (11:10–26)

This last section of the first pentad corresponds to the second section, which traces descent from Adam to Noah (5:1–32). It too has a linear genealogy segmented only at the end and concluding with three sons. The formulas are also identical, except that the birth of other sons and daughters and the death notice are missing. The only other difference is that the postdiluvian list has nine rather than ten members. LXX has rectified this anomaly by adding Kenan between Arpachshad and Shelah, and several commentators have taken this to be the more original reading. The only addition to the list is the notice that Shem begot Arpachshad two years after the deluge (11:10b). If this is a gloss, as is sometimes suggested (e.g., Skinner 1930 2d ed., 232), it still calls for an explanation. Perhaps it was intended either to avoid placing Arpachshad's birth in the year of the deluge, to accommodate the overall chronological schema, or to introduce a correction into an existing schema.

The names in the Shem genealogy suggest a work of *bricolage,* an artificial composite put together to serve as a parallel to the antediluvians and bridge the gap between the deluge and Abraham, first of the Hebrews. The first five names also occur in the "table of the nations" immediately preceding (10:21–25), presenting us with a problem not unlike that of Gen 5:1–32 in relation to 4:17–26. The genealogy is filled out with both ethnic names (e.g., Arpachshad) and place names (Serug, Nahor, Terah in Northern Mesopotamia). It ends by narrowing down to one of the three great branches of the human family, arriving via Eber, eponymous ancestor of the Hebrews, to Abraham.

Little need be added to what has already been said about the chronological schema into which the life spans of the postdiluvians have been fitted. Assuming that MT represents the earliest version, it is interesting to note that both LXX and the Samaritan Pentateuch have added 100 years to the ages of all but three of these ancestors (Shem, Terah, and Nahor) at the birth of a son. The idea may have been to avoid the embarrassment of making Noah a much older contemporary of Abraham but, needless to say, other suggestions have been put forward (e.g., Klein 1974, 255–63). Cassuto (1964, 255–59) attempted to demonstrate that the numbers are based on the Mesopotamian sexagesimal system, but in several cases had to settle for approximations. His calculation of 365 years from the birth of Arpachshad to the migration of Abraham (by adding the total of the ages at the birth of sons to the seventy-five years of Abraham at the migration, Gen 12:4) corresponds to the length of a solar year and to the life span of Enoch, but what we are to make of this remains uncertain. That the life span of the postdiluvians is much less than their predecessors before the flood (a total of 2,996 years against 7,625 years) at least fits the pattern of progressive degeneration noted earlier. The same conclusion holds for the significantly higher figures for Shem, since he is the only one born before the deluge and therefore in a different epoch.

With the Terahite line begins a new epoch marked by momentous events for the future of humanity, and to this corresponds a new series of *toledot*.

Some Provisional Conclusions

It will be appreciated that in this kind of inquiry, and especially at this point in the ongoing investigation of the Pentateuch, the most we can aim for is to elevate a possibility to a serious probability. With this proviso we may summarize the conclusions reached to date. We have identified the fivefold *toledot* scheme as the most salient structural feature of Genesis 1–11 and the deluge narrative as its central and structurally most important panel. Each of the five parts contains summary and narration in unequal proportions, the latter generally serving to explicate and further develop the former. The source division of the documentarians was accepted in its main lines, but with some important modifications. There can be little doubt that the Priestly strand (P) is basic, providing as it does the genealogical and chronological framework that holds the entire unit together. It has been filled out at several points with narrative expansions—corresponding to the J of the documentary hypothesis—whose characteristic language, point of view, and cross-references strongly suggest a common source. Whether these expansions belonged at one time to a continuous and coherent narrative of origins we cannot say for certain. What we can say is that in their extant form, as part of a larger narrative structure, they do not. While some are quite extensive, others are very brief and unconnected and make sense only as additions to the base narrative (e.g., 5:29; 7:16; 10:8–12). While it is theoretically possible that a final editor has filled out the P narrative with material earlier than P, we have seen that the arguments for a date in the early monarchy are unpersuasive and that, on the contrary, all the indications favor a date several centuries later. This led to the proposal that these passages constitute a reflective and discursive commentary, in the sapiential mode, on the base narrative which is itself a response to the fears and hopes of a defeated and exiled people.

Though structurally and thematically a self-contained unit, Genesis 1–11 also serves as a preface to the history of the nation Israel, and in this respect it may be compared with other historiographical works from antiquity. For its basic structure and major themes it has drawn on a well-established literary tradition best represented by the Mesopotamian

Atraḥasis text, and in this limited respect it is comparable with the work of early Greek mythographers. That it is in this sense derivative in no way diminishes its intrinsic value, however. On the contrary, it brings out more clearly in its adaptation of that tradition the particular emphasis of the biblical authors on the problematic nature of human existence, the reality of sin and judgment, and the character of a God who does not give up on his creation.

NOTES

1. It has been suggested that the noise and tumult *(rigmu, ḫubūru)* refer to rebellion against the gods resulting in the punishment of the deluge; see G. Pettinato, "Die Bestrafung des Menschengeschlechts durch die Sindflut," *Or* 47 (1968) 165–200; R. A. Oden, "Divine Aspirations in Atrahasis and in Genesis 1–11," *ZAW* 93 (1981) 197–216. But the explicit allusion to population growth preceding the divinely inflicted pestilence and drought, and the circumstances after the deluge restricting human fertility (barrenness, infant mortality, celibacy) point in a different direction; see H. Schwarzbaum, "The Overcrowded Earth," *Numen* 4 (1957) 59–74; Anne Kilmer, "The Mesopotamian Concept of Overpopulation and Its Solution as Reflected in the Mythology," *Or* 41 (1972) 160–77; Tikva Frymer-Kensky, "The Atrahasis Epic and its Significance for our Understanding of Genesis 1–9," *BA* 40 (1977) 147–55.

2. On the king lists, see A. L. Oppenheim in *ANET* 265–66; T. Jacobsen, *The Sumerian King List* (Chicago, 1939); J. J. Finkelstein, "The Antediluvian Kings: A University of California Tablet," *JCS* 17 (1963) 39–51; W. W. Hallo, "Antediluvian Cities," *JCS* 23 (1970) 57–67; T. C. Hartman, "Some Thoughts on the Sumerian King List and Genesis 5 and 11B," *JBL* 91 (1972) 25–32.

3. Published by Arno Poebel in 1914; see S. N. Kramer in *ANET* 42–44; T. Jacobsen, "The Eridu Genesis," *JBL* 100 (1981) 513–29.

4. The only other *toledot* formula in the Pentateuch, Num 3:1, introduces the Aaronite Priestly line. It may well have been suggested by the Genesis series but is certainly not integral to it, *pace* T. L. Thompson, *The Origin Tradition of Ancient Israel* (Sheffield, 1987) who extends the series to include Exodus 1–23. The *toledot* superscript for the Esau line is repeated after the listing of his wives and sons (Gen 36:9), but vv 9–14 are an expanded version of vv 1–5, and therefore the repetition is not structurally significant. On the *toledot* in general, see Karl Budde, "Ellä Toledoth," *ZAW* 34 (1914) 241–53; "Noch einmal 'Ellä Toledoth,'" *ZAW* 36 (1916) 1–7; O. Eissfeldt, "Biblos geneseōs," *Festschrift Erich Fascher* (Berlin, 1958), 31–40 (= *Kleine Schriften III* [Tübingen, 1966], 458–70; "Toledot," *TU* 77(1961) 1–8; J. Scharbert, "Der Sinn der Toledot-Formel in der Priesterschrift," in H. J. Stoebe (ed.), *Wort-Gebot-Glaube. Walther Eichrodt zum 80. Geburtstag* (Zurich, 1970), 45–56; P. Weimar, "Die Toledot-Formel in der priesterschriftlichen

Geschichtsdarstellung," *BZ* 18(1974) 65–93; S. Tengström, *Die Toledotformel und die literarische Struktur der priesterlichen Erweiterungsschicht im Pentateuch* (Gleerup, 1981); T. L. Thompson, *The Origin Tradition of Ancient Israel* (Sheffield, 1987), 61–131.

5. In Gen 2:25–3:1 there is a play on *ʿarôm,* "naked," and *ʿarûm,* "crafty." The snake has wisdom from living on earth, but it is also naked when compared with other animals.

6. L. Alonso-Schökel, "Motivos sapienciales y de alianza en Gn 2–3," *Bib* 43 (1962) 295–316, finds several pairs of verbs *(lāqaḥ/hinnîaḥ, ʿābad/šāmar, ʿāzab/dābaq)* reminiscent of prophetic discourse; G. E. Mendenhall, "The Shady Side of Wisdom: The Date and Purpose of Genesis 3," in H. N. Bream *et al.* (ed.), *A Light Unto My Path. Old Testament Studies in Honor of Jacob M. Myers* (Philadelphia, 1974) 319–34, adds a few other terms and takes the opportunity to air some of his antifeminist prejudices.

7. Evading death and living forever are made possible through partaking of a plant and lost through the intervention of a snake; in the first stage of his existence Enkidu lived with the animals, as did the Man in Genesis, and his initiation into a new phase came through the Woman and involved sexuality; the Woman clothed him and declared him wise and godlike ("you are wise, Enkidu, you have become like a god"), in spite of which he became subject to death, etc.

8. There has been much discussion as to where this narrative begins, several scholars tracing it even further back than Chapter 9. My own view has remained unchanged that it included only the history dealing with David's sons, with the first incident spliced into the account of the second Ammonite campaign (2 Sam 11:1, 26–31).

9. I pointed out these parallels in "Theme and Motif in the Succession History (2 Sam xi 2ff) and the Yahwist Corpus," *VTSup* 15 (1966) 44–57, at which time, however, I followed the consensus on the date of J.

10. The word *robēṣ* cannot be a participial since the governing noun *ḥaṭṭāʾt* is feminine; it must therefore be a substantive. In that case it is most likely the Hebrew equivalent of the Akkadian *rābiṣum,* a demon of a kind thought to lurk at the entrance to buildings; see H. Gunkel, *Genesis,* 43; E. A. Speiser, *Genesis,* 32–33; C. Westermann, *Genesis 1–11,* 299–300.

11. Since it was Cain who named the city, it was probably he and not his son who built it. Karl Budde's emendation of *kĕšēm bĕnô ḥănôk* to *kĕšēm bišmô* is arbitrary; see his *Die Biblische Urgeschichte (Gen 1–12.5) untersucht* (Giessen, 1883), 120–21.

12. Differences between the genealogies in the two chapters are now being explained by "genealogical fluidity" following R. R. Wilson's *Genealogy and History in the Biblical World* (New Haven & London, 1977). D. T. Bryan, "A Reevaluation of Gen 4 and 5 in Light of Recent Studies in Genealogical Fluidity," *BA* 99 (1989) 180–88, assumes that there were originally two distinct genealogical traditions which were partially conflated, but it seems more likely that we have two different and purposeful manipulations of a common source.

13. K. Budde, *Die Biblische Urgeschichte,* 93–103, found the turning point at the beginning of the second half of the genealogy signified by the name Jared, understood to derive from the verbal stem *yrd,* "descend." If, regardless of etymology, the name was understood in this way, we would have name symbolism at the beginning, in the middle, and at the end of the list, and also a contrast with the ascent of Enoch in the following position.

14. See C. Westermann, *Genesis 1–11,* 379–81. On the Catalogue of Women, see M. L. West, *The Hesiodic Catalogue of Women, Its Nature, Structure and Origins* (Oxford, 1985); J. Van Seters, "The Primeval Histories of Greece and Israel compared," *ZAW* 100 (1988) 1–22; R. S. Hess, "The Genealogies of Genesis 1–11 and Comparative Literature," *Bib* 70 (1989) 251–53.

15. On the Ugaritic background of Isa 14:12–20 see Otto Kaiser, *Isaiah 13–39. A Commentary* (Philadelphia, 1974), 38–40.

16. The reading *mēʿôlām* instead of MT *mēʿărēlîm* follows LXX *apʾaiōnos.*

17. *yādôn* is hapax and of uncertain meaning; for the range of opinion see Westermann, *Genesis 1–11,* 375.

18. Thus Umberto Cassuto, *A Commentary on the Book of Genesis II* (Jerusalem, 1964 [first published in Hebrew in 1949]), 30, describes it as a perfectly integrated narrative and presents a detailed analysis attempting, unsuccessfully I believe, to prove that it is. More recently G. J. Wenham, "The Coherence of the Flood Narrative," *VT* 28 (1978) 336–48, argues for a palistrophic structure with fifteen items before and after the turning point of 8:1; similarly, S. E. McEvenue, *The Narrative Style of the Priestly Writer* (Rome, 1971), 22–89, and B. W. Anderson, "From Analysis to Synthesis: The Interpretation of Genesis 1–11," *JBL* 97 (1978), 23–29, both of whom, however, admit a plurality of sources. A different approach to the unity of the narrative is taken by Y. T. Radday, "Chiasmus in Hebrew Biblical Narrative," in J. W. Welch (ed.), *Chiasmus in Antiquity* (Hildesheim, 1981), 99–100. In Y. T. Radday and H. Shore, *Genesis: An Authorship Study in Computer-Assisted Linguistics* (Rome, 1985), however, P turns out to have a quite distinctive character from JE. The problems inherent in these and other attempts to eliminate the combination of sources from the flood narrative are exposed by J. A. Emerton, "An Examination of Some Attempts to Defend the Unity of the Flood Narrative in Genesis," *VT* 37 (1987) 401–20 and 38 (1988) 1–21.

19. The chronology of the deluge continues to exercise the ingenuity of commentators; witness the essays of N. P. Lemche, "The Chronology of the Story of the Flood," *JSOT* 18 (1980) 52–62 (a combination of three systems corresponding to J, P, and a redactor); F. H. Cryer, "The Interrelationships of Gen 5:32; 11:10–11 and the Chronology of the Flood (Gen 6–9)," *Bib* 66 (1985) 241–61 (the flood lasted two solar years in P, one lunar year in J); L. M. Barré, "The Riddle of the Flood Chronology," *JSOT* 41(1988) 3–20 (based on a schematic 360-day year).

20. The term *mabbûl* occurs in Ps 29:10 and in Genesis predominantly in P passages, in some instances referring to the deluge as event; but it also appears in passages assigned to J (7:7, 10, 17), perhaps from the hand of the final editor. See J. Begrich, "Mabbûl. Eine exegetisch-lexikalische Studie," *Zeitschrift für Semitistik* 6 (1928) 135–53.

21. C. Westermann, *Genesis 1–11,* pp. 396–97, holds that J has in most cases been worked into a basic and intact P narrative which, given Westermann's acceptance of the conventional early date for J, presumably implies that a redactor later than P has supplemented P with older material. P. Weimar, *Untersuchungen zur Redaktionsgeschichte des Pentateuch* (Berlin, 1977), 145, picks out words and phrases attributable to the redactor: the animal series (6:7; 7:3, 8; 8:20), the execution formula (7:9), the sending out of the raven (8:7), the couplet about the seasons (8:22) and Ham, father of Canaan (9:18).

22. The parallels between the P flood narrative and certain passages in Ezekiel deserves further investigation. In the present paragraph, note, for example, the phrase "corrupted its way" *(hišḥît ʾet-darkô),* cf. Ezek 16:47; *qēṣ kol-bāśār bāʾ lĕpānay,* cf. Ezek 7:2, 6; violence *(ḥāmās),* cf. Ezek 7:11, 23; 8:17; 12:19; 28:16. In this last passage the king of Tyre, once blameless *(tāmîm),* is punished because of violence.

23. Karl Elliger, "Sinn und Ursprung der priesterlichen Geschichtserzählung," *ZTK* 49 (1952) 121–42; H. Cazelles, "Les écrits sacerdotaux," in A. Robert and A. Feuillet (eds.), *Introduction à la Bible* I (Paris, 1959) 373–74; R. Kilian, "Die Hoffnung auf Heimkehr in der Priesterschrift," *Bibel und Leben* 7 (1966) 39–51; W. Brueggemann, "The Kerygma of the Priestly Writer," *ZAW* 84 (1972) 397–414; R. W. Klein, *Israel in Exile* (Philadelphia, 1979), pp. 125–48; E. Zenger, *Gottes Bogen in den Wolken* (Stuttgart, 1983), pp. 43–49.

24. *EncJud* 12:189–91.

25. The meaning of *lipnē YHWH* here is uncertain; some have taken it as a kind of superlative.

CHAPTER 4

THE STORY OF THE ANCESTORS

(GEN 11:27–50:26)

CONTENTS AND STRUCTURE

The fairly brief story that unfolds in these chapters is most simply described, to begin with, as a family history traced through four generations. In at least this respect, therefore, it could be compared with such fictional but realistic works as Thomas Mann's *Buddenbrooks* or John Galsworthy's *The Forsyte Saga*. In contrast to the history of early humanity preceding it, it has little of what Alter calls "summary" or what Westermann terms "the numerative element." Apart from the *toledot* superscriptions and brief chronological markers, very few genealogies or lists interrupt the narrative flow.[1] There is also very little authorial comment on the characters or their actions. These actions, described in episodes of varying length, are allowed to speak for themselves. The deeper significance of the events and their interconnectedness are brought out principally by means of strategically placed pronouncements of the deity or, less commonly, revelatory dreams.[2] It is also by these means that the ancestral history is integrated into the larger narrative context—that of the Pentateuch in the first place, and then the entire historical corpus from Genesis to Kings.

From the literary point of view there are also significance differences between larger sections of the story. The characters receiving most attention are Abraham, Jacob, and Joseph. While the Abraham story consists of about twenty fairly brief episodes (the one exception, Genesis 24, deals rather with Isaac and his bride-to-be Rebekah), the nucleus of the Jacob story is a lengthy and continuous account of a twenty-year exile in Mesopotamia, with the events leading up to and following it described more briefly (Chapters 27-33). The Joseph story, on the other hand, though logically part of the Jacob narrative since Jacob is alive and well almost to its conclusion, has a highly distinctive novelistic character that sets it apart from the rest of the ancestral history. These prominent stylistic differences would give some plausibility, initially at least, to the theory of distinct origin and formation of the major components (Rendtorff 1977, 22; Blum 1984).

The *toledot* Structure

While it is common practice to divide the story into three sections corresponding to the principal characters (12-25; 25-36; 37-50), the most explicit structural feature, as in Genesis 1-11, is the fivefold *toledot* arrangement. Since this is the way the text is actually organized it would be reasonable to take it as the starting point of our investigation. It is not, in any case, absolutely incompatible with the more usual arrangement. The *toledot* structure singles out Ishmaelites as a separate branch of the Terah-Abraham line, and Esau as a separate but related branch of the Isaac family, but with the advantage of bringing out more clearly the progressive narrowing of the genealogy, begun in Genesis 1-11, to the seventy descendants of Jacob who went down into Egypt.

This second genealogical pentad is arranged as follows:

1. 11:27-25:11   Terah (Abraham)
2. 25:12-18   Ishmael
3. 25:19-35:29   *Isaac (Jacob)*
4. 36:1-37:1   Esau-Edom
5. 37:2-50:26   Jacob (Joseph and his brothers)

The same structure as in the early history of humanity is therefore replicated, with the difference that in 1, 3 and 5 the narrative deals with a descendant or descendants of the eponym rather than with the eponymous ancestor himself. Here, too, the fivefold structure directs attention to the central panel: in Genesis 1-11 Noah and the deluge, in Gen 12-50 Jacob, his exile in Mesopotamia and return to the homeland. We shall see in due course that here too the structure provides a clue to the situation which the narrative reflects.

We now turn to a brief overview of each of the five panels, leaving aside for the time being the complex and controversial matter of their formation.

I.   11:27–25:11 Terah (Abraham)

The first episode (11:27–32) begins and ends with familiar genealogical formulas relating to Terah. Terah links the story of the ancestors with the first postdiluvians, a point clearly indicated by the much longer life span allotted to him. It is therefore this brief notice about the Terahites rather than the programmatic statement of the deity in Gen 12:1–3 that connects with the early history of humanity (Crüsemann 1981, 11–29). Starting out from this point, and covering a period of 100 years, the following narrative moves through a series of crises to a partial resolution. The forward movement of the story is not, however, entirely even and sequential. Subsidiary themes are intertwined in such a way that any one of them can be dropped and picked up again at a later point without obscuring the central thrust of the narrative line.

All of the themes that follow are present implicitly in this *mise en scène:* the first stage of the journey to the promised land, the infertility of Sarah, the presence of Lot, son of Haran. Taken together, the prominence of Lot as a participant in this two-stage journey and the notice that Sarah is infertile suggest that Lot was at this stage the intended heir of Abraham. We are in any case alerted to follow closely the fortunes of these two characters as the story unfolds. What is only implicit in the first stage of the emigration is stated explicitly in the communication from YHWH to Abraham in Haran (12:1–3). This will be recalled as an important point of reference at significant junctures of the ongoing narrative (18:18; 22:18; 24:7; 26:4; 28:13–14). It is worth repeating that, contrary to a widely accepted assumption (e.g., von Rad 1961, 46; Wolff 1966, 131–58), this programmatic statement does not provide the primary link between the early history of humanity and the ancestral history. Nothing in Genesis 1–11 prepares us for it, the blessing of Abraham does not remedy the situation described in these early chapters (the curse on the soil, the confusion of tongues), and the language and style have few if any common features. The juxtaposition of command ("go to the land") and promise suggests that the commitment to make of Abraham a great nation and a blessing to humanity is contingent on occupation of the land, that this is what first must be done. Hence Abraham's perambulations from one sanctuary to another: from Shechem (12:6–7) to Bethel (12:8; 13:3–4), then Mamre (13:8) and, later, Beersheba (21:32; 22:19). These apparently random movements are explained by the command to walk the length and breadth of the land in anticipation of possessing it (13:17). In this connection, it is worth recalling that establishing a new cult ("calling on the name of YHWH") was the standard way of staking a claim to the territory on which the cult was established. Saul, for example, erected an altar to YHWH immediately after conquering territory previously held by the Philistines (1 Sam 14:35).

The issue of an heir focuses, as we have seen, on Sarah and Lot. We detect some tension between the roles assigned to these two, since the infertility of Sarah (11:30) would seem to consign her to at best a walk-on part in the unfolding drama. This, however, does not happen. Abraham is twice in danger of losing her to foreigners attracted by her beauty (12:10–20; 20:1–18). According to the logic of the narrative these are not parallel versions of the same episode, since Abraham had anticipated that this would happen more than once (20:13). Something of the same must be said about the narratives dealing with the attempt to have an heir through Hagar, Sarah's proxy (16:1–6; 21:8–21), for Hagar is cast out, returns, and then is dismissed again for a quite different reason. The resolution comes with the birth of a child to Sarai/Sarah against all odds (21:1–7), and this leads to the most dramatic moment of the last-minute rescue of the child from an attempted human sacrifice. As John Osborne's Luther puts it, "If God had blinked, Isaac would have been dead" (22:1–19). There follows the death and burial of Sarah in Ephron's field at Machpelah (23).

The presence of Lot, Haran's son, is emphasized from the beginning and at each stage of the journey in and through Canaan (11:27, 31; 12:4–5; 13:1). His separation from Abraham is part of a larger process by which Abraham's descendants in direct line are set apart from the Aramean kingdoms descended from Nahor (22:20–24), the Arabs from Abraham's marriage with Keturah (25:1–6), those descended from Ishmael (25:12–16), the Edomites from Esau (26), and Moab and Ammon from Haran and Lot (19:30–38). The account of the actual separation (13:2–13) seems to imply that by inviting Lot to occupy the land to the north or the south, Abraham intended to share the land of Canaan with him as his presumptive heir. Lot, however, chose the *kikkār* instead, that part of the Jordan basin lying outside the boundaries of the land (Vawter 1977, 184–85; Helyer 1983, 78–80). It nevertheless remained for Abraham to rescue his nephew from enemy action (14) and from the effects of the divine judgment visited on the cities of the plain (the *kikkār*, 19:1–29). Lot does not come out too well from all of this. To borrow an expression from Mark Twain, he was a good man in the worst sense of the term. The last we hear of him is in the story of the incestuous union with his daughters, to which disreputable origin Moabites and Ammonites are traced (19:30–38).

Abraham's relation to the land is also paramount in two other episodes. The first (21:22–34) records a troubled period when he was residing in a part of the Negev controlled by Abimelech, later identified as king of the Philistines (26:1, 8). The question at issue was the disputed ownership of a well dug by Abraham, and the issue was settled in Abraham's favor by a solemn oath sworn by Abimelech. Thus the first installment of the promised land was nothing more than a hole in the ground. The second episode has Abraham negotiating with Hittites for the purchase of a cave and field in the neighborhood of Mamre north of Hebron (23). This was to be the burial site for the recently deceased Sarah and, in due course, Abraham himself and his descendants (25:9–10; 49:29–32; 50:12–13). The importance of this transaction is indicated by the close attention to the legal formalities. It takes place in the open plaza by the city gate and in the presence of the property-owning citizens; the distinct stages of the negotiations are carefully noted and the dialogue recorded, as in certain contracts extant from the Neo-Babylonian and Persian periods. The exact price is recorded, a very high price which Ephron either thought Abraham would not be able to raise or which was intended as the overture to the kind of negotiations still conducted in Middle Eastern souks. Finally, the payment of the price in full is put on record. Apart from a parcel of land purchased by Jacob from the Shechemites (33:19–20; cf. the alternative tradition in Gen 48:22, according to which he seized it by force of arms), this was to be the only part of Canaan legally appropriated by the ancestors. And this, in its turn, suggests that the land theme in the ancestral stories would more naturally refer to the reappropriation of land after the return from exile than to the conquest tradition in Joshua.

The mission of Abraham's servant going to Mesopotamia to find a bride for Isaac (24) assures the continuity of the line uncontaminated by Canaanite intermarriage. But the focus is no longer on Abraham but on Isaac, and it is with Isaac in the Negev, not with Abraham at Mamre, that the return journey terminates. There remains only to record the Arab line through Abraham's second wife, Keturah, the disposal of his goods, his death, and his burial in the field bought from Ephron (25:1–11).

II. 25:12–18 Ishmael

The title of this second panel has been prefixed to a list of twelve Arab settlements—described as sons of Ishmael and princes—which has its own title and concluding formula (25:13–16). The Ishmael *toledot* itself is rounded off in the conventional way with the length of his life span and his death (17). The final notice about his location is an expanded form of information given previously (16:12b). The reader mindful of the contemporary situation in the Middle East cannot fail to be impressed by the sense of a close ethnic bond between the descendants of Abraham in direct line and the Arab peoples (cf. 10:25–30; 25:1–4).

The role of Ishmael in relation to Isaac parallels that of Esau in relation to Jacob, hence the correspondence between the second and the fourth panels of this second pentad. Both embody the common motif of the elder son supplanted by the younger, and this in spite of the fact that Ishmael is circumcised, and therefore enters the covenant, before the birth of Isaac (16:15–16; 17:23–27). It is also important that both Ishmael and Esau, following the example of Lot, are removed outside the boundaries of the land promised to Abraham (cf. 36:6–8). Both too are recipients of a subsidiary blessing (cf. 27:39–40), though the promises addressed to Ishmael on several occasions (16:10; 17:20; 21:13, 18) have more substance. In the overall scheme, however, the relative absence of narrative in the Ishmael and Esau *toledot* serves to emphasize their function as counterpoint to the development of the main theme.

III. 25:19–35:29 Isaac (Jacob)

This central panel begins by recapitulating the birth of Isaac and his marriage to Rebekah (cf. 21:2–5; 24) and ends in the usual formulaic way with his life, death, and burial (35:28–29). The narrative in between, however, deals almost exclusively with Jacob and his relations with his brother Esau and his cousin Laban. This story is told with compelling psychological insight and narrative skill—not least in combining a personal life story with the representative function of the characters. It has understandably attracted a vast amount of literary analysis to which, unfortunately, we cannot do justice in this study.[3] Close attention has also been paid to structure, the key to which is often sought in a chiastic arrangement (Fishbane 1979, 40–62). While there is no doubt that chiasm is a feature of some biblical narratives, it suffers somewhat from overuse; and in this instance the attempt is vitiated either by lumping distinct episodes together or by selecting only those that fit the scheme. What is clear at least is that this story, like the story of Gilgamesh and the Odyssey, is organized around the journey away from the homeland and the eventual return to it. The point of departure is Beersheba, with Isaac ostensibly on his deathbed (26:23; 28:10). The terminus is Mamre, where Isaac finally dies (after a twenty-year interval) and is buried (35:27–29). The deeper level of meaning is revealed through numinous encounters at the points of departure and return (28:10–22; 32:2–3 [32:1–2]; 32:23–33 [22–32]; 35:9–15). These experiences also invite us to read it as a story of transformation through suffering and conflict—*tō pathei mathos,* as the Greeks would say—the outcome of which is that Jacob is enabled to bear a new name and the destiny that goes with it.

Birth and infancy narratives generally have the purpose of saying something about the character and destiny of the child or, as here, the children. Like the other matriarchs, Rebekah is initially infertile. Then, as a result of prayer, she gives birth to twins in a manner unique in the history of obstetrics, if not of folklore. There is usually something ominous about the birth of twins, and here we have the additional complication of the struggle in the womb, reminiscent of Acrisios and Proitos, sons of the king of Argos, as reported by Apollodorus (Gunkel 1964, 294). Esau, the firstborn, is ruddy (*'admônî*) and covered with hair (*śē'ar*), like Enkidu in *Gilgamesh*—characteristics appropriate for the eponymous ancestor of Edom/Seir. Jacob's grabbing his brother's heel (*'āqēb*) anticipates his role as trickster or deceiver (stem *'qb*, 27:36). In keeping with a common folktale motif, he is destined to supplant his brother. The story goes on at once to relate how this happened, in the incident in which Esau surrendered his birthright (*bĕkorāh*) for some red stuff (borscht?) which, as a glossator hastens to add, explains why he was also called Edom, meaning "Red Man." As is so often the case in the ancestral history, the episode can be understood at different levels: an incident in a family history characterized by strife; a culture myth bearing on the relations between sheep rearers and hunters; and finally, as an ethnic etiology, a political satire or spoof directed against the Edomites.

However *the origin* of the following episode about Rebekah masquerading as Isaac's sister is explained in relation to similar incidents recorded earlier (12:10–20; 20:1–18), the narrator insists that it is a distinct event (26:1 cf. 12:10). One difference, easily overlooked, is that in this instance Isaac is forbidden to leave the land as Abraham had in similar circumstances. The following narrative (26:1–33), in which Jacob plays no part, is generally thought to be a foreign body, a later intrusion into the Jacob story (e.g., Westermann 1985, 408). But if we may assume that in the context of the ancestral history as a whole Esau's forfeited birthright, like that of Ishmael, included the promised land, it would be of the greatest importance for Isaac to remain in the land and renew the claim on the first installment occupied by Abraham (21:25–34). This is in fact what he does, and in the process there is a further separation, this time from Abimelech, king of the Philistines (26:12–22).

The lengthy account of the usurpation of the deathbed blessing which follows (27:1–40) is not presented as a parallel to the earlier deception practiced on Esau (25:29–34), for Esau himself clearly distinguishes between the theft of the birthright (*bĕkorāh*) and the blessing (*bĕrākāh*), the latter depriving him of political dominance as well as the more favored habitat. (We note how the two deceptions are tied together by a palpable play on the words for "birthright" and "blessing.") The style of narration illustrates very well the significant difference between the cycles of Jacob and Abraham. That the former incorporates folktale motifs and illustrates one or other of Axel Olrik's laws of folk narrative (e.g., the law of the single strand) does not oblige us to call it a folktale or describe it as the product of oral tradition. It is a product of literary art that happens to use folktale motifs, as do many other literary works both ancient and modern. In the larger narrative context the deceptions prepare Jacob for his flight to Mesopotamia by providing a compelling motive—the threat of death at the hands of his brother (27:41–45). A subsidiary motive, already hinted at (26:34–35), is the need to avoid marriage with a local woman (27:46–28:9), perhaps the most transparent clue in the Jacob story to an exilic or post-exilic situation (Westermann 1985, 446).

In strictly topographical terms the outbound journey begins at Beer-sheba, and the return after twenty years' absence ends at Hebron/Mamre with intermediate stops at Ephrath and Migdal Eder. But the significant point of both departure and return is Bethel, where the promise is made and renewed (28:13–15; 35:11–12) and the vow to set up a sanctuary is made and honored (28:22; 35:7, 14–15). During the intervening two decades the only divine communication to Jacob is the command to return (31:3), repeated in a dream (31:10–13). The central event is the birth of children (29:31–30:24) whose names are recapitulated at the end of the narrative (35:22b–26). The children, all except Benjamin born in Mesopotamia, are grouped with their mothers as follows:

Leah: Reuben, Simeon, Levi, Judah, Issachar, Zebulon, Dinah

Zilpah, Leah's proxy: Gad, Asher

Rachel: Joseph

Bilhah, Rachel's proxy: Dan, Naphthali

Leah, therefore, has seven children, but Dinah will be excluded, since in consequence of the rape she will not have a husband. This makes room for Benjamin, who restores the number twelve, and the twelve then fall into a pattern of six pairs, in keeping with a very old and widespread tradition (e.g., Romulus and Remus, Castor and Pollux).[4] With the passing of time other expedients will be needed to maintain the statutory duodecimal arrangement of the tribes.

The subsidiary motif of the acquisition of property, reminiscent of the "despoiling of the Egyptians" theme in the exodus narrative (Ex 12:36), is introduced in the curious incident in which Jacob outwits Laban by a kind of prenatal conditioning of the flocks (30:25–31:16). Much more attention is paid to the return than to the outbound journey. Rachel's theft of the teraphim (31:17–42)[5] provides another instance of the "endangering of the ancestress" theme by virtue of Jacob's unwitting pronouncement of the death penalty on her (31:32). The eventually friendly resolution of Jacob's problems with Laban and Esau also extends the theme of topographical separation introduced in the stories about Lot and Ishmael (31:43–54; 33:1–17). Encounter with a unit of God's army patrolling the borders of the promised land (32:1–2 [31:55–32:1]; cf. Deut 3:16; Josh 12:2) prepares Jacob for the life-threatening struggle with the mysterious assailant at Wadi Jabbok, which in its turn prepares him for the final encounter with his estranged brother.[6] The penultimate stopover at Shechem (33:18–35:4) allows Jacob, following the example of Abraham, to buy a parcel of land, illustrates further the problematic relations, marital and otherwise, with the native population (34:1–31), and provides an occasion for the abjuration of foreign cults in preparation for the final stage of the homecoming (35:1–4).

IV.   36:1–37:1 Esau-Edom

Structurally parallel with the Ishmael panel (II), this Edomite chapter has preserved a great deal of onomastic material—about eighty names—presented in familiar schematic arrangements: three branches of the Esau line and three "sons" of Esau by his wife Oholibamah, seven chieftains of the Eliphaz line and seven Horite, twelve descendants of Esau by Adah and Basemath (9–14), and perhaps originally twelve (in the present state of the text, eleven) chieftains of Esau (40–43; cf. the twelve Ishmaelite leaders in 25:16). The Edomite king list also follows an ancient pattern (cf. the Sumerian king list) in presenting the eight rulers in chronological sequence, though it is quite clear that there is no dynastic succession.

The listing of the immediate family of Esau—three wives and five sons —and the account of their territorial separation from Jacob (1–8) is clearly distinct from the following lists (9–43). A *toledot* formula has been added to these lists (9) which are rounded off with an inclusion identifying Esau as the father of Edom, quite different, therefore, from 1–9, in which Esau *is* Edom. It appears likely that the compiler of 1–9 has made use of the lists to put together his own brief narrative, though this would not exclude the possibility that the lists were appended subsequently.

The main purpose of this section is to record the territorial separation of the brothers. The history of sibling rivalry is thus brought to a conclusion favorable to Jacob's family, and their claim to Canaan survives unchallenged. The same point is made at the end of the section, with Edomites settled in their territorial patrimony while Jacob continues to dwell in the land of his father's sojournings (36:43–37:1). The five archival lists of Edomite clans (9–14), Edomite and pre-Edomite chieftains (15–19, 20–30, 40–43), and Edomite kings (31–39) are perhaps intended to show the development from family beginnings to nationhood in fulfillment of the birth oracle (25:23). There is very little narrative expansion, but what there is illustrates once again the close relation between genealogy and historiography.

V.   37:2–50:26 Jacob (Jacob's sons)

This last and longest section is distinctive in several respects, not least in its literary character. The story of Joseph's treatment at the hands of his brothers, his rise to power in Egypt, and his eventual reconciliation with his family has generally been characterized as a Novella (Gunkel 1964, 6th ed., 395–401; Donner 1976), though one which has incorporated a number of subsidiary genres (Coats 1983, 259–315). It is the longest continuous narrative in Genesis, and it is interrupted by very little non-narrative material—the list of Israelites in 46:8–27 and the deathbed oracles of Jacob in 49:1–27. Several commentators have also been impressed by its sapiential character, reflected in the themes of retribution and providence (45:5–8; 50:20) and in the figure of Joseph as wise administrator and interpreter of dreams (von Rad 1966, 292–300). Its distinctiveness should not, however, be exaggerated. It continues the family history begun with Abraham; it too features sibling rivalry with eventual reconciliation, speaks of the birth of sons and subversion of the primogeniture principle (Zeiah and Perez, Manasseh and Ephraim), and entails the overarching theme of exile and return. This last comes to expression in the words of the dying Joseph which anticipate the next chapter of the history (50:24–25).

While narrative interest in this final *toledot* obviously focuses on Joseph, it still keeps to the pattern of dealing with the family of Jacob as a whole, and indeed with Jacob himself, the final chapter of whose life history comes only near the very end (47:27–50:14). Several of Joseph's brothers—Judah, Reuben, Simeon, and Benjamin—have important support roles, and others are mentioned. The story as a whole serves as a bridge between Canaan and Egypt, a vehicle for transporting the entire three-generational family into the next chapter of its history. This important structural fact leads us to suspect that the list of seventy members of that family (46:8–27) may at an earlier stage have served as the finale to the ancestral history. It connects with a shorter version of the same list, with the same title ('*ēlleh šĕmôt*, "these are the names"), at the beginning of Exodus, and the few events narrated after the list—Jacob's audience with the Pharaoh; Joseph's administrative measures during the famine; Jacob's final disposition, death, and burial; and the death of Joseph himself —could as well have been located in the next or Egyptian phase of the history.

The story of Judah and Tamar (Chapter 38) has generally been read as an intrusive element spliced into the Joseph story with the purpose of providing additional genealogical information on one important branch of the Jacob/Israel family.[7] It does, of course, interrupt the story of Joseph's misadventures at the point where he is being sold as a slave—by Midianites in 37:36 and by Ishmaelites in 39:1—but perhaps we should allow the author the privilege of introducing an interesting subplot which inevitably delays the forward movement of the narrative. Judah has, in any case, already been introduced (37:26), and the birth of the two sons, also listed in the final summary (46:12), is an obviously important aspect of the family history (cf. the two sons of Joseph, 41:50–52, and of Reuben, 42:37). It also embodies motifs prominent throughout the ancestral history: the overcoming of childlessness, the birth of twins under extraordinary circumstances, the subversion of primogeniture, and problematic relations with the Canaanite population.

This, then, is the way in which the great medley of stories about Israel's ancestors has been put together. The fivefold arrangement of the early history of humanity and the history of the ancestors looks like a well-planned narrative continuum from creation to the descent into Egypt. It also confers on Genesis a highly distinctive character that sets it apart from the other books of the Pentateuch. I have suggested that this structuring inscribes or encodes into the narrative the theme of exile and return, near extinction and survival, as an interpretative clue of (literally) central importance. In due course the same pattern was replicated in the Pentateuch as a whole, and here too the cultic enactments of Leviticus, forming the central panel, constitute an essential point of reference. It was in this way that those to whom Iranian hegemony provided the opportunity to return from exile and establish a new commonwealth recomposed a usable past which both reflected and consolidated their identity as Israel.

GENEALOGY AND CHRONOLOGY

Though genealogies and lists take up little space in the story of the ancestors, the entire narrative is presented within a complex genealogical structure encompassing four generations. The fictive nature of this structure is apparent in the conventional arrangement of the names. Just as Adam, Lamech, and Noah had three sons, so the ancestral line begins with the three branches of the Terahite family, and Judah also has three sons (38:1–11). There is also a marked predilection for sevens: the seven children of Leah (29:31–35; 30:17–21), seven descendants of Gad, Asher, and Judah (46:12, 16–17), and several sevens in the Edomite lists (36:20–21, 29–30, 31–39). The twelve sons of Jacob and his seventy descendants also conform to a schematic principle that will be invoked often in compositions of the Second Temple period, including early Christianity.

If the genealogy is viewed, so to speak, horizontally, in its various segmentations, the emphasis will be seen to fall on relations with other ethnic groups: Arameans (Nahor-Bethuel), Moabites and Ammonites (Haran-Lot), Arabian tribes (from Abraham's marriage with Keturah), Ishmaelites (from Hagar), Edomites and "Hittites" (Abraham-Esau). Viewed vertically, along its linear axis, it exhibits a successive narrowing down, leaving the descendants of Abraham in the direct line as sole claimants to the land of Canaan. In counterpoint to the social realia expressed by genealogy, we note also a repeated subversion of the principle of primogeniture. Isaac is preferred over Ishmael, Jacob over Esau, Ephraim over Manasseh, and Perez, ancestor of David, over Zerah. Viewed in its totality, the genealogical schema exhibits the fulfillment of the creation command to increase and multiply, while at the same time embodying tension between universalism and particularism, a central feature of the emergent Judaism of the Second Temple period.

Little need be added to what was said above about the chronological framework of the Genesis narrative (see the table on p. 48). Following the MT data, the history of the ancestors forms a distinct segment of 215 years' duration from entry into Canaan to descent into Egypt, i.e., from A.M. 2021 to A.M. 2236. At significant moments the ages of the ancestors are carefully noted,[8] and these notations have been synchronized with the overall chronological system. Abraham, therefore, is allotted twenty-five years in Canaan to the birth of Isaac, Isaac sixty to the birth of Jacob, and Jacob one hundred and thirty years in Canaan before going down into Egypt. Chronology therefore plays an important integrative role, obliging the attentive reader to place this sequence of episodes within the forward movement of a history the goal of which lies in the distant future.

THEME

What is the theme of the ancestral history? The problem of definition was discussed a few years ago by David Clines in his monograph *The Theme of the Pentateuch* (1978), to which the reader is referred. Theme is not merely a summary of the content or plot of a work. It should also be distinguished from motif, understood as "a type of incident, a particular situation, an ethical problem, or the like, which may be treated in a work of imagination" *(Oxford English Dictionary)*. The analogy with music is not very helpful, since this distinction does not seem to be operative; as, for example, when one speaks of the theme song of a film. A satisfactory solution would be to accept Clines's working definition of theme as the central or dominating idea of a literary work which serves to orient the reader and constitutes a proposal about how best to approach it (Clines

1978, 18). But then a problem arises as to whether the Pentateuch and, a fortiori, the story of the ancestors, both forming part of a more extensive narrative, can be described as literary works. The practical solution seems to be that while the larger context cannot be ignored (the chronology helps to remind us of it), both the Pentateuch and the ancestral history have their own narrative integrity within this larger context. An analogy might be Dostoevsky's *The Brothers Karamazov,* which was planned as part of an even larger work to be entitled *Memoirs of a Great Sinner.* It helps to know this, but one can read *Karamazov* as a fully integrated and fully intelligible work of art without knowing it.

Another consideration is that we would expect to find some correlation between theme and structure. I suggested that the *toledot* structure invites us to concentrate on Jacob's exile from and return to the land as the central peripety of the story. If now we consider the beginning and end of the work, we see that the story begins in Mesopotamia and ends in Egypt. Otherwise stated, it begins with a command to go to the land (12:1) and ends with an assurance of return to it (50:24). We are therefore led to conclude that *the land of Canaan* is somehow of central importance, and yet at the decisive points of the narrative, at the beginning, in the middle, and at the end, we find the protagonists outside of the land. It seems, then, that any statement of theme must in some way explicate this paradoxical situation.

The narrative itself provides a kind of explanation, by means of pronouncements of the deity occurring at key points in the story. The first of these, delivered before Abraham entered the land, is clearly intended to be programmatic:

> Go from your land, your kin, and your father's house to the land that I will
> show you. I am going to make you into a great nation; I will bless you and
> make your name great, so that it will be used as a blessing. I will bestow
> blessing on those who bless you, and those who curse you I will account
> accursed. All the families of the earth will find blessing through you[9] (Gen
> 12:1–3).

The tendency in recent and not-so-recent scholarship has been to concentrate massively on the formation or prehistory of the "promise tradition," and especially on the question of which has priority, the promise of an heir, of posterity, of blessing, or of land. But attention has not always been paid to the syntactical relation between them as expressed in this programmatic statement and subsequent pronouncements of the same kind. In Gen 12:1–3 they are not simply juxtaposed. Everything that is promised is contingent on Abraham's obeying the command to leave his old world behind him and go to the land he will be shown. The land, therefore, has logical priority in that everything else depends on the promise that he and his descendants will possess it. This first statement provides a point of reference throughout the narrative (18:18; 22:18; 26:4, 24; 28:13–14; 31:2, 13), and the promise of the land implicit in the call to enter it is also repeated at significant junctures (12:7; 13:14–17; 15:7–21; 17:8; 26:2–4; 28:13; 35:12; 46:2–3). But it soon becomes apparent that this promise is subject to postponement, a point made explicitly in 15:7–21, which speaks of a return to the land in the fourth generation of the Egyptian diaspora (v 16). It is this delay which, again following the logic of the narrative, gives urgency to the continuation of the line—the deferred promise of land cannot be honored if there is no one to give it to. In this sense, therefore, possession of the land of Canaan is the basic component in the theme of the ancestral history, a conclusion confirmed by the structural features just noted.

THE FORMATION OF THE ANCESTRAL HISTORY

If the formation of the narrative in Genesis 12–50 was a matter of dispute during the heyday of the documentary hypothesis, it is now even more increasingly called into question. Probably the first thing to say is that there is no prospect of a comprehensive explanation or new consensus emerging in the near future. It is also important to affirm that in this kind of work our gains are incremental. As William McKane put it, "Biblical criticism requires that we should always have a sense of the cumulative gains of criticism—an awareness that other men [and women] have laboured and we have entered into their labours" (McKane 1979, 13). The most we can strive for is a reasonable degree of probability, and the method that seems to hold out the best prospects of success is to work backward from the text as we have it rather than forward from its hypothetical origins in ancient traditions in oral or written form.

The documentary hypothesis works with the assumption that Genesis 12–50 resulted from the combination of at least two ancient sources (J and E) with P. It remains a matter of dispute whether P stands for a redactor of the earlier sources or an independent narrative source, and therefore whether the combination of JE and P requires a redactor (R) responsible for the final shaping of the story. It has been widely but by no means universally assumed that there is little if any contribution from a Deuteronomic writer (D). There has also been broad agreement that these literary sources incorporate traditions which originated and were transmitted for the most part orally, and a great deal of energy and ingenuity has been expended in tracing the stages by which these traditions, originating in different localities, generally cult centers, were combined in a sequential and comprehensive narrative. This traditio-historical investigation *(Traditionsgeschichte)* is especially associated with the names of Gunkel, Alt, von Rad, and Noth (see Chapter 1), and it has an obvious bearing on the historicity of the ancestral narratives.[10]

In recent years debate has tended to concentrate on those pronouncements of the deity in which the ancestors were assured of the continuance of their line, numerous progeny, nationhood, secure possession of the land of Canaan, and a state of blessedness in general. The major points at issue, none of which can be said to have been resolved to the general satisfaction, include the following: Does the promise of an heir represent the earliest stage? Are single promises (e.g., of an heir, of land) chronologically prior to multiple ones, and unconditional to conditional? Does the "great nation" theme reflect the situation under the United Monarchy, or at least the early monarchy, or does it rather come from a time when national identity was either in jeopardy or a thing of the past? Since the answers to such questions have to be based exclusively on literary criteria (e.g., as to which of the pronouncements is more firmly embedded in the narrative), the most that can be hoped for is a plausible explanation of the process by which the narrative, including the pronouncements, reached its present form.[11]

There is, however, one resource which, if it cannot break the deadlock, may at least serve as a control, and that is the fact of so many allusions to the ancestors in the Hebrew Bible outside of Genesis. Since the so-called wisdom books (Job, Proverbs, Ecclesiastes, Song of Songs) nowhere refer to them, we are limited to the narrative material in Exodus, Leviticus and Numbers, the Deuteronomistic corpus including Deuteronomy, and the prophetic books. Psalms, notoriously difficult to date, contain occasional allusions that at best serve a corroborative function. We shall therefore survey this material to see what contribution it can make to an eventual solution.

The Ancestors in the Prophetic Books

We begin with the prophetic books since, in spite of the problems posed by their often complex editorial history, they seem to offer the best prospect for sequential dating. A survey of retrospective allusions to ancestors in these books permits the following conclusions:

1. In numerous instances the term "fathers" *('ābôt)* refers to the forebears of Israel subsequent to Abraham, Isaac, and Jacob, and the emphasis is more often than not on their religious infidelity.[12]

2. In several of these instances the allusion is more specifically to the ancestors of the exodus and wilderness period. The D editor of Jeremiah speaks of a covenant made with the fathers at the time of the exodus from Egypt (Jer 11:3–4; 31:32; 34:13). That the reference is to the Sinai-Horeb covenant is clear from the allusion to the law governing the manumission of slaves in Jer 34:13 (cf. Ex 21:2; Deut 15:12). It is equally clear that in these texts the honoring by YHWH of the oath made to *previous* ancestors is contingent on Israel's observance of the terms of that covenant (Jer 11:5). We find a similar situation in Ezekiel's magisterial review of Israel's history, a history beginning with a revelation in Egypt and the oath to bring Israel out from there into a land flowing with milk and honey (Ezek 20:4–6, 42). Comparison with Ex 6:2–9 (P) shows that here too a promise or oath made *before* the sojourn in Egypt is presupposed (*pace* Van Seters 1972, 448–49).

3. In pre-exilic prophetic texts the population of one or other of the two kingdoms is referred to frequently by the designation Jacob,[13] less frequently Isaac (Amos 7:9, 16) and Joseph (Amos 5:5, 15; 6:6). Since all three are personal names, this usage implies a collective consciousness of descent from individuals so named—whether real or fictitious need not be decided—and the plurality of designations further suggests a genealogical connection of some kind between them, though not necessarily a developed narrative tradition about them. It is particularly noteworthy that there is no reference to Abraham in prophetic texts prior to Ezekiel (33:24).

4. In those places where pre-exilic prophets appeal to historical traditions, the allusions generally go back no further than the sojourn in Egypt, the wilderness experience, and the occupation of the land. But there are exceptions. The spectacular destruction of the cities of the plain is a topos of fairly frequent occurrence in prophetic diatribe, though the fact that Lot is never mentioned in this connection may mean that these two traditions had not yet been combined.[14] Jer 31:15 speaks of Rachel weeping for her children in Ramah of Benjamin (cf. 1 Sam 10:2, where her tomb is located at Zelzah in Benjamin), so this matriarch at least was known at the time of writing. Allusions to Esau (Edom) in Obadiah also suggest some acquaintance with the narrative tradition about enmity between the two brothers, as does the opening paragraph in Malachi (1:2–5). But the most extensive reference to the ancestors in early prophecy occurs in Hos 12:4–5, 13 [12:3–4, 12], which speaks of Jacob. Hosea appears to be acquainted with the following traditions: the birth of twins, the wrestling with God or an angel, the dream theophany at Bethel, the flight to Mesopotamia, and Jacob's service there as a herdsman. However, there is no reference in Genesis to Jacob weeping; Edwin Good (*VT* 16[1966] 137–51) suggested a

connection with the place name Allon-bakuth (Oak of Weeping, Gen 35:8), but the etiology is preempted by the death of Deborah, Rachel's nurse. The parallels are obviously quite close, but they do not imply that Hosea was familiar with a continuous narrative such as Genesis 25–35. Nor can we be certain that these allusions are native to their present context. The indictment in which they occur is directed against the people designated Jacob (cf. 10:11), and their evil deeds are neither explained nor illustrated by the reference to the deeds of Jacob the individual. It seems, therefore, that either Hosea is *contrasting* the conduct of his contemporaries with that of Jacob (Ackroyd 1963, 245–59) or, a more likely alternative, a glossator has been led by the reference to the deeds of Jacob the people to expatiate, somewhat inappropriately, on those of the patriarch. If the latter hypothesis is correct, the same hand may have added the line about the flight to Mesopotamia (12:13 [12:12]), which is even less at home in its present context.

5. In exilic prophetic texts, especially Ezekiel and Second Isaiah, we find a very noticeable preference for Jacob as an ethnic designation (e.g., Isa 41:8; 44:1–2; Jer 30:10; 46:27–28; Ezek 28:25). This preferential usage will help to explain why the narrative tradition about this patriarch, especially his exile and return, makes such a close match with the historical situation through which these prophets were living. Now too for the first time we begin to hear of Abraham (Isa 29:22; 41:8; 63:16; Micah 7:20; Jer 33:26), with special reference to his call and blessing (Isa 51:1–2; 63:16) and his claim on the land (Ezek 33:23–29). Sarah too is named for the first and only time (Isa 51:2), and we cannot fail to note the association with Zion, the barren woman who nevertheless will be blessed with children after the return from exile (Isa 49:21; 54:1–3). I take this to be one of several indications that historical experience has played an important part in shaping the stories about the ancestors as we find them in Genesis.

The Ancestors in the Deuteronomistic Corpus

The Deuteronomistic corpus includes the book of Deuteronomy, conventionally dated to the seventh century B.C., the Deuteronomistic History (Dtr hereafter), from the mid-sixth century B.C., and editorial expansions of prophetic books, especially Jeremiah, from about the same time. While the composition of Deuteronomy and the associated matter of dating continue to be discussed, we can accept as a working hypothesis that Deut 4:44–28:68 forms the core of the work from the time of the late monarchy, while Deut 4:1–40 and a good part of 29–30 constitute an exilic expansion. The historical introduction (1–3) and the final chapters (31–34) present special problems and will be dealt with separately. A corresponding double redaction of Dtr (hereafter Dtr[1] and Dtr[2]) has also been argued, and is accepted here. These proposals will be scrutinized more closely in a later chapter, but for the present they may serve as a point of departure.

In all these parts of the corpus we find a preponderant emphasis on the gift of the land as the fulfillment of a commitment made to the ancestors. But at the same time we note that wherever historical reminiscence is introduced, the perspective goes back no further than the descent into Egypt of Jacob and his seventy descendants (Deut 10:22; 26:5–9). As in the prophetic books, the only exception is the destruction of the cities of the plain, four of which are named in Deut 29:22 [29:23] and two in Deut 32:32. In D[1], the core of the work, the fathers are referred to on numerous occasions as the beneficiaries of a promise and oath dealing primarily with the land and secondarily with numerous descendants. For the most part these fathers are unnamed, but on three occasions (Deut 6:10; 9:7, 27) Abraham, Isaac, and Jacob stand in apposition to "fathers." Van Seters has nevertheless argued that the gift of the land is not associated with these early ancestors in Deuteronomy, but that the reference is to fathers of the exodus generation (Van Seters 1972, 448–59). But neither text-critical considerations nor the context justifies deleting the names, and there are instances where the names do not occur which refer explicitly to a period prior to the exodus and wilderness (Deut 8:3, 16; 10:22). We may therefore conclude that at the time of writing, perhaps during the reign of Josiah (640–609 B.C.), at least the names of the three prominent ancestors were known in the order in which Genesis presents them.

We find much the same situation in D[2], the exilic expansion, in which Abraham, Isaac, and Jacob are also named (Deut 29:12 [29:13]; 30:20), in a context identical to that in which unnamed fathers are referred to (4:37; 30:5, 9; 31:7, 20). In this section the Horeb covenant is also made with "the God of their fathers" (29:24 [29:25] cf. Jer 11:3–4; 31:32; 34:13), which emphasizes once again the conditional nature of the promise to the ancestors according to this theological perspective. The same situation obtains in the historical introduction (1:8, 10–11, 21, 35) and in the final scene in which Moses surveys the land which he was forbidden to enter (34:4).

The author of Dtr[2] also introduces, as the occasion warrants, allusion to the three ancestors (1 Kings 18:36; 2 Kings 13:23), and refers to Jacob's descent into Egypt in his rendering of Samuel's valedictory address (1 Sam 12:8; cf. Deut 10:22; 26:5–9). But the most interesting passage is Joshua's discourse preceding the Shechem covenant (Josh 24:2–15). In it he presents an outline of the entire ancestral history from Terah to the descent into Egypt. There are, of course, omissions, but few significant differences from what we find in Genesis: there are two rather than three sons of Terah, and there is the fact that the ancestors worshipped other gods before leaving Mesopotamia. The ceremony following the address is also quite clearly related to the abjuration of foreign gods by Jacob's household as reported in Gen 35:1–4, and both take place at the tree sanctuary of Shechem. Since the Shechem cult tradition appears to have left its mark on Deuteronomy (Deut 11:26–32; 27), it is safe to conclude that the episode in the Jacob story has drawn on Dtr at this point, which would also increase the probability that the ancestral history as a whole is a greatly expanded version of the kind of summary represented by Joshua's address.

What we find in the Deuteronomistic additions to Jeremiah is consistent, as we would expect, with the situation in Deuteronomy and Dtr[2]. There are numerous allusions to unnamed fathers, generally of a derogatory nature,[15] some of them belonging to the generation of the exodus and wilderness (Jer 7:14, 22–23; 11:7; 31:32; 34:13). But it is worth repeating that where fathers are mentioned as receiving the promise and oath concerning the land,[16] the allusion is to an earlier time, the time of Abraham, Isaac, and Jacob. This is transparently clear in Jer 11:1–5, certainly of Deuteronomistic vintage (cf. the term "iron furnace," referring to Egypt in Deut 4:20), where a divine pronouncement to the exodus generation refers to the oath sworn to *their* fathers. It is also clearly stated or implied that the fulfillment of the oath is contingent on observance of the (Deuteronomic) law.

An interesting feature of this extensive editorial rewriting is the explicit parallel drawn between the exodus and the return from exile:

See, the days are at hand (oracle of YHWH) when people will no longer say, "By the life of YHWH who brought the Israelites up from the land of Egypt," but rather, "By the life of YHWH who brought the Israelites up from the land of the north . . . for I will bring them back to their own land which I gave to their ancestors" (Jer 16:14–15; cf. 23:8; 31:8).

A similar parallelism exists between the "exodus formula" ("I am YHWH your God who brought you up from the land of Egypt") and the declaration of YHWH preceding the "covenant of the pieces" in Genesis 15 ("I am YHWH who brought you up from Ur of the Chaldees to give you this land to possess"; Van Seters 1972, 455). Ur of the Chaldees has simply replaced the land of Egypt, another indication of the way in which Genesis 12–50 has been formed on the basis of confessional and interpretative schemata emerging at different times throughout the history of Israel.

The Ancestors in Exodus–Numbers

An interesting feature of the narrative from Exodus to Deuteronomy, one easily overlooked, is the relative paucity of reference back to the story of the ancestors in Genesis 12–50. The P narrative strand is a special case, since it is in evidence throughout the Pentateuch and, as we shall see, beyond it. It is in P that we read that God heeded the oppression in Egypt and remembered his covenant with Abraham, Isaac, and Jacob (Ex 2:24). The same assurance is repeated in Lev 26:42 in a context which speaks explicitly of Israel in exile. The P version of the revelation to Moses, which takes place not in the Midianite wilderness but in Egypt, identifies the one who addresses him as El Shaddai who appeared to the ancestors (Ex 6:2–9). The reader is therefore assured that Israel in exile may still count on the god who made these ancient commitments to honor them by bringing his people back to their land.

Apart from P, however, there is surprisingly little reference to the ancestors in the story of the exodus, Sinai, and the wilderness. At the burning bush the deity reveals himself as the god of Abraham, Isaac, and Jacob (Ex 3:6, 15–16; 4:5), but the names of the three patriarchs occur in what is clearly an *additional* locution of the deity (3:6, 15–16). The awkward syntactic construction in 4:5 likewise leads us to suspect an addition from an editor eager to identify the god of the theophany with the god worshiped by the early ancestors, the god who swore to give them the land. The three ancestors are mentioned again in the intercessory prayer of Moses after the incident of the golden calf (Ex 32:13), a prayer which is very close to that of Moses in Deut 9:27. The promise of the land in Ex 33:1 and Num 32:11 is also reminiscent of Deuteronomic formulations (e.g., Deut 34:4), suggesting the conclusion that a Deuteronomic editor has inserted the promise theme at crucial junctures of the narrative—at the beginning of the exodus history and at the point where its successful outcome was threatened by apostasy.

From this brief survey we may draw the following conclusions. Before the publication of Deuteronomy during the later period of the monarchy, the patriarchs, with the probable exception of Abraham, were known by name. Of these the most prominent was Jacob, about whom several traditions were in circulation, whether in written or oral form we do not know. The tradition about the destruction of the cities of the plain was also known, though apparently not yet connected with the Lot story, closely associated as it is with Abraham. With the appearance of Deuteronomy, the promise of secure possession of the land, now conditional on observance of the law, became prominent, and understandably so in view of the expectation of political emancipation, including the emancipation of the provinces to the north already incorporated in the Assyrian empire. By the

time of the Babylonian exile—dating from the first deportation in 598/597
B.C.—there existed, at least in outline, a consecutive history from entry
into Canaan to descent into Egypt, with the three great ancestors in chronological and presumably also genealogical sequence. This must be regarded as only an assured minimum since it is based on the relatively few
writings which have come down to us. But it may nevertheless serve as a
useful control as we go on to ask what conclusions may be drawn from an
examination of the ancestral history itself.

THE ANCESTRAL HISTORY AND ITS SOURCES

The story of Israel's ancestors can be read through from beginning to
end as a reasonably coherent narrative without regard to sources. That, in
fact, is how it was read for centuries before the rise of historical criticism,
and that is how many people still read it today with profit. The matter of
sources only assumed importance with the need to understand the development of religious thinking in Israel, the different ways in which successive historical situations, especially political disaster, affected the way people in Israel understood their relation to God. To the extent that an
understanding of the past, individual and collective, is an essential aspect
of self-understanding and identity, that need still exists. There is therefore
no need to apologize in advance for attempting to understand something
of the formation and development of the biblical narrative. To take an
example analogous to the ancestral history, the development of Christian
theology has been deeply influenced by competing views of the development of earliest Christianity, views which were based on different con-
structions of the literary history of the extant texts and their sources.

To begin with what is least subject to doubt: there is still a broad
consensus on the existence of a Priestly source (P) which has provided the
skeletal framework of the narrative. This consensus is based on the occurrence of characteristic linguistic, stylistic, and thematic features, several
of which were noted in the previous chapter.[17] Whether P should be
regarded as a quite distinct source or merely an editorial strand, a
Bearbeitungsschicht (as maintained, e.g., by Cross 1973, 324–25 and
Rendtorff 1977, 139–42) depends largely, it seems to me, on the answer
one gives to the question whether P responsible for the final shaping
of the narrative. In the previous chapter we saw reason to believe that this
is not the case. We cannot reasonably maintain that P deliberately omitted
the distinction between clean and unclean and the sacrifice in the deluge
narrative and, then, as final redactor, reintroduced both of these features.
It is also difficult to see why the Priestly writer, who gives pride of place to
Aaron, would, as final redactor, have left unchanged the golden calf inci-

dent, which hardly does credit to the founder of the priesthood. If, then, we posit a final redaction other than and later than P, we may accept that an independent P narrative has been used, perhaps selectively, to provide the basic narrative line, including the numerous chronological indications and perhaps also the *toledot* superscripts.[18]

Consistent with this view of the matter is the fact that the passages attributed to P in the ancestral history add up to a reasonably coherent narrative.[19] In the Terah-Abraham *toledot* it recounts the move from Ur of the Chaldees to Haran (11:27–32),[20] Abram's journey from Haran to Canaan (12:4b–5), his separation from Lot, which left him as sole claimant to the land (13:6, 11–12), Hagar's appointment as proxy for the infertile Sarah and the birth of Ishmael (16:1, 3, 15–16), the covenant of circumcision and promise of an heir (17), the rescue of Lot from the doomed city (19:29), the birth and circumcision of Isaac (21:2–5), the death of Sarah and Abraham's purchase of the field and cave at Machpelah (23), and finally the death and burial of Abraham (25:7–11).

After the interstitial Ishmael section listing his "sons" and recording his death (25:12–17), there follows the Isaac-Jacob *toledot* in which P records the marriage of Isaac and Rebekah and the birth of their two sons (25:19–20, 26b), the unfortunate marriages of Esau with foreign women (26:34–35), and the sending away of Jacob to Mesopotamia to avoid following his example (27:46–28:9). After noting how Jacob prospered in the land of his exile (31:18), P goes on to record his return to Bethel (35:6), where El Shaddai appeared to him, changed his name to Israel, and renewed the promise of nationhood and land (35:9–13). This section ends with the list of twelve sons and the death of Isaac (35:22b–29). At least the first part of the Edomite list is from P, incorporating the important theme of topographical segregation which has appeared more than once already. In the final *toledot* P deals almost exclusively with Jacob rather than with Joseph which, given the superscript, suggests rather strongly that Joseph is a latecomer to the section. P, therefore, records only the relocation in Egypt of Jacob and the seventy members of his extended family (46:6–27), his audience with Pharaoh (47:5–11, uncertain), and the prosperity attained during Jacob's seventeen years in the land of exile (47:27–28). It concludes with the deathbed scene, in which Jacob recalls the theophany at Bethel, adopts Ephraim and Manasseh as his own sons (48:3–6), and gives instructions concerning his burial (49:28–33), and Jacob's burial in Abraham's cave at Machpelah (50:12–13).

Looking over the entire Genesis narrative, we can now see more clearly some of the main concerns of the Priestly writer. One of the most prominent of these has to do with the covenant. The displacement backward from Sinai to human origins in Genesis 9 and the origins of Israel in Genesis 17 implies a radical rethinking of the covenant idea in response to the pressure of new situations and new exigencies. YHWH, the God of Israel, is identified with the creator-God who was worshipped from the beginning and whom the ancestors worshipped as El Shaddai (17:1; 28:3; 35:11; 48:3), and it is this God who has established a relationship with humanity long before Israel appeared on the scene of history. Israel's special status, of which the sign is circumcision, is established by an equally indefectible covenant, a běrît ʿôlām which, unlike other covenants, does not require periodic renewal. All that is required is that God *remember* his covenant, which he does when his people are languishing in exile (Ex 2:24; 6:5; Lev 26:42–45). This covenant is also unconditional, since neither the Noachide laws nor circumcision are presented in P as conditions on which the honoring of the covenant is contingent. In P, therefore, běrît means more a dispensation than a covenant, defining in advance God's relation first to humanity, then to Israel.

Apart from the establishment of the běrît in Genesis 17, the only other P narrative of significant length in the ancestral history is the account of the purchase of the Machpelah cave in Chapter 23. I suggested earlier that the careful and detailed description of the negotiations reflects the importance of land claims after the descendants of the deportees began to return to the province of Judah in the Persian period (6th–4th centuries B.C.). This point is confirmed by the progressive elimination of other claimants— Lot, Ishmael, Esau—corresponding to the situation which obtained after the expropriation of ancestral holdings at the time of the deportations (e.g., Ezek 11:14–17). Several other aspects of the P narrative reflect the same historical situation, including the emphasis on avoiding marriage with the "women of the land" (Gen 27:46; also 26:34–35; 27:46–28:9) and on the prosperity of the ancestors which came to them in spite of unpropitious circumstances (12:5; 13:6; 31:18; 36:7; 46:6).

There are therefore sufficient indications to suggest that P reflects the experience of exile and the hopes for a better future after the destruction of the state apparatus by the Babylonians in the early sixth century B.C. This conclusion has been widely accepted, but we must bear in mind that the exile did not end with the Persian conquest of Babylon in 539 B.C. As little as we know of life in the Jewish settlements in the alluvial plain of southern Mesopotamia, we may be sure that there existed a social substructure capable of sustaining the kind of priestly and scribal learning which found eventual expression in the Pentateuch. (If we are to believe Ezra 8:15–20, for example, Ezra was able to recruit Levites and other cultic personnel from an establishment at Casiphia under the regency of a certain Iddo, presumably a priest.) At any rate, whether in the Nippur region or back in the Judean homeland, learned priests and their associates were engaged in constructing, in response to the experience of deprivation and exile, a conceptual world of meaning in which historical reconstruction, the recovery of a usable past, played an important role. We have good reason to find in Genesis 12–50, and elsewhere in the Pentateuch, the fruits of these labors.

Once we move beyond the Priestly narrative we enter a very gray area indeed, especially now that the consensus or near-consensus on the extent and date of the early sources (J and E) has begun to disintegrate. Even in the heyday of the documentary hypothesis it was acknowledged that there are passages which cannot be assigned to these sources, or at least do not readily lend themselves to the kind of analysis on which the existence of the sources was postulated. A case in point is the account of Abraham's rescue of Lot after defeating a coalition of eastern kings (Genesis 14). Over the years the events narrated in this chapter, and sometimes the chapter itself, have been placed in the third millennium B.C., in the Hasmonean period, and at several points in between (Emerton 1971, 24–47; Westermann 1985, 182–208). Whatever the date, it has nothing in common with either J or E. Also sui generis is Abraham's pleading for the doomed citizens of Sodom (Gen 18:22–23). I argued some years ago that it is a type of narrative unique in Genesis and that in view of the identification of Jerusalem with Sodom in prophetic diatribe, it may be read as an addition reflecting the religious crisis of the sixth century B.C. and addressing, somewhat in the manner of midrash, the issue of the fate of the righteous caught in the destructive flow of events attributed to divine causality (Blenkinsopp 1982, 119–32). To these we may add other passages which have resisted alignment with J and E, e.g., the mission to find a wife for Isaac and the theft of the deathbed blessing by Jacob (Westermann 1985, 383–84, 435).

We have seen that the Elohist source (E), deemed to originate in the Northern Kingdom in the eighth century B.C., has been under a cloud from the early days of critical inquiry. And in fact a survey of the passages usually assigned to E (Eissfeldt 1966, 200–1; Noth 1972, 263–67) reveals that those which to some degree satisfy the accepted criteria, especially use of the designation "Elohim" for the deity, are set not in the Northern Kingdom but in the Negev, more often than not in the Beersheba region (20; 21:8–21, 22–34; 22:1–19). Other passages often assigned to E, especially the "covenant of the pieces" in Genesis 15, which some have taken to be its opening scene, and the "binding of Isaac" in Genesis 22, do not satisfy the criteria at all. The former will call for comment shortly. The latter was never in serious contention since it is associated with a Yahwistic cult place (v 14), features the angel of YHWH (v 11), and is located in the Beersheba region (v 19).

One basic assumption of most documentary critics is that E is genetically related to D, in that both exhibit prophetic influence, use similar terminology (e.g., Horeb rather than Sinai) and originate in the Northern

Kingdom. At the same time, most documentarians have been influenced by Martin Noth's Tetrateuch hypothesis in ruling out any significant D (Deuteronomic or Deuteronomistic) contribution to the Genesis narrative. Some have hedged their bets by allowing for proto-Deuteronomic traits, but without clarifying how such traits differ from E and D. Our survey of references to the ancestors in the D work, and especially the D formulation of the promises in Exodus (3:6, 15–16; 32:13; 33:1), might however at least lead us to suspect that similar formulations in Genesis derive from the same source. A particularly strong case can be made where the promise is linked with observance of the law, as in the following passages:

> YHWH said, 'Shall I conceal from Abraham what I am about to do, in that Abraham is destined to become a great and powerful nation through whom all the nations of the earth will receive blessing? I have surely chosen him, so that he may charge his sons and his household after him to observe the way of YHWH, to act with righteousness and justice, so that YHWH may bring on Abraham what he has promised him' (18:17–19).

> By myself I have sworn (oracle of YHWH) that because you have done this thing . . . I will indeed bless you and increase your descendants like the stars of the sky and the sand of the seashore; your descendants shall possess the gate of your enemies, and all the nations of the earth shall find blessing through your descendants since you have obeyed my voice (22:16–18).

> I will multiply your descendants like the stars of the sky, I will give your descendants all these lands, and all the nations of the earth shall find blessing through your descendants, because Abraham obeyed my voice, observing my charge, my commandments and laws (26:4–5).

This kind of language is indistinguishable from the homiletic and hortatory style of the Deuteronomists. Similar language occurs at intervals throughout the ancestral history (e.g., 16:10; 26:24; 28:15; 35:1–4), allowing for the possibility that a D writer has edited narrative source material in a manner analogous to the presentation of prophetic narratives in Dtr, e.g., the stories about Elijah and Elisha.

Of particular interest in this regard is the vision report in Genesis 15 which for the first time takes up the theme of delay in the fulfillment of the promises. It is here that the Elohist was thought by many to make his first appearance, in spite of the fact that the name YHWH occurs throughout. While it is possible with a little goodwill to read the chapter as a coherent and seamless account, indications are not lacking that at least two sources have been conflated. The vision takes place initially at night (v 5), but shortly thereafter we hear that the sun is just setting (v 12); Abraham believes YHWH in the first instance (v 6), and then entertains doubts and seeks for reassurance (v 8). There are also duplicated locutions ("Abraham said" in vv 2 and 3), and the phrase "on that day" *(bayyôm hahû',* v 18) suggests an addition, as often in prophetic books. Indications of a later date are also present. The episode is introduced as a vision report, using a form of speech attested in Dtr and later prophets, especially Ezekiel. ("The word of YHWH came to X in a vision.") The initial injunction not to fear belongs to the category of salvation oracle of a kind frequent in Second Isaiah (Isa 40:9; 41:10, 13, 14, etc.). As with Ezekiel, the visionary is led in the vision to a place where a further revelation takes place (cf. Ezek 8:3). The communication of information about the future course of events (vv 13–16) is also characteristic of later prophecy, including prose narratives about prophets in Dtr (e.g., 1 Sam 2:30–36; 2 Sam 7:12–17; 2 Kings 22:15–20). And, finally, the fixing of the boundary of the land at the Euphrates is certainly Deuteronomic (Deut 1:7; 11:24; Josh 1:4).

It is therefore hardly surprising if several recent commentators have concluded that a D author has either composed or extensively edited this crucial chapter.[21] There is also the interesting connection between faith and righteousness in Gen 15:6, which would seem to indicate a mature stage of theological reflection, anticipating the later presentation of Abraham as the father of those who believe. This same verse implies, if it does not state, a connection between the commitment of YHWH to his word and the appropriate human response, and in this respect it recalls the Deuteronomic view that without faith Israel cannot fulfill its destiny (Deut 1:32; 9:23). We also owe to the Deuteronomists the formulation of the promises in terms of a covenant (Perlitt 1969, 68–77), and we have seen that the statement "I am YHWH who brought you up from Ur of the Chaldees" (15:7) is modeled on the self-presentation of YHWH as the God of the exodus (Ex 20:2; Deut 5:6).[22] It should be obvious that the occurrence of the ritual severing of animals in connection with covenant making in ancient Mesopotamian texts—from Mari in the eighteenth century B.C.—tells us nothing about the date of this passage; and in fact the only other biblical allusion to this practice is in Jer 34:18, roughly contemporary with Deuteronomy. We may therefore conclude that this pivotal incident in the ancestral history was either written or extensively rewritten by a D author at a time when possession of the land, and indeed the continuing existence of Israel, could no longer be taken for granted.

Turning now to the Yahwist source (J), it is easier at this stage to state the problems under which it labors than it is to propose an alternative hypothesis. It has always been assumed that J is a continuous narrative covering the period from early humanity to the occupation of the land, or at least to the death of Moses. But we have seen that there is little in common between narrative attributed to this source in Genesis 1–11 and Genesis 12–50, and that linkage between these two sections was established only at a relatively late date by the genealogical schema. The same can be said of the larger narrative corpora in Genesis 12–50. The highly individual character of the Joseph story and the difficulty of reducing it to a combination of J and E have been widely acknowledged, and we have seen that it appears to have been incorporated into the larger complex at a relatively late date. The Abraham cycle of stories is also significantly different from the Jacob cycle. The latter abounds in detail and presents a psychologically realistic portrait of the protagonist, while the former is quite schematic, presenting Abraham more as an ideal and typical figure than a fully developed character. Thus the first part of the Abraham story is little more than an itinerary, and the descent into Egypt and temporary separation from Sarah are told with a minimum of narrative development. Apart from the destruction of the twin cities and the incestuous union of Lot with his daughters, in neither of which Abraham makes an appearance, the only episodes told at any length are the dismissal of Hagar and the promise of a child (Gen 16; 18:1–16).

While arguments from silence are seldom definitive, it would be imprudent to overlook the total absence of any reference to Abraham in pre-Deuteronomic writings. Isaac, too, is alluded to only by name, and just twice; and though some traditions about Jacob were in circulation at a relatively early time, we have no assurance that they existed then in the form of a consecutive narrative.

The fragility of the arguments for dating J to the early monarchy, perhaps the United Monarchy, have also been increasingly exposed in recent studies. One cannot argue for an early date on the basis of a nomadic or semi-nomadic setting (as Eissfeldt 1966, 198–99 with respect to his Lay Source), as if a later author could not, like the author of the Book of Job, compose such a setting for his characters. Nor can we appeal to a "proud and grateful delight in people, land, cultus, and kingdom" (Eissfeldt 1966, 200 with respect to J), as if a later author could not express these sentiments in the hope and expectation of a future restoration. Some recent authors (Wagner 1972, 131–36; Van Seters 1975, 151–53) have also attacked the frequently propounded thesis of an association between Abraham and David (e.g., Hans Walter Wolff 1966, 131–58; Ronald E.

Clements 1967). If Abraham was such an important figure for the "theologians" of David and Solomon as Wolff and Clements assume, it is surprising that he is never mentioned in the record of their reigns, or that there is no allusion to kingship in the J record about Abraham (oddly enough, such allusions occur only in P), or that we pick up no hint in the same record of the life-and-death struggle with the Philistines. A more plausible alternative would be that Abraham is being presented as an example for those in the Babylonian diaspora who answered the call to return to the homeland and rebuild the nation. He is at least mentioned in texts from that time.

Our discussion of the formation of Genesis 12–50 leads to the following conclusions. The final edition was organized around the Priestly work with its concern for precise chronology and its highly distinctive ideology. This edition incorporated a Deuteronomic-Deuteronomistic strand with its own understanding of promise and covenant and a marked emphasis on possession of the land. We could therefore compare narrative techniques, editorial methods, and historiographical procedures in the ancestral history with those in Dtr. In both we find free compositions, old stories retold to fit new situations, and entire narratives of considerable length incorporated with little or no alteration. It appears, for example, that the Joseph story has been incorporated completely into the larger narrative complex in much the same way that the Succession History (2 Sam 11–20 and 1 Kings 1–2) has been incorporated into Dtr.

Comparison between the two works may also help to put in perspective the criterion of divine names which has played such a large part in the debate since the early days of critical inquiry. In both Genesis 12–50 and Dtr there are many episodes in which YHWH and Elohim are used interchangeably. In the story of Gideon (Judges 6–8) and the announcement of the birth of Samson (Judges 13), for example, the supernatural emissary is referred to as both the angel of YHWH and the angel of Elohim. In the Saul narrative, likewise, both designations occur (e.g., 1 Sam 10:9), and the author refers in the same episode to the spirit of YHWH and the spirit of Elohim (1 Sam 10:6, 10). There are, however, a few instances of parallel accounts in which the titles are differentiated. Saul's attempt to pin David to the wall with a spear is narrated twice, and in one version we hear of an evil spirit from Elohim (1 Sam 18:10), while in the other the evil spirit is from YHWH (1 Sam 19:9). The incident of the famine brought to an end by ritual sacrifice concludes by saying that Elohim heeded supplication for the land (2 Sam 21:14), while the more-or-less parallel account of the census and ensuing pestilence concludes with YHWH doing the same (2 Sam 24:25). In other parallels, however, the divine names are not differentiated (e.g., David sparing Saul's life: 1 Sam 23:14–24:22; 26:1–25). There are a few narratives—perhaps only those dealing with Gideon's fleece

(Judg 6:36–40) and Abimelech (Judges 9)—that are entirely Elohistic, and the reason may be that neither exhibits much in the way of religious interest.

THE QUEST OF THE HISTORICAL ANCESTORS

Since so many readers of the Bible today have a stake in the historical accuracy of the narrative contained in it, it is still necessary to insist that we cannot even begin to address historical issues until we have come to terms with the literary problems. As the philosopher and historian Robin George Collingwood reminded us years ago, the first question to ask in reading such texts is not "Did it really happen?" but "What does it mean?" Meaning can be conveyed in many different literary forms of which history is only one. Moreover, historiography as understood today, based on the accurate reporting of events and the careful evaluation of sources, is a relatively recent phenomenon, perhaps datable to Gibbon's *Decline and Fall of the Roman Empire,* completed in 1788. Biblical texts which narrate past events work with different assumptions and must therefore be approached with somewhat different expectations. We cannot assume in a simplistic way that the accurate rendering of past events and characters was the principal goal of the authors of Genesis 12–50, and in fact there are plenty of indications that this was not the case.

The first requirement for saying anything, however speculative, about the historicity of the ancestral narratives is the identification of the traditions incorporated in the text. We noted in the opening chapter how Hermann Gunkel made a first move in this direction by attempting to isolate and describe the smaller units of tradition that served as the building blocks of the narrative. Gunkel assumed that these were both composed and transmitted orally, and thought it possible in principle to reconstruct the social situation (the *Sitz im Leben*) which generated an individual tradition. This method of investigation was further developed by a great number of scholars, conspicuous among whom were Albrecht Alt, Gerhard von Rad, and Martin Noth. By means of impressive hypotheses they aimed to explain the origin of the traditions in the social activity, and especially the cultic activity, of the Israelite tribes in the pre-state period, and to show how these traditions eventually coalesced into continuous narrative form.

Traditio-historical investigation, therefore, shifted the focus from the time of composition of the documents to the period in which the traditions behind the documents originated. The task then was to corrolate these traditions with the (imperfectly preserved) archaeological record bearing on the social and cultural history of the ancient Near East. Where a reasonably close correlation could be achieved, it was then thought possible to affirm the essential historicity of the tradition in spite of a gap of many centuries between the epoch in question and the date assigned to the document in which the tradition appeared. In recent years the problems inherent in these procedures have become more and more apparent. The example of the Book of Job will suffice to make the point that creating a plausible social setting does not necessarily confirm the historicity of the characters and events placed in that setting. Many of the scholars in question also operated with ideas about oral tradition which anthropological field work and theoretical studies based on it have shown to be questionable. There was a tendency toward hasty conflation of the biblical data with the necessarily provisional results of archaeological excavation, rather than investigating both sets of data independently. In the very influential work of William Foxwell Albright in particular, there also lurked the naive idea that archaeological data have an objectivity which confers on them a privileged status and finality denied texts. It is therefore not surprising that so many claims for historicity once confidently advanced have more recently been called into question.

The present situation, then, is this: in the current state of our knowledge there is no realistic expectation of establishing the historicity of the ancestors. The most that can be hoped for is to propose a plausible setting for the stories in the context of the social and political history of the ancient Near East studied independently of the biblical traditions. Over the last half century the preferential option has been for the early second millennium B.C., corresponding to the Middle Bronze period—either MB I (ca. 2100–1900) or MB IIA–B (ca. 1900–1600). With varying degrees of emphasis and variations in detail this view has been held by many British, American, and French biblical scholars and archaeologists—Rowley, Kenyon, Cazelles, Albright, Wright, and de Vaux, to name some of the more prominent[23]—and has been repeated in any number of books written for the general public. It appears in the third edition of John Bright's widely read *History of Israel* (1981) in a form practically unchanged from the first edition published twenty-two years earlier, and this in spite of the fact that it has come increasingly under attack, most impressively in detailed studies by Thomas L. Thompson (1974) and John Van Seters (1975).

Space permits only the briefest summary of the current debate on the historicity of the ancestral narratives. The choice of a date in the early second millennium may have been originally suggested by the biblical chronology which stipulates 430 years for the sojourn in Egypt (Ex 12:40) and 480 years from the exodus to the beginning of the building of the temple in the fourth year of Solomon's reign (1 Kings 6:1). If this event took place c. 960 B.C. we arrive at a date of c. 1870 B.C. for the relocation of Jacob's family in Egypt. It was gratifying that this conclusion seemed to be supported by archaeological data gleaned from such sites as Mari (Tell el-Ḥariri) on the Upper Euphrates, Nuzi (Yorghan Tepe) in northeast Iraq, Alalakh (Tell Atchaneh) in Syria, Ugarit (Ras Shamra) on the Syrian coast opposite Cyprus, and Tell el-Amarna between Thebes and Memphis on the east bank of the Nile. To these we must add the Cappadocian Tablets from Kanish (Kültepe), an Assyrian trading colony in eastern Turkey, the Execration Texts from Egypt of the nineteenth and eighteenth dynasties, and the results of excavations and surveys in the Cisjordanian and Transjordanian regions.

Even before we begin to match up the biblical narratives with the archaeological data, there is a problem which though obvious has not been given due weight. On the assumption that the sources have faithfully preserved traditions current in ancient Israel either shortly before or shortly after the rise of the state, an assumption which we have seen is not free of difficulties, we would have to conclude that these traditions, recording the names and activities of ancestors in distinctive social settings, have been accurately transmitted *orally* over a period of roughly eight centuries (i.e., from MB I or IIA to Iron I). While this is not impossible, studies of oral tradition in comparable cultures (e.g., Vansina 1965 [1961]; Culley 1976) suggest that it has a very low percentage of probability, and in fact no advocate of the high date has given a plausible explanation of how it might have happened.

Our suspicion is also aroused by the steadily increasing number of features which the proponents of an early second millennium date are obliged to bracket as anachronisms. A long-standing problem is created by the dealings of Abraham and Isaac with the Philistines (Genesis 21 and 26) who are known to have arrived in the area no earlier than the twelfth century B.C. It has also been pointed out that the term *kaśdîm* (Chaldeans) belongs in the first rather than the second millennium, that references to Hittites (e.g., in Genesis 23) reflect a designation of the region current in the Neo-Assyrian period, and that the strongly attested Aramean connection points to the early first rather than the early second millennium B.C.

It must also be said that none of the arguments for an early second millennium setting has survived unscathed. The names of the patriarchs (usually only the males are considered) draw on the common stock of west Semitic nomenclature by no means confined to that period. The link between the tribe of Benjamin and the "Benjaminite" nomads in the Kingdom of Mari in the eighteenth century B.C. has not held up. The birth of this "son" of Jacob/Israel, and this one alone, in Canaan (Gen 35:16–18) points in a different direction, and suggests that the name (literally, sons of the right hand or the south) can more readily be explained by its location as the southern branch of the Joseph tribes. The semi-nomads or pastoralists of the Mari texts provide a useful analogy to certain aspects of the social milieu described in Genesis 12–50, but the same situation obtained long before and long after the existence of the Kingdom of Mari. The hypothesis linking the movements of the Terahites with an Amorite migration westward in MBI has also turned out to be questionable, depending principally as it does on a dubious reading of the Egyptian Execration Texts.

The popularity of E. A. Speiser's commentary on Genesis in the Anchor Bible series has ensured that the best-known archaeological parallels are those drawing on the Nuzi tablets from the fifteenth century B.C. Several of these texts illustrate various aspects of customary law in force among the predominantly Hurrian population in and around Nuzi, and these seemed to parallel rather closely certain features of the Genesis stories that had puzzled earlier commentators. The principal examples have to do with adoption (Gen 11:29; 12:10–20; 15:2–4), the role of the brother in the marriage of his sister (Genesis 24), the provision of a proxy by an infertile woman (16; 21:1–21; 30:1–8), and Rachel's theft of Laban's household gods (31). But it is now beginning to appear that either the Nuzi text in question has been misunderstood or the biblical context has been neglected. To take only one example: it is by no means clear that possession of the household gods conferred the right of primogeniture at Nuzi, and in any case there is no hint in the biblical text that Jacob aspired to be Laban's heir and inheritor of his property (Greenberg 1962, 239–48; Thompson 1974, 277–78). More generally, we cannot assume that this kind of customary law was confined to one ethnic group or one specific epoch. In fact, Speiser himself put the ancestors in the early second millenium, while Cyrus H. Gordon, who also made much of the Nuzi parallels, dated them to the Amarna period in the early fourteenth century B.C.

SOME PROVISIONAL CONCLUSIONS

To repeat a point made earlier, it is necessary to appreciate the literary character of the text, its structures and lines of force, and the intentions and motivations that have gone into its making before we can say anything about its historical character. It is also important to bear in mind that even in explicitly historiographical writing we have no direct line to the *nuda facta historica*. What we have is an interpretation, a construct, put together by a certain selection and arrangement of sources and data informed by certain conscious and unconscious authorial processes. Understood in this sense, the past can change in relation to the changing perspective of the time of writing, just as an object seen on the horizon can reveal itself differently as the observer moves further along on a plane of observation. The peculiarity of the ancestral story, as of the Pentateuch in general, is that it incorporates not just sources, in the manner of Herodotus and other early Greek historians, but different constructs of the past seen from the perspective of different situations in the history of Israel. In this sense the biblical authors would, I believe, agree with Kierkegaard that it is not worthwhile to remember that past which cannot become a present.

In this chapter I have taken the position that the latest, and therefore the most clearly identifiable, of these constructs are those traditionally designated Priestly (P) and Deuteronomistic (D). While both are intelligible in themselves, the former belongs to a more extensive Priestly composition, to which we shall return, while the latter has to be taken in tandem with the Deuteronomistic History (Dtr) with which it has several features in common. This matter of a D component in Genesis (and, as we shall see in due course, in Exodus and Numbers also) represents a relatively new departure in Pentateuchal studies and contradicts assumptions long taken for granted. It is still *sub iudice,* but if it turns out to be correct we shall either have to think of the D edition of the history up to the time of Moses as a long preface to Dtr or of one continuous Deuteronomistic History extending from creation to the Babylonian exile. The last stage of formation, by which the Pentateuch emerged from the incorporation of Deuteronomy into the Priestly history, will be dealt with in our final chapter.

In different ways both P and D reflect the experience of destitution and exile and the hope for the rebirth of a viable community in continuity with the past. Around this nucleus have been assembled other narratives and narrative chains, for the most part of indeterminate origin. If we continue to use the designations J and E, it will be more to maintain continuity in the scholarly tradition than for the reasons for which they were postulated in the first place, for we have seen that the criteria according to which these two sources are identified have proved to be generally unsatisfactory. Some of these narratives may have been transmitted more or less unaltered from an early date, while others have been heavily edited; some may be based on oral tradition, while others appear to be free compositions. All, in one way or another, express deeply held convictions about the corporate identity and destiny of Israel and, beyond that, about human existence *coram Deo.* For this reason their interpretation constitutes an important chapter in the history of the communities within which they have continued to be read.

NOTES

1. Gen 11:27–32; 22:20–24; 25:1–6, 12–18; 35:22b–26; 36:1–5, 9–43; 46:8–27.

2. Pronouncements: Gen 12:1–3, 7; 13:14–17; 15:1, 4–5, 7–9, 13–16, 18–21; 16:10–12; 17:1–16, 19–21; 18:9–10, 13–14, 17–21; 21:12–13, 17–18; 25:23; 26:2–5, 24;

31:3; 32:28; 35:1, 9–12; 46:2–4; 48:3–4; Dreams: 20:2–7; 28:13–15; 31:11–13, 24; 37:5–10; 40:5–19; 41:1–8.

3. J. P. Fokkelman, *Narrative Art in Genesis: Specimens of Stylistic and Structural Analysis* (Amsterdam, 1975), 83–241; A. de Pury, *Promesse divine et légende cultuelle dans le cycle de Jacob. Genèse 28 et les traditions patriarcales.* 2 vols. (Paris, 1975); M. Fishbane, *Text and Texture. Close Readings of Selected Biblical Texts* (New York, 1979), 40–62; R. Alter, *The Art of Biblical Narrative* (New York, 1981), 42–46, 137–40; G. W. Coats, *Genesis with an Introduction to Narrative Literature* (Grand Rapids, 1983), 177–246; S. Bar-Efrat, *Narrative Art in the Bible* (Sheffield, 1989), 99–101, 103–105.

4. This point about the tribal groupings I owe to Professor David Noel Freedman.

5. There is considerable disagreement as to exactly what these *těrāpîm* were. Since Jacob speaks of them as his gods, they must have been idols and were small enough to be hidden in a camel saddle (31:34), though the one placed by Michal in David's bed to simulate his body must have been larger (1 Sam 19:13–16). The *těrāpîm* in Micah's shrine, however, is distinct from his graven image (Judg 18:14). They were therefore probably household gods, similar to the Roman *penates,* and could be used for purposes of divination (Ezek 21:26 [21:21]; Zech 10:2). Together with other idolatrous objects, they were proscribed during Josiah's reform (2 Kings 23:24). Moshe Greenberg, "Another Look at Rachel's Theft of the Teraphim," *JBL* 81 (1962) 239–48, rejects the view, based on a Nuzi parallel, that possession of the teraphim implied title to inheritance. Taking a clue from Josephus, he suggests instead that women departing for a foreign land took them with them to promote fertility.

6. The Wadi Jabbok narrative has given rise to an immense amount of commentary, including the highly original structuralist reading of Roland Barthes, "La Lutte avec l'ange," in *Analyse Structurale et Exegèse Biblique* (Paris, 1971), 41–62 (= *Structural Analysis and Biblical Exegesis: Interpretational Essays* [Pittsburgh, 1974], 21–33). Bibliography in Westermann, *Genesis 12–36,* 512.

7. John A. Emerton has dedicated several studies to this chapter: "Some Problems in Genesis xxxviii," *VT* 25 (1975) 338–61; "An examination of a recent structuralist interpretation of Genesis xxxviii," *VT* 26 (1976) 79–98; "Judah and Tamar," *VT* 29 (1979) 403–415.

8. Gen 11:32 (Terah); 12:4; 16:3, 16; 17:1, 24; 21:5; 25:7 (Abraham); 17:17; 23:1 (Sarah); 17:25; 25:17 (Ishmael); 25:20, 26; 35:28 (Isaac); 26:34 (Esau); 47:9, 28 (Jacob); 41:46; 50:22, 26 (Joseph).

9. Or: will bless themselves or each other with reference to you; as, for example, "may I/you be as blessed as Abraham."

10. See William McKane, *Studies in the Patriarchal Narratives* (Edinburgh, 1979) for a thorough and well-balanced evaluation of traditio-historical research.

11. Among the more significant studies of the promise theme in recent decades are J. Hoftijzer, *Die Verheissungen an die drei Erzväter* (Leiden, 1956); C. Westermann, *The Promises to the Fathers. Studies on the Patriarchal Narratives* (Philadel-

phia, 1980 [1976]); J. A. Emerton, "The Origin of the Promises to the Patriarchs in the Older Sources of the Book of Genesis," *VT* 32 (1982) 14–32.

12. Amos 2:4 (perhaps editorial); Jer 2:5; 3:25; 9:13, 15 [9:14, 16]; 11:10; 14:20; 16:11–13, 19; Isa 43:27–28; Ezek 2:3; 20:4, 27, 36; Hag 2:2; Zech 1:2, 4–6; 8:14; Mal 3:7.

13. E.g., Amos 3:13; 6:8; 7:2, 5; 8:7; 9:8; Hos 10:11; 12:3 [12:2], though the preferred term in Hosea is Ephraim; Isa 2:5, 6; 8:17; 10:20–21; Micah 1:5; Nah 2:3 [2:2]; Jer 2:4; 5:20.

14. Amos 4:11; Hos 11:8; Isa 1:9–10; 3:9; Zeph 2:9; Jer 23:14; 49:18; 50:40; Ezek 16:49–50.

15. Jer 9:13, 15 [9:14, 16]; 11:10; 16:11–13; 19:4; 23:39; 44:3, 9–10, 21.

16. Jer 3:18; 7:7; 11:5; 16:15; 24:10; 25:5; 30:3; 32:22; 35:15.

17. Lexical items exclusive to or highly characteristic of P are: *rěkûš*, "property" (Gen 12:5; 13:6; 31:18; 36:7; 46:6); *'ăhuzzāh*, "possession, inheritance" (17:8; 23:4, 9, 26; 36:43; 47:11; 48:4; 49:30; 50:13; *'ereṣ měgurîm*, "land of sojourning" (17:8; 28:4; 36:7; 37:1; 47:9); *zarʿăkā 'aḥărēkā*, "your descendants after you" (17:7–10, 19; 35:12; 48:4); *běnē-ḥēt* rather than *ḥittîm*, "Hittites" (Chapter 23 *passim;* 25:10; 27:46 and cf. *běnôt ḥēt*, "Hittite women," 49:32); *bě'eṣem hayyôm hazzeh*, "on this very day" (17:23, 26 cf. 7:13; Ex 12:17, 41, 51, etc.). Carried over from Genesis 1–11 is the creation command to be fruitful and increase (28:3; 35:11; 47:27; 48:4); *běrît 'ôlām*, "perpetual covenant" (17:7, 13, 19), which El Shaddai (17:1; 28:3; 35:11; 48:3) remembers (19:29; cf. 8:1; 9:15–16; Ex 2:24; 6:5; Lev 26:42–45). On the Priestly "execution formula" ("X did according to all that God commanded him"), see Blenkinsopp, "The Structure of P," *CBQ* 38 (1976) 275–92.

18. G. von Rad, *Die Priesterschrift im Hexateuch* (Stuttgart, 1934), 33–34, argued for a distinct *toledot*-book incorporated into the P work.

19. J. A. Emerton, "The Priestly Writer in Genesis," *JTS* 39 (1988) 381–400.

20. Gen 11:28–30 is often assigned to J (e.g., by Westermann, 1985, 134, 136), but there is nothing specifically "Yahwistic" about these verses, and "Ur of the Chaldees" occurs in v 31, which is certainly from P.

21. J. Van Seters, *Abraham in History and Tradition,* 249–78; H. H. Schmid, *Der Sogenannte Jahwist,* 35–36; R. Rendtorff, "Gen 15 im Rahmen der theologischen Bearbeitung der Vätergeschichten," in R. Albertz *et al.* (ed.), *Werden und Wirken des Alten Testaments: Festschrift für Claus Westermann zum 70. Geburtstag* (Göttingen, 1980), 74–81; "Covenant as a Structuring Concept in Genesis and Exodus," *JBL* 108(1989) 391–92; J. A. Emerton, "The Origin of the Promises to the Patriarchs in the Older Sources of the Book of Genesis," *VT* 32 (1982) 17; M. Anbar, "Genesis 15: A Conflation of Two Deuteronomic Narratives," *JBL* 101 (1982) 39–55; John Ha, *Genesis 15: A Theological Compendium of Pentateuchal History* (Berlin, 1989).

22. The continuation of this formula—*lātet lěkā hā'āreṣ hazzo't lěrištāh,* "to give you this land to possess"—is clearly Deuteronomic. The verb *yrš* in connec-

tion with the land occurs some sixty times in Deuteronomy and the phrase *lĕrištāh* twenty-five times.

23. Extensive bibliographies in T. L. Thompson, *The History of the Patriarchal Narratives,* 336–78 and J. H. Hayes and J. Maxwell Miller (eds.), *Israelite and Judaean History* (Philadelphia, 1977), 70–148.

CHAPTER 5

FROM EGYPT TO CANAAN

EXODUS, LEVITICUS, NUMBERS

The opening paragraph of Exodus (1:1–7) recapitulates the longer list of the extended family of Jacob in Gen 46:8–27. It also signals a new chapter in the history, and therefore justifies a new book, by noting that the entire generation of which we were reading in the latter part of Genesis has passed away (1:6). No doubt it is this clear distinction between generations that explains why the division into books occurs at this point rather than with the list of family members in Genesis 46. If, however, we look ahead, we see no such clear demarcation separating Exodus from Leviticus nor Leviticus from Numbers. Leviticus contains cultic ordinances revealed to Moses at Sinai, beginning in the twenty-fourth chapter of Exodus (vv 15b–18a), and the divine pronouncements from the tent of meeting in the wilderness spill over from Leviticus into Numbers. We can therefore state more precisely a point made earlier, that the division of this long central section of the Pentateuch into three books was dictated neither by the logic of the narrative nor by purely practical considerations of scroll production, since it could easily have been accommodated on two scrolls. The division into three allowed the final editor to place Leviticus, easily the shortest of the five books, in the central position between Exodus and Numbers, of almost exactly equal length,[1] the entire section being then enclosed by the much more distinctive and self-contained first and fifth books. One of our aims will be to understand the exegetical significance of this structuring device.

Unlike Genesis 12–50, the narrative of these three central books does not break down into discrete sections with markers comparable to the *toledot* superscripts. In Genesis 12–50 the divisions correspond to the dominant roles of individuals, principally Abraham, Isaac, Jacob, and Joseph, but in these books the only comparable *dramatis personae* are Moses and Aaron. One way of construing the narrative would be to read it as a biography of Moses preceded by a long introduction consisting of Genesis and the first chapter of Exodus. It begins with his birth and his rescue from death as an infant (Ex 2:1–10) and, if we include Deuteronomy, ends with his death in Moab (Deuteronomy 34). In between these it recounts significant events in his life, including marriage (Ex 2:11–22), the commission to rescue his enslaved people (2:23–4:31), the carrying out of this task (5:1–15:21), and his leadership of that people for forty years, including the giving of a constitution designed to preserve Israel's identity after settlement in the land (Ex 15:22–Deut 33:29). It is not, of course, a biography comparable to modern or even ancient examples of the genre (e.g., those of Xenophon and Plutarch), but several studies have shown that we can learn much from reading the narrative biographically.[2] It is worth noting that in late antiquity Philo and, in a somewhat different way, Josephus *(Ant* 2:201–4:321) wrote lives of Moses, who also seems to have been the object of biographical interest for earlier Jewish writers whose works have survived only in fragments.[3] But having said all this, we cannot avoid the impression that the focus of interest is not so much on Moses himself as on the broad theme of the creation of a people with a special relationship to a God (YHWH) who nurtures it into viable existence, preserves it, and prepares it to play its preordained role among the nations of the world.

This last point will be confirmed by an examination of the narrative structure of the three books. The story begins not with Moses but with the suffering of a new generation under a new ruler in Egypt. It is thereby made clear from the outset that the role of Moses is subordinate to the destiny of the people. The story then unfolds in a fairly straightforward way with the mission to Pharaoh, the plagues, and the escape and deliverance at the sea (Ex 2:1–15:21). There follow the vicissitudes of the people in the wilderness, a jumble of episodes most of which are associated with stopovers in the rather bewildering itinerary from Goshen to Moab. At this point we come up against the structural anomaly referred to earlier: that in the context of the journey narrative a disproportionate amount of space is given to the Sinai episode, roughly one-fifth of the Pentateuch (Ex 19:1–Num 10:28). It is now time to examine this feature more closely.

Scattered throughout Exodus and Numbers are topographical notices about the stages in Israel's uneven progress through the wilderness. The Israelites set out from Raamses in Egypt (Ex 12:37) and end in Moab, across the Jordan from Jericho (Num 22:1). The basic formula used gives the point of departure and the destination of each leg of the journey— "they set out from X and camped at Y"—but a considerable amount of narrative has clustered around several of the locations named. These stages or stations *(mas'îm)* are also set out in a separate list in Numbers 33 with only a minimum of narrative accretion. The introduction to this list, the precise dates attached (33:3, 38), and the emphasis on the station at which Aaron died (33:37–39; cf. 20:22–29), justify attribution to the Priestly writer who, however, has certainly used more ancient topographical source material. All but two of the stations in the section between Egypt and Sinai are mentioned elsewhere in the wilderness narrative in Exodus or Numbers and could therefore have been taken from that source. But those between Sinai and the Jordan are, for the most part, unattested elsewhere; hence the plausible suggestion of Martin Noth that they reproduce in inverse order a list of stations on the pilgrimage route from the land of Israel to Sinai.[4]

The most interesting feature of the chapter for our present purpose is that the wilderness of Sinai is listed without comment as the fifteenth of the forty-two stations of the itinerary. Nothing at all is said about the giving of the law and the all-important role of Moses, an omission which would seem to call for an explanation. The name Sinai occurs in one or two poems of uncertain date (Deut 33:2; Judg 5:5; Ps 68:9, 18), but not in connection with Moses and the giving of the law; apart from these occurrences it is not attested outside of the Pentateuch in any pre-exilic text. There are also recitals of the story from exodus to the occupation of the land, introduced quite incidentally,[5] in which Sinai is conspicuously absent. The most interesting of these is the reply of Jephthah to the Ammonite king justifying the Israelite occupation of Transjordanian territory:

Jephthah sent envoys once again to the king of the Ammonites with this message: Thus says Jephthah: Israel did not seize the land of Moab and the land of the Ammonites. For on their way up from Egypt Israel went through the wilderness in the direction of the Red Sea and arrived at Kadesh. Israel then sent envoys to the king of Edom with the message, Let us pass through your territory, but the king of Edom would not listen. They also despatched envoys to the king of Moab, but he was unwilling to consent. Israel therefore remained at Kadesh. Then they continued through the wilderness, skirting the territory of Edom and that of Moab, arriving to the east of Moabite territory. They set up camp on the other side of the Arnon without crossing the boundary of Moab, for the Arnon marks the Moabite boundary (Judg 11:14–18).

What is interesting here is not just the absence of even a passing reference to Sinai as a stage in the journey, but the distinct impression conveyed that Kadesh was the destination of the Israelite trek from the beginning and the staging area for the occupation of Canaan. It remains for us to see whether this is consonant with the wilderness narrative in Exodus and Numbers.

Kadesh or Kadesh-barnea is a large oasis in the Northern Sinai, about fifty miles southwest of Beersheba. The narrative tradition locates it in both the wilderness of Paran (Num 13:26) and the wilderness of Zin (Num 20:1; 27:14), and with it are closely associated the names Massah and Meribah. Several of the incidents in the wilderness narrative are located in the region of this oasis during what must have been a lengthy stay ("So you remained at Kadesh many days," Deut 1:46). These include the provision of water from the rock (Ex 17:1–7; Num 20:2–21) and the successful campaign against the Amalekites (Ex 17:8–16). The visit of the Midianite priest, father-in-law to Moses, follows immediately; and though the place of the encounter is not given, it too appears to belong to the same local tradition complex (Exodus 18). This important narrative tradition locates the Israelite encampment at "the mountain of Elohim" (Ex 18:5), often dismissed as a gloss incorrectly identifying this site with Horeb. But a Mount Paran (perhaps Jebel Fārān, west of the Gulf of Aqaba/Elath) occurs in poetic compositions as a place of theophany (Deut 33:2; Hab 3:3), and this could well represent an alternative tradition to Horeb. The reconnaissance of the land also originates at the Kadesh oasis (Num 12:16–14:45), and it is clearly stated elsewhere that Kadesh was the staging area for the conquest (Num 32:8; Deut 9:23; 14:6–7). The last event recorded as taking place there is the death of Miriam, sister of Moses (Num 20:1).

It appears, then, that Kadesh represents a distinct phase intermediate between Egypt and Canaan. There are also indications of judicial and legal activity there, suggesting an obscure but important early stage in the development of Israel's legal traditions (in which respect it is interesting that the former name of Kadesh was En-mishpat, Judgment Spring, Num 14:7). The blessing on Levi in Deut 33:8–11 associates the priestly tasks of teaching and handing down legal decisions with Massah and Meribah, and of course Moses was himself a Levite. The encounter between Jethro and Moses (Exodus 18), which the tradition seems to locate in the Kadesh region, assumes that legal enactments *(mišpaṭîm,* vv 16, 20) have already been promulgated, and that all that is needed are proper judicial procedures and a program of instruction in the law. This apparent anticipation of the law-giving at Sinai has bothered exegetes since at least the Middle Ages. Sacrifices are also offered, and there is a sacrificial meal in which Moses (unnamed but certainly present), Aaron, and the Israelite elders participate, and this too seems to anticipate the sealing of the covenant in Exodus 24 (vv 1–2, 9–11). There is no certain answer to this complex of problems, which has given rise to a great deal of speculation,[6] but a plausible explanation is that Exodus 18 has transmitted an alternative version of the origins of the legal tradition, perhaps connected with a Midianite-Israelite covenant at Kadesh, one which in the course of time was displaced and marginalized by the dominant Sinai tradition.

Other clues to this alternative tradition have been pursued at one time or another by exegetes of the wilderness narratives. The little story about the healing of the bitter water at Marah (Ex 15:23–26) speaks of the promulgation of a statute and ordinance *(ḥoq ûmišpāṭ).* It also has YHWH "testing" the people, with the verb *nissāh* elsewhere associated with Massah at Kadesh (Ex 17:2; Num 14:22; Deut 6:16; 33:8). Putting all this together, it seems reasonable to suggest that the Sinai law and covenant tradition has been superimposed on a more ancient Kadesh tradition, and that this superimposition corresponds at the literary level to the insertion of the massive Sinai pericope (Ex 19:1–Num 10:28) into the wilderness narrative. The hypothesis is strengthened by the fact that the departure of the Midianite priest to his own country, recorded immediately before the solemn introduction to the Sinai pericope (Ex 18:27), is repeated immediately after it (Num 10:29–32), illustrating a resumptive technique of frequent occurrence in the Hebrew Bible.

Allowing due weight to this important structural feature, I propose to deal with this central part of the Pentateuch in the following order: (1) Israel in Egypt (Ex 1:1–15:21); (2) Israel in the wilderness, including its progress through the Transjordanian region (Ex 15:22–18:27 + Num 10:11–36:13); (3) Israel at Sinai (Ex 19:1–Num 10:10). The first two will occupy us for the remainder of this chapter, and the third, which takes up the complex issue of Israel's legal traditions, will be dealt with separately in Chapter 6.

ISRAEL IN EGYPT (Ex 1:1–15:21)

This first section tells a fairly straightforward story of rescue from a life-threatening situation and of conflict leading to the victory of the weak over the strong, the oppressed over the oppressor. Beginning with small

victories—the unnamed Pharaoh outwitted by the Hebrew midwives
(1:15–21), a brutal Egyptian foreman assassinated by Moses (2:11–15)—it
moves to the contest in magic between Moses and Aaron on the one hand
and the Egyptian sorcerers on the other (7:8–13), and eventually to a
protracted trial of strength with a stubborn Pharaoh culminating in the
death of the Egyptian firstborn, emigration en masse, and the crowning
victory at the sea. Recounting a rescue operation by divine intervention,
the story is held together by the theme of the endangered firstborn. The
genocidal campaign launched against the Hebrew slaves at the beginning
culminates in a direct threat to their male children, and therefore also to
their firstborn (1:15–22). Right from the start, therefore, we have a
prefiguring of the threat to Israel as the firstborn of YHWH (4:22–23).
After Moses is saved from death by the timely circumcision of his own
firstborn by Zipporah (4:24–26), the protracted refusal of the Pharaoh to
release Israel from slavery, in spite of a series of crushing disasters, leads
to the death of his own firstborn and those of his subjects. This application
of the *lex talionis* is first threatened (4:23), then announced (11:4–9; 12:12–
13), then effected (12:29–32). Escape from death is then turned into victory which is celebrated by hymns of praise as this part of the story reaches
its conclusion (15:1–21).

One structural feature of this narrative calling for comment is the inordinate length of the description of the ten plagues (7:14–10:29; 12:29–32).
The events leading up to this series of disasters is narrated vividly but with
all due economy: the group is identified, the situation under a new political
regime is described, the leadership is introduced, a first mission ends up
making things worse, then a renewed attempt (originally a different version of one and the same mission) leads to the inflicting of disasters on the
Egyptians. The climactic disaster, the death of the firstborn, achieves dramatic effect by the interposing of the Passover ritual between the announcement and the event itself. From one point of view, the plague series
could be seen as a development from the signs worked with the magical
wand, the original purpose of which was to persuade the doubting
Hebrews of the legitimacy of Moses' mission (4:1–9). The first of these, the
transformation of the wand into a snake, is repeated before Pharaoh (7:8–
13), and the third and last, the changing of the Nile water into blood,
becomes the first of several ecological disasters in the series (7:14–24). But
it could also be argued that the logic of the narrative requires only the
death of the Egyptian firstborn, a culmination for which, as we have seen,
the narrator has prepared us from the outset. The nine preceding disasters
would then serve to heighten the dramatic impact of the final one by
postponement, in a manner somewhat similar to Abraham's brave but
futile attempt to reduce the odds against the doomed inhabitants of
Sodom (Gen 18:22–33).

For the creation of such a series abundant material was at hand in the form of curses attached to covenants or treaties (e.g., boils or ulcers in Deut 28:27, 35) and prophetic oracles of judgment. Amos 4:6–12, for example, lists a series of seven disasters—literally, "acts of God"—visited on unfaithful Israel: famine, drought, blight and mildew, locusts, an unspecified pestilence, military defeat, and earthquake. These too were designed to bring about a divinely willed effect; they were equally unsuccessful, and the last is clearly the climactic one in the series. The anti-Egyptian oracles in Ezekiel (Chapters 29–32) may also have some bearing on the plague narrative, especially in view of the acknowledged links between Ezekiel and the Priestly matter in the Pentateuch. In both Ezekiel and the P contribution to the plague narrative the "acts of God" are described as "judgments" (*mišpaṭîm*, Ezek 30:19; Ex 7:4), and are punctuated by the concluding declaration "they shall know that I am YHWH" (Ezek 29:9, 16, 21; 30:19, 26; 32:15). The first and ninth plague also echo the threat of blood and darkness throughout the land of Egypt in the Ezekiel oracles (Ezek 30:18; 32:6–8).

We should add that explanations of this string of disasters with reference to natural phenomena encountered from time to time in Egypt (e.g., red sediment washed down the Nile after heavy rainfall) or spectacular natural disasters (e.g., the volcanic eruption on the island of Thera/ Santorini) have been around for a long time and continue to be proposed.[7] One may admire their ingenuity, but they add little if anything to our understanding of the narrative. Attention to detail (e.g., the bloody water was not confined to the Nile) will show fairly clearly that plausibility was not a major concern.

As the text now stands, there are nine plagues leading up to the climax in the death of the firstborn:

1. Blood (7:14–24)
2. Frogs (7:25–8:11 [7:25–8:15])
3. Gnats (8:12–15 [8:16–19])
4. Flies (8:16–28 [8:20–32])
5. Murrain (9:1–7)
6. Boils (9:8–12)
7. Hail (9:13–35)
8. Locusts (10:1–20)
9. Darkness (10:21–29)

While there seems to be no clear rationale for the order, it does not require a very close reading to detect two contrasting ways in which the

episodes are presented. According to one—the J of the documentarians—
YHWH communicates directly to Moses, who himself manipulates the
wand, the effect of which is described in some detail. Pharaoh generally
relents and pleads, Moses intercedes, Pharaoh makes concessions which
prove to be unacceptable, we are told that the land of Goshen was not
affected by the disasters, and Pharaoh's heart is, literally translated,
"made heavy" (kābēd, 7:14; 8:11, 28 [8:15, 32]; 9:7, 34; 10:1). In the strand
identified as of Priestly origin, on the contrary, YHWH communicates to
Aaron through Moses, Aaron manipulates the wand in 1, 2, and 3, Moses
acts alone in 7, 8, and 9, and both act together in 6. In the first three
involving Aaron, he is in competition with the Egyptian sorcerers, and in
general the universal incidence of the disasters is stressed. For the hardening of Pharaoh's heart, clearly a basic leitmotif, the verb ḥzq, indicating
"strength and obduracy," is employed (7:22; 8:15 [8:19]; 9:12, 35; 10:20,
27).

It is also worth noting that two of the plagues (2 and 6) are recognized
to be exclusively Priestly, while two others (4 and 5) betray no trace at all
of the Priestly style. This points to two parallel series of seven, the same
number as attested in Psalm 105 and perhaps also Psalm 78, which series
were combined in such a way as to give a total of ten including the death
of the firstborn. There was probably no esoteric reason for these arrangements; sevenfold series are numerous, and that ten was considered a practical and convenient number hardly needs emphasizing. Equally apparent
is the function of the series in the context of Exodus 1–15 as a whole. The
explicitly stated purpose is the demonstration of the universal lordship,
incomparability, and power of the God of the Hebrews (8:18 [8:22]; 9:14–
16, 29; 10:2). But as we read of the great cry that went up throughout
Egypt at the death of the firstborn (12:30), it is difficult to avoid asking
whether a demonstration of overwhelming divine power, specifically in the
application of the lex talionis, justified such a great burden of human suffering. Perhaps all we can report is the conviction, apparent throughout,
that God has a design for this people, and through them, for humanity;
and that the opposition to that design, then as often since, inevitably
brings suffering in its wake.

THE LITERARY CHARACTER AND FORMATION OF THE EXODUS STORY

Any interpretation of a biblical text, as of any text, is conditioned by
the assumptions, conscious and unconscious, of the reader. Obviously
there must be some criteria for discriminating between good and bad interpretations, but there is no such thing as an objective and definitive
interpretation of a text. After the interpreter's work is done, the text is still

there, to question past readings and invite future interpretations. Perhaps, therefore, the best advice one could give the interpreter is to be as clear as possible about presuppositions, aims, and methods. It was noted earlier that many today work with the assumption that the circumstances of the production and acceptance of a text are irrelevant to its contemporary meaning. Once produced, the text exists in its own right and is to be interpreted as a closed system exclusively within its own terms of reference. At the risk of appearing naive, however, one might ask whether any social and cultural product, and a text is certainly that, can be adequately understood apart from the social situation that generated it. The question also arises whether such a hermeneutic preserves the necessary distance between text and reader, the kind of distance and balance required for a successful conversation (the analogy is that of Hans-Georg Gadamer).

Whatever its faults and exaggerations and in spite of the aesthetic insensitivity of many of its practitioners, the historical-critical reading of texts at least acts as a constraint on the tendency for the text to be subjugated to the self-understanding and agenda of the interpreter. Alter, we noted, decried the "excavative techniques" employed by biblical scholars, but if understanding a text implies something more than aesthetic appreciation, excavation is really not such a bad metaphor. We recall a similar metaphor of Claude Lévi-Strauss (in *Tristes Tropiques*), suggested by his early fascination with geology. He makes the point that a landscape, however beautiful, presents itself as a chaotic phenomenon until one realizes that its different features are to be explained by what lies below the surface, and therefore by their previous history. Like the formation of a landscape, the formation of a text is part of its total, contemporary meaning.

Also to be considered is the fact that these texts have been and continue to be accorded a special status in what Stanley Fish has called "interpretative communities." In such communities, continuity with the past, in the form of a collective remembering, memorializing, and reactualizing, is a constitutive factor. It is therefore no exaggeration for Gerhard Ebeling to say that the history of the Church is in large measure the history of the interpretation of the Bible. For our present purpose what needs to be added is that this interpretative process—with respect to the exodus, for example—can not only be traced back into the biblical period but can also, in principle, be reconstructed in its earliest stages from the biblical text itself. This is what we will be trying to do in the remainder of this section of our study.

It is safe to say that no narrative in the Hebrew Bible has played such a central role in the Jewish and Christian interpretative communities, and in sub-groups within these communities, as the exodus story. Liturgical recital has had a great deal to do with this, though there is now little support for the view that the story itself originated as the festive legend for Passover (Johannes Pedersen 1934, 161–75). Its paradigmatic status is clearly expressed in the Passover seder:

bĕkol-dôr wādôr ḥayyāb ʾādām lir'ôt
ʾet-ʿaṣmô kĕʾillû hûʾ yāṣāʾ mimmisrāyim

In every generation one must look upon oneself as if one
had in one's own person come out of Egypt.

We can do no more than give one or two examples of what has been called the exodus pattern in the Bible (David Daube 1963). It forms the subtext for the historian's description of the crossing of the Jordan (Josh 3:13–17, 23). It comes through very clearly in the way the exilic Isaiah (Isaiah 40–55) looks forward to an exodus from Babylonian captivity and return to the land.[8] It is no accident that the (certainly very foreshortened) account of the return in Ezra 1–6 ends with the celebration of Passover, and we are meant to infer that Ezra himself and his caravan celebrated the same festival shortly after their departure from Mesopotamia (Ezra 8:31). It seems that the compiler of Chronicles-Ezra-Nehemiah omitted the narrative of the founding events at the beginning to introduce them typologically at the end, presenting the establishment of a new commonwealth as the outcome of a new exodus from captivity and occupation of the land. And, to take a final example, the same pattern persisted in early Christian communities, not least in the association of the redemptive death of Jesus with Passover.

What then can we learn from Exodus 1–15 about the earliest stages in this ongoing interpretative process? While there have been, and still are, numerous differences of opinion about individual sections and verses, most adherents of the documentary hypothesis agree that final copy resulted from the combination of a basic J source, a more fragmentary and incomplete E account, and a P expansion of the JE complex. Analysis of the narrative along these lines was laid out for English language readers by Samuel Rolles Driver in his commentary of 1911 and his *Introduction to the Literature of the Old Testament* (pp. 22–42) published two years later. (A convenient tabulation of Driver's results is available in the article of Moshe Greenberg in *EncJud* 6:1058). Much of this is also reproduced in more recent commentaries, though no one now assigns the Song at the Sea to E. Building on the results of our analysis of Genesis in the two preceding chapters, we will now go on to test the validity of the following propositions concerning the formation of Exodus 1–15. (1) The narrative comes in its final form from a post-exilic compiler who arranged the material at his disposal to form a coherent and compelling story. (2) As in Genesis, the Priestly source (P) provided the basic framework, either in the form of brief summaries or, less often, in more extensive narratives at particularly important junctures. (3) There are also indications of a Deuteronomic-Deuteronomistic redaction (= D) especially in the commissioning of Moses (3:1–6:1) and the injunctions about the feast of Unleavened Bread and offering of the firstfruits (13:3–16). (4) Both P and D are parts of more extensive literary works beginning in Genesis and continuing on beyond Exodus. (5) Both have selectively incorporated existing narrative traditions from different sources, which traditions seem to have little in common with the Genesis narrative. If we continue to refer to these as J and E, it will be principally to maintain some continuity in the scholarly *diadoche,* since the criterion of divine names is even less helpful here than in Genesis.

We shall now take a closer look at Exodus 1–15 with a view to testing these theses. No attempt will be made to offer a verse-by-verse exegesis, for which the reader is referred to the commentaries.[9]

The Oppression (1:1–22)

This introductory mise en scène corresponds to the first Masoretic *sĕtuma* section divided into three paragraphs, each of seven verses, with a concluding verse, an arrangement that happens to align with the P passages vv 1–7 and 13–14. The immigrant list (vv 1–5) is a greatly abbreviated version of Gen 46:8–27 (also P) with much the same title and conclusion. The total of seventy corresponds to the sum of the nations in Genesis 10 and also, probably not by coincidence, to the number of deities in the Canaanite pantheon, the "seventy sons of Athirat" of the Ugaritic Baal text (II vi 44–46). The connection is made in an interesting couplet in the Song of Moses (Deut 32:8–9):

> He fixed the bounds of the peoples
> According to the number of the sons of God.

Following the tradition in Deut 10:22 and these lists in Genesis and Exodus, MT has "sons of Israel," but LXX, apparently supported by a Qumran reading,[10] has preserved the original sense that one of the seventy members of the pantheon has been assigned to each of the nations as a tutelary deity. Israel is therefore the microcosm within the macrocosm of the Gentile world. Ex 1:6 ("Joseph died, and all his brethren, and all that generation") may have been added by the redactor (R) to make a clean break between epochs, and therefore between books, just as the deaths of Moses and of Joshua mark the end point of the two epochs following (Deut 34:10–12; Josh 1:1–2; Judg 2:10). We see here, and in the dying out of the first generation in the wilderness (Num 14:20–38 P), a covert allusion to the situation in the Babylonian diaspora preceding the return of a new generation to the homeland. But P goes on to tell us (Ex 1:7) that the dying out of the first generation was followed by a phenomenal demographic explosion in keeping with the creation command (Gen 1:28), repeated after the mass death in the deluge (Gen 9:1). This also may be seen to correspond to the demographic increase under Neo-Babylonian and Achemenid rule following on the enormous loss of life during and immediately after the conquest of Judah and Jerusalem.

P has also provided, in 1:13–14, a typical summary of the oppression in which the key phrase "with rigor" *(bĕpārek,* only here, in Lev 25:43, 46, 53 and Ezek 34:4) occurs near the beginning and end, forming an elegant inclusion.

The rest of the narrative records the accession of a new ruler, corresponding to the new Israelite generation, and his embarking on a series of increasingly drastic measures, the last of which leads directly into the account of the birth of the savior figure and his remarkable rescue from death shortly after birth. There are some puzzling features in this story. Why, for example, would the Pharaoh want to exterminate his work force, especially after expressing anxiety that they might walk off the job? Was he acting in the belief that increasing the workload would decrease the birth rate, perhaps by making them too tired to procreate? And assuming that, for reasons best known only to him, he decided to exterminate them, why kill off the males rather than the females? Would he have dealt directly with Hebrew midwives (only two for a population shortly to be estimated in the millions, Ex 12:37), and did he and his daughter have the services of an interpreter?

It has been common practice to explain at least some of these puzzling features as resulting from a conflation of sources, the first stage of the oppression (1:8–12) and the decision to drown the male infants (1:22) belonging to J, and the story about the midwives (1:15–21) to E.[11] Here as so often elsewhere, however, the linguistic criteria for source division are far from decisive. Elohim occurs in vv 15–21, but without the contrasting use of YHWH in the rest of the narrative; the J sections refer to the oppressor as Pharaoh (vv 11, 22), while E has "the king of Egypt" (vv 15, 17, 18) but also Pharaoh (v 19); the oppressed are "Hebrews" in E (vv 15, 16, 19) and "the people of Israel" in J (vv 9, 12), but J also refers to Hebrews (v 22 with LXX and the Samaritan Pentateuch). The compiler, therefore, doubtless drew on narrative traditions in either written or oral form, but they are not clearly identifiable as segments of continuous sources carried over from Genesis.

While it is obviously of interest to identify sources where it can be done with a reasonable degree of assurance, it is more important to grasp the kind of writing with which we have to deal. Thus we note that the Pharaoh's policy toward his prolific Hebrew subjects unfolds in three stages, each announced in direct speech and recording the success or failure of the plan. This threefold repetition, so common in traditional narrative, reaches a climax with a decree that prepares directly for the emergence, rescue from death, and mission of the savior figure. In the first stage (vv 8–12) the edict is so garbled that we may suspect the intention of exhibiting the stupidity of the would-be outwitter of the Hebrews. The second stage (vv 15–21) achieves the same effect by showing how the Pharaoh, inheritor of a long tradition of wisdom, is himself outwitted by two simple Hebrew women. (That there are only two is, of course, a requirement of the narrative genre.) The final stage (v 22), concentrated in a direct and brutal decree of the oppressor, forces the reader to turn the page, so to speak, and continue reading to discover the outcome. We note, finally, that proper names are used sparingly. The principal actor is not Seti or Ramses but simply Pharaoh, type of the oppressive ruler. Even the names of the midwives, Shiphrah ("Beauty") and Puah ("Splendor"), are typical rather than realistic, and are borne by no other Israelite women that we know of.[12]

Moses Is Introduced and Escapes Death Twice (2:1–22)

The story continues with the birth of the savior and his two escapes from death, first as an infant, then as a young man. The two episodes (vv 1–10, 11–22) are linked as stages in his growth *(wayyigdal,* 10, 11) and the second indicates the passage of a considerable amount of time by the vague temporal phrase "in those days" *(bayyāmîm hāhēm,* v 11). In the first episode we note again how the characters—Moses' parents and sister and Pharaoh's daughter—are unnamed; attention is concentrated on the name of the central protagonist and its meaning is revealed at the end. The second episode also ends with a name, that of Moses' son, but even here it refers not to the child but to Moses in this second stage of his career ("I was an alien in a foreign land," v 22). Here, too, there are puzzles for the modern reader. The introduction of a grown sister is surprising, to say the least, after we have been given to understand that Moses was the first child of this Levite marriage. Pharaoh's daughter may have happened to have been in the right place at the right time, and it is just possible that she was in the habit of bathing in the Nile, but could she adopt an abandoned child of a people condemned by her father to extermination? And did she know just enough Hebrew to give him an ostensibly Hebrew name?

   Source criticism will not help the reader solve any of these problems, and in fact, neither episode offers much scope for the source critic, especially in the absence of divine names. The second episode is generally assigned to J notwithstanding, surely because the priest of Midian bears the name Reuel rather than Jethro, the name assigned to him in passages attributed to E (Ex 3:1; 4:18; 18). The occurrence of different names for this important figure certainly suggests a conflation of different traditions (*pace* Albright 1963, 1–11, who emends to "Jethro, son of Reuel" in Ex 2:18 and argues for three different people), but it is not clear that this is much help in distinguishing between J and E, in the sense that any passage not belonging to the one must belong to the other. The first episode (vv 1–10) has in fact been assigned to both J (e.g., by Noth) and E (e.g., by Driver and Childs).

Here too, therefore, a more rewarding approach is through close attention to the literary character of the episodes. The reader who has been brought up on folk tales, or who is otherwise at home with traditional storytelling, will have no difficulty detecting the motifs or functions. One of the most familiar of these is the birth of the hero (or less commonly, the heroine) and the threat of death in infancy and rescue by some extraordinary combination of circumstances. One of the closest parallels to Ex 2:1–10 is the often-quoted legend of Sargon of Akkad (c. 2334–2279 B.C.), founder of the Assyrian empire (*ANET* p. 119):

Sargon, the mighty king, king of Agade am I.
My mother was a changeling [?], my father I knew not.
The brother(s) of my father loved the hills.
My city was Azupiranu, which is situated on the banks of the
    Euphrates.
My changeling mother conceived me, in secret she bore me.
She set me in a basket of rushes, with bitumen she sealed my lid.
She cast me into the river which rose not [over] me.

The river bore me up and carried me to Akki, the drawer of water.
Akki, the drawer of water, lifted me out as he dipped his ewer.
Akki, the drawer of water, [took me] as his son and reared me.
Akki, the drawer of water, appointed me as his gardener.
While I was a gardener, Ishtar granted me [her] love,
And for four and [.....] years I exercised kingship.

There are some obvious differences between the legends of Sargon and Moses, but they conform to the same basic pattern. Herodotus tells a similar story about the birth of Cyrus, the designs of the Median king Astyages on his life, the command to expose the infant, leaving him at the mercy of wild animals, and the child's adoption by the cowherd

Mitradates, whose wife substituted her own stillborn son for the infant (Her. 1:107–13). Other instances are tabulated in a well-known paper of Lord Raglan on "The Hero of Tradition" published in 1936 (repr. in Dundes, *The Study of Folklore* [Englewood Cliffs, 1965] p. 142–57). These parallels justify describing the Moses story as heroic saga (Coats 1983, 33–44; 1988 *passim*), but it is nevertheless important to distinguish between traditional narrative and the work of an author who consciously incorporates traditional themes and patterns.

Other noteworthy features are the stereotypical numbers, e.g., the three months during which the infant was hidden and the seven daughters of the Midianite priest. The second episode is also arranged in a triadic structure. The first excursion of Moses from the Egyptian court leads to the assassination of the overseer (vv 11–12), and the second, in which Moses attempts to mediate in a brawl, shows that the deed has been discovered (vv 13–15a), thus leading directly to the third and climactic exodus, anticipating the exodus of the entire people (vv 15b–22). The encounter at the well corresponds to a familiar scene, generally resulting in betrothal and marriage (cf. Gen 24:11–27; 29:1–12; see Alter 1981, 52–58). The well, however, also functions in a more general sense as a point intermediate topographically and symbolically between phases of existence. For Moses it is a place of destiny, since if he had not defended the women against the shepherds he would not have married Zipporah, and if he had not married Zipporah he would not have survived the mysterious onslaught on his way back to Egypt (4:24–26). This third excursion, finally, is dictated by the logic of the narrative since, for this author but not for P, YHWH cannot appear and cult cannot be offered to him in a land polluted by idolatry (cf. Ps 137:4).

Moses Receives His Call and Mission at the Burning Thornbush (2:23–4:17)

After a considerable lapse of time (years rather than months) during which another Pharaoh passed from the scene (2:23 cf. 1:8) and Moses' second child was born (4:20 cf. 2:22; 18:3–4), the moment of redemption was at hand (2:23–25). In the course of an extraordinary experience in the wilderness Moses was charged to tell Pharaoh to release his Hebrew slaves which, however, first required that he convince the slaves themselves that they should choose freedom. Moses' own reservations were finally overcome when he was promised the assistance of Aaron as spokesman (4:10–17).

The mysterious revelation at the burning thornbush is one of the exegetical pressure points of the Torah history and as such has been the object of an immense amount of interpretative activity. Biblical interpretation is the lifeblood of the Jewish and Christian communities, and we have seen that its earliest stages are embedded in the biblical texts themselves. Reflecting along these lines, Frank Kermode has made the point that the Torah has something in common with midrash understood as "narrative interpretation of a narrative, a way of finding in an existing narrative the potential of more narrative" *(The Genesis of Secrecy* [Cambridge, Mass., 1979], xi). It is this character of biblical narrative that justifies the long-standing and now widely maligned attempt to reconstruct something of the history which made the text what it is.

A case in point is the revelation of the Tetragrammaton, the divine name, in Ex 3:13–22. After receiving his commission, Moses requests the name of the deity who has revealed himself as the God of the Hebrews. To this question he receives not one but three answers with three distinct introductions: "God said to Moses" (v 14a), "he said" (v 14b), "God said once again to Moses" (v 15). However one translates the first of these, the mysterious *'ehyeh 'ăšer 'ehyeh,* it is not a name at all but a phrase which, echoing the assurance that "I will be with you" *('ehyeh 'immāk,* 3:12), is meant to convey something about presence and assistance in the uncertain events about to unfold. The second, *"'ehyeh* has sent me to you," seems to make of the first a kind of name, one which is used as a name even by Hosea ("you are not my people and I am not your *'ehyeh,"* 1:9), but not a name by which the deity can be addressed. Only in the third is the name YHWH given as a personal and proper name—"this is my name for ever; this is my title throughout all generations."

It therefore seems right to conclude that we have here successive stages in the interpretative process referred to a moment ago. A further stage is introduced by P with the simple announcement "I am YHWH" with which the P version of the commissioning begins and ends (6:2–8). In this as in other respects P is much more explicit and schematic, for the progressive revelation of divine names in P—first Elohim, then El Shaddai, finally YHWH—corresponds to successive dispensations in God's relationship with the world and with his people. We may then trace the process further through the Old Greek translator, the authors of the targums, the rabbis and fathers of the church, on down into the present. (For some aspects of that history, see Childs 1974, 80–87.)

These indications of cumulative interpretation at a point of great exegetical density provide a clue to the formation of the section as a whole. Following our procedure of starting from what is least controvertible, we note that P has a typical summary serving as a transition to the central event, the rescue operation led by Moses and Aaron (2:23–25). It is therefore not very important to decide whether this summary concludes the preceding narrative (as Childs 1974, 32) or introduces the one following.

As God remembered Noah at the time of the deluge (Gen 8:1), so now he remembers the covenant with the ancestors, and remembering is of course an assurance of intervention. The final phrase, *wayyēda' 'ĕlohîm*, literally "and God knew," should read with LXX *wayyiwwāda' 'ălēhem*, "he made himself known to them," thus anticipating the revelation of the name which is the focal point of the narrative (6:3). As noted earlier, this fits the situation of the diaspora communities which may well have thought themselves to be abandoned and forgotten by God.

In our discussion of Genesis 12–50 we saw reason to endorse the view, now gaining ground, that D also has made a contribution to the history of the ancestors. In Exodus the first signs of the characteristic thematic and style of D occur in this part of the narrative and will be increasingly in evidence as the story unfolds. While they do not add up to a coherent narrative, they are congruent with the kind of editorializing easily identified in various episodes in Dtr. It is also worth noting that the exodus story appears frequently in Deuteronomy and is familiar even to outsiders like Rahab (Josh 2:10), the Gibeonites (Josh 9:9), and the Philistines (1 Sam 4:8; 6:6). In Exodus, affinity with D is often found in passages described by most documentarians as later additions to J or E (e.g., Noth 1962, 41–46); and even Martin Buber, no conventional documentary critic, identified Ex 3:16–22 as a supplement in the late Deuteronomic style *(Moses. The Revelation and the Covenant* [New York, 1959], 39). Among the clearer examples of D themes and language are the description of the land "running with milk and honey" and the listing of its indigenous populations (3:8, 17), the ancestral promise of land (3:16–17), and the combination of believing and heeding God's voice or that of his representative (4:9; cf. Deut 9:23). Commentators have also noticed the structural and verbal parallels in the commissioning of Moses and the call of Jeremiah (Jer 1:1–19), a passage generally thought to be the first of many in the book composed or edited by a D writer.[13] Both expostulate, claiming an inability to speak in public, and both are reassured that God will be with them and will put his words in their mouth (cf. Deut 18:18). Since according to D, Moses was the protoprophet, the prophet *par excellence* (Deut 18:15–18), it is hardly surprising that his commissioning is presented after the manner of the great pre-exilic prophets of whom Jeremiah was the last.

Since the existence of early *continuous* sources was a basic axiom of the classical documentary theory, the first stage of analysis was the identification of J and E on the basis of certain criteria, especially the incidence of divine names. Whatever was left over was assigned to P or described more vaguely as a later addition. In this section the revelation in the thornbush (3:1–8), the command to take the message to the Israelites (3:16), the magical acts worked with the help of the wand (4:1–9, an attempt to give the story some Egyptian coloring), and the appointment of Aaron as spokesman (4:10–16) were generally assigned to J. E was thought to have expanded and touched up the J narrative (part or all of 3:1, 4, 6; 4:17), but the main E contribution was the commissioning of Moses and revelation of the divine name in 3:9–15. If these results can no longer be taken for granted, it will be in good part because the criteria were applied somewhat mechanically, disregarding other possible explanations. The most obvious example is the revelation of the Tetragrammaton (3:9–15) in which the narrator could hardly have referred to the deity otherwise than as Elohim. Also neglected was the evidence, discussed above, for a cumulative process of interpretation in this passage.

We should therefore be under no illusions about the chances of recovering the earliest stages in the long process which ended when the Pentateuch attained fixity, that is, when the interpretative process could no longer be incorporated in the text. What we can say is that the large-scale narrative works identified by the sigla D and P used a variety of sources, including at times parallel versions of the same episode, in somewhat the same way in which Dtr incorporated source material into the history, often with minimal editorial embellishment (e.g., the two versions of David sparing Saul's life, 1 Sam 23:14–24:22 and 26:1–25). What cannot be taken for granted at this stage is the confident identification of two distinct and parallel sources extending from Genesis to Numbers or even further, dated to the early period of the monarchy (10th–8th centuries B.C.).

The Failure of the First Mission (4:18–6:1)

As we approach the moment of Moses' return to Egypt, the reader needs to be aware of the passage of time, not always explicitly noted by the narrator. The time spent in Midian did not perhaps amount to forty years (as Acts 7:30), but enough time had passed for the situation of the Hebrew slaves to have reached such a critical point that Moses could wonder whether they were still alive. Different accounts of the return must have been in circulation. According to one version, Moses obtained permission to return from Jethro (4:18), while the other speaks of a direct divine command (4:19). We are also left in doubt as to whether he took his family with him (4:20) or left them with his father-in-law (18:1–4). So far only one son has been introduced (2:22), and the story of the dangerous encounter in the wilderness gives the impression that only one son is present (4:24–26); for the introduction of the second son, Eliezer, the reader must wait quite a while (18:4). This unevenness is no more than we might expect in narrative of this kind; it does not require a division of this first paragraph into J (vv 19–20a) and E (vv 18, 20b). The second address of YHWH to Moses focuses on the motif of the firstborn, as is clearly indicated by the way it is crafted (italics mine):

My firstborn son is Israel.
I say to you, let my son go that he may serve me.
If you do not let him go
I will kill *your firstborn son.*

The prefatory "thus says YHWH" and the form of the saying align it with prophetic oracles, and the presentation of Israel in Egypt as YHWH's son in Hosea (11:1) suggests that at this point, as in the call of Moses, the narrative bears the mark of pre-exilic prophecy.

The same motif is given a surprising turn in the following narrative describing an event at a caravanserai on the way (4:24–26). This all-too-succinct account bristles with difficulties: the respective roles of father and son, whose "feet" (i.e., genitals) were touched, the meaning of the key phrase "bridegroom of blood" *(ḥătan dāmîm),*and why YHWH would want to kill his envoy when the mission was just getting under way. It seems to have been drawn into the narrative by the allusion to the threat of death hanging over the firstborn of both Hebrews and Egyptians. YHWH claimed the firstborn as his own (Ex 13:1–2, 11–16), and the time-honored way to acknowledge his ownership was by the death of the firstborn (cf. Gen 22:1–19). If the blood of the circumcision served as a ritual substitution for transfer of ownership by death, it may also have been thought to have saved the life not just of the son but the father also— perhaps, as Wellhausen suggested, by a kind of proxy circumcision— touching the genitals with the child's foreskin. This, at any rate, is the approach taken in LXX and the targums. There is also the fact that in Hebrew father-in-law and son-in-law are called respectively "circumciser" and "circumcised," suggesting a pre-marital ritual carried out by the father-in-law to ward off danger attending this crucial rite of passage. This ritual Moses had neglected to perform, but was saved from the consequences by the timely intervention of Zipporah. For the wide-ranging discussion on circumcision as apotropaic ritual, Midianite folklore, and desert demons, the reader is referred to the commentaries.[14]

The encounter with Aaron at the mountain of God, not here identified with Horeb (as in 3:1), is reminiscent of the later meeting with Jethro, apparently at the same location (18:5). According to this tradition, which antedates what is said of Aaron in P, Aaron not only served as Moses' spokesman, as Hermes did for Zeus, but also performed the signs with which Moses had been charged (4:17). The positive outcome of their combined mission contrasts with the less favorable results reported by P (6:9). The ensuing encounter with Pharaoh seems to be modeled on the prophet-ruler confrontation occurring so frequently in Deuteronomy. Moses' complaint to YHWH after the failure of the mission (5:22–23) is also reminiscent of the "confessions" of Jeremiah. The report ends with a prediction of the plagues, the account of which follows the alternative P version of the mission which, in the narrative context, actually constitutes a second mission.

The Second Mission (6:2–7:7)

After the failure of the first mission, Moses embarks on a second attempt to free his people, this time with the assistance of Aaron. It is abundantly clear that this entire passage was originally the alternative P version of the mission just recorded. We recognize as characteristic of P the declarative formula "I am YHWH" at the beginning and end of divine speech, the referring back to the title El Shaddai, the remembering of the covenant, "the land of sojournings" (*'ereṣ měgurîm*), "you shall know that I am YHWH," and similar linguistic features. P is usually content with summaries and genealogies, but at certain crucial junctures provides a full-scale narrative in which divine speech is prominently featured. The genealogy may have been inserted by a later Priestly scholiast with a view to introducing the *dramatis personae* in an appropriate fashion and, at the same time, enhancing the status of the eponymous ancestor of the priesthood. We note, in fact, how the resumptive verses 6:28–30 connect with the expostulation of Moses immediately preceding the genealogy, and how the genealogy itself borrows from other P lists (Num 3:17–39; 26:5–14). It encodes different aspects of the history of priestly families, their reciprocal relations, and the struggle for ascendancy among them. Regrettably, however, the history of the Israelite priesthood remains very obscure indeed.[15]

The question arises why at the final redaction the two accounts of the mission (3:1–4:17; 6:2–7:7) were not simply conflated, in the same manner in which parallel versions of the deluge and the plagues have been combined. Since the intention was clearly to present two distinct missions, it would be interesting to note how the second differs from the first in its theological perspective and point of view. One obvious difference is the enhanced role of Aaron, eponym of the priesthood, who is also assigned a greater age than that of Moses and a superior position as firstborn of Amram. It is also worth noting that the revelation of the divine name takes place not in Midian but in Egypt (6:28), in agreement with the historical perspective of Ezekiel (Ezek 20:5), to whom the deity also appeared in the land of exile. Both of these features can be related to the situation of exile which called for a basic reassessment of many traditional assumptions. The further point that Israel will recognize the reality and power of their God when they see what happens to Pharaoh may also be read as a reflection on current political realities under Neo-Babylonian and Achemenid rule, in which respect comparison with Second Isaiah would be instructive. We shall see that the same kind of political commentary forms a kind of subtext to the plague narrative that follows.

The First Nine Plagues (7:8–11:10)

Little need be added to the remarks made earlier on this long passage forming a bridge between oppression and liberation. A close reading reveals the care with which the editor has arranged the material at his disposal to communicate a message. The passage leading up to the plague narrative (7:2–6) speaks of the signs to be performed, the hardening of Pharaoh's heart, and the departure of the Israelites from his land, all of which feature in the inclusion at the end (which, like certain passages noted earlier [Gen 1:27; 7:17b–20], is couched in an elevated style) a kind of recitative reminiscent of the rhymed couplets closing out scenes in Shakespeare's plays:

> ûmošeh wĕʾahăron ʿāśû ʾet-kol-hammopĕtîm
>   haʾēlleh lipnē parʿoh
> wayĕḥazzēq YHWH ʾet-lēb parʿoh
> wĕloʾ-šillaḥ ʾet-bĕnē-yiśrāʾēl mēʾarṣô

> Moses and Aaron performed all these wonders before Pharaoh;
> but YHWH hardened Pharaoh's heart,
> and he would not let the Israelites go out of his land.

The nine afflictions fall into a pattern of three triads with progressively destructive effect, and the connections between them are effected by structural and linguistic features that can be easily identified once the pattern is perceived. Thus the introductory formulas of the first, second, and third in each triad are of the same kind, and the effect on the Pharaoh is similarly described in the first and fourth, second and fifth, third and sixth.[16] We also saw that the compiler had before him two series, each with seven plagues. The P series (1, 2, 3, 6, 7, 8, 9 in the tabulation on p. 140) is organized in a 3 + 1 + 3 pattern with the plague of boils in the center, and each of the seven concludes in much the same way, though the formula is less clear in the last three:

> Pharaoh's heart was hardened, and he would not heed them,
> as YHWH had said.

The emphasis in P is as much on the demonstration of divine power as on punishment; there is no letting up on Pharaoh and no possibility of intercession. P also presents the plagues as a contest between intermediaries, specifically between Aaron, representing the Israelite priesthood, and the Egyptian sorcerers, who were also priests and who controlled access to the divine world, according to the Egyptian point of view. These Egyptian intermediaries are involved in the first three—blood, frogs, and gnats—but are forced to admit defeat in the third ("this is the finger of God," Ex 8:19). In the fourth and central plague—boils—they themselves are infected, rendered ritually unclean, and thus eliminated from the contest. Logically, therefore, they do not figure in the last three, which means that Aaron can now withdraw, leaving Moses to operate by himself. The defeat of the spiritual agencies of the kingdom paved the way for political collapse and the enfranchisement of the enslaved. As noted earlier, this message matches the aspirations of a people for whom, whatever accommodations might be suggested by the political realities of the moment, subjugation to a foreign power remained basically unacceptable.

Death of the Firstborn and Preparations for Departure (11:1–13:16)

The account of the final stage of the long sojourn in Egypt incorporates extensive ritual prescriptions. The Passover ritual (12:1–28) is preceded by the announcement of the tenth plague (11:1–8) which follows immediately afterward (12:29–36), and other ritual law has been spliced into the account of the departure (12:43–49; 13:1–16). Also folded into the story at this point is the theme of the "despoiling of the Egyptians," one which has disconcerted interpreters since antiquity.[17] The biblical author has felt obliged to explain this improbable development by attributing it to the high esteem in which the Egyptians held Moses and his people (11:3), which is, to say the least, surprising after all that happened. An explanation of a different order would relate this topos to the wealth of those *olim* who returned to the Judean homeland in the early Persian period. The connection is most clearly perceived in Ezra 1:6, referring to the bullion donated to the departing Judeans by their Babylonian neighbors, but the emphasis on wealth is apparent throughout the Ezra narrative (Ezra 1:4; 2:69; 7:15–16; 8:25–27, 33–34; cf. Zech 6:9–11). The economic disparity between these diaspora Jews and those who had never left the province would in the course of time create severe social problems (see especially Nehemiah 5).

The account of the Passover ritual, which serves to delay and thus strengthen the impact of the mass death of the Egyptian firstborn, has incorporated an older version with closer links to this climax of the plague narrative (12:21–27). It places greater emphasis on the sprinkling of blood as an apotropaic rite, adds the prohibition of leaving the house during the celebration, and assigns the role of destructive agent to the Exterminator *(mašḥît)* rather than to YHWH himself. Both versions connect the Pass-over ritual *(pesaḥ)* with the event by means of the verbal form *pāsaḥ,* referring to YHWH passing over or skipping the houses marked with the blood (12:13, 23, 27). In point of fact, the verb means "to limp" or (in Piel) "to engage in a kind of limping dance" (1 Kings 18:26), which has led to speculation that at one time the spring festival of Passover involved such a ritual dance, also attested in other cultures. But the origins of Passover are, as the saying goes, lost in the mists of time and need concern us no further here.[18]

The beginning of the P version of the ritual (12:1–2) implies that this is the first stage in the formation of the liturgical calendar the essential pre-conditions for which were established on the fourth day of creation (Gen 1:14–19). The only ritual enactment preceding this point in P is circumci-sion (Genesis 17), an essential requirement for participating in the festival (Ex 12:44, 48). Following the Babylonian calendar familiar to the depor-tees, the first month is Nisan (previously Abib, Ex 23:15; 34:18; Deut 16:1), permitting a combination of Passover with the originally quite distinct spring Festival of Unleavened Bread *(maṣṣôt)*. Detailed prescriptions cover the timing of the successive phases from the tenth to the twenty-first day of the month, the ritual status of the animal, how it is to be prepared (roasted, not boiled, as in Deut 16:7) and eaten, and, in a supplementary section, who may and may not participate. Further stipulations appear in Lev 23:4–8, Num 9:1–14 (the delayed Passover), Num 28:16–25 (offerings to be made) and, comprehensively, in the Mishnaic tractate *pesaḥim.*

It is interesting to note that those to whom the Passover ritual is ad-dressed are described as already forming an *'ēdāh,* a politico-religious entity organized according to ancestral houses, that is, extended kinship groupings named for a real or fictive ancestor. This *bēt-'ābôt* unit (liter-ally, "fathers' house") was a form of social organization characteristic of the post-exilic rather than the pre-exilic period, and one which it would therefore be reasonable to surmise took shape in the Babylonian dias-pora.[19] This assembly or commonwealth included both the native-born *('ezraḥ)* and the resident alien *(gēr),* defined the conditions for member-ship in it, and exercised the right of exclusion or excommunication—wit-ness the formula in Ex 12:15, 19 and frequently in P, and the similar formula in Ezra 10:8. Like the annual reception of the sacrament in the Anglican Church following the act of 1673, participation in the Passover festival seems to have become the test case of membership in the *'ēdāh* (e.g., Ezra 6:19–22). The reason, no doubt, is that what constitutes the community at the deepest level is not its organizational apparatus but *anamnesis,* a collective remembering of events which grounds the exis-tence of the group and confers on it its distinctive character. In Ex 12:14 the designation *zikkārôn* ("memorial") is used of Passover, but the sense is probably that God will remember Israel rather than that Israel must remember God's deeds on its behalf. It is probably this meaning which the term *anamnesis* bears in early Christian accounts of the Lord's Supper (Lk 22:19; 1 Cor 11:24–25).

In typical fashion, the P account of the sojourn in Egypt concludes with the exact calculation of the time spent there—430 years to the day— though it is unclear whether the day in question is the last day of the festival, the twenty-first of the month, or, as in Num 33:3–4, the fifteenth day of the month, at which time the Egyptians were still engaged in burying their dead.

The additional instructions about the consecration of the firstborn (13:1–2, 11–16) and Unleavened Bread (13:3–10) were added for good measure and are clearly Deuteronomic in character (cf. Deut 15:19–16:8). The description of the land and its inhabitants, the ancestral promise of land, emphasis on family instruction (13:8, 14–15), and allusion to frontlet bands or phylacteries (13:9, 16 cf. Deut 6:8; 11:18) provide further confirmation. With this supplement the Egypt narrative is brought to a close and a new phase of the story can begin.

Departure from Egypt, Deliverance at the Sea (13:17–15:21)

The question now arises: Where does Egypt end and the wilderness begin? The itinerary in Numbers 33 states that the Israelites left Raamses the day after Passover, that is, on the fifteenth of Nisan, but entered the wilderness only after crossing the sea. Logically, therefore, the first four stages— Raamses to Succoth; Succoth to Etham, on the edge of the wilderness; from there in the reverse direction to Pi-hahiroth; and thence across the sea—would be intermediate between Egypt and the wilderness. By bringing the Egyptian phase to a solemn conclusion in Ex 12:40–42 (repeated in 12:50–51 after the supplementary legislation), P also distinguishes between the exodus and the crossing of the sea. The non-P material makes no such distinction between phases. It has the 600,000 adult male Israelites[20] journey from Raamses to Succoth (12:37–38), and from there take the wilderness route to the Reed Sea[21] rather than the more direct coastal route, arriving at Etham on the edge of the wilderness (13:17–20). It is nevertheless clear that the wilderness phase has already begun. Divine guidance by means of the pillar of cloud and fire is available (13:21–22), the people are grumbling (14:10–12), and there is no crossing of the Sea to mark a decisive divide between regions and corresponding phases (Coats 1967, 253– 65; Childs 1970, 406–18).

This reading of the narrative is confirmed by those liturgical hymns that speak of YHWH leading his people out of Egypt but either do not mention the Sea episode (Pss 78:32; 80:9; 105:37; 135:8–9), or allude to it as a distinct episode without reference to the exodus (Ps 106:7–12), or as an event subsequent to their being led by YHWH out of Egypt (Ps 136:10–15; Neh 9:9–11).

The prose account of Israel's deliverance at the Sea in Exodus 14 can be read as a complete and reasonably coherent story (Auffret 1983, 53–82; Ska 1986), but it is nevertheless clear that the narrator has combined two narrative strands presenting two distinct versions of how the deliverance came about. In the P version (most of vv 15–18, 21–23, 26–29) Moses is commanded to cleave the Sea so that the Israelites can pass through dry-shod; he does so, the water forms a wall on either side of them, the Egyptians follow, and the water returns and drowns them to the last man. In the alternative version the seawater is pushed away by a strong east wind, the Egyptian pursuit is bogged down in the mud, and in attempting to withdraw, the Egyptians are overtaken by the returning water. The Israelites do not cross over the water; as Moses predicted (14:14), all they have to do is stay put. It is not even clear that they witnessed the event, for the final paragraph (vv 30–31) may simply mean that they understood what had happened after seeing the Egyptian corpses washed up on the shoreline.

Yet another account of the incident is given in the "Song beside the Sea" (15:1–18), which is juxtaposed with the prose narration in much the same way as the prose and verse accounts of the battle beside the river Kishon (Judges 4–5). That this poetic composition was introduced as a grand finale to the Egyptian phase of the history is suggested by the inclusion and summary in 15:19, which repeat the original P conclusion in 14:26–29. This conclusion is also couched in the elevated recitative noted earlier (see the comment on 11:10):

> Pharaoh's horses with his chariotry and cavalry went into the sea
> YHWH brought back upon them the waters of the sea
> While Israel walked on dry land in the midst of the sea.

The following verses (15:20–21), of Deuteronomic flavor, may then be read as the extension of the alternative version, taking up from 14:31 or even from 14:25. This would imply that the "Song of Miriam" is not the title of the preceding poem (as Cross 1973, 123) but a snatch or refrain that is part of the story, rather like the singing of the women in celebration of David's prowess–also accompanied by percussion and dancing (1 Sam 18:7; 21:12 [21:11]).

The "Song beside the Sea," which takes off from Miriam's refrain, is not so much a victory song as a thanksgiving hymn, and is in no essential respect different from other examples of the genre in Psalms and elsewhere in the Hebrew Bible (e.g., that of Jonah while traveling in the whale). Its opening words—"let me sing to YHWH"—set the tone (cf. Pss 69 and 101), and its conclusion is reminiscent of the so-called enthronement psalms (cf. Pss 96 and 99). It uses much of the conventional language familiar from this type of liturgical composition: v 2b is, for example, identical with Ps 118:14, and such phrases as "the God who works wonders" and "who is like you among the gods?" are often attested (e.g., Pss 77:14–15; 89:7). The song, therefore, conforms to the practice, well attested in biblical and post-biblical literature, of rounding off a prose narrative with a hymn of praise or thanksgiving.

It is still frequently maintained that this composition is one of the most ancient poems in the Hebrew Bible, and it has even been claimed that it was written by an eyewitness of the event—most recently, to my knowledge, by C. R. Krahmalkov in *BAR* 7.5 (1981) 52. Albright dated it to the thirteenth century,[22] Cross and Freedman, more realistically, to the late twelfth or early eleventh century.[23] Arguments for such an early date rely heavily on tense usage in the poem and what many would consider a very rigid theory of prosodic typology which makes generous use of the Late Bronze Age epic poetry from Ugarit-Ras Shamra. It would be possible to speculate that the first half of the poem (vv 1–10) is based on an old victory chant, perhaps from a collection such as *The Book of the Wars of YHWH* (Num 21:14–18). But neither the juxtaposition of yaqtul and qatal forms ("imperfect" and "perfect"), nor such features as climactic parallelism, internal rhyme, and assonance, are peculiar to this composition. We have also seen that it reproduces much of the conventional terminology found in liturgical compositions which few if any would care to date earlier than the monarchy.

More significantly, the incident at the Sea, as described in the song, is part of a historical recital including the wilderness experience, the conquest of the Transjordanian kingdoms, entry into Canaan, and the eventual establishment of the sanctuary in Jerusalem. According to Albright, followed by Cross and Freedman, "the mountain of your inheritance" *(har naḥălātkā,* v 17a) also describes the residence of Baal in the Ugaritic poems, and so should be taken to refer to Sinai rather than to Jerusalem. Albright therefore concluded that "there is no longer the slightest valid reason for dating the Song of Miriam after the thirteenth century B.C." *(The Archaeology of Palestine,* 233). But Albright failed to note that the terminus of YHWH's loving guidance of his people (v 13a) is also described as "thy holy habitation" *(něveh qodšekā,* v 13b), a term elsewhere used of Zion (2 Sam 15:25; Isa 27:10), "the foundation for your dwelling" *(mākôn lěšibtěkā,* v 17a), a description of the temple in 1 Kings 8:13 (cf. Isa 4:5; Dan 8:11), and "the sanctuary which your hands have established" *(miqdāš konĕnû yādēkā,* v 17b), frequently used in apposition to Zion (e.g., Ps 48:9; 87:5). This last phrase would be particularly inappropriate if it referred to Sinai. It would seem, then, that the reign of Solomon is the earliest, but by no means the latest, possible date for the composition of the poem in its final form.

Since the poem makes generous use of mythological motifs involving the watery abyss *(tĕhomôt,* v 5) and the underworld *('eres,* v 11), in which respect it differs not at all from similar compositions (e.g., Pss 68:23; 69:3, 16; Jonah 2:4, 6), it is not easy to form a picture of the event as described by the poet. There can be no doubt that the pursuing Egyptians drowned (vv 1, 4, 9–10), and in describing how this came about the author invokes both a sudden violent wind (v 10) and the piling up of the waters to form a wall or dam (v 8), both of which figure in the prose account, as we have seen. The question of priority cannot easily be decided, a circumstance obliging us to be very cautious in using the poem as an independent source of information on what actually happened.

From the perspective of the historical and literary critic, the story in Ex 1:1–15:21 is a work of *bricolage* put together out of diverse materials including folk tale, heroic saga, etiology, prophetic commination, priestly lore, and psalmody. It has also incorporated and combined sources of which the most clearly discernible is the segment of the P narrative carried over from Genesis. We might be tempted to conclude that this is not the best way to put together a story, but this story has demonstrated its capacity age after age to generate new meanings and create new futures, to sustain community, to inspire and transform.

JOURNEY THROUGH THE WILDERNESS (EX 15:22–18:27; NUM 10:29–36:13)

While the account of what happened at Sinai in Ex 19:1–Num 10:28 is integral to the wilderness narrative and contains many of its themes—e.g., divine guidance and rebellion—both its length and the complex issues involved in its interpretation counsel separate treatment. The journey begins at Raamses in Egypt and ends in the plains of Moab, east of the Jordan, but in its final phase it includes an account of the conquest of territory in the Negev and Transjordan region together with measures preparatory to the conquest and occupation of Canaan (Num 20:14–36:13). Israelite tradition attests that it is this complex of events, transpiring outside of the land and before the foundation of the monarchy, rather than the historical experience of statehood, that was decisive for the identity and self-understanding of Israel. Our principal task, therefore, is to arrive at some understanding not so much of what actually happened as of the different ways in which the narrative embodies and reflects that self-image.

As a potent if ambivalent symbol, the wilderness evoked a powerful emotional response in antiquity, as it does today. Those who venture into it leave behind the security of settled existence and enter a physical and spiritual region of danger and liminality. It is "the great and terrible wilderness, with its fiery serpents and scorpions and thirsty ground where there is no water" (Deut 8:15), the abode of demons and spirits (Isa 34:13–14; Lk 11:24), a place that tests the body and tempts the soul. At the other end of the spectrum, however, it was for some of the prophets a time of innocence and intimacy with God, a kind of utopia that came to an end when Israel succumbed to the corrupting influences of the fertile land (e.g., Hos 2:16–17 [2:14–15]; 11:1–4; Jer 2:1–3). To find the courage to continue, and to escape the threat of death, Elijah journeyed back into the wilderness (1 Kings 19:4–18). The Rechabites, to whom we suspect these early "primitives" among the prophets were in some way related, kept alive the wilderness ideal by a radical rejection of the amenities of civilization. The same primitivist strand persisted into late antiquity with the first *ḥăsîdîm,* including the Qumran community and the Therapeutae, and in due course early Christian monasticism.

The vicissitudes of Israel in the wilderness also provided scope for allegorical and spiritual interpretation for exegetes both Jewish and Christian. This is a vast sea in which one could trawl with profit and pleasure, but the scope of the present work requires that we limit ourselves to the earliest stages of interpretation incorporated in the biblical texts themselves.

The Itinerary

The Pentateuch contains one complete and two fragmentary itineraries of Israel's trek from Egypt to the border of the promised land (Num 33:1–49; 21:10–20; Deut 10:6–9). To these we can add numerous topographical notices in the journey narrative in Exodus and Numbers. We have seen that the principal source (Numbers 33) is of Priestly origin. Suffice it to mention its interest in Aaron, the notice of whose death on Mount Hor is the only significant narrative development in the list (vv 38–39). In his careful study of the itineraries, G. I. Davies *(The Way of the Wilderness* [Cambridge, 1979], 59–60) states that the non-P topographical notices in the journey narrative have been taken from the itinerary in Numbers 33 and probably inserted by a Deuteronomistic redactor, and that therefore they have no independent value for reconstructing the direction of the journey. The issue cannot be settled beyond doubt, but it seems more likely that the itinerary in Numbers 33 is a late addition compiled on the basis of the narrative together with other material no longer extant. This would more readily explain the misplaced encampment by the Red Sea *(yam sûp)* in

Num 33:10, which appears to be based on a misunderstanding of Ex 15:27b, reporting the Israelites' encampment by the water after coming to Elim. On this reading, then, the itinerary—for which Mosaic authorship is claimed (Num 33:2)—would be the work of a later member of the priestly-scribal class.

Excluding the original point of departure in Egypt, forty stages are listed, perhaps corresponding to the forty years in the wilderness (Deut. 2:7; 8:2; etc.), though of course not on a one-to-one basis. Needless to say, the itinerary cannot serve as a Blue Guide for a tour of the Sinai and Aravah. While there has been no lack of more or less plausible guesswork on the location of the stations mentioned (see Cazelles 1955, 321–51; Davies 1979, 120–51), no more than three or four of them have been identified with a reasonable degree of probability. Problems also arise when we try to match the itinerary with the mainline wilderness narrative. Thus, Kadesh occurs only in the last part of the itinerary (Num 33:36) and is located in a different part of the wilderness (Zin rather than Paran). We would be inclined to suspect that whatever the value of the available sources, the compiler of the list himself did not have first-hand topographical information on the eastern edge of the Nile delta and the Sinai peninsula.

The shorter and more fragmentary lists in Num 21:10–20 and Deut 10:6–9 cover only the last phase of the journey, the passage through the Aravah and then east of the Dead Sea in the direction of Moab. Deuteronomy also is interested mainly in this final phase. It says nothing about the first stage from Egypt to Horeb, corresponding to the first eleven stages in the itinerary. It reports first an eleven-day journey from Horeb to Kadesh-barnea via Mount Seir (Deut 1:2, 19), then a protracted stay at Kadesh (1:46). The journey from Kadesh to Wadi Zered, the crossing of which marked the next decisive phase, occupied thirty-eight of the forty years (2:13–14), and was followed by transit through Edom into Moab, ending in the valley opposite Baal-peor (3:29). While the Numbers 33 itinerary has little in common with the D presentation, it seems to have drawn on the same source as the short list in Deut 10:6–9, since four of the five place names in the latter occur in the itinerary. This circumstance helps to explain why the itinerary concentrates on the last phase of the journey, namely, the passage northward through the Aravah in the direction of Moab.

At this juncture we return briefly to a point mentioned earlier, about Kadesh and the hypothesis of an early tradition of legal and judicial activity associated with this important stage en route to the land. It is at Kadesh that, according to P, Aaron died and Moses miraculously, if for some obscure reason reprehensibly, provided water (Num 20:1–13). The latter incident is also located at the Waters of Meribah (cf. Meribath-kadesh, Num 27:14 and Deut 32:51, both P), and the variant tradition in Ex 17:1–7 is also associated with Meribah as well as Rephidim. Since the narrative appears to be presented in roughly chronological order, we may also conclude that the victory over Amalek (Ex 17:1–7) and the visit of Jethro (Ex 18:1–27) are located in the same region. Finally, Kadesh was the point of departure for the reconnaissance mission and the staging area for the conquest (Num 20:14–21; Deut 1:19–46; Josh 14:6–7).

Kadesh, then, represented a distinct and important phase in the wilderness experience of Israel. As noted earlier, the hypothesis of an early stage of legal activity associated with this area rests on an obscure but nevertheless impressive convergence of indications: the judicial dispositions following on Jethro's visit, the prerogatives of the Levitical priests as described in the oracle on Levi in Deut 33:8–11, the names Massah and Meribah, and En Mishpat as the alternative name for Kadesh itself (Gen 14:7). If Wellhausen *(Prolegomena,* 343) was correct in assuming that the giving of a statute and ordinance at Marah (Ex 15:25) is a displaced Kadesh tradition, the case would be considerably strengthened.

Wellhausen went on to argue that the arrangement of the wilderness narrative supports the view that Sinai has displaced Kadesh and that on the literary level the vast and complex Sinai tradition has been inserted into an account of what happened at Kadesh, the insertion constituting what he called "a most melancholy, most incomprehensible revision" *(Prolegomena,* 342). Leaving aside Wellhausen's well-known prejudice against Israel's legal tradition, it is true that events narrated before arrival at Sinai in Exodus 19 are repeated after Israel moves on in Numbers 10: the manna and quails (Ex 16:1–36; Num 11:4–35), the miraculous provision of water from the rock (Ex 17:1–7; Num 20:2–13), and the administration of justice (Ex 18:13–27; Num 11:10–17, 24–30). More specifically, the account of Jethro's visit immediately before arrival at Sinai is completed immediately after departure (Num 10:29–32). These literary data have important implications for the formation of the legal traditions which will be taken up in the following chapter.

The Final Stages of the Itinerary (Num 13–21)

The mainline P narrative envisages a successive movement from one wilderness to another—from Sinai to Paran and from Paran to Zin—none of which, unfortunately, can be identified. There is, at any rate, a gradual movement in the direction of the border of Edom. P has created some confusion by locating Kadesh in the wilderness of Zin (Num 20:1) rather than in the wilderness of Paran (Num 13:26). The phrase "at Kadesh" in Num 13:26 has generally been attributed to J, but it more probably represents an editorial harmonizing with D, for whom the reconnaissance mission certainly sets out from Kadesh.

The main lines of the P account can fairly easily be disengaged from the elements of an alternative version which has supplemented P. This supplementary account betrays at several points affinity with D, and specifically with the account of the same events in Deut 1:19–46. It shows considerable interest in the Calebite clan which in the course of time amalgamated with Judah, gives prominence to Moses as prophetic intercessor (Num 14:13–19; cf. Ex 32:9–14, also in the D style), and emphasizes possession of the land as contingent on obedience to and trust in God (e.g., Num 14:11). P presents Israel as a well-organized cult community, an *ʿēdāh*, gives prominence to divine intervention in the form of the effulgence (*kābôd*) associated with the tent of meeting (*ʾohel môʿēd*), and highlights the role of Joshua. It also extends the reconnaissance to the entire land as far north as present-day Lebanon (13:21), and assigns the task to a group representative of the twelve tribes (13:1–16). If the widely held view that P was writing for the Babylonian diaspora communities is correct, we can appreciate how this narrative would be read as reflecting the fears and hopes of those contemplating return to Judah: conflicting reports about the unfavorable economic conditions obtaining there, the attitude of the native population, and so on. Prominent use of the duodecimal system, in both P and Ezra-Nehemiah (Ezra 2:2 cf. Neh 7:7; Ezra 6:17; 8:24, etc.), is also symptomatic of a strongly felt need for continuity with ancient Israel, an impulse expressed in much of the literature of the Second Temple period.

The reconnaissance is followed by a long section (Numbers 15–19) dealing with cultic matters and the prerogatives, perquisites, and responsibilities of the clergy. Commentators have long been exercised with the question why this material was placed precisely here. It is clearly intended as preparatory to the occupation of the land ("when you come into the land . . . ," 15:1, 8), but the main point seems to be that this is just about the last opportunity for introducing supplementary ritual legislation and stressing the prerogatives of the priesthood before the death of Aaron recorded at the next but one station on the route (20:22–29). There can be little doubt that these chapters constitute "one of the very latest sections of the Pentateuch" (Noth, *Numbers,* 1968, 114). Much of the legislation supplements laws in Leviticus, and thus represents the final stage in the evolution of midrash halakah before canonical closure. Sabbath observance provides an interesting example. The decalogic prohibition of any kind of work obviously called for further specification. It had long been understood, for example, that trading on Sabbath was forbidden (see Amos 8:5), but it appears that Nehemiah extended the prohibition to purchasing from Gentiles (Neh 13:15–22 cf. 10:32 [10:31]). The case of the woodgatherer could in like manner be understood as an extension of the prohibition of lighting a fire on sabbath (Num 15:32–36).[24] If they are to remain active, laws must be adapted to new situations and therefore the process continued beyond canonical closure with the Mishnaic treatise *Shabbat,* the Gemarah, and halakic decisions corresponding to conditions obtaining in the modern world.

Much of the material in this late section therefore reflects the situation of the Judean community during the early post-exilic period. From the writings which have survived from this period, especially Ezra-Nehemiah, we know something of the problems facing this community, the issues being debated, and the factional struggles that were going on. The ascendancy of the Aaronite priesthood and the demotion of other priestly families to subordinate status are also reflected in the suppression of Korah's revolt and the blossoming of Aaron's rod in the sanctuary (Numbers 16–17). The moral is clearly spelled out: no non-Aaronite need apply for admission to the priestly office (Num 17:5 [16:40]). The care with which the priestly perquisites in produce and specie are specified also confirms the impression of an increasing commercialization of the office, and reminds us that the sacrificial system was also a significant aspect of the economic life of the province. The regulation concerning the Levitical tithe (Num 18:21–24) recalls Nehemiah's concern for the economic maintenance of this ancillary clerical order on which he could count for support in his often acrimonious relations with the priesthood (Neh 13:10–14). The requirement that 10 percent of this tithe be passed on to the priests (Num 18:25–32) is an even later development first attested in the covenant stipulations in Nehemiah 10 (v 38 [39]), probably from a time subsequent to Nehemiah's tenure of office.

The ritual of the red heifer, an ancient practice incorporated into a ceremony of purification (19:1–10), and the procedures for dealing with corpse contamination (19:11–22) likewise illustrate the concern for ritual purity which became a defining characteristic of early post-exilic Judaism. In this entire section, therefore, we are observing the Judean community identifying itself with the Israel of the wilderness period and, in the process of doing so, forming its own polity and defining its own way of life.

According to the P author the deaths of Miriam, Aaron, and Moses take place successively at the three last stations of the journey: Kadesh, in the wilderness of Zin (20:1), Mount Hor (20:22), and the plains of Moab (22:1). The water miracle following the death of Miriam (20:2–13; cf. Ex 17:1–7) is told in such a way as to explain why Moses and Aaron did not lead their people into the promised land. While the D author understands Moses to have taken on himself the sin of the people, and therefore absolves him of any wrongdoing (Deut 1:37–38; 3:25–26), P explains his death outside the land as punishment for a failure of faith, in that he struck the rock rather than merely commanding it to yield water. But the inconsequential nature of the act suggests that the author is interested not so much in the circumstances leading to the deaths of the two men as in the important issue of succession to office and continuity of leadership. The investiture of Eleazar is therefore carefully described (20:22–29), forming a kind of diptych with the installation of Joshua as successor to Moses (27:12–23). Since according to the Priestly view the civic leadership cannot function legitimately without the hereditary priesthood, it was appropriate that the appointment of Eleazar should precede that of Joshua, and therefore that Aaron should die before Moses. In this respect also, therefore, the P narrative serves to legitimate the polity of the early postexilic cult community.

The same narrative has been filled out with other episodes connected more directly with the early phase of the conquest. One of these is the curious incident of the bronze snake icon set up by Moses (21:4–9). In the course of his religious reform Hezekiah destroyed a cult object in the form of a snake believed to have been made by Moses but probably associated with a Canaanite fertility cult. This object was known and venerated under the name Nehushtan (2 Kings 18:4). Num 21:4–9 seeks to explain that the setting up of the icon in the wilderness was intended not as part of a permanent cult but as an ad hoc measure designed to counter the bite of poisonous snakes that infested the terrain (cf. Deut 8:15; Isa 30:6). The connection was therefore not with fertility but with healing, an association well-attested in antiquity and still apparent in the caduceus, emblem of the medical profession. The incident also served to illustrate one more time the consequences of lack of faith and to provide a final example of Moses as mediator and intercessor.

In the Plains of Moab (Num 22–36)

After arrival at the final staging area for the occupation of Canaan (Num 22:1; cf. 33:49), no further movement forward is recorded. From this point to the end of the book, and in fact until the end of the Pentateuch, the Israelite base of operations is in the plains of Moab by the Jordan, opposite Jericho. The length and complexity of the account of this interval between wilderness journey and occupation are a measure of its importance in the context of the story as a whole. All we can do here is provide some pointers to the structure and arrangement of the section, in the hope of discovering clues to the formation of the Pentateuch as a whole.

The narrative between the last of the topographical notices in Num 22:1 and the recapitulation of the journey in Chapter 33 deals with the conquest of the Transjordanian region and measures preparatory to the occupation of Canaan. Negotiations with Edom have already been reported (20:14–21); the Israelite horde did not pass through Edomite territory (21:4), and its conquest, predicted by Balaam (24:18), lay in the future. The breakdown of negotiations with the Transjordanian Amorites, on the other hand, led to the conquest of the kingdoms of Sihon and Og (21:21–35; cf. Deut 2:26–3:11), an event much celebrated in liturgical hymns and prayers (Pss 135:10–12; 136:17–22; Neh 9:22). The main purpose of the Balaam pericope (22–24) is to record the defeat of the spiritual powers opposing the onward progress of the Israelites, and thus prepare for the eventual overthrow of the Moabite-Midianite confederacy (24:17; 31:1–54). The incident at Baal-peor (25:1–18) follows naturally, since the women are of the same nationality as the enemy in the Balaam pericope and the apostasy is attributed to Balaam's influence, leading to his death in the war against Midian (31:8, 16). This early phase of the conquest is then rounded off with the distribution of Transjordanian territory to Reuben, Gad, and the half-tribe of Manasseh (32:1–42) followed by the itinerary.

The stated purpose of the census (26:1–65) is to prepare for the allotment of land holdings (naḥălôt) after Canaan was conquered. The point is made that with the exception of Caleb and Joshua, this is a new generation replacing those who died in the wilderness. The sum total is not much below that of the Sinai census (26:51; cf. 1:46), and represents an enormous demographic expansion from the seventy who went down into Egypt. To the census has been added an appendix dealing with the case of Zelophehad of the tribe of Manasseh, who died in the wilderness without a male heir but was not among the 250 lay adherents of the rebellious Korahite Levites (27:1–11; cf. 26:33). The petition of his five daughters to inherit the property belonging to their father's bēt ʾābôt led to a decision handed down by the civic and religious leadership of the ʿēdāh. Couched in the form of apodictic law, this decision provided an occasion for regulating inheritance of property in the absence of a male heir. It was later found necessary to add a codicil to this ruling preventing the female heir from marrying outside of the tribal structure and thus alienating tribal property (36:1–12). This codicil appears to be a last-minute addendum tacked on after the book was essentially complete.[25] It is one of several legislative supplements in Numbers, including those concerning offerings and the status of vows made by women (28–30).

To the new generation replacing those who died in the wilderness corresponds new leadership. If, as will be argued later, the death of Moses was originally recorded in Num 27:12–23 (P), its postponement was dictated by the need to include the Deuteronomic law and complete some unfinished business in the final chapters of Numbers. If this is so, the instructions and lists in Numbers 28–36 must have been added at the final stage of the redaction of the Pentateuch.

WILDERNESS THEMES

Guidance, Providence, Presence

It would not be surprising if the historical experience of Israel, including the experience of exile, contributed to shaping the story of its founding events. The basic conviction expressed in the wilderness part of that story is that the successful negotiation of life-threatening perils was due to the constant if at times elusive presence of a merciful and demanding God. Wherever the wilderness is recalled a similar note is sounded: God led them (Deut 8:15; Amos 2:10; Ps 136:16), guided them (Hos 11:3), carried them in his arms (Deut 1:31; Hos 11:3), bore them aloft like an eagle (Ex 19:4; Deut 32:11–12), even dragged them along (Hos 11:4), with the result that in spite of themselves they reached their destination. In only one instance do we hear of a human guide. As he was about to depart from Sinai, Moses invited his father-in-law, the Midianite Hobab (elsewhere Reuel and Jethro), to accompany them; he at first declined, but Moses eventually prevailed on him to act as guide (Num 10:29–32). But then we hear no more of Hobab acting in that capacity, and the narrator goes on to speak of the ark and the cloud going ahead to establish their camping grounds (10:33–34). This may be an example of what Samuel Sandmel called "neutralizing by addition" *(JBL* 80 [1961] 120), the neutralizer in this case being a Deuteronomic editor. (The terms *'ărôn běrît-YHWH* and *měnûhāh* are of frequent occurrence in Deuteronomy and Dtr.)

The guidance theme is developed with the help of several topoi which coalesce into a rich theological mosaic. The column of cloud by day and of fire by night appeared as the Israelites prepared to enter the wilderness, and stayed with them throughout the journey. Exceptionally, the cloud moved behind them at the Reed Sea, serving as a kind of smokescreen during their encounter with the Egyptians (Ex 14:19b–20). This symbolic representation, generally attributed to J, may have been suggested by phenomena accompanying volcanic activity, though probably without assistance from the volcanic eruption on the island of Thera/Santorini.[26] It is closely related to the Sinai epiphany, and is intended to provide visible assurance of divine presence and assistance.

The cloud is also associated with the oracular tent in which Moses received communications concerning the governance of the people (Ex 33:7–11). Its presence signified divine authentication of decisions promulgated from the tent, e.g., concerning the subdelegation of authority to the seventy elders (Num 11:25) and the rejection of the claims of Miriam and Aaron (Num 12:5, 10). The P author incorporated this topos into his view of the journey as a cultic procession (Num 10:11–28). When the cloud covered the tent they stayed in camp; when it was taken up they moved on (Ex 40:34–38; Num 9:15–23). This kind of guidance was available only from Sinai, for the obvious reason that the wilderness sanctuary was constructed only then. The ideological intent was to stress the role of the priesthood as mediator of the divine will. Guidance for the life of the community is not to be left to the vagaries of individual inspiration but is to be sought in the temple and the spiritual resources dispensed by its personnel.

Closely associated with these epiphenomena in P is the *kābôd* ("effulgence"), a technical expression for the visible manifestation of the invisible God. In using this term, P was drawing on an old representation associated with the ark at Shiloh during the life-and-death struggle with the Philistines (1 Sam 3:3). Whatever the original function of the ark (the Hebrew term *'ărôn* means "chest" or "container"), it seems by this time to have come to represent an empty throne, and was carried into battle like the early Arabic *qubba* (1 Sam 4:3–11; cf. Num 10:33–36) and used occasionally for purposes of divination. After its capture by the Philistines, the daughter-in-law of the priest Eli gave her newly born son the name Ichabod, meaning probably "alas, the effulgence!", with the explanation that "the effulgence has departed from Israel for the ark of God is taken" (1 Sam 4:19–22). This idea of the exile of the *kābôd* and its eventual return from exile provided the priest-prophet Ezekiel with a way of speaking of divine presence and absence at the time of the deportations (Ezek 9:3; 10:4, 18–19; 11:22–23; 43:1–5). For the P narrator of the wilderness journey it was a way of solving the problem of combining divine transcendence with presence. Moses, therefore, was allowed to see not the face of God but the mysterious divine effulgence (Ex 33:18–23). It filled the mobile tent-sanctuary, and its presence could be either salvific (e.g., Ex 29:43) or ominous (e.g., Ex 16:7, 10–12; Numbers 16), depending on the situation. It expresses the conviction that there can be no guidance for the conduct of life apart from the divine presence in the sanctuary.

A quite different theologoumenon is the accompanying messenger or angel of God (Ex 14:19; 32:34; 33:2; Num 20:16). The older commentators took this to be the E counterpart of J's columns of cloud and fire, but there are better grounds for assigning it to D. The most extensive reference occurs, in fact, in the short homily, unmistakably Deuteronomic, attached to the so-called Covenant Code (Ex 23:20–33), with which we might compare the discourse of the *mal'ak YHWH,* who brought Israel out of Egypt (Judg 2:1–5). In Ex 23:20–33 the angel will guard Israel on the way and bring them to their destination; he must be obeyed; he will not pardon those who rebel against him; the divine name is in him. The *mal'ak* is therefore no human agent but a manifestation or hypostasis of the deity. It is closely related to the divine presence *(pānîm,* literally "face") that accompanies Israel on the journey (Ex 33:14; Deut 4:37; cf. *mal'ak pānāw,* "the angel of his presence," in Isa 63:9). In brief, what we are witnessing in these affirmations about the *kābôd,* the *mal'ak,* and the *pānîm* is the transformation of old mythic representations—the appearance of the deity in the storm cloud, visitation by divine emissaries—into theological symbols of divine presence and assistance.

Deuteronomy and liturgical compositions of Deuteronomic inspiration constantly remind the reader of the providential supplying of daily necessities to Israel on its journey through the "great and terrible wilderness" (Deut 2:7; 8:3–4, 15–16; Pss 78:15–16; 106:15; Neh 9:15). Of these necessities the most basic is water, as the Israelites discovered three days into the wilderness. At this point the P travelogue has been filled out with an old story about the healing of brackish water by Moses at a place appropriately called Marah (Ex 15:22b–25a), a story reminiscent of the prophetic legend of the purifying of water at Jericho by Elisha (2 Kings 2:19–22). It is widely agreed that the Marah story has been expanded by a kind of miniature homily in the D style referring to the giving of a statute and ordinance and to divine testing (vv 25b–26; see Noth 1962 [1959], 127–29; Coats 1968, 47–53). But it is also possible that it was the D author who introduced the story in the first place, in much the same way in which short narratives of a similar kind are presented in Dtr. In the account of the water miracle at Massah and Meribah, it is the people who test God—as frequently in Deuteronomy—by doubting his ability to provide for them (Ex 7:1–7). This is one of the incidents repeated in a revised and expanded form after the Sinai pericope (Num 20:2–13). In this case P has reworked the story to explain why Moses was not permitted to lead his people into the land (cf. Num 27:12–23; Deut 32:48–52).

The providential supplying of food is also narrated both before and after Sinai (Ex 16:1–36; Num 11:4–34). In spite of some unevenness noted by the commentators (Noth 129–37; Childs 271–304; Coats 1968, 83–96), Ex 16:1–36 is a fairly straightforward story told in the P manner. An old tradition probably circulated about people surviving in the Sinai by eating manna, a flaky, sticky substance deposited mysteriously each morning on the ground.[27] The narrator makes the point that just enough was given for each day; there was no surplus and no shortage, and it went bad if stored overnight. This, therefore, was Israel's "daily bread" in the strict sense of the term. The message, taken up in the Sermon on the Mount (Mt 6:11, 25–34), is about abandoning a false sense of security. P also uses the story to anticipate the sabbath command (Ex 20:8–11; 23:12). Though the observance of sabbath is encoded in the P creation account, as we have seen, the word itself occurs here for the first time. In the post-Sinai version (Num 11:4–34) dissatisfaction with the thin fare of manna is countered, not without irony, by a surfeit of quail resulting in a deadly epidemic; hence the name Kibroth-hattaavah, "Graves of Craving." In another narrative (Num 21:4–9) the outcome, death by poisonous snakebite, was no better. Disconcertingly, this disaster was mitigated by erecting a bronze snake icon on a pole.

Complaints about food and drink are symptomatic of a hankering for security, even the security of slavery, and a disinclination to accept the risky consequences of freedom. Some commentators (e.g., Fritz 1970) have speculated that an older narrative theme about divine providence in the wilderness has been reworked with a view to presenting the wilderness as the place and period of disobedience and apostasy–a plausible if unprovable hypothesis. As the narrative now stands, the themes of divine providence and human failure are combined in a sequence covering the entire itinerary from the Reed Sea onward. To the extent that we can detect a development here, the complaints in the later strands are more clearly formulated in legal terms. We also note how the assessment of Israel's response to the divine initiative becomes increasingly negative. The complaining escalates into open rebellion and apostasy, especially in the P narrative sections. At this point we are close to the decidedly negative evaluation of the wilderness period in Ezekiel's diatribe (see especially Chapter 20). Where precisely Ezekiel stands in relation to the P authorial-editorial school is a matter of dispute, but it is noteworthy that all of his indictments of Israel in his survey of the wilderness period, with the exception of the enigmatic "statutes that were not good and ordinances by which they could not have life" (20:25),[28] correspond to episodes in Exodus and Numbers.

Authority and Institution

According to the P narrative in Exodus and Numbers, the Israel of the wilderness is routinely described as an *ʿēdāh* or a *qāhāl,* in other words, as a distinct polity or commonwealth. The basis of its organization is the twelve-tribal system that has retained something of its military substructure (division into 1000s, 100s, 50s, and 10s; see Num 31:4–5; cf. Deut 1:15). The individual tribes are divided into ancestral houses *(bātē ʾābôt,* e.g., Num 26:1–2, the *bēt ʾābôt* being a unit distinct from the *bēt ʾab* and characteristic of the Second Temple period, as we have seen). Leadership of the tribe and tribal phratry is entrusted to the *nāśîʾ* ("chieftain"), and the *zāqēn* ("elder") also has an important leadership role. The membership includes both the *ʾezraḥ* ("native-born") and the *gēr* ("resident alien"), the latter enjoying, theoretically at least, equal legal status (Ex 12:49; Num 9:14, etc.). Participation in the cult served as the basic criterion for membership (e.g., Ex 12:43–49; cf. Ezra 6:21), and the *ʿēdāh* also exercised the right to exclude or excommunicate for a variety of offenses (e.g., Ex 12:15, 19; Num 19:13, 20; cf. Ezra 10:8).

It seems clear that this organizational apparatus corresponds to the situation obtaining in the province of Judah after the return, and perhaps also, in some respects at least, to the situation of those Jews in the Mesopotamian diaspora who, as we know, were permitted to maintain their own identity and organization as one of several ethnic minorities settled in the alluvial plain. The decisions which Moses and the *ʿēdāh* were called upon to make all point in the same direction. Land tenure (Num 26:52–56; 34:1–29), exogamous marriage (Num 25:1–15), alienation of tribal land (Num 27:1–11; 36:1–2), and the prerogatives and perquisites of the clergy (Num 15:1–31; 18:1–32; 28–29; 35:1–8) were all major issues in the Judean temple community during the first two centuries of its existence.

During the wilderness sojourn the ultimate authority, as communicator and interpreter of the divine will, was of course Moses. In the most general sense the authority of Moses stands for the authority of the revealed law, but law requires interpretation, and interpretation derives from specific individuals and groups with their own agendas and interests. The identity of the originating party is easily perceived in the many instances in which Aaron functions in tandem with Moses. But there are civic as well as religious authorities—the king and court during the existence of the Judean state, the governor and ruling families after the return from exile. There is therefore some point to the contention of J. R. Porter *(Moses and the Monarchy. A Study in the Biblical Tradition* [Oxford, 1963]) that Moses functioned as a paradigm for the monarchy, at least in the sense that, in the absence of a native dynasty, other institutions had to take over monarchic functions, including the promulgation of law.

The basis for a claim to exercise authority often emerges more clearly when that authority is challenged. Moses confronts challenges to his leadership with the counterclaim that to challenge him is to oppose God (Ex 16:8; 17:2). The accusation directed against him by Miriam and Aaron—not here represented as his siblings—that he had limited access to revelation to himself (Num 12:1–16) raises the fundamental issue of control of the redemptive media, and therefore of the religious legitimation of political power. The resolution of this dispute, delivered in an oracle from the Tent of Meeting (12:6–8), distinguishes between prophetic modes of revelation (visions, dreams, riddles) and the "face-to-face" (literally, "mouth-to-mouth") kind unique to Moses. The intent appears to be to limit the claims of institutionally unattached prophets to play an important role in the political process, and the implication is that at some undetermined point in time the leadership felt itself threatened by the contemporary phenomenon of prophecy. Coming as it does immediately after the prophesying of the seventy elders (Num 11:14–17, 24b–30), it may also be another example of "neutralizing by addition" (cf. Noth, *Numbers,* 93, who reads it as an expansion and correction of the preceding pericope).

In Num 16:1–17:15 [16:1–50] the editor has more or less skillfully conflated two episodes involving defiance of the leadership: an older tradition (cf. Deut 11:6) about two Reubenites, Dathan and Abiram, who reject his authority, perhaps by refusing to take part in the conquest; and opposition by a lay faction of 250 prominent members of the assembly in alliance with Korahite Levites. (For a more detailed reconstruction of the literary history of the passage, see Budd 1984, 181–91). In both the lay and Levitical protests the basic issue is that of hierarchy and authority in the assembly according to preestablished degrees of holiness, the kind of system schematically set out in Ezekiel 40–48. If the episode is read in the light of what we know of the temple community in the Persian period (6th–4th centuries B.C.), the protest of the 250 leading figures in the assembly (*něśî'ê 'ēdāh,* 16:2) would have to do with lay participation in control of the temple and its considerable revenues, while Korah would represent those Levites opposing the hegemony of the priestly aristocracy. Control of the temple and its operations and its revenues was a major issue during the governorship of Nehemiah, a layman, and there are indications that he and Ezra each had considerable support from both laity and Levites in their difficulties with the temple priesthood (Ezra 9–10; Neh 8:1–9:5; 13:4–14, 28–29).

The Moses of the wilderness period not only mediates the law but also interprets, teaches, and administers it. Since this was obviously too much for one person, the creation of a comprehensive judicial system was called for, and it was put in place following advice from Jethro (Ex 18:13–27). Moses was to represent the people before God, continue his teaching function (cf. Deut 1:5; 4:1, 5, etc.), and deal with extraordinary cases, meaning those without precedent in law. All other cases were to be dealt with at the local level by exemplary individuals appointed for that purpose. The same principle of subdelegation figures in the similar account of the commissioning of the seventy elders (Num 11:4–35) effected by the transfer to them of some of Moses' spirit. And since to speak of spirit (*rûaḥ*) inevitably brings prophecy to mind, they exhibited the efficacy of the act by engaging in prophetic activity. Attached to Moses, this part of the story is often understood as a legitimation of ecstatic prophecy, and Eldad and Medad, who prophesied even though they were not commissioned at the sacred tent, represent prophecy exercised outside of the cultic sphere. But as the story now stands, the principal issue is the governance of the community, and we are dealing with essentially the same issue as in Exodus 18.

The Deuteronomic law mandates the setting up of judicial procedures throughout the country and the creation of a central judiciary composed of priests, Levites, and laity to deal with cases of special difficulty (Deut 16:18–20; 17:8–13; cf. 1:9–18). Whether this was a genuinely new measure or a confirmation of existing practice we cannot say. 2 Chron 19:5–11 records that King Jehoshaphat (mid-ninth century B.C.) established precisely such a system, adding only that the priest dealt with religious matters and the layman with those belonging to the secular sphere. While this may be historical, it is also possible that Jehoshaphat's name ("YHWH establishes justice") suggested attributing to him the Deuteronomic measures, adding only a distinction obtaining in the author's own day (cf. the distinction between the "law of your God" and the "law of the king" in Ezra 7:26). However the system originated, it is reasonably clear that here too the wilderness period has provided a paradigm for the institutional life of the community.

EPILOGUE: THE HISTORICAL REALITY BEHIND THE TEXTS

The interest of the contemporary reader of the Bible tends to focus, much more than his counterpart in antiquity, on historical issues. In fact, for many Christians today, assent to the historical accuracy of the Bible is a major, if not *the* major, criterion of orthodoxy. Much of the contemporary interest in archaeology, evident in the wide readership of publications like *Biblical Archaeology Review,* derives from the expectation of finding support for the dogma of historical accuracy and inerrancy. In fact many of the early practitioners of "biblical archaeology," at least from the English-speaking world, were seminary professors who were motivated by something of the same expectation.

It may therefore be useful to state certain facts bearing on this issue of historicity. The first is that with the exception of the Merneptah stele from the last decade of the thirteenth century B.C., no source external to the Bible prior to the ninth century B.C. provides any direct information on the history of Israel. The most that can therefore be expected from archaeology is the reconstruction of a plausible setting for events recorded in the Pentateuch. In the pursuit of this limited goal, moreover, our expectations must be tempered by an acute sense of the limitations inherent in archaeology. First and most obviously, the results of archaeological excavation always remain subject to revision or even subversion as a result of further excavation on the same site or on others. Less obviously, the artifactual data obtained are no less subject to interpretation than are texts. They are not endowed with an objectivity that compares favorably with the subjectivity inseparable from literary analysis. An indication of the greater maturity of the discipline today is that conclusions once confidently proclaimed are now being called into question. Site identifications once regarded as certain (e.g., Debir/Tell bet-mirsim, Egion/tell el-hesi, Heshbon/Hesban) have now either been rejected or are being questioned, the number of cities that may have been, or even could have been, destroyed during the Israelite occupation has shrunk dramatically, and the thesis of a united conquest, confidently propounded by W. F. Albright, G. E. Wright, and others has been widely abandoned, largely as a result of more sophisticated methods, including regional surveys (e.g., Finkelstein 1988).

Much confusion has been caused over the last few decades by a methodologically unsound conflation of archaeological and literary (biblical) data. It is now widely agreed that the solution is to interpret and evaluate each set separately, on its own terms and with its own distinctive methods, before attempting a correlation where this seems feasible. This brings us to our second point, about the limited potential of the biblical texts as historical source material. The story of Israel from Egypt to Canaan was put together in its final form no earlier than the fifth century B.C. Its major components, designated P and D, cannot be dated earlier than the previous century, though both include material of greater antiquity. Older narratives, conventionally designated JE, have been incorporated that resist even approximate dating, but are probably not as old, not as numerous, and certainly not as continuous as was once thought. In the narrative surveyed in this chapter the oldest components are probably the brief excerpts from the Book of the Wars of YHWH (Num 21:14–15, 17–18, 27–30). For the most part, therefore, the narrators stand at a very considerable distance from the time when the events recorded are deemed to have taken place.

It should also be obvious that literary analysis must precede historical reconstruction. This includes an appreciation of the different genres, including folk tale, heroic tale, legend, etiology, each with its own intentionality and mode of communication, which have gone into the literary construct we have been considering in this chapter. The schematic, programmatic, and didactic character of the P narrative has also been abundantly in evidence. Israel in the wilderness is fully organized as a twelve-tribal polity deployed around the sanctuary, moving processionally from one station to the next under clerical and lay leaders with well-defined functions. The many improbabilities we have encountered—an unnamed Pharaoh negotiating directly with his slaves and their midwives, the astonishing demographic expansion of the enslaved, the precisely engineered earthquake that disposed of Korah and his faction—serve not to discredit the biblical narrative but to draw our attention to its true literary character.

However discouraging it may seem, the net result of a more discriminating approach to both artifactual and literary data is that we are much less certain today about what really happened than we were two or three decades ago. All we can do here is report briefly on the present state of the discussion with respect to the Egyptian sojourn, the exodus, and the settlement in Canaan. While we cannot agree with Bright (*A History of Israel,* 121) that the biblical tradition demands belief since no people would invent such discreditable origins, it seems plausible that some Hebrew ancestors of the Israelites spent time in Egypt, together with other Western Semites, and were engaged in building projects. This part of the story is supported by the tradition of entry into Canaan from the south and east rather than via the usual northern route, and there is no reason to follow those who deny any validity to the tradition at this point. Needless to say, not all the tribes were in Egypt. The tribal structure came into existence in Canaan, some of the tribal names deriving from Canaanite topographical features (e.g., Josh 11:21; 20:7; 21:11, 21), and many would now argue that the twelve-tribal system is no earlier than the United Monarchy. The incidence of Egyptian names in the tribe of Levi (Moses, Hophni, Phineas, Merari, and perhaps Aaron) does not prove that this tribe was in Egypt, since it can be explained by pervasive Egyptian influence in Canaan down to the end of the eleventh century at least. It is agreed that the biblical Hebrews (*ʿibrîm*) cannot simply be identified with the *ḥabiru/ʿapiru,* a category of stateless people attested in Egypt from the fifteenth century, and several scholars deny any connection at all, philological or sociological.[29]

Since the narrator does not name the Pharaohs with whom the Hebrews had to cope, the issue of dating has always focused on the store cities Pithom and Raamses, built with Hebrew labor (Ex 1:11). Pithom (pr ʿtm = house of Atum) is identified with either tell er-reṭābeh or tell el-mašḥūta in the Wadi Tumelat, and Raamses (pr rʿmś-św = house of Ramses) with the Pharaonic residence during the nineteenth and twentieth dynasties, rebuilt on the site of Avaris, the former Hyksos capital. Since many building projects were undertaken in the eastern delta by the Pharaohs of the nineteenth dynasty, it was and still is widely assumed that the oppressor of the Hebrews and the Pharaoh of the exodus were respectively Seti I (ca. 1305–1290) and Ramses II (ca. 1290–1224). This also seemed to make a good fit with the mention of Israel on the Merneptah stele (ca. 1207), the encounter with Edomites and Moabites in the final stages of the wilderness journey (Numbers 20–21), and the archaeological evidence for destruction in Canaan at the end of Late Bronze (ca. 1200 B.C.).

Unfortunately for peace and concord in the scholarly community, these conclusions have all been questioned. The Egyptologist Donald Redford noted several years ago *(VT* 13 [1963] 408–13) that the two store cities were known under these names long after the Ramessid period and suggested that Ex 1:11 was a post-exilic interpolation designed to give an archaic flavor to the narrative. The surface exploration of Transjordan carried out by Nelson Glueck in the 1930s[30] led to the conclusion of an occupational gap in that region during MB II and LB, that is, from the nineteenth to the thirteenth centuries B.C., thereby ruling out a date earlier than the thirteenth century for the events related in Numbers 20–21. But later surveys conducted in the same region have shown that there was no occupational gap and no rash of new settlements at the end of LB. If these conclusions are sustained, they would not undermine the generally accepted date for the exodus and settlement but would at least remove one obstacle to an earlier date.

In the third and most recent edition of his *A History of Israel* (1981), John Bright acknowledged some of the problems involved in dating the occupation of Canaan to the mid-thirteenth century, but the problems are rather more severe than he was prepared to admit. According to the summary of the conquest in Joshua (12:7–24) thirty-one "cities" were occupied by the all-conquering Israelites, but the narrative of the conquest itself speaks explicitly of the destruction of only four of these: Jericho, Ai, Hebron, and Hazor. Of these four, only Hazor has provided archaeological evidence of occupation at the end of LB, and the same conclusion has had to be drawn for other sites said to have been taken over by the invaders—Gibeon (el-Jib), Debir (Khirbet Rabūd), Arad (Tel Malhata), and Hormah (Tel Masos?). Hazor (Tell el-Qedaḥ) was destroyed at the end of LB but the archaeological data do not permit us to say by whom. Moreover, the destruction or abandonment of sites toward the end of the thirteenth century and the beginning of the twelfth is not confined to Palestine/Israel, and the notable change in material culture between LB and Iron I may be due to factors other than military conquest by new arrivals on the scene.[31]

The erosion of evidence for military conquest toward the beginning of the twelfth century has opened up the *theoretical* possibility for an earlier dating, but attempts to establish such a dating, e.g., that of John J. Bimson, are unsupported by archaeological evidence, and they labor under other difficulties as well.[32] We note a growing sense that some elements of what was eventually to become Israel, including the "Israel" of the Merneptah stele, were already settled in Canaan before the Iron Age, and recent regional surveys on the surface suggest a notable increase in settlements in the hill country toward the beginning of Iron I.[33] Open conflict with the major Canaanite urban centers would presumably have been feasible only after considerable time had passed. We can conclude that at this writing all of the older theories, including the seminal work of Albrecht Alt (1966

[1925] 133–69), and all more recent ones, including those of Mendenhall and Gottwald, are in the process of being re-evaluated.[34]

While the question of the historical setting of the narrative in Exodus and Numbers has been at the center of scholarly discussion in recent years, other issues continue to be debated, including the historicity of Moses, the origins of the YHWH cult, the plagues, and the wilderness itinerary (northern or southern route). Space permits only a brief reference to the historical role of Moses, a subject which will come up for discussion again in the following chapter. The reader will find a solid treatment of the literary character of the Moses narratives in George W. Coats, *Moses. Heroic Man, Man of God* (Sheffield, 1988) and a succinct statement of some of the major historical issues in a contribution to the G. Henton Davies *Festschrift* by Geo Widengren *(Proclamation and Presence* [Richmond, 1970], 21–47). However we describe its literary character (Coats uses the term "heroic saga"), the Moses narrative stands at the end of a long traditioning process. That so little attention is paid to Moses in pre-exilic texts has persuaded several scholars, beginning with Eduard Meyer, that the presentation of Moses' career in the Pentateuch is essentially unhistorical.[35] This leaves us wondering how a figure who, if he existed at all, played a very minor role, came to be considered the founder of a people and a religion. The question is not unanswerable, but it is fair to say that those who have taken a radically negative position have not adequately addressed it.

On a more balanced view, one that would still be widely shared, we can extract from the biblical story a critical minimum of historically reliable information. This would include his Egyptian name, his marriage into a Kenite or Midianite family (Judg 1:16; 4:11; cf. Num 10:29), his marriage to another foreign woman (Num 12:1), at least two of his sons (Ex 18:3–4), and his membership in the tribe of Levi (Ex 2:1). To take a leaf out of Bright's book, the foreign marriages would hardly have been invented by an Israelite author of a later day. It seems to have been by virtue of his tribal affiliation that both the connection with Kadesh and his role as proclaimer of the law developed (cf. Deut 33:8–10), the latter escalating into massive proportions in the course of centuries. The tradition of his death and burial outside the promised land (Deut 34:6) would also appear to be solid and unimpeachable. As I have said, this is a critical minimum. Many would be prepared to go further, and they may well be justified in doing so, but there is enough here to explain how Moses came to occupy a position of such overwhelming importance in the collective consciousness of Israel.

NOTES

1. F. I. Andersen and A. D. Forbes, "Prose Particle' Counts of the Hebrew Bible," in C. L. Meyer and M. O'Connor (eds.), *The Word of the Lord shall go forth. Essays in Honor of David Noel Freedman* (Winona Lake, Ind., 1983), 172, count 16,713 words for Exodus, 16,413 for Numbers, and 11, 950 for Leviticus.

2. E.g., Martin Buber, *Moses. The Revelation and the Covenant* (New York, 1958 [1946]); David Daiches, *Moses. The Man and His Vision* (New York, 1975); George W. Coats, *Moses. Heroic Man. Man of God* (Sheffield, 1988).

3. Eupolemus, Aristobulus, Artapanus, and Ezekiel the Tragedian. On the life of Moses in late antiquity, see D. L. Tiede, *The Charismatic Figure as Miracle Worker* (Missoula, 1972), 101–37; C. H. Holladay, *Theios Aner in Hellenistic Judaism* (Missoula, 1977), 67–73.

4. M. Noth, "Die Wallfahrtsweg zum Sinai," *PJB* 36 (1940) 5–28; *Numbers. A Commentary* (Philadelphia, 1968 [1966]), 242–46. On the itinerary in general, see G. W. Coats, "The Wilderness Itinerary," *CBQ* 34 (1972) 132–52; G. I. Davies, *The Way of the Wilderness* (Cambridge, 1979).

5. Excluded, therefore, are the texts discussed by Gerhard von Rad in connection with his "little credo" theory; see his *The Problem of the Hexateuch and Other Essays* (Edinburgh, 1966 [1958]), 1–78.

6. The Kadesh traditions were important for Wellhausen, *Prolegomena to the History of Israel* (New York, 1957 [1883]), 342–43 followed by Eduard Meyer, *Die Israeliten und ihre Nachbarstämme* (Darmstadt, 1967 [1906]), 51–71, and more recent studies, e.g., M. L. Newman, *The People and the Covenant. A Study of Israel from Moses to the Monarchy* (Nashville, 1962). This approach was criticized by Martin Noth, *A History of Pentateuchal Traditions* (Englewood Cliffs, N.J., 1972 [1948]), 164–66.

7. E.g., G. Hort, "The Plagues of Egypt," *ZAW* 69 (1957), 84–103; Z. Zevit, "Three Ways to look at the Ten Plagues," *BR* 6.1 (1990), 16–23, 42–43.

8. W. Zimmerli, "Le Nouvel Exode dans le message des deux grands prophètes de l'exil," in *Hommage à Wilhelm Vischer* (Montpellier, 1960), 216–27; B. W. Anderson, "Exodus Typology in Second Isaiah," in B. W. Anderson and W. Harrelson (eds.), *Israel's Prophetic Heritage* (New York, 1962), 177–95; J. Blenkinsopp, "Scope and Depth of the Exodus Tradition in Deutero Isaiah," *Concilium* 2(1966) 41–50; Hans Barstad, *A Way in the Wilderness. The "Second Exodus" in the Message of Second Isaiah* (Manchester, 1989).

9. Among the more substantial recent commentaries available in English are those of Martin Noth (1962 [1959]) and Brevard Childs (1974), but the older commentary of S. R. Driver (Cambridge, 1911) is well worth consulting. From the Jewish side, see Umberto Cassuto, *A Commentary on the Book of Exodus* (Jerusalem, 1967 [1951]), for the most part a paraphrase of the biblical text from a traditional perspective, and Moshe Greenberg, *Understanding Exodus* (New York, 1969) and *EncJud* 6:1050–67.

10. 4QDeutq reads *bny* '*l* [. . .], so it is not clear whether the reading was '*el* or '*ĕlohîm;* see Patrick W. Skehan, "A Fragment of the 'Song of Moses' (Deut 32) from Qumran," *BASOR* 136 (1954) 12–15.

11. See the commentaries of Noth and Childs *ad loc.* and, for the chapter as a whole, T. C. Vriezen, "Exodusstudien, Exodus 1," *VT* 17 (1967) 334–53; O. Eissfeldt, "Die Komposition von Exodus 1–12," in *Kleine Schriften* (Tübingen, 1963) vol. II, 160–70; G. Fohrer, *Uberlieferung und Geschichte des Exodus. Eine Analyse von Exodus 1–15.* (Berlin, 1964), 9–23.

12. On the literary qualities of Exodus 1–2, see James S. Ackerman, "The Literary Context of the Moses Birth Story (Exodus 1–2)," in K. R. R. Gros Louis *et al.* (eds.), *Literary Interpretations of Biblical Narratives* (Nashville, 1974), 74–119; Michael Fishbane, *Text and Texture,* 63–76; C. Isbell, "The Structure of Exodus 1:1–14," in D. J. A. Clines *et al.* (eds.), *Art and Meaning. Rhetoric in Biblical Literature* (Sheffield, 1982), 37–61.

13. In addition to the commentaries, see W. L. Holladay, "The Background of Jeremiah's Self-Understanding," *JBL* 83 (1964) 153–64; 85 (1966) 17–27; E. W. Nicholson, *Preaching to the Exiles* (Oxford, 1970), 113–15; W. Thiel, *Die Deuteronomistische Redaktion von Jeremia 1–25.* (Neukirchen, 1973), 62–72.

14. In addition, C. Houtman, "Exodus 4:24–26 and Its Interpretation," *JNSL* 11 (1983) 83–105, provides an overview of the history of exegesis. More recently Herbert Rand, "Moses at the Inn: New Light on an Obscure Text," *Dor leDor* 14 (1985) 31–38, has revived the old idea that the attack is a metaphor for an illness of the psychological kind. For a different and even more recent approach, see B. P. Robinson, "Zipporah to the Rescue: A Contextual Study of Exodus iv 24–6," *VT* 36 (1986) 447–61.

15. See A. H. J. Gunneweg, *Leviten und Priester* (Göttingen, 1965); A. Cody, *A History of Old Testament Priesthood* (Rome, 1969); F. Moore Cross, *Canaanite Myth and Hebrew Epic,* 195–215; M. Haran, *Temples and Temple Service in Ancient Israel* (Winona Lake, Ind., 1985), 58–111.

16. See the careful analysis of Moshe Greenberg, "The Redaction of the Plague Narrative in Exodus," in Hans Goedecke (ed.), *Near Eastern Studies in Honor of William Foxwell Albright* (Baltimore & London, 1971), 243–52.

17. Some early interpretors took the despoiling to be a loan, based on a possible meaning of the verb *š'l* (see LXX, Vulgate, and Mekhilta on Ex 12:36) which, however, leaves the departing Israelites in a morally dubious position. The problem is avoided if the valuables were taken as payment due to a manumitted slave in the year of release (Deut 15:13: "you shall not send him away emptyhanded"), a possibility suggested by Cassuto in his commentary (1983 [1951], p 46) and, with a different nuance, Daube (1963, 55–61). If, on the other hand, Ex 11:1b is translated "as one dismisses (i.e., divorces) a newly wedded wife *(kallāh)* so will he surely drive you away hence," the supplying of provisions could be seen as the return of the bridal dowry, which would also explain why the women make the request.

18. On the different hypotheses, see R. de Vaux, *Ancient Israel. Its Life and Institutions* (New York, 1961 [1957], 484–93 and *Studies in Old Testament Sacrifice* (Cardiff, 1964), 1–26.

19. Joel Weinberg, "Das Bēit 'ābōt im 6.-4. Jh.v.u.Z.," *VT* 23 (1973) 400–14.

20. Since the number is exclusive of dependents (12:37), the grand total must have been in excess of two million, an obviously fantastic figure. Both rationalist critics like Reimarus and liberal exegetes like Bishop Colenso made much of this figure; for examples, see John Rogerson, *Old Testament Criticism in the Nineteenth Century. England and Germany* (Philadelphia, 1985), 25, 182, 221–22.

21. The traditional designation "the Red Sea" derives from the OG *eruthra thalassa* and Vulg. *mare rubrum*, and in some texts (1 Kings 9:26; Jer 49:21; perhaps Ex 23:31) *yam sûp* must refer to the Gulf of Aqaba/Elath that empties into the Red Sea. But the Hebrew term can only mean "Reed Sea" or "Papyrus Sea" and the topographical indications, obscure as they are, favor one of the lagoons east of the delta region. The term would be appropriate for either Lake Manzala or Lake Bardawil (Sirbonis).

22. *The Archaeology of Palestine* (Baltimore, 1960 [1949], 232–33; *From the Stone Age to Christianity* (Garden City, N.Y., 1957, 2nd ed.), 14; *The Biblical Period from Abraham to Ezra* (New York, 1963 [1949], 21; *Yahweh and the Gods of Canaan* (London, 1968), 1–46.

23. Frank Moore Cross, Jr., and David Noel Freedman, *Studies in Ancient Yahwistic Poetry* (Missoula, 1975 [1950]), 45–65; "The Song of Miriam," *JNES* 14 (1955) 237–50; D. N. Freedman, "Archaic Forms in Early Hebrew Poetry," *ZAW* 72 (1960), 105; *Pottery, Poetry and Prophecy. Studies in Early Hebrew Poetry* (Winona Lake, Ind., 1980), 179–227; F. M. Cross, *Canaanite Myth and Hebrew Epic*, 112–44. By comparing its morphological and syntactic features with those of the Ugaritic texts, D. A. Robertson, *Linguistic Evidence in Dating Early Hebrew Poetry* (Missoula, 1972), attempts to show that the Song is one of very few poetic compositions (Job is another) containing very early features, and the only one without grammatical forms characteristic of standard poetic Hebrew. He assumes that it cannot be dated on any other grounds including historical allusions, which we have seen is not the case.

24. J. Weingreen, "The Case of the Woodgatherer (Numbers xv 32–36)," *VT* 16 (1966) 361–64; A. Phillips, "The Case of the Woodgatherer Reconsidered," *VT* 19 (1969) 125–28. On Neh 13:15–22, see J. Blenkinsopp, *Ezra-Nehemiah. A Commentary* (Philadelphia, 1988), 357–61 and M. Fishbane, *Biblical Interpretation in Ancient Israel* (Oxford, 1985), 129–34.

25. The close connection between marriage and property was also a factor in the measures taken to promote endogamy as recorded in Ezra-Nehemiah. The problem would of course be more severe if a Judean woman who had inherited property married outside of the Israelite kinship system. On the stipulations in Numbers, see J. Weingreen, "The Case of the Daughters of Zelophehad," *VT* 16 (1966) 518–22.

26. A connection between the eruption on Thera in the Cyclades and the biblical account of the exodus was first suggested, as far as I know, by Immanuel Velikovsky. It is defended, surprisingly, by the Egyptologist Hans Goedicke, whose theory is discussed in *BAR* 7.5 (1981) 42–50; 7.6 (1981) 46–53. More recently the eruption has been backdated to the late seventeenth century.

27. The explanation of manna as the sap of the tamarisk secreted and excreted by certain insects seems to have been widely accepted; see F. S. Bodenheimer, "The Manna of Sinai," *BA* 10 (1947) 2–6.

28. The following verse (Ezek 20:26) has suggested to some commentators that the reference is to the crematory sacrifice of the firstborn. Jo Ann Hackett, *The Balaam Text from Deir ʿAllā* (Chico, Calif., 1984), 75–89, finds a reference to child sacrifice in the second combination and suggests a connection, albeit obscure, with the allusions in Psalm 106 to sacrifices offered to the dead at Baal-peor and the sacrificing of children to demons *(šēdîm,* cf. the *šdyn* deities of the inscriptions).

29. On the *habiru/ʿapiru* problem, see J. Bottero, *Le problème des Habiru* (Paris, 1954); M. Greenberg, *The Hab/piru* (New Haven, 1955); R. Borger, "Das Problem der ʿApiru (Habiru)," *ZDPV* 74 (1958), 121–32. The issues are discussed at length by M. Weippert, *The Settlement of the Israelite Tribes in Palestine* (London, 1971 [1967]), 63–102.

30. Nelson Glueck, *The Other Side of the Jordan* (Cambridge, Mass., 1940; 2nd ed., 1970).

31. The collapse of the Mycenean civilization about the same time (Late Helladic IIIC) offers an interesting parallel, to explain which different theories have been proposed, including invasion (by Dorians or Sea Peoples) and internal strife. The view that drastic climatic changes contributed to or even induced cultural, political, and demographic decline in the Aegean, Asia Minor, and Syria-Palestine cannot be excluded; see Rhys Carpenter, *Discontinuity in Greek Civilization* (Cambridge, England, 1966); William H. Stiebing, "The End of the Mycenean Age," *BA* 43.1 (1980) 7–21.

32. J. J. Bimson, *Redating the Exodus and Conquest* (Sheffield, 1981, 2nd ed.); J. J. Bimson and D. Livingston, "Redating the Exodus," *BAR* 13:5 (1987) 40–53, 66–68.

33. The most important recent study is Israel Finkelstein, *The Archaeology of The Israelite Settlement* (Jerusalem, 1988).

34. The "peasant revolt" theory of G. Mendenhall ("The Hebrew Conquest of Palestine," *BA* 25 [1962] 66–87) and the related but much more developed construct of Norman K. Gottwald (*The Tribes of Yahweh* [New York, 1979]) were subjected to a detailed critique by Niels Peter Lemche, *Early Israel. Anthropological and Historical Studies on the Israelite Society Before the Monarchy* (Leiden, 1985). Lemche's own drastically reductionist assessment of the biblical material is restated in *Ancient Israel. A New History of Israelite Society* (Sheffield, 1988).

35. E. Meyer, *Die Israeliten und ihre Nachbarstämme* (Halle, 1906), 451. Martin Noth, *A History of Pentateuchal Traditions,* 156–75, limits Moses' role to the story of the conquest and finds the burial tradition the one reliable point of reference in the biblical tradition.

CHAPTER 6

SINAI, COVENANT AND LAW

THE SINAI NARRATIVE (EX 19:1–NUM 10:28)

Though laws take up the greater part of the space in this central section of
the Pentateuch, a series of events is recorded beginning with the arrival in
the Sinai wilderness and ending with the move to the next stopping place.
The delivery and promulgation of the laws are therefore part of the story,
and this circumstance invites the conclusion that they are to be understood
in the context of the narrative to which they belong. But the course of
events in that narrative presents some puzzling features. The reader may
wonder why Moses repeatedly goes up the mountain, on one occasion only
to hear that he has to go down again and repeat an instruction already
given (Ex 19:20–23). (If the mountain in question is identified with either
jebel mūsa, 7647 ft., or jebel qāterīn, 8649 ft., all this activity would represent no mean feat of stamina and endurance). The introductory address
(Ex 19:7–8) seems to assume that the laws or "words" (děbārîm) have
already been given, and there are conflicting accounts of how the closing
ceremonies were carried out, where they took place, and who participated
in them (Ex 24:1–11). To take a final example, Moses intercedes successfully for the apostates after the Golden Calf episode (Ex 32:14), but a
plague follows with yet more punishment in store (Ex 32:34–35).

If we are not to put these and similar inconcinnities down to the ineptitude of the author or compiler, we will have to make an effort to grasp the special characteristics of this kind of paradigmatic narrative, a difficult task without some idea of how the story was put together. This is not to imply that it is nothing more than a collage of different sources put together with scissors and paste. There is an overall pattern the principal features of which are the making, breaking, and remaking of the covenant. This could be stated abstractly as the passage from guilt and sin to forgiveness and acceptance, but we shall see that the pattern encodes a theological interpretation of the history of Israel viewed from the other side of political disaster. We are therefore invited to think of the extinction of the two kingdoms, Israel in the eighth century and Judah in the sixth, the deportations that followed, and the hope for a new beginning.

Other structural and stylistic features help to hold the narrative together. There is the chronological scheme, with dates reckoned from the exodus at the beginning and end (Ex 19:1; Num 10:11). Internal correspondences include the two forty-day absences of Moses on the mountain, the first ending with the breaking of the law tablets and the second with the making of new tablets (Ex 24:18; 34:28). The theme of divine guidance precedes the making of the old and the new covenant (Ex 23:20–33; 33:1–3). Also not to be missed is the device of "bracketing": the decalogue is located between the theophany and the reaction of the people to it (19:16–20:20), and the Golden Calf incident separates the instructions for the establishment of the wilderness sanctuary and their implementation (24:15b–31:17; 31:18–34:35; 35–40). Since these and similar procedures arise from a cumulative redactional process, they necessarily lead to a consideration of sources and the successive stages of composition that they represent.

In keeping with the practical rule followed in the preceding chapters, our procedure will be to begin with what is least obscure, which in effect means working back from the final form to increasingly hypothetical earlier stages of formation. Since sources are rarely quoted verbatim in the Pentateuch, we have to rely on the cumulative effect of different stylistic, lexical, and ideological indicators and look out for obvious inconsistencies and discontinuities, of which there happen to be quite a few in the Sinai pericope. The analogy of Chronicles and its use of sources is useful, but the obvious difference is that in this case the principal source, namely 1–2 Kings, is extant in its entirety. The process, however, is not the merely mechanical one of adding one source to another like the courses of a brick wall or the layers of a cake. As a recent contributor to the discussion put it, "Redaction is fundamentally a hermeneutical activity concerned with the receiving and reconceiving of continually valid tradition in all the relativities of new historical circumstances" (Johnstone 1987, 17). It is only by pursuing this line of inquiry that, for example, we can form some idea of when and under what impulses the covenant became a dominant organizing concept in religious thinking, or how the figure of Moses came to assume a dominant place in Israelite and Jewish religious consciousness.

The Formation of the Narrative: (1) P

The P strand in the Sinai pericope is part of an extensive narrative work beginning with creation. Its terminus continues to be disputed, but we shall see that there are good reasons for taking it down to the establishment of the wilderness sanctuary in Canaan and the allotting of tribal territory under the leadership of the priest Eleazar and Joshua (Joshua 18–19).[1] While the main-line P narrative bears the stamp of an individual author, it has been expanded at various points. The laws, many of which are older than the narrative, have also undergone considerable development, as is to be expected. The siglum P, therefore, like D, to be considered shortly, stands for the literary production of a "school," a class of learned individuals sharing the same general ideology and active over several generations, comparable in some respects to the rabbinic houses and the early Christian Alexandrian and Antiochean exegetical schools. We noted earlier that it seems advisable to distinguish between P and the final redaction of the Pentateuch. It is unlikely that the P narrator would have included incidents that show Aaron in an unfavorable light, especially the Golden Calf episode, and in spite of the rather lame attempt to shift the blame elsewhere (Exodus 32). There are also incidents of uncertain provenance but probably later than P, including Moses' vision of the divine effuigence (Ex 33:12–23) and his transfiguration on the mountain (34:29–35).

According to this source, then, Israel arrived at the mountain in the wilderness of Sinai (Ex 19:1–2; cf. Num 33:15), whereupon Moses immediately entered the cloud blanketing the mountain in order to receive instructions for the setting up of the sanctuary and its cult (Ex 24:15–18a). There is therefore no theophany, apart from the vision vouchsafed to Moses, and no covenant.[2] We pass directly from arrival to ascent of the mountain and communications concerning the cult, the resumptive verse "and Moses went up the mountain" (24:15a) connecting with "and Moses went up to God" (19:3a). The cultic instructions are presented with the attention to detail characteristic of P (25:1–31:17), and the equally detailed account of their implementation (35–40) follows the breaking and remaking of the covenant (31:18–34:35). While this command-execution pattern is a characteristic of P, in this case the repetition in practically identical terms was deemed necessary by a later scholiast in order to make the point that the instructions had not lost their validity because of the intervening lapse involving Aaron, eponym of the priesthood. The main point, closely related to the theology of Ezekiel, is that the new dispensation rests directly not on the human response to the remade covenant but on the divine presence in the sanctuary. And in keeping with this basic conviction, the cultic laws in Leviticus and Numbers place the emphasis on holiness rather than on covenant fidelity.

Here as elsewhere in the P history the key dates are carefully noted. Israel arrived at Sinai on the first day of the third month (19:1), counting from the exodus, and departed on the twentieth day of the second month in the following year (Num 10:11) after the tabernacle had been erected on New Year's Day of the second year (Ex 40:1, 17). The creation of the world, the emergence of the new, postdiluvial world after the flood (Gen 8:13), and the setting up of the sanctuary all therefore fall on New Year's Day. That Moses received instructions for the establishment of the sanctuary and its cult on the seventh day (Ex 24:16) reinforces the homology between cosmos and temple and therefore also the cosmic significance of the cult as basic thematic and structural features of the P narrative.

The Formation of the Narrative: (2) D

At several points in our survey of the story from Genesis 12 to the end of Numbers we had occasion to note language and thought patterns characteristic of D. Even Martin Noth, whose distinction between the Tetrateuch and Dtr prefaced by Deuteronomy has been so influential, conceded that several passages in the Sinai pericope betray the hand of a D redactor (e.g., Ex 19:3–9a; 23:20–33; 32:9–14; see his *Exodus,* 157, 192–94, 244). One of the most disputed issues now on the agenda in Pentateuchal studies is the extent of the D contribution to the story of the founding events in Genesis 12–50, Exodus, and Numbers, and in view of its pivotal position in the narrative and its crucial theological importance, the Sinai pericope is at the center of the debate. At one end of the band there are those who hold the more traditional view that it is essentially a JE composition expanded by P but with only very minor D editorial retouchings; while at the other end there seems to be an increasing disposition, much influenced by the work on the covenant of the German scholars L. Perlitt (1969) and E. Kutsch (1973), to read it as basically a work of D provenance incorporating some early traditions and expanded by P. A brief examination of the narrative sections of the pericope, leaving aside for the moment the complex issue of the legal material, is therefore in order.

Before proceeding with this examination, however, we might note that in this instance we have the advantage of external evidence for the D understanding of the Sinai/Horeb event, and the covenant in general, in Deuteronomy itself (principally Deut 4:10–14; 5:2–33; 9:8–10:11). As presented in Deuteronomy in the form of historical reminiscence put in the mouth of Moses, the sequence of events is as follows. The Israelite assembly was convened by Moses at the foot of the mountain. In the course of a theophany YHWH delivered the decalogue ("the ten utterances") directly to the people, wrote them on stone tablets, and instructed Moses to teach the people statutes and ordinances (i.e., detailed stipulations of law as opposed to the ten utterances). It is emphasized that only the decalogue was promulgated at that time *(lo' yāsap,* "he added no more," 5:22) since the people, fearful of further exposure to the divine presence, requested Moses to act as mediator, which he agreed to do. In that capacity he went up the mountain to take delivery of the tablets, stayed there, fasting forty days and nights, and was instructed to go down again, since the people had persuaded Aaron to make them a molten image of a calf. Moses went down, smashed the tablets in the sight of the assembly, interceded for Aaron and the people during a second forty-day fast, and reduced the calf to dust, which he threw into a stream flowing from the mountain. At YHWH's bidding he made two new tablets and took them up the mountain, and during a third forty-day period of intercession YHWH wrote on them the same utterances as before. The narrative ends with instructions to continue the journey and occupy the land promised by oath to the ancestors.

This, then, is the story as told in Deuteronomy. In the Sinai narrative in Exodus, the opening address of YHWH to Moses and his reporting back and forth between the deity and the people (19:3–9a) provide a first hint of the difficulties inherent in source criticism. Cazelles, for example, assigns this opening address to P, many of the older and some of the more recent commentators opt for E (e.g., Beyerlin 1965 [1961], 67–77), after some hesitation Childs comes out in favor of a D redactor (Childs 1974, 360–61), and this option is adopted wholeheartedly by Perlitt (1969, 167–81). Linguistic evidence would certainly seem to support this choice. The designation "house of Jacob" occurs predominantly in texts later than the dates usually assigned to J and E; the appeal to what you ("your eyes") have seen is a mark of the D homiletic style (Deut 3:21; 4:3, 9; 10:21; 11:7; 29:1 [29:2]; Josh 23:3); YHWH carrying (verbal stem *nś'*) Israel through the wilderness is a D topos (e.g., Deut 1:31), and the beautiful image of being borne on eagles' wings occurs in the Song of Moses (Deut 32:11). The idea that future blessing is contingent on observance ("if you will truly obey my voice and keep my covenant," Ex 19:5) is unmistakably Deuteronomic (cf. Deut 11:13; 13:18; 27:10; 28:1, 15; 30:10), as is the heavily charged term *sĕgullāh,* "special possession" (Deut 7:6; 14:2; 26:18). The much discussed designation "a kingdom of priests and a holy nation" *(mamleket kohănîm wĕgôy qādôš,* v 6)[3] does not occur in Deuteronomy, but is consistent with its presentation of Israel as a holy people (Deut 7:6; 14:2, 21; 26:19; 28:9) and a *gôy* (Deut 4:6–8, 33–34, in a passage from the exilic Deuteronomist). And, as noted at several points in Genesis, the emphasis on the need for believing (v 9) is characteristic of the D outlook (Deut 1:32; 9:23; 2 Kings 17:14).

These linguistic features are confirmed by the structure of the address, which conforms to a pattern frequently attested in Deuteronomy and D-edited passages, e.g., Joshua 24 and 1 Sam 12:6–25. The recounting of the beneficent actions of YHWH in the past (cf. Deut 11:2–4; 29:1 [29:2]) is followed by the promise of future blessing, or a special relationship, contingent on obedience and law observance, the passage from past to present and future being marked by the formulaic "and now" *(wĕʿattāh . . .)*. There then follows the assent of the hearers: "all that YHWH has spoken we will do." Since, incidentally, this response presupposes knowledge of what is to be done, the "words" *(dĕbārîm)* transmitted by Moses must refer to the decalogue, as in the similar passage Ex 24:3. This opening discourse, therefore, may be read as a D summary of the Sinai/Horeb event placed at the beginning, a summary encapsulating some of the most basic tenets of the D school: covenant resting on divine initiative and human response in obedience to the law, the unique status of Israel among the nations, and the mediatorial role of Moses as promulgator of the law.

At the conclusion of this address the phrase "YHWH said to Moses" is repeated in order to introduce instructions to prepare for what is to follow on the third day (v 10a). The consecration and washing of clothing are reminiscent of preparations for the Shechem covenant in Gen 35:1–4 (cf. also Josh 3:5 and 7:13), the people are to stay distant from the sacred temenos under pain of death, and the event is to be announced by the blowing of the ram's horn. The injunction of sexual abstinence (cf. 1 Sam 21:5–6 [21:4–5] and Lev 8:33), added by Moses, was implied in the consecration, since bodily discharges created a state of impurity (cf. Deut 23:11–12 [23:10–11]). All of this has the effect of representing what follows as a religious ceremony. It is conventionally assigned to J, but more by default than for any positive identifying features (e.g., Noth, *Exodus,* 158).

There is broad agreement that the description of the theophany (Ex 19:16–25, with its sequel following the decalogue in 20:18–20) combines two different scenarios: a violent storm on the mountain with thunder, lightning, and dense clouds (19:16–17, 19; 20:18), and volcanic phenomena including a column of smoke, fire, and tectonic movement (19:18, 20; 20:18). The trumpet blast was added as a summons of the people to a religious ceremony (cf. Josh 2:15; Isa 27:13; Ps 81:4). Based on the incidence of divine names, the volcanic scenario has been assigned to J and the storm to E. The problem then would be that the former is closer to the description of the event in Deuteronomy (4:11–12; 5:4–5) than the latter, which is problematic in view of the alleged association between E and D. The rather enigmatic sequel in 19:20–25, where Moses goes up the mountain and then, after what would seem to be a quite reasonable protest, goes down again, is generally labeled "secondary," meaning that it cannot easily be attributed to either J or E (e.g., Noth, *Exodus,* 160); and in fact the reaction to the theophany in 20:18–20, following the promulgation of the decalogue, follows on naturally from 19:19. The sequence of events is exactly as described in Deuteronomy (5:2–33), in which the decalogue alone is promulgated there and then and the "statutes and ordinances" are revealed to Moses privately. The content of this private revelation is contained in the "book of the covenant" or "covenant code," as it is sometimes called (20:23–23:19). The D author accounts for the promulgation of a different law book (Deuteronomy 12–26) at a later point in time, one which supplements the "book of the covenant," with reference to the Golden Calf incident, which necessitated a new covenant and a new law.

The brief introduction to the covenant book, with its appeal to the Israelites to recall what they themselves have seen, is cast in the by now familiar D style (20:21–22). The same must be said for the sequel to the laws which introduces the theme of divine guidance and the conquest of the land (23:20–33). While the guiding messenger or angel *(mal'ak)* cannot be identified with Moses, it occupies a place intermediate between YHWH and Moses in his role as prophetic agent, leader, and guide. Deut 18:15–18 derives the prophetic function from the mediation of Moses at Horeb, and the prophet, like the *mal'ak,* is to be heeded and obeyed, since he speaks in YHWH's name. In one of the few pre-exilic allusions to Moses, Hosea (12:13) describes him as prophetic guide and preserver in the wilderness, and the association between the "angelic" and the prophetic function may help to explain why *mal'ak* came to serve as a synonym for prophet (e.g., Hag 1:13). There is therefore a thematic link between the preface and the conclusion to the covenant book. The conclusion is replete with Deuteronomic themes: the extermination of the indigenous peoples and destruction of their cult objects, the prohibition of making covenants with these peoples, the native deities as a snare *(môqēš,* cf. Deut 7:16), the language of the holy war (hornets appear only here, in Deut 7:20 and Josh 24:12), and the ingenious reason offered for the delayed completion of the conquest (cf. Deut 7:22; different reasons in Judg 3:1–6).

Exodus 24 has always been the pivotal chapter in the interpretation of the Sinai pericope, and at the same time the passage most resistant to the usual source-critical procedures. As Perlitt put it, sources might as well be assigned by drawing straws (a rough translation of "durch Losorakel," *Bundestheologie,* 181). Dillmann, S. R. Driver, von Rad, Hyatt, and many others assigned vv 1–2 + 9–11 to J, mostly because the bracketed passage, vv 3–8, had already been reserved for E. Noth *(Exodus,* 196) and Beyerlin *(Origins and History,* 27–35), however, reverse the order. Most documentarians therefore have assigned vv 3–8 to E, even though the divine name is YHWH throughout, no doubt because they had already decided that the J covenant is recorded in Chapter 34. The only major exception is the Norwegian scholar Sigmund Mowinckel, who here as elsewhere *cantat extra chorum.* If the passage is read as a continuous and coherent account, we have a summons to ascend the mountain addressed to a limited group including Moses, a delay allowing for the ceremony at the foot of the mountain, and the crowning event of the vision and the meal on the summit. At this point we would have to assume a hiatus, since another summons to go up is addressed to Moses who, however, is already there (v 12). We may content ourselves with this if we wish, but it remains true that a surface reading of this kind in no way exhausts the meaning of a narrative that embodies centuries of religious experience and theological reflection.

To begin with what is least subject to doubt, the chapter contains four strands, each with its own cast of characters, location, and action.

(1)   1–2, 9–11. In obedience to a summons from YHWH, Moses, Aaron, Nadab, Abihu, and seventy elders go up the mountain, are granted a vision of the enthroned God of Israel, and partake of a meal. (Ex 24:2 is often taken to be a later addition from an editor who wanted to preserve the special status of Moses in the group, and in fact in vv 9–11 no distinction is made between the participants, all of whom are described as *’aṣîlîm,* "community leaders").

(2)   3–8. Moses and the people, including young men who perform the sacrifices, engage in a ceremony at the foot of the mountain including the public reading and assent to the law (twice). Then Moses writes the words of YHWH, an altar with twelve columns is set up, and a blood ritual is carried out. (From the point of view of later priestly praxis, the role of the youths is of course quite unorthodox).

(3)   12–15a + 18b. Moses is summoned to ascend the mountain with his servant Joshua to receive the law tablets written by YHWH. The sequel to this strand is the Golden Calf episode and the reissue of the tablets (31:18–34:35).

(4)   15b–18a. Moses goes up the mountain, enters the cloud, and receives instructions for the establishment of the wilderness sanctuary and its cult. This strand is continued in 25:1–31:17.

The arrangement of these strands illustrates the bracketing technique spoken of earlier. That 3–8 is bracketed by 1–2 and 9–11, and 15b–18a by 12–15a and 18b, suggests that the point of the arrangement is to highlight the bracketed passages, therefore those numbered 2 and 4 above. Attention is therefore focused on the conceptual messages which they encode, in the one instance the connection between covenant and law, and in the other divine presence in the act of worship. Perhaps this means that to take seriously the final form of the text, as many are now urging us to do, implies serious attention to its internal organization which results from a long historical process. We do not have to choose between synchronicity and diachronicity.

In the first of the four strands (vv 1–2, 9–11) the main point of contention has to do with the interpretation of the vision and meal on the mountain. Until fairly recently, most commentators took the meal to be the final sealing of the covenant between the God of Israel and his people (e.g., Noth 1962 [1959], 194; Beyerlin 1965 [1961], 33–35; McCarthy 1978 (2nd ed., 264). Others, however, have pointed out that there is no mention of covenant making, and that the emphasis is on the vision rather than the meal (Perlitt 1969, 181–90; Schmid 1976, 110–12; Nicholson 1986, 121–33, who takes the eating and drinking to mean simply that they survived direct encounter with the deity). These objections are difficult to answer, and I would suggest the alternative explanation that this strand derives from the Kadesh tradition, having migrated (as traditions tend to do) from the other mountain of God. Kadesh is also the scene of a meal "before God" in which Moses, Aaron, and the elders participated (Ex 18:12).

The bracketed episode at the foot of the mountain (vv 3–8) begins by repeating 19:7–8 almost verbatim and continues with Moses writing the words (dĕbārîm, identified with the decalogue; cf. Ex 20:1 and Deut 5:19) and reading the covenant book, the stipulations of which the people agree to observe. After sacrifices are performed by the youths, blood is sprinkled on the altar and the people, accompanied by words explaining the ritual, words which were to find their way into the Christian eucharist. The problem of sources proved to be particularly severe in this passage, for although the name YHWH occurs throughout, it was assumed that the J version of the covenant, including the J version of the decalogue, occurs only in Chapter 34. Here, too, Perlitt has pioneered a quite different approach by concentrating on those features of the narrative clearly reminiscent of Deuteronomy, namely, the reading of the decalogue and the covenant book followed by the assent of the people (vv 3, 7). He concluded that we have here a D reinterpretation of ancient tradition originating no earlier than the time of Josiah (Perlitt 1969, 190–203), a view which has won considerable support (e.g., Zenger 1971, 75–76; Kutsch 1973, 89; Schmid 1976, 112–14).[4] How old the tradition about the altar, the twelve pillars (maṣṣēbôt), the sacrifices and blood rite may be, we do not know. The Shechem tradition reproduced in Deut 27:1–8 and Josh 8:30–35 also features the building of an altar, the setting up of (presumably twelve) stones, burnt offerings, peace offerings, and a written law. Perhaps, then, it is this tradition at an early stage of its formation which has served as the basis for the D covenant ceremony reported here.

According to the third narrative strand (24:12–15a, 18b; 31:18–34:35), Moses is summoned yet one more time to the mountaintop to receive the stone tablets on which the decalogue was written (34:28; Deut 4:13; 5:22; 10:4),[5] while Aaron, his shadowy companion Hur, and the elders are left in charge at the foot of the mountain. The scene is set for the rejection of Moses' leadership by the people who persuade Aaron without much difficulty to make them a calf image out of melted-down gold ornaments. There has been considerable discussion as to the implications of this act and the nature of the sin. For Aaron at least, who goes on to proclaim a feast in honor of YHWH, it consisted not in idolatry but in a violation of the decalogic prohibition of making an image. The cult performed before the image is also reprehensible because of the arbitrary and ad hoc fixing of the date and the nature of the celebration which is of the orgiastic kind; the "playing" has a sexual connotation (cf. Gen 26:8), and there are also dancing and loud singing which could be heard from afar (32:18–19).

All critical commentators agree that this episode reflects the religious measures of Jeroboam I following on the division of the kingdom after the death of Solomon (1 Kings 12:28–33). The setting up of the gold calf icons at Bethel and Dan is accompanied by the same acclamation—"These are your gods, O Israel, who brought you up out of the land of Egypt"—a circumstance which may explain the use of the plural in Ex 32:8. Both Jeroboam and Aaron also play fast and loose with the liturgical calendar (1 Kings 12:32–33; cf. Ex 32:5). This being the case, the episode cannot be the work of a J author from the time of the United Monarchy. Since it is generally agreed that other parts of the narrative, especially the intercessory prayer of Moses (32:11–14, 30–35), are cast in the D style, it seems more likely that the entire episode is a D composition. Whether it is to be dated to the reign of Hezekiah, whose religious reforms were motivated in good part by the collapse of the Kingdom of Samaria in 722 B.C. (e.g., Zenger 1971, 164), or to the reign of Josiah, who destroyed the separatist Bethel sanctuary (2 Kings 23:15) (e.g., Perlitt 1969, 208–9), cannot easily be decided.

In the final episode in Chapter 34 Moses is told to cut two new tablets on which YHWH will write the same words as on the broken ones; he does so and takes them with him in yet another ascent of the mountain (vv 1–4). YHWH descends in the cloud, proclaims himself as the merciful, forgiving, and just God, and hears Moses' renewed intercession for the obdurate people (vv 5–9). The announcement of a (new) covenant is followed by a series of laws in the apodictic or direct command/prohibition form (vv 11–26) which Moses writes down in the course of a forty-day fast on the mountain (vv 27–28). The episode ends with Moses descending the mountain with the tablets, his face transformed by direct encounter with the godhead (vv 29–35).

Following Wellhausen, most documentary critics find in this chapter the J account of the covenant, and therefore the earliest extant version. Those who hold this view argue that the situation has been obscured by the secondary attachment of this version to the Golden Calf episode, which had the effect of transforming it into the renewal of a covenant previously made and then broken. Originally, however, it followed immediately after the J version of the theophany in Chapter 19. The transformation was effected by two simple additions: the remade tablets were to be "like the former ones" (kāri'šonîm, 34:1–4) and their content consisted in "the ten utterances" (34:28). It was implied, however, that the allusion was no longer to the decalogue in Ex 20:1–17, attributed to E, but to the "cultic decalogue" in 34:11–26. The sequence of events according to the J version, therefore, allowing for minor variations of this or that commentator, would be as follows: YHWH comes down on the mountain in smoke and fire (19:18, 20; 20:18); he proclaims his identity (34:5–7) and his intention to make a covenant (34:10); he gives them a series of laws, originally ten, and commands Moses to write them down, which he does (34:11–28).

Needless to say, this standard solution to these difficult chapters did not solve all problems. One of these, noticed long before Wellhausen by Goethe, no less, is that the laws in 34:11–26 are not identical with the ethical decalogue and their number exceeds ten. Another is that Moses is commanded to write the laws and does so in spite of YHWH's proposal at the outset to write them himself. It was also conceded that several passages sounded much more like D than J. Preserving the Yahwistic character of the pericope, therefore, called for a quite inordinate amount of textual surgery. In Martin Noth's commentary, for example, only eight of the twenty-eight verses survived intact (Noth, *Exodus,* 258–67).

In view of this situation, it would seem reasonable to look for a different approach to the formation of the Sinai pericope. An essential feature of the reconstruction of Noth and others is the secondary and editorial connection between Chapters 32 and 34. But if it could be shown that this is not the case, but rather that Chapters 32–34 form essentially one continuous narrative, the case for a primitive J version of covenant making collapses. In recent years several scholars, conspicuously Lothar Perlitt (1969, 203–32), have made out a strong case for the basic unity of this part of the Sinai pericope. (See also Nicholson, 1986, 134–50, for a critical review of this alternative). It has been pointed out that the stone tablets constitute a major topos throughout the section (Ex 24:12; 31:18; 32:15–16, 19; 34:1–4, 28), and that this topos is also prominent in Deuteronomy (4:13; 5:22; 9:9–10:5) but nowhere in evidence in passages assigned to J. Read consecutively, Chapters 32–34 also conform to the pattern of sin, punishment, and forgiveness encountered frequently in Deuteronomy and Dtr. They also fit the D concept of serial covenant making, beginning with the covenant in Moab which, as we are explicitly informed, was distinct from the Horeb covenant (Deut 28:69 [29:1]). The remade covenant at Sinai/Horeb also adumbrates the new covenant necessitated by the spiritual failure of Israel (Jer 31:31–34, a D-edited passage), a point of great theological importance to which we shall return.

At the present state of inquiry, therefore, it seems reasonable to propose as a working hypothesis that the Sinai/Horeb pericope is essentially a production of the scribal school from which Deuteronomy and Dtr derive and the Priestly school in which much of the ritual law originated. This does not exclude the possibility of older traditions having been taken over and reinterpreted (e.g., in 24:3–8) and additional material having been inserted prior to the final redaction. It should also be added that the sigla stand for schools active over more than one generation. But, to repeat once again, the methodologically sound approach is to work backward from these latest forms rather than to start out from the earliest and most hypothetical stages in the process of formation.

The Formation of the Narrative:
(3) Early Traditions and Final Additions

While arguments from silence are rarely if ever decisive, and therefore should be used with great caution, it is worth pointing out that Sinai is mentioned in pre-exilic texts only once or twice in poems and with no allusion to the covenant and the giving of the law (Judg 5:5; Ps 68:9, 18). In Jer 15:1 Moses and Samuel are the paradigms of prophetic intercession, but in prophetic writings earlier than Jeremiah Moses is mentioned by name only in Micah 6:4, a verse often assigned to a later editor. (He is probably alluded to but not named in Hos 12:13, "by a prophet YHWH brought Israel up out of Egypt.") The origins and early development of the traditions about Moses continue to be debated. Probably few scholars today would subscribe to the minimalist view of Martin Noth, who shrinks the original historical nucleus to the grave tradition (Noth 1972 [1948], 156–75). In our survey of the wilderness story we noted several markers pointing to a Midianite-Kenite connection (see also Judg 1:16 and 4:11), and specifically to the Kadesh oasis, from which point the figure of Moses seems to be firmly embedded in the final stages of the journey and preparations for the occupation of the land. I also suggested that the same tradition, closely related to the encounter of Moses with Jethro in Exodus 18, has been worked into the D version of the vision and meal on the mountain of revelation in Ex 24:1–2, 9–11. In somewhat similar fashion, an old tradition of Shechemite origin underlies the account of the ceremonies recorded as taking place at the foot of the mountain (Ex 24:3–8).

Ancient tradition has also been transmitted in the account of the oracle tent at which Moses received communications from God (Ex 33:7–11). Unlike the Priestly tent or tabernacle in the center of the camp (Ex 25–31; Num 2:17; etc.), this tent sanctuary was located outside, and therefore people had to leave the encampment in order to "consult YHWH." Consultation was mediated through Moses, whose unique relationship with God is expressed in the idiom of face-to-face encounter (Blenkinsopp 1977, 89–95). Of particular interest is the role of Joshua described in Ex 33:7–11 as *mĕšārēt* ("cultic servant") and *na'ar* (literally "youth," but probably with the meaning "cult official").[6] The implication seems to be that Moses, though enjoying the unique privilege of direct encounter with God, also used the services of a prophetic intermediary, somewhat like the prince of Byblos in the story of Wen-Amon who received a communication from a deity through a possessed youth *(ANET* 26). This reproduces a feature clearly more archaic than the representation of Joshua in the book named for him (Möhlenbrink 1942/1943, 14–58; Dumermuth 1963, 161–68). Ex 33:7–11 has generally been assigned to E (e.g., Beyerlin 1965 [1961], 112), though Noth derives it from a "special tradition," no doubt on account of the divine name YHWH that occurs throughout (Noth, *Exodus,* 255). All we can safely say is that it represents a fragment of pre-Deuteronomic tradition deemed appropriate for the literary context in which it has been inserted.

The context in question, Exodus 33, consists in a series of paragraphs, located between the breaking and remaking of the covenant, and bearing on the crucial theme of divine presence and guidance, now rendered problematic after the lapse into false worship. How could the divine presence be experienced once Sinai was left behind? Did Israel have to resign itself to the absence of its God, or at best to some surrogate for the divine presence? This is the issue which a people threatened with exile, or actually experiencing it, would find themselves confronting. These episodes, and indeed the entire Sinai pericope in its final form, were designed to address this problem.

The command to leave Sinai behind is repeated (33:1 cf. 32:34), but in this last phase of the journey YHWH will no longer be with them in person but will be represented by the angel-emissary, an eventuality anticipated earlier (23:20–23). On hearing the bad news the people give expression to their mourning and repentance by removing the jewelry that had been the occasion for their downfall. This last point is one of several indications that 33:1–6 continues the story of the apostasy and its aftermath, and is therefore of D provenance (Noth, *Exodus* 1962 [1959], 253 against Beyerlin 1965 [1961], 98–112 who divides it between J and two strands of E). Pointing in the same direction are the role of the *malʾak* (cf. 23:20 and 32:34), the list of indigenous peoples, and such typically Deuteronomic expressions as "the land running with milk and honey" and "the stiff-necked people." Ex 33:12–17 pursues the same theme of presence and guidance, but Moses seems to be unaware of the promise of the angel-emissary as guide. This section, closed in with an inclusion (vv 12 and 17), also has some affinity with the larger context (cf. 34:9) but may well be a later elaboration. It recalls the guiding presence alluded to in Deut 4:37—in an exilic passage—and "the angel of his presence" in a lamentation preserved in Isa 63–64 (63:9).

The account of the remaking of the covenant (34:1–28) is preceded and followed by passages the purpose of which is to explore the unique status of Moses (33:18–23; 34:29–35). We have had occasion to note this structuring device of framing or bracketing more than once; in this instance it seems to have the purpose of expatiating on certain features of the bracketed narrative. It may therefore be suggested that the preceding paragraph is interpreting the phrase "YHWH passed before him (i.e., Moses)" in 34:6 which, when transposed into the first person, is rephrased, "I will make all my goodness pass before you" (33:19).[7] In other words, the passage sets out to explain, after the manner of midrash, how YHWH could have passed in front of Moses without causing his death; for it is axiomatic that no one can see (the face of) God and live. The solution provides a good example of narrative generating more narrative. YHWH covered Moses' face with his hand so that Moses saw the godhead only after he had passed by. The explanation also posits a relationship between the face *(pānîm)* and the effulgence *(kābôd),* perhaps in the sense that they are, so to speak, respectively the recto and the verso of the godhead. These speculations take us back to the experience of worship, for it is in the act of worship that one "sees the face." [8] And beyond that again, we hear the language of age-old courtly protocol as, for example, when a petty Asiatic ruler, writing to the Egyptian chancellery, asks rhetorically, "when shall I see the face of my lord the king?"[9]

The paragraph following the remade covenant (Ex 34:29–35) records how, when Moses finally came down the mountain with the two "tablets of the testimony," his face was transformed from intimate contact with the godhead. The verb *qāran,* which occurs three times here but is otherwise unattested, was interpreted by Aquila in the second century A.D. to mean that Moses had sprouted horns during his stay on the mountain. It was this idea, perpetuated through Jerome's Vulgate *(ignorabat quod facies eius cornuta esset),* which gave rise to the strange iconographic tradition best known from Michelangelo's statue in the Church of San Pietro in Vincoli in Rome. The reason for this strange aberration is the similarity between this rare verb and *qeren, qarnayim* ("horn, pair of horns") but, needless to say, the context demands the idea of shining, glowing, or something of the sort.[10] That Moses covered his face with a veil or scarf *(masweh,* unfortunately another hapax legomenon) except when communicating with God was clearly not in order to protect the onlookers from this fearful and numinous phenomenon; for if he could speak to them without the *masweh,* why put it on afterward? The point seems rather to emphasize the divine origin and radiance of the law revealed by God and the unique status of Moses as intermediary, which is also the meaning hinted at by Paul in 2 Cor 3:7. Together with the passage preceding the remade covenant, 34:29–35 belongs to a late, perhaps the latest stage in the compilation of the Sinai story. It is both a fitting conclusion to that story and an appropriate introduction to the setting up of the instruments of worship which follows.

THE COVENANT LAW BOOK (Ex 20:21–23:19)

This earliest compilation of Israelite laws takes its name from the document written by Moses and read publicly by him as an essential feature of the Sinai/Horeb covenant (Ex 24:3–8).[11] According to the narrative context it was delivered privately to Moses following the promulgation of the decalogue and the request of the faithful, fearful of longer exposure to the divine presence, that Moses act as intermediary. The course of events as described in Deuteronomy 5 follows the same order, with the important difference that the Deuteronomic law (12–26) takes the place of the covenant law book.[12] We are no doubt meant to understand that the promulgation of this updated law book on the eve of the occupation of the land was necessitated by the illegitimate cult offered at the altar built by Aaron (Ex 32:1–6). And in fact the most prominent difference between the two collections is the altar law that introduces both (Ex 20:24–26; Deut 12:1–28).

Arrangement of the Laws

The covenant law book begins and ends with cultic prescriptions (20:23–26; 23:13–19), providing one more illustration of bracketing or ring composition. More precisely, the final admonition against invoking deities other than YHWH (23:13) forms an inclusion with 20:23–26 prohibiting the making, and presumably also the invoking, of images of deities. This overall structure carries the message that societal relations are to be regulated in a context in which the proper relationship to God is first defined. The final section (23:14–19), which is closely related to the so-called cultic decalogue (34:17–26), has been tacked on as an appendix.

There can be no doubt that, with the exception of some editorial embellishments, this compilation existed independently prior to its insertion into the Sinai/Horeb story. The prohibition against making gold or silver images of deities (20:23) connects with the decalogue (20:3) and anticipates the Golden Calf incident and the remaking of the covenant (32; 34:17). This prohibition differs from the injunctions following in the use of the plural form of address; since the preceding verses are cast in the D style, it may be read as the D introduction to the compilation. The altar law, which assumes the legitimacy of multiple places of worship and sacrifice, is abrogated by the D law of cult centralization and points to an important innovation introduced by D. According to Dtr the suppression of the provincial sanctuaries was an important aspect of the reforms of both Hezekiah and Josiah (2 Kings 18:4; 19:22; 23:5, 8–9, 19–20). Archaeological evidence from the Judean sanctuary at Arad has been adduced in support of the historicity of these reforms,[13] but it would be rash to conclude from this one piece of evidence that the measure was uniformly successful.

Ex 21:1 introduces a series of sixteen ordinances *(mišpātîm)* in the form of case law, of a kind attested in all the extant collections from the ancient Near East. These legal decisions form the nucleus of the first part of the document (21:1–22:19 [21:1–22:20]), and the nucleus has been expanded by the addition of apodictic laws covering acts subject to the death penalty (21:12–17; 22:17–19 [22:18–20]). The scope of the case law collection is quite limited, covering as it does such diverse matters as slavery or indentured service, torts, injury inflicted by rogue oxen, bailment, sheep rustling, and property damage, including loss resulting from the seduction of an unmarried virgin daughter. These stipulations are far from comprehensive in scope and therefore in no way constitute a law code as we would understand the term. They contain only a selection of remedial measures concerning problematic issues arising in the course of time. What was part of familiar and unproblematic customary law, falling under the jurisdiction of the paterfamilias, was passed over in silence.

All but one of the apodictic sentences specifying the death penalty are in the participial form. The first of the seven, dealing with homicide, may serve to illustrate this terse and forceful legal genre:

makkēh ʾîš wāmēt môt yûmāt, literally

the striker of a man so that he dies shall surely be put to death

The peremptory requirement of this particular penalty is emphasized by the threefold repetition of the verb "to die" in a sentence of five words. In this instance, however, a codicil is added distinguishing between kill-

ing without premeditation and homicide with malice aforethought, and
therefore between cases where the law of sanctuary applies and where it
does not. Four of these death penalty sentences interrupt the series of case
laws (21:12–17), the insertion no doubt having been suggested by the case
of nonfatal injury inflicted in a brawl (21:18–19). The other three,
specifying the death penalty for sorcery, bestiality, and non-Yahwistic cult
acts (22:17–19 [22:18–20]), have been added as a coda at the end. Since the
last of the three proclaims the sovereignty of YHWH in the legal
community, it is probably not accidental that it stands exactly at the
midpoint of the document (Halbe 1975, 421).

The second half of the document (beginning at 22:20) is in several
respects quite different. In the first place, most of the stipulations are of
the apodictic kind, and of these the majority are in the negative ("you
shall not"), though there are instances of contamination with the casuistic
or case law type (22:24, 30 [22:23, 29]; 23:4–5). Then also, it is only in this
section that motivation is provided for the observance of the laws, and it
will be obvious that these motivation clauses are significant for grasping
the fundamental intent of the laws (Gemser 1953; Sonsino 1980). The two
legal statements about the resident alien *(gēr)* seem to have been placed
deliberately at the beginning and end of a section dealing primarily with
matters of social justice (22:20 [22:21]; 23:9), and this arrangement may be
taken to convey a message about the point and purpose of the law in
general. Only here is appeal made to the collective historical memory of
the community:

> You shall not wrong an alien or oppress him; for you were
>   aliens in the land of Egypt.

> You shall not oppress an alien; you know what it means to
>   be an alien, for you were aliens in the land of Egypt.

This stylistic inclusion sets the tone for the other laws designed to protect
the disadvantaged in that society, including widows and orphans (i.e., the
fatherless), fellow-Israelites forced into debt by indigence, the debtor who
has been obliged to pawn his outer garment (a law alluded to in Amos
2:8), and even the straying or distressed animal of a competitor. The laws
are therefore the means toward realizing an ideal of justice consonant with
the historical consciousness of Israel. The unique element is not so much
in the humanitarian provisions themselves, most of which can be
paralleled in other ancient Near Eastern compilations, but in the different
ways in which they give form and substance to a historically specific
societal ideal.

Some of the apodictic sentences in this second section appear to be more directly related to actual judicial procedures involving the activity of judges, plaintiffs, and witnesses. The suggestion has in fact been made that the laws in 23:1–3, 6–8 constitute a decalogue reflecting usage in a Hebrew court of law, perhaps even serving as an inaugural oath for judges (McKay 1971, following Auerbach, *VT* 16 [1966], 255–76). The original form of the decalogue, it is argued, would have been something like the following:

1. You shall not utter a false report
2. You shall not conspire with the one in the wrong by being a malicious witness
3. You shall not follow the majority in evildoing
4. When testifying, you shall not follow the majority in perverting justice
5. You shall not be partial to a person of standing in his suit[14]
6. You shall not pervert the justice due to the poor person in his suit
7. Be far removed from a false charge
8. Do not slay the innocent or the one in the right
9. Do not give judgment in favor of the one in the wrong[15]
10. Do not accept a bribe

It will be seen that here, as in the more familiar decalogue, most but not all of the stipulations are in the negative. While the decalogue hypothesis, elaborated with the help of some textual emendation, may be correct, it was certainly not for the exclusive use of judges who, among other things, did not serve as witnesses. It seems more likely that it would have served to guide the entire community in the vital task of preserving the judicial process from subversion and corruption.

Early Stages in the Development of the Legal Tradition

Our brief analysis of the components of the covenant law book provides a fairly broad sample of Hebrew law at an early stage of development. Many attempts have been made to fix the date of the compilation more precisely, ranging from the time of Moses (e.g., Cazelles 1946) to the reign of Jehu in the ninth century. Perhaps all we can safely say is that (1) its final redaction antedates the Deuteronomic law book, and (2) the *mišpāṭîm* presuppose a peasant agrarian society (pastureland, vineyards, oxen, etc.), and therefore a situation obtaining some time after settlement in Canaan. The almost complete absence of allusion to political institutions[16]

—in marked contrast to the Deuteronomic law—does not necessarily pre-suppose origin in the prestate period. The scope is clearly more limited than the D compilation, and it is also possible that the compiler aimed to present an idealized traditional society over against the pretensions of the monarchy and the state apparatus (Halbe 1975). While there are many incidents recorded in the Pentateuch and Dtr illustrative of legal custom at the time indicated, or at least at the time of writing, few if any of them clearly and unambiguously refer to stipulations in the covenant law book. We have seen that Amos castigates his contemporaries for failing to return the pawned cloak at nightfall (Amos 2:8), which suggests that this law, and perhaps the collection as a whole, was known in the eighth century B.C. The closest estimate may therefore be some time during the two centuries prior to the fall of the Northern Kingdom in 722 B.C.

Before the beginning of the present century it was possible for all sorts of claims on behalf of Israelite law to go unchallenged, since the laws in the Hebrew Bible were the only ancient Near Eastern laws then known. This was to change when, during the winter of 1901 and 1902, the French archaeologist Jacques de Morgan unearthed the law stele of the Babylo-nian king Hammurabi in the citadel of Susa (Shushan), ancient capital city of the Elamites. The stele, now in the Louvre, represents the king receiv-ing the laws from the god Shamash, who had presumably written them himself. The 282 laws, couched in the casuistic form, are enclosed within a lengthy prologue and epilogue praising the king as the protector of justice *(ANET* 163–80). They were engraved toward the beginning of Hammu-rabi's reign (ca. 1728–1686 B.C.), but of course derive from a legal tradition of greater antiquity. Since the discovery of this important text other collec-tions, for the most part fragmentary, have come to light. These include laws promulgated by Ur-Nammu, founder of the third dynasty of Ur, in the late third millennium *(ANET* 523–55), the laws of Lipit-Ishtar, ruler of Isin, about two centuries later *(ANET* 159–61), laws of the city of Eshnunna excavated at Tell Abū Harmal near Baghdad *(ANET* 161–63), Hittite and Assyrian laws from the fourteenth and twelfth centuries re-spectively, and finally, Neo-Babylonian laws from the sixth century B.C., the only ones later in date than the covenant law book *(ANET* 180–98). To these we can add the edict *(mišarum)* of Ammisaduqa king of Babylon (second half of the seventeenth century B.C.), the only fairly complete example of the genre *(ANET* 526–28), treaty stipulations illustrative of what might be called international law, and numerous contracts exemplify-ing different aspects of customary law regarding property, marriage, inher-itance, and the like.

Reading the covenant law book against the background of this exten-sive corpus of cuneiform law reveals the extent to which early Israel ap-propriated an ancient and widespread legal tradition. It would be natural to assume that this appropriation took place via Canaanite common law, though unfortunately no Canaanite laws have come down to us. More specifically, the first section of the law book containing the *mišpāṭîm* betrays very little of a uniquely Israelite character. There is the law concerning Hebrew slaves–if the term is understood to be a gentilic–and the oath in the name of YHWH (22:19 [22:20]), but that is all. The second section, on the contrary, with its appeal to historical memory, has a more marked Israelite character, especially since the prohibition of non-Yahwistic cults occupies the center of the compilation (22:19 [22:20]). It is therefore principally, though not exclusively, in the case law that we find agreement with the common legal tradition that was taken over in most parts of the Near East, with local adaptations, from the Sumerian city states of the third millennium B.C.

It lies beyond the scope of our study to engage in a detailed comparative study of these case laws; suffice it to say that practically all of the *mišpāṭîm* in the first section can be paralleled more or less closely in cuneiform law. The parade example is the case of the goring ox, either onetime offender or recidivist, and the various penalties and remedies for injuries inflicted on persons or animals (Ex 21:28–32, 35–36). Fairly close parallels exist in the Sumerian laws *(ANET* 163, 526) and in the Hammurabi Code (#250–52; *ANET #*176). We note a peculiar feature of the biblical laws, that the rogue ox which has killed is subject to judicial execution and its flesh is taboo on account of blood guilt. It is claimed that this follows from a specifically Israelite religious premise (cf. Gen 9:5: "for your lifeblood I will surely require a reckoning; of every beast I will require it, and of man"), but it must be added that there are other examples in legal history of judicial guilt contracted by animals. It should also be noted that the death sentence for criminal negligence on the part of an animal's owner can be commuted.[17]

A more interesting and controversial case is that of injury to a pregnant woman resulting in miscarriage. This difficult text (Ex 21:22–23) may be translated more or less literally as follows:

> When men fight and injure a pregnant woman so that her children come out but there is no serious harm, he [i.e., the party responsible] must surely be fined according as the woman's husband shall impose on him, and he shall pay as the assessors determine. But if serious harm follows, you shall give a life for a life.

The following points call for comment: (1) it is assumed that the injurious act is unintentional, and therefore a civil tort rather than subject to criminal proceedings; (2) "her children" *(yĕlādēhā)* may be a textual error (plural instead of singular), or it may refer to the dislodging of parts of the fetus, but in any case does not limit the scope of the law to multiple births; (3) the "serious harm" (*'āsôn,* a word of infrequent occurrence) refers to the mother rather than the fetus, and the concluding part of the law implies a fatal injury; (4) "as the assessors determine" *(biplilim,* only here, in Deut 32:31 and Job 31:11) is quite uncertain, but it probably refers to a restriction on the discretionary power of the husband; (5) the concluding part of the law imposing the death penalty if the woman dies (depending on the meaning assigned to *'āsôn,* above) is problematic; it is in the second rather than the third person, and would constitute a notable exception to the otherwise widely attested distinction in Israelite law between intentional and unintentional acts; (6) if the preceding conclusions are correct, it would appear that the fetus is not regarded as a person subject to the protection of the law.

It should be emphasized that this is only one of several interpretations of this difficult law, and it should be noted that LXX translates the crucial term *'āsôn* with the Greek *exeikonismenon [paidion],* meaning "fully formed." This means that the Greek translator has shifted the focus from the mother to the fetus by introducing a distinction between different stages of pregnancy. Here, too, comparison with cuneiform law is illuminating, but not to the point of solving all the outstanding problems. In most cases the injury to the woman is deliberately inflicted, the only exception being a Sumerian law which distinguishes between intentional and unintentional acts *(ANET* 525). The Hammurabi Code specifies that compensation is for the loss of the fetus, not because the fetus enjoyed legal rights but because children were a particularly valuable commodity in that society. It adds, however, that if the woman dies as a result of the injury, the daughter of the offending party is to be put to death *(ANET* 175). The Middle Assyrian law is even harsher, in that the wife of the offending party is to be put to death to compensate for the loss of the fetus resulting from a non-fatal injury. In the event of a fatal injury, or a nonfatal·injury to a childless woman resulting in a miscarriage irrespective of the sex of the child, the offending party himself is subject to the death penalty *(ANET* 184–85). The Hittite laws alone distinguish between stages of pregnancy, imposing a fine of ten shekels of silver for the tenth month and half of that sum for the fifth month *(ANET* 190).

The biblical law has been rounded off with the *lex talionis* (an eye for an eye, a tooth for a tooth, etc.), a legal axiom often quoted by the uninformed as typifying an Old Testament (and therefore Jewish) ethic as opposed to the Christian love ethic (cf. Mt 5:38–42). Suffice it to say that the axiom is by no means confined to the Hebrew Bible. It occurs, and is applied literally, in the Hammurabi Code and in Roman law, and it is very probable that in Israelite legal practice, in which mutilation is extremely rare (Lev 24:19–20 and Deut 25:11–12 are the sole instances, and we have no evidence that they were implemented), the *lex talionis* came to stand for equivalent monetary compensation. And even where it was understood literally, as in the Hammurabi Code, its intent was not only retributive but restrictive, substituting the principle of equity for recourse to the wholesale and indiscriminate settling of accounts.[18]

APODICTIC LAWS IN SERIES: THE DECALOGUE

Apodictic Law

As the name suggests, a case law is a specific kind of legal article that states the facts of the case in the protasis ("when a person does X") and the legal consequences in the apodosis ("then Y follows"). A common-law tradition develops through the gradual accumulation of such precedents covering different aspects of the social life of the individual. Our information on the judicial mechanisms by which such decisions were reached, formulated, and implemented in early Israel is not, sadly, very abundant. Like other traditional societies, Israel in the earliest period was organized according to a network of kinship relationships. Kinship structures in such societies, including Israel, have been much discussed in recent years. If we are guided by the incident in which Achan was identified as the violator of the ban during the conquest (Josh 7:16–18), we would have the following picture: the nuclear unit was the household or extended family *(bayit)*, several of which formed a clan or phratry *(mišpāḥāh)*, a number of such units constituting a tribe *(šēbeṭ)*. As long as this form of social organization was maintained as constituting the principal coordinates of the social life of the individual, legal authority was vested in the clan and tribal elders *(zĕqēnîm)*, with certain functions—the administration of oaths and decision by sacred lot—reserved to the local priesthood (e.g., Ex 21:6; 22:7, 8, 10 [22:8, 9, 11]). Within the kinship network an ethical consensus could be reached and transmitted without great difficulty, and a wide range of resources were at hand to enforce compliance.

With increasing urban development this basic system would clearly have undergone modification, as a comparison between the covenant law book and the Deuteronomic law will show (e.g., in the latter the parents no longer have absolute discretion in dealing with an ungovernable son; Deut 21:18–21). The more formal procedures now in place were administered by a panel of city elders, the preferred location being the open plaza by the city gate complex (e.g., Ruth 4:1–6). The scope of intratribal jurisdiction would have been further limited by the state bureaucracy and the creation of a distinct judiciary with a central court of appeal composed of clerical and lay members. According to the Chronicler this new instrument was created during the reign of Jehoshaphat in the ninth century (2 Chron

19:5–11; cf. Deut 17:8–13). In due course a distinct class of law scribes came into existence—we hear of these "handlers of the law" for the first time in Jer 2:8 and 8:8—and it is reasonable to assume that it was to such legal experts that we owe the drafting of collections of case law.

Case law presupposes an underlying ethical consensus transmitted from one generation to the next within the kinship network. Certain attitudes and kinds of behavior are recognized as incompatible with the common ethos of the social group; certain things are "not done in Israel" (e.g., Judg 19:30; 2 Sam 13:12). This moral consensus finds expression in a variety of forms, including traditional narrative, proverbs, and instructions handed down within the family. Similar in function are those ethical and legal sentences classified as apodictic law that help to shape and maintain Israel as a moral community. Discussion of this category of statement continues to pivot on the seminal paper of Albrecht Alt written more than half a century ago in which the term "apodictic law" first appeared (Alt 1966 [1934], 79–132). Alt identified several different types of apodictic sentence which, unlike case law, dealt in broad moral imperatives and prohibitions universally binding as a direct expression of the divine will. He concluded that these apodictic sentences of law were peculiar to Israel, that they originated in the earliest period of its history, and that they were recited in the covenant renewal festival of the Israelite amphictyony before the emergence of the state.

In the decades since Alt wrote, it has become part of the received wisdom to reject his claim that the apodictic formulation is a uniquely Israelite creation. Several scholars have pointed to similarities with the stipulations of vassal treaties (following the well-known essay of Mendenhall, 1955), others have sought parallels in Egyptian and Mesopotamian instructions, especially in prohibitions addressed to the "son" (i.e., the pupil), and comparisons have also been made with the Egyptian Books of the Dead containing lists of forbidden acts (e.g., stealing, adultery, pederasty) and with Assyrian lists of sins. Alt's cultic setting for the apodictic laws is also frequently rejected in favor of the kind of collective wisdom transmitted by the tribal elders (Gerstenberger, 1965). All these comparisons are, however, seriously vitiated by the failure to distinguish between different kinds of formulation covered by the apodictic category. Alt himself made the necessary distinctions but failed to consider the possibility that each type might have a distinct origin and social location. A survey of the laws in the Pentateuch as a whole obliges us to distinguish between the following kinds of formulation:

(1) Legal sentences referring in the participial form to those guilty of acts subject to the death penalty, attested in the covenant law book (Ex 21:12–17; 22:18–19 [22:19–20]) and infrequently elsewhere (Lev 24:16, 18,

21b). An example already cited would be: "The striker of a man so that he dies must surely be put to death" (Ex 21:12). Other capital punishment sentences are formulated differently (Lev 20:2, 9–16; 24:17; Num 35:16–21).

(2) Sentences placing under a curse those guilty of particularly heinous offenses (Deut 27:15–26). Example: "Cursed be he who dishonors his father or his mother" (Deut 27:16). These deal with acts committed in secret (Deut 27:24) and which can therefore be detected and punished only by God, hence the curse formula.

(3) Brief statements prohibiting certain acts ("You shall not . . ."), therefore formulated with few exceptions in the negative. Several examples have been noted in the covenant law book, but they are of fairly frequent occurrence elsewhere; e.g., in the so-called ritual decalogue (Ex 34:17, 25, 26b) and a list of forbidden sexual relations (Lev 18:6–23). See also Lev 19:2–18, in which the forms are mixed, and Deut 25:13–15.

There are significant differences between these types of legal or quasilegal sentences. While they would certainly have required further interpretation, those listing capital offenses are quite specific, and the same can be said for several of the prohibitions, especially the detailed list of forbidden sexual relations in Leviticus 18. In this respect they differ notably from the general and comprehensive articles of the decalogue. The curse formulas in Deuteronomy 27 are also distinctive not only in formulation but also in specifying acts committed in secret. They are also the only ones placed in an explicitly cultic setting. These distinctions, often overlooked, must be borne in mind in any discussion of the origin and development of Israel's legal traditions.

The Decalogue

Apodictic laws are characteristically presented in series. This does not emerge very clearly in the covenant law book since they have been edited into the larger framework of a collection of case law. The seven apodictic sentences in the first section have, in fact, been inserted at two different points, as have the prohibitions, possibly amounting to ten, in the second section (23:1–3, 6–9). A decalogue has also been identified in Ex 34:13–26, though in its present form the covenant contains either eleven articles or twelve if v 13 is included. Some commentators have also reduced the twelve curse formulas in Deuteronomy 27 to a decalogue by redescribing the first and last as prologue and epilogue. Our final example is the list of twelve forbidden degrees of sexual relationship in Leviticus 18. In this instance Elliger has transformed a dodecalogue into a decalogue by the more dubious procedure of omitting two of the articles (in vv 17–18) as "secondary" (Elliger, 1955).

The most familiar of these series is, of course, the one that is explicitly designated a decalogue in the biblical record (Ex 34:28;[19] Deut 4:13; 10:4). The Pentateuch contains two versions (Ex 20:2–17; Deut 5:6–21), another version has come down to us in the Nash papyrus from about 100 B.C., and fragments of the decalogue have turned up at Qumran, including the phylacteries published by Yigael Yadin *(Tefillin from Qumran* [Jerusalem, 1969]). While the version in Deuteronomy fits naturally into the narrative context, which speaks of a revelation at Horeb during which YHWH promulgated the decalogue directly to the assembly, it is generally assumed that the Exodus version was at some point inserted into the narrative. On the assumption, defended earlier, that a D editor played an important part in the production of that narrative, it is entirely possible that the same hand was responsible for the insertion.

Several commentators give the impression that the Exodus version represents P and the Deuteronomy version D, but the evidence for this is exiguous at best. The sabbath command in Ex 20:11 does refer back to creation, but without using language characteristic of P *('āśāh* not *bārā', wayyānah* not *wayyišbot).* A closer scrutiny will in fact show that the language of Ex 20:2–17 is no less Deuteronomic than that of Deut 5:6–21. The following list of typically Deuteronomic expressions and turns of phrase speaks for itself:

The introductory address ("I am YHWH your God . . ."); cf. Deut 6:12; 7:8; 8:14. "YHWH your God" is one of the most characteristically Deuteronomic ways of referring to the deity.

"other gods" *('ĕlohîm 'ăḥērîm),* also frequent in D material

"graven image and likeness," *(pesel, tĕmûnāh)* terms occurring together only in Deuteronomy (4:16, 23, 25).

YHWH, a jealous (passionate) God *('ēl qannā'),* occurring only in D writings (Ex 34:14 [D]; Deut 4:24; 6:15).

The connection between loving God and keeping the commandments is typically Deuteronomic (Deut 6:5)

"the alien in your gates"; cf. Deut 14:21, 29; 16:14; 31:12.

"that your days may be long in the land . . ." cf. Deut 4:40; 11:9; 25:15; 30:18; 32:47.

false witness *('ēd šeqer);* cf. Deut 19:18.

It is therefore quite clear that *both* versions have a marked Deuteronomic character. Since most of the features listed occur in what .appear to be amplifications of originally terse apodictic sentences, all but two of which are prohibitions, we are dealing with Deuteronomic refashioning of a brief catechism of basic ethical imperatives. Several attempts have been made to reconstruct the original series (see Stamm and Andrew 1967 [1958]; Nielsen 1968 [1965] and commentaries). On the assumption that the original form has been preserved in some of the stipulations (murder, adultery, stealing, bearing false witness), it would have looked something like the following:[20]

1. You shall have no other gods before me
2. You shall not make for yourself a graven image
3. You shall not utter YHWH's name for wrong purposes
4. Observe the sabbath day to keep it holy[21]
5. Honor your father and your mother
6. Do not commit murder
7. Do not commit adultery
8. Do not steal
9. Do not bear false witness against your neighbor
10. Do not covet your neighbor's house

The two variants would therefore represent more developed forms of a kind of moral catechism listing basic obligations to God and the neighbor. Some of these (1, 4, 10) have been considerably amplified, and others (2, 3, 4, 5) have acquired motivation clauses. By the time of the D redaction the order was standardized, though this did not prevent them being cited in a different order at a latter time (e.g., Mt 19:18–19; Rom 13:9).

Little can be said with any assurance about the origin and early development of this proto-decalogue prior to its adoption and expansion by the Deuteronomists. Sigmund Mowinckel of Oslo University, one of the most prolific Old Testament scholars of the first half of this century, was the first to draw attention to a decalogue of requirements in Ps 15 which he took to be part of an entrance liturgy, defining ethical qualifications for participating in worship (Mowinckel, 1927). This led him to propose a cultic origin for the decalogue, a suggestion taken up in the important essay of Albrecht Alt referred to earlier. Alt, however, transferred the decalogue to the center of the covenant renewal liturgy celebrated every seven years at the feast of Sukkoth (Deut 31:10–13). The reading of the decalogue may well have been a feature of such occasions, but that is not to say that it originated in or was generated by the cult in the way Mowinckel seemed to suggest. It would be safer to assume that it developed as a distillation of the ethical *sensus communis* of the community over a long period of time. Thus, it is no surprise to find prophets appealing to these basic ethical requirements in their teaching:

> There is swearing, lying, killing, stealing, and committing adultery;
> they break all bounds, and murder follows murder (Hos 4:2).

> Will you steal, murder, commit adultery, swear falsely, burn incense to Baal, and go after other gods that you have not known, and then come and stand before me in this house? (Jer 7:9–10)

The different order confirms the suspicion that several versions may have been in circulation before standardization by the Deuteronomists.

Somewhat surprisingly, the decalogue did not play a prominent role in the formative period of Judaism following on the revolts against Rome. Nor did it provide the basis for the vast and complex legal system of the Mishnah, which in fact refers to it only twice (m. Tamid 5:1; m. Taanit 4:6). One reason may have been the Christian appropriation of the decalogue as a basis for moral instruction (e.g., in the *Didache),* especially in view of the prominence given to it at the expense of the ritual law. According to m. Tamid 5:1 it was recited during the period of the Second Temple, and should have been joined to the Shema, but its recital was discontinued "due to the cavils of the heretics *(minîm)"*—presumably Christians. It has continued to function, nevertheless, as a fundamental statement of moral requirements for many Jews and Christians down to the present.

THE SECOND LAW

The Laws in Deuteronomy

The title Deuteronomy, with its even less elegant derivatives Deuterono-mic and Deuteronomistic, comes to us from the Old Greek (LXX) translation of Deut 17:18 and Josh 8:32. These texts refer to the writing, by the king and Joshua, respectively, of a copy *(mišneh)* of the law of Moses, and it is generally assumed that the Greek version mistakenly took this to mean a second law. But it is difficult to imagine how the translator could have made such a mistake with such a common and straightforward word as *mišneh,* and use of *deuteronomion,* rather than *deuteron nomon* (second law), suggests that this title was already in use at the time of writing. This in its turn leads us to conclude that the character of the book, as a law and covenant additional and subsequent to those of Sinai/Horeb, was already recognized at that time—not surprisingly, since that is what the book itself says (Deut 28:69 [29:1]).

The account of Joshua's covenant making at Shechem in Josh 8:30–35, clearly of D origin, states that he constructed the altar according to the law in the book of the covenant (Ex 20:25) and read aloud the blessing and the curse contained in the book of the law. Since the book of the covenant contains no blessings and curses, it would appear that the author envisages both Exodus 20–23 and Deuteronomy as comprising the revealed law of Moses. This seems to point to a very late stage when the different legal compilations had been brought together into a comprehensive collection. The implication would then be that the laws in Deuteronomy 12–26 were understood as an exposition, expansion, and, at certain points (e.g., the altar law), correction of the covenant law book delivered at Horeb. We have no reason to believe that the covenant law book and the Deuterono-mic law were thought to be so mutually contradictory that they could not coexist in one and the same comprehensive legal corpus.

It therefore seems mistaken to conclude (with Eissfeldt 1966, 221) that the Deuteronomic law was intended to supplant the covenant law book. There are cases where an earlier stipulation is modified or neutralized by a later provision, but without necessitating the suppression of the former. The redactor of the sanctuary law in Deuteronomy 12, for example, was perfectly aware that the older stipulation no longer met the needs of the contemporary situation (Deut 12:8–9). That only slightly more than one third of the articles in the covenant law book appear in Deuteronomy, for the most part with considerable modification and in a different sequence, would not have constituted an insuperable obstacle. The redactor(s) of the laws in Deuteronomy would, we imagine, have seen the task as reformu-lating and expanding the Horeb legislation in keeping with the more evolved social situation at the time of writing. Hence the emphasis on the city (e.g., Deut 13:12–18; 16:18–20; 22:23–29), on trade practices (e.g., 25:13–16), and especially on the role of different institutions, including the cult, within a centralized state system (e.g., Deuteronomy 12:17–18).

Many attempts have been made to discover a basic organizing principle behind the order in which the laws in Deuteronomy 12–26 are presented (Merendino 1969; Seitz 1971, 92–95; Carmichael 1985; Braulik 1985, 252–72). Since none of them has proved to be entirely convincing, we should perhaps simply note that the first half of the corpus (Chapters 12–18) deals for the most part with cultic matters, while the second half (19–25, omit-ting the distinctive final chapter) has to do for the most part with judicial and, in the broad sense, secular affairs.[22] This rough division draws our attention to the passage about the role of Moses and of prophets in the line of succession to Moses located at the center of the law (18:15–22). Since according to the D perspective the prophet has the divinely commissioned task of proclaiming the law, this passage in context serves to validate the Deuteronomic law and legitimate those responsible for its promulgation and implementation.

Whatever order may have existed has, at any rate, been obscured by displacements and additions made from the time it was first drafted, probably during the reign of Josiah (640–609 B.C.), to the point at which it achieved canonical fixity. It is still possible, notwithstanding, to pick out some of the individual units of which it is composed. The law of the sanctuary at the beginning and the offering of firstfruits and tithes at the end (12:2–27; 26:1–15) serve as bookends, emphasizing the intimate link in Deuteronomy between the law and the gift of the land. The sanctuary law also illustrates the cumulative editorial process behind the final draft, since an original nucleus (12:13–19) has been expanded with an amendment (vv 20–27) and a parenetic introduction characteristic of the exilic Deuteronomist (vv 1–12, or at least 8–12) (Seitz 1971, 187–222; Mayes 1979, 221–30). The position of the sanctuary law at the beginning of the compilation (cf. Ex 20:24–26; Lev 17:1–9) corresponds to the societal role of the temple as an emblem of collective identity in the ancient Near East in general and the Second Commonwealth in particular.

Another distinct section follows consisting in three anti-idolatry laws modeled on the case law formula and framed by exhortation in the characteristic protreptic D style (12:28; 13:19 [13:18]). The first of these, dealing with apostate prophets, may at one time have belonged to a series of death penalty sentences ending with the formula "you shall purge the evil from your midst" (17:7, 12; 19:13, 19; 21:9, 21; 22:21, 22, 24; 24:7) (L'Hour 1963, 1–28; Merendino 1969, 336–45). The following purity laws, also rounded off with an inclusion ("you are a people holy to YHWH your God," 14:2–21), catalogue clean and unclean fauna. This section too has a history of its own, since it appears to be an alternative version of the catalogue in Leviticus 11 augmented with a list of ten clean animals (14:4–5). It may be one of several examples of late Priestly editing, perhaps from the time when Deuteronomy was incorporated into the P history.

There follows a series of religious duties including the annual and triennial tithes, the septennial remission of debt and manumission of slaves, the pilgrim festivals, and the obligation incumbent on males to visit the sanctuary three times a year (14:22–16:17). The section has a certain unity, since it is an updated version of Ex 23:10–19 and 34:18–26, but it differs from these earlier enactments in its strongly educational and exhortatory character and its evident intent to foster a sense of national unity through worship. It also manifests a stronger sense of social responsibility, particularly in evidence in the innovation of the triennial tithe for the disadvantaged (14:28–29) and the more humane provisions of the slavery law, especially with respect to female slaves (15:12–18; cf. Ex 21:2–6).

Even more distinctive in character is the section following (16:18–18:22), in which the character of Deuteronomy as a civic constitution, a *politeia,* is most clearly in evidence. It deals with various aspects of the state apparatus, including the judiciary, monarchy, cult personnel and, most significantly, prophecy. The enactment concerning judges, in which prophetic influence is most clearly discernible ("justice, only justice you shall pursue"), is followed by three apodictic laws concerning cultic offenses, a good example of the close association between ethics and cult (16:21–17:1). The last of these is one of several "abomination" laws (featuring the word *tôʿēbāh),* probably quite ancient, dealing primarily with cultic disorders (see also 18:12; 22:5; 23:18; 24:4; 25:16).

Order is less apparent in the later part of the compilation, though there is some grouping of stipulations concerning homicide (19:1–21) and the conduct of warfare (20:1–21:14). Of particular interest is the "law of the assembly," which excludes certain categories from membership in the commonwealth *(qāhāl),* and therefore from participation in worship (23:2–9 [23:1–8]). Those excluded are (1) the sexually mutilated, an extension to the entire community of the provisions governing eligibility for the priesthood (Lev 21:17–21); (2) "bastards" *(mamzĕrîm),* widely understood as offspring of incestuous unions (cf. 23:1 [22:30]), though the only other occurrence of the word in the Hebrew Bible refers to the hybrid population of Ashdod (Zech 9:6; cf. Neh 13:23–27); (3) Ammonites and Moabites *in perpetuum,* though the acceptance into the Jewish community of Ruth from Moab and Achior from Ammon (Judith 14:10) illustrates the survival of a more open policy; (4) first- and second-generation Edomites and Egyptians. This law is of uncertain origin. Several scholars have followed Kurt Galling (1950, 176–91), who argued that these disqualifications were applied in border sanctuaries in the pre-monarchic period. But this explanation does not cover physical disabilities, and it seems more likely that the individual stipulations, some of which may well be ancient, were assembled by the more exclusivist elements in the post-exilic temple community whose position is well documented in Ezra-Nehemiah. The law was certainly of actuality at that time (e.g., Neh 13:1–3), and indeed long afterward (e.g., in the Qumran community; see 1QSa 2:4–9). That it did not go unchallenged is apparent from Isa 56:1–8, which in effect abrogates a point of law on prophetic authority, a precedent of some significance for the future.

The Framework of the Laws

Compared with the covenant law book, or the Code of Hammurabi with its prologue and epilogue, the laws in Deuteronomy are presented in a highly distinctive fashion. Scholars are accustomed to speak of the law code in Chapters 12–26 and the framework to the code in the remaining chapters, but the laws are simply a continuation of the first-person discourse of Moses addressed to the Israelite assembly. The exhortatory or comminatory tone of this last discourse of Moses, delivered on the day of his death, is carried over into the laws, motivation is provided for their observance, past experience is recalled, and future possibilities are entertained. The "second law" is therefore not a law code in anything like the sense in which we would use the term today. It is more a program than a code, and its utopian character is frequently in evidence (e.g., "there shall be no poor among you," 15:4). In short, it is more a sustained rhetorical composition than a law book (von Rad 1953 [1948], 11–16).

We may nevertheless speak of a rhetorical framework to the laws, and it is clearly the result of a long process of editorial amplification that can be reconstructed only very tentatively. Indications of this process include repetitions and changes from the singular to the plural form of address, but the clearest is the series of headings or superscriptions throughout the book. The first of these, 1:1–5, leads us to expect laws or legal exposition, but what follows in the first three chapters is not law but historical reminiscence. A similar heading in 4:44–49 announces "statutes and ordinances," but introduces instead a review of the Horeb event beginning with the theophany and the decalogue. In like manner 6:1 also promises laws but delivers a sermon, and only from Chapter 12 are laws forthcoming. Then, toward the end of the book, 28:69 [29:1] introduces the covenant in the land of Moab which continues down to 32:47, and 33:1 is the heading for the blessings pronounced by Moses on the tribes.

The debate on the origin and formation of Deuteronomy, which has been going on since the early nineteenth century, and continues unabated, has generated an enormous secondary literature. All we can hope to do here is indicate some of the points at which a broad but by no means universal agreement has been reached. Thus there is something approaching a consensus that 4:44–49 marks the original introduction to the law book including the blessings and curses in 28:1–68. But we must then go on to note that this initial paragraph combines two introductions only the second of which (4:45), taken up again in 6:1, refers to the laws in 12–26. The more comprehensive allusion to the Torah in the previous verse (4:44) was probably added when the Horeb decalogue was brought in as a preface to and recapitulation of the individual stipulations of law. The insertion of the decalogue, connecting an originally independent law book with the Horeb event, has then occasioned what might be called a sermon on the first commandment contained in 6:1–11:25. (For different analyses of these chapters, see Lohfink 1963 *[Das Hauptgebot];* Seitz 1971; Lopez 1978; Mayes 1979; Brekelmans 1985). We note further that the anticipation of a covenant ceremony to be carried out at Shechem after the occupation of the land serves to bracket the recital of the laws (11:26–32; 27:1–26). While this Shechem covenant tradition may be quite ancient, the concluding ceremony has gone through several editions, as may be seen in the different roles assigned to Levites in it (27:9, 12, 14).

A rare instance of almost complete acceptance of a hypothesis in biblical studies is Martin Noth's Deuteronomistic History (Dtr) consisting of Joshua to 2 Kings with Deuteronomy as a prologue providing the key to the interpretation of the history and the criteria according to which the characters in it are evaluated (Noth 1943, 1957, 2nd ed.). Noth's thesis was taken further by Frank Moore Cross, who distinguished between a seventh century edition of the history, from the time of Josiah (Dtr[1]), and the final exilic edition from the mid-sixth century (Dtr[2]), each with its own distinctive point of view and theology (Cross 1973, 274–89). This conclusion has also been widely accepted, and has been further developed by several of Cross's students (Friedman 1981; Nelson 1981; Peckham 1985). It was then natural to assume that the D law book, including the framework, would have had a similar editorial history. While there are passages referring explicitly to the exilic experience, it is not always easy to distinguish between earlier and later editions. Most commentators would nevertheless agree that 4:1–40 aligns with Dtr[2] and that the Moab covenant text in 28:69–32:47 [29:1–32:47] was either composed or greatly expanded at the same time, for it is clear that both can best be explained as passages addressed to the Babylonian diaspora after the fall of Jerusalem and subsequent deportations.[23] Noth took the first three chapters of the book, which retell the history from Horeb to Moab, to be the beginning of Dtr. But since it is in the form of personal reminiscence of Moses, and therefore in that respect quite unlike Dtr, it seems better to read it as the historical link between the two covenants, beginning as it does with departure from Horeb and ending in the valley opposite Beth-peor where the Moab covenant was enacted (3:29 cf. 4:46). The final and extremely important editorial stage coincides with the incorporation of the book into the P history, but of this, more in Chapter 7.

Who Wrote Deuteronomy?

It will be obvious by now that there can be no simple answer to this question, if only because of the successive editions through which the book has passed. Since the famous "Critical Dissertation" of de Wette early in the nineteenth century, a connection with the religious reforms of Josiah (640–609 B.C.) has been more or less taken for granted. In 2 Kings 22–23 the historian records how in the eighteenth year of Josiah's reign, therefore 622/621 B.C., the high priest Hilkiah reported the discovery of "the book of the law" during repair of the temple fabric. The king reacted to the reading of this document with consternation and dismay, no doubt because of the curses attached to the nonobservance of its clauses. The dire consequences of its neglect were confirmed by Huldah the prophetess, consulted on behalf of the king, whereupon Josiah enacted a covenant in the temple to put its stipulations into effect and proceeded at once to implement it by carrying out a thorough religious reform. Since these measures tally fairly closely with the corresponding cultic laws in Deuteronomy, it was concluded that the book in question contained at least these laws with the curses and blessings attached to them.

The historicity of this report, which comes to us from the author of Dtr for whom the Deuteronomic law was of paramount importance, has been variously assessed (Nicholson 1967, 1–17; Mayes 1979, 85–103). De Wette accepted its substantial historicity, but suggested that the law book had been "planted" by the priests and then "rediscovered" in order to instigate a religious reform. One problem with this opinion is that, according to 2 Chron 34:3, the king initiated the reforms six years before the discovery of the book. While the historical information offered by the Chronicler is generally, and rightly, greeted with skepticism, this earlier date has the advantage of aligning the religious reform more closely with the transfer of power in Assyria, generally a good time to make a bid for independence. (Ashurbanipal abdicated in 631 and died in 627). Another problem is that Deuteronomy does not seem to reflect the point of view and ethos of the Jerusalem priesthood.

A possibility not easily discounted is that the discovery of the book is a fiction of the historian the purpose of which was to explain how this allegedly Mosaic and therefore ancient text could have been unknown and neglected for so long. In other words, the report served to authenticate what was in effect a pseudepigraphal work of recent composition, perhaps from the last years of Josiah's reign. It would also serve to exhibit Josiah as a good king judged by Deuteronomic criteria, in contrast to his immediate predecessors Manasseh and Amon. The author would have taken his cue from the cultic reforms of Josiah, the account of which in 2 Kings 23:4–20 does not so much as mention the law book, understood as an essential corollary of his bid for independence from Assyria and recovery of the lost northern provinces. Also, this seems to have been an epoch that felt the need to preserve the legacy from the distant past. In Egypt Psamtik I (Psammeticus I), a leader of the anti-Assyrian forces, encouraged nativist tendencies, including the revival of religious ideas, art, and literature from the Old Kingdom, and in Assyria itself Ashurbanipal's scribes were busy copying an impressive range of ancient texts for his library in Nineveh.

If, then, as seems likely, the D law was drafted by legal experts during Josiah's reign, we would have a ready explanation for the many scribal features the book contains, as also for the structural and thematic parallels with Assyrian international treaties from the same century (Frankena 1965; Weinfeld 1972). Jeremiah's disparaging allusions to "handlers of the law" and "the false pen of the scribes" (Jer 2:8; 8:8), from about the same time, would also be consistent with this hypothesis. But since there is much in Deuteronomy that cannot easily be explained by scribal authorship or draftsmanship, many scholars have looked elsewhere in attempting to account for the characteristic features of the book. One line of inquiry, represented by older scholars like Burney and Welch in England and Causse in France, and more recently by Ernest Nicholson of Oxford University (Nicholson 1967, 58–82), has emphasized the links with the Ephraimite prophetic tradition and especially with Hosea, its most distinguished representative. There can be no doubt that Deuteronomy has been deeply influenced by prophetic preaching. But apart from the fact that Hosea shows little interest in such issues as social justice, national identity, and the conduct of war, issues that loom large in Deuteronomy, the distinctly deterrent attitude to prophecy in the book is difficult to reconcile with prophetic authorship. The social legislation of Deuteronomy is much closer to the concerns of Judean country prophets, especially Micah from Moresheth in the Judean foothills, than it is to Hosea and other Ephraimite prophets. We note that Micah's preaching had a direct effect on the reforms of Hezekiah (see Jer 26:16–19), and there are numerous points of contact between his denunciations and the social program of the law book.[24]

Micah's religious conservatism, his guarded and critical attitude to state institutions, and his fierce denunciation of those who were undermining a traditional agrarian way of life by enclosure, foreclosure, bribery, and other abuses suggest strongly that he spoke for the independent farmers of the Judean countryside. This religiously and socially conservative class, known to the historian as "the people of the land" (*'am hā'āreṣ*), began to play an important political role from about the mid-ninth century B.C., supporting the coup that deposed the Baalist queen Athaliah, and playing a decisive role in the accession of Joash and his grandson Uzziah (2 Kings 11:13–20; 14:21). It was they too who put Josiah on the throne (2 Kings 21:24) and, in all probability, played a leading part in the religious reforms begun during his minority and the movement for political independence from Assyria that accompanied them—we note that they are numbered among the war party in Jer 34:19 and 37:2, and were among the first to be executed after the Babylonian conquest (2 Kings 25:18–21). Von Rad pointed out that the religious and political views of these people were shared by those country priests referred to in Deuteronomy as "the Levites within your towns," including, no doubt, some of the descendants of those clergy excluded from service in the state temples of the erstwhile Northern Kingdom (1 Kings 12:31) (Von Rad 1953 [1948 2nd ed.], 60–69). Whoever it was that actually wrote the book, it seems that it was this constituency that found a voice, the voice of Moses, in the political, social, and religious program of Deuteronomy.

The Cultic Laws

The Narrative Framework

As a distinct narrative, or at least a distinct and late stage in the editorial process eventuating in the Pentateuch, P was the last of the sources to emerge from the travail of critical debate in the modern period. It has also proved to be the most durable. In our first chapter we saw how it was first identified as a strand of the foundational E document by Ilgen in the late eighteenth century, and then more clearly by Hupfeld some fifty years later. The decisive move, however, was the displacement of P from the beginning to the end of the historical process, first as a result of de Wette's study of Chronicles, then in the cumulative studies of cultic institutions by Reuss, Graf, and Wellhausen. Though often challenged, this conclusion is still by and large intact a century after Wellhausen. Not surprisingly, many issues are still being disputed, especially concerning the unity and extent of P and its relation to the rest of the narrative content of the Pentateuch or Hexateuch. Uncertainty about these issues has not, however, inhibited the publication of numerous studies of the P narrative, often designated P[G] to distinguish the *Grundschrift* or core narrative from later additions and the vast amount of cultic material designated by the same siglum.[25]

The recurrence in the P narrative of formulaic expressions, and especially expressions indicating the completion of a significant work commanded or (in one case) carried out by God, highlight aspects of a clearly articulated and carefully designed structure. Without going into detail, we may note simply that the most solemn of these conclusion formulas occur at three points of the P history:

(1) Creation of the world (Gen 2:1–2): "Thus the heavens and the earth were finished and all their hosts . . . God finished his work which he had done."

(2)   Construction of the wilderness sanctuary (Ex 39:32; 40:33): "Thus all the work of the tabernacle of the tent of meeting was finished . . . so Moses finished the work."

(3)   Setting up of the sanctuary in Canaan and allotment of territory (Josh 19:51): "So they finished dividing the land."

The creation of the heavenly bodies "for signs and seasons, days and years" on the fourth day, and the rest of God on the seventh, indicate that worship is rooted in the created order and is the means of conforming to that order, and not just for Israel. The place of worship is a scaled-down cosmos, and its appointments and architecture encode a cosmic symbolism bearing directly on the meaning of the acts that take place within it.[26] The temple is constructed according to a heavenly model. Gudea, king of the Sumerian city of Lagash, received the model of the temple of Ningursu from the deity in a dream, and Moses is shown the plan *(tabnît,* Ex 25:9, 40) of the wilderness sanctuary on Mount Sinai. In a certain sense, therefore, the construction of the sanctuary is the completion of the work begun in creation, a conclusion towards which P leads us by the parallel wording of the two narratives:

Creation of the world	Construction of the sanctuary
And God saw everything that he had made, and behold, it was very good (Gen 1:31).	And Moses saw all the work, and behold, they had done it (Ex 39:43).
Thus the heavens and the earth were finished (Gen 2:1).	Thus all the work of the tabernacle of the tent of meeting was finished (Ex 39:32).
God finished his work which he had done (Gen 2:2).	So Moses finished the work (Ex 40:33).
So God blessed the seventh day (Gen 2:3).	So Moses blessed them (Ex 39:43).

The parallelism is completed by the injunction to observe sabbath which concludes the instructions for the setting up of the cult and is repeated immediately before the account of their implementation (Ex 31:12–17; 35:1–3).

It is difficult to avoid the conclusion that this basic structure of the P narrative is related in some way to the project of rebuilding the temple and restoring the cult in the land of Israel, reduced to a small and impoverished province after the Babylonian conquest. Consistent with this historical connection is the care with which P notes the establishment of circumcision, Passover, and sabbath, all of which assumed great importance from the time of the Babylonian exile. None of these practices requires either temple or priesthood, and consequently they are all instituted before the sanctuary is erected and the priesthood confirmed in office. As the sign of the covenant people, circumcision is traced back to the early ancestors (Gen 17:9–14). Whatever its actual origin and early use, its importance for membership in the diasporic and reconstituted Judean *qāhāl* can hardly be doubted. Passover, prescribed before the departure from Egypt (Exodus 12), marks a new beginning and, as such, was celebrated by the golah-community immediately after the dedication of the rebuilt temple (Ezra 6:19–22). While its observance was anticipated in the wilderness (Ex 16:5, 22–30), the sabbath command is given following instructions for the erection of the sanctuary, the implication being that Israel must rest after work as God rested after creation (Ex 31:12–17). The practice is certainly ancient, but here too we note that it comes into its own as a confessional mark of identity only from the time of the Babylonian exile.[27]

We saw how the P version of the Sinai event consists exclusively in the revelation of instructions for the setting up of the cult and the showing of the model according to which the sanctuary is to be built. The dates of arrival at and departure from Sinai are carefully noted in the manner characteristic of P (Ex 19:1; Num 10:11). All the ritual legislation in Leviticus is therefore promulgated at Sinai after the erection of the sanctuary, as is explicitly noted in the solemn conclusion in Lev 26:46, repeated after the addition of an appendix dealing with vows in Lev 27:34. Up to this point the narrative line is maintained, though it is somewhat obscured by the insertion of a great mass of ritual legislation. The vision on the mountain with the detailed prescriptions for worship is followed by the equally detailed account of their implementation, concluding with the setting up of the sanctuary and its occupation by the divine presence in the form of the mysterious effulgence. The crucial significance of this juncture is also marked by a precise date (Ex 40:2, 17). Thereafter, all of Israel's movement through the wilderness will be controlled from the sanctuary (Num 9:15–23), which corresponds to the dominant role, social and political as well as religious, which the priesthood aimed to fill after the collapse of the state.

In Leviticus the narrative continues with the ordination of the priests and their inaugural sacrifices (Lev 8:1–9:24). The elimination of Nadab and Abihu (10:1–7) and the ritual faux pas of his remaining two sons (10:16–20) follow the by now well established pattern of a new beginning followed by a deviation, as in the Golden Calf incident, in which Aaron was also involved and of which he was somewhat unconvincingly exonerated. The only other piece of narrative in Leviticus is the trial and execution of a blasphemer (24:10–23), which is of a kind with other exempla from the wilderness period—the sabbath violator (Num 15:32–36), the rebellion of Korah (16:1–17:15 [16:1–50]), Aaron's blossoming wand (17:16–28 [17:1–13]), and the war against Midian (31).

The same narrative line continues into the first part of Numbers down to the departure from Sinai (Num 9:15–10:28). This solemn finale takes up where Ex 40:38 left off, repeating the description of the cloud and fire over the tabernacle that now dictate the tempo and direction of the march. The date of departure, the twentieth of the second month, accommodates the supplementary Passover law allowing for a month's delay for the ritually unclean (9:1–14). Much of the remaining material in this section is preparation for the journey: the census of laity and Levites (1:1–54; 4:1–49), dispositions of the camp (2:1–34; 5:1–4), and regulations concerning Levites (3:1–51; 8:1–26). It is worth noting that legislation concerning Levites is found in Numbers, not in Leviticus, the latter known more appropriately in Jewish tradition as *tôrat kohănîm,* the law concerning priests. The miscellaneous legislation in the rest of Numbers, in some instances loosely connected with the narrative line—e.g., the request of Zelophehad's daughters for their tribal inheritance (27:1–11)—is located in the plains of Moab (36:13), and therefore in this respect parallels the Deuteronomic law. It consists for the most part in legislation supplementary to the Sinaitic laws in Leviticus.

The Major Collections of Ritual Law

Most discussions of the subject in Old Testament scholarship of the last two centuries have been colored in one way or another by assumptions about the place of ritual in *Christian* practice. Throughout the nineteenth century the tendency in liberal Protestantism was to identify morality as the core of Christianity and therefore of true religion in general, and to interpret progress as a gradual abandonment of the archaic, materialistic, and magical world view in which rituals of avoidance played a dominant role. This tendency can be seen very clearly in the interpretation of the taboo, a Polynesian term introduced into the English language by Captain Cook in 1784. The reader will find an admirable survey of the use of this term during the late nineteenth and early twentieth centuries in a monograph of Franz Steiner published posthumously in 1956. In his article under that title in the great ninth edition of the *Encyclopaedia Britannica* (1875–1889), Sir James Frazer, of *Golden Bough* fame, took it to be a relic of primitive superstition from which, however, ideas of law and morality developed in the course of time. It is of interest to note that this compendium of the Victorian enlightenment also contained the article of William Robertson Smith on the Bible which led to a famous heresy trial, and that of Julius Wellhausen on Israel which identified the cultic and ritual laws as the heathen element in the Old Testament. While the attitude toward Christianity of Robertson Smith was very different from that of his friend James Frazer, his views on the ritual laws were not essentially different. The irrationality of the purity laws, he maintained, is so manifest that they must necessarily be seen as having survived from an earlier form of faith and society (The Religion of the Semites [London, 1889], 449). For Wellhausen also the ritual law is the least edifying and least rational element in the religious system of early Judaism, and of Judaism tout court, and one which stands in antithesis to the exalted moral teaching of the prophets (Prolegomena, 509 and passim).

A survey of some of the more influential theologies of the Old Testament and monographs on biblical law written by Christian scholars in the present century will, I believe, show how persistent this prejudicial view of the ritual law has proved to be.[28] It is only in recent decades that a serious effort has been made, with the help of anthropologists such as Victor Turner and Mary Douglas, to understand it as part of a consistent world view rather than dismissing it as deviating from the norms dictated by our own—often confused and unreflective—perceptions of order and rationality. The first stage toward understanding, I suggest, is a close and unprejudicial reading of the individual compilations of ritual law accompanied by an effort at detecting something of their underlying rationale and the ends which their observance was intended to promote. Space does not permit us to study, or even survey, all the material, but we can make a start by listing and briefly commenting on the principal collections in Leviticus.

Sacrifices (Lev 1:1–7:38)

The insertion of a manual on sacrifice at this point interrupts the narrative connection between the instructions for the establishment of the priesthood in Exodus 29 and the ordination ceremony, and therefore the official inauguration of worship, in Leviticus 8–10. This insertion was necessitated by the instructions concerning the disposal of offerings by the priests in Lev 9:12–20 which otherwise would remain unexplained. It will be noted that the ordination ceremony lasts seven days (Lev 8:33; 9:1), and therefore parallels the seven days of creation and divine rest in Gen 1:1–2:3. Worship, which is according to the Priestly view the goal of creation, can therefore begin on the eighth day. The extent of the manual on sacrifice is clearly marked by an introduction (Lev 1:1) and a conclusion (7:37–38), the latter of a kind occurring, perhaps not by accident, seven times in the first half of Leviticus (7:37–38; 11:46–47; 12:7b; 13:59; 14:32; 14:54–57; 15:32–33).

There are two kinds of sacrificial offerings: those that are optional and unscheduled (1–3) and those mandated for the removal of sin and culpa-

bility (4–5). The first kind includes the following: the burnt or whole offering, perhaps the oldest *('olāh,* 1:3–17); the cereal or tribute offering
(minḥāh, 2:1–16), probably the most popular because the least expensive
(Anderson 1987, 27–34); the peace or well-being offering *(zebaḥ šĕlāmîm,*
3:1–17), eaten by the donor and his family (Levine 1974, 3–52). Of the two
kinds of mandatory sacrifice, the purgation offering *(ḥaṭṭā't,* 4:1–35) is
required for the removal of involuntary infractions and specifies the offerings to be made by the high priest,[29] the congregation as a whole, a tribal
head,[30] and a member of the common people (Milgrom 1983, 67–95).
There follows a list of borderline cases (5:1–13) the first of which, the case
of one who refuses to testify, appears to be an exception to the principle
that the purgation offering can atone only for involuntary acts disruptive
of an objective order. (Cf. Num 15:22–31 read as an exegetical commentary on this section; see Fishbane 1985, 190–94, 223–25). The reparation
offering *('āšām,* 5:14–26 [5:14–6:7]) is intended for more severe cases of
desecration, meaning the violation of the restrictions placed on the laity
with respect to the sanctuary and its prerogatives. (On this idea of en-
croachment see Milgrom, *IDBSup* 264–65). But it also covers deliberate
acts including theft, cheating, and extortion, and the offering must be accompanied by restitution plus 20 percent of the value of the stolen property. The saying of Jesus linking offerings at the altar with reconciliation
(Mt 5:23–24) is therefore in line with this requirement and not, as often
stated, a break with the contemporary Jewish understanding of sacrifice.

The supplement covering procedural matters and the disposal of the
offerings (6:1–7:38 [6:8–7:38]) lists the sacrifices in a different order and
adds the consecration offering to align the section more completely with
the narrative context. It may have been added at a later time, together
with other supplementary material (Num 7:1–89; 15:1–36; 28–29).

Clean and Unclean (Lev 11:1–15:33)

The fivefold occurrence of a recapitulatory conclusion formula ("This is
the law of X") divides this manual into the following sections: clean and
unclean animals (11:1–47); uncleanness resulting from childbearing
(12:1–8); skin diseases and, by extension, rot or mildew in buildings and
clothing (13:1–59); the appropriate rituals of purification (14:1–57); uncleanness through bodily discharges (15:1–33). This, too, was originally a
separate booklet, for the following chapter, prescribing the ritual for the
Day of Atonement, is the narrative sequence to the desecration of the
sanctuary by the priests Nadab and Abihu (16:1 cf. 10:1–7). The Day of
Atonement stands on its own as the centerpiece of Leviticus, and therefore indicates by its position the fundamental importance of the removal
of sin and impurity.

The criteria according to which living things are categorized as clean and unclean are clearly stated, but the rationale determining the criteria has long been a matter of speculation. The general idea behind this taxonomic system seems to be to preserve the order and distinctness of the original creation, the importance of which can be gauged from the tenfold occurrence of the phrase "according to its/their kind" in Genesis 1. An important corollary was therefore the exclusion of the anomalous. Thus the bat is unclean since, though it is equipped with wings, it has fur instead of feathers; the eel is excluded because its mode of locomotion does not conform to that of scaly and finned aquatic creatures; the ostrich has wings but doesn't fly; and so on. Land animals and birds that feed on carrion are unfit for human consumption. Pork is eschewed not because of the danger of contracting trichinosis, unknown before the nineteenth century, but because the pig figured in pagan rituals (e.g., Isa 65:4–5; 66:17; see de Vaux 1971, 252–69). Whatever the explanation, these distinctions helped to keep alive a reverent regard for the created order and a discriminating ethical attitude to the taking of life for food, a possibility granted only as a concession in the new dispensation following the deluge (Milgrom 1963, 288–301; Douglas 1966, 40–57).

Bodily discharges—blood, semen, pathological exudates—rendered unclean and caused secondary uncleanness by contact as a kind of violation of the integrity of the human body. Childbearing, therefore, called for a ritual quarantine followed by a ritual of purification because of the discharge of the afterbirth, the longer period of quarantine for a female child probably dictated by the vaginal emission of the infant caused by the hormones secreted by the mother. The Hebrew term ṣorāʿat, often translated "leprosy" (Hansen's disease), should instead be taken to cover a wide range of skin disorders (e.g., psoriasis, seborrhea, scabies) which also required ritual quarantine and, on recovery, validation by a priest and a ceremony of purification. Here too we are dealing with aspects of a symbolic system that has more to do with inculcating a certain ethic of bodily existence in the world than with medicine and hygiene.

The So-called "Holiness Code" (Leviticus 17–26)

Since the suggestion was first made by the German scholar August Klostermann in 1877, there has been broad agreement that this latter part of the book, excluding the final chapter, which is an appendix dealing with vows, constitutes a distinct corpus of ritual law, from either the late preexilic or exilic period, which was eventually incorporated into the P complex. The name "Holiness Code" (Heiligkeitsgesetz) was suggested by the frequent repetition of the call to imitate the holiness of God ("you shall be holy, for I YHWH your God am holy"). It was also noted that, like the

Deuteronomic law, the corpus begins with the limitation of animal sacrifice to the central sanctuary (17:1–9) and ends with blessings and curses (26:3–39). The result was that H entered the critical mainstream along with the other alphabetical sigla.

While it is true that this second half of Leviticus following the centrally placed ritual for the Day of Atonement is distinguished from the first half by a quite different kind of recapitulatory formula (to be noted presently), the chapters assigned to H come without a title and manifest too little internal coherence to suggest a quite distinct document. Moreover, the call to holiness referred to a moment ago occurs only in Chapters 19–22. We would therefore be better advised to be guided by the incidence of such formal features as we have identified in the first half of Leviticus. Of these the most prominent is an exhortation placed at the end of the different sections, the fifth and last of which is much longer than the four preceding it (18:24–30; 20:22–26; 22:31–33; 25:18–24; 26:3–45). This gives us the following sections which betray no evidence of having belonged to any larger unit other than Leviticus and the P corpus of which it is a part. We can do no more than list these divisions:

(1) 17–18 Sacrificial butchering; the blood prohibition; forbidden sexual relations

(2) 19–20 Prescriptions on various ethical matters and corresponding penalties

(3) 21–22 Regulations for priests

(4) 23–25 Functioning of the cult, including the liturgical calendar; sabbatical year and Jubilee (with a supplement in 25:25–55)

(5) 26 Final injunctions and concluding homily (with a supplement on vows in 27:1–33 and the final conclusion to the Sinaitic laws in the following verse)

A consecutive reading of the homiletic conclusions to the sections will highlight the connection between observance of the ethical and ritual law and secure possession of the land. The tone, and sometimes the language, is reminiscent of D, but there are equally clear traces of Ezekiel and P, a combination strongly suggesting a very late date for the redaction of this part of the Sinai pericope. Emphasis on the land is consistent with the situation of those among the deportees in Babylon who anticipated and were actively preparing for return to the homeland, and in fact the exilic situation is clearly and explicitly referred to in the final homily.

. . .

In his essay "The Laws in the Pentateuch," Martin Noth traced the development of the legal tradition in Israel, a development which he believed came to a dead end when law became what he called "an absolute entity" *(eine absolute Grösse)* in the post-exilic period.[31] What he meant by this was an inauthentic reliance on law detached from its ancient foundations in covenant faith; and we may be sure that when he went on to speak of "dead ordinances and statutes" he had in mind the ritual law in particular. A concern to regulate human activity by law can certainly degenerate into formalism and legalism, no less in Christianity than in Judaism. Whether this actually became a dominant trait in the emergent Judaism of the Second Commonwealth could, however, be determined only after a survey of all the writing from that time, including those passages that speak of the law as a source of wisdom, enlightenment, and joy; and this Noth failed to do. Our study of the Sinai story has shown that laws, whenever enacted and promulgated, had to be brought into relation with certain events in which the presence and action of God were discerned. It is this remarkable and possibly unique feature of the legal traditions of Israel which, it seems to me, provides a more basic explanation of the covenant relationship than the treaty analogy. Noth may also have overlooked the fact that the Pentateuch itself, in which law and narrative are inseparably united, is after all the most impressive literary product of the emergent Judaism of which he so strongly disapproved.

NOTES

1. H. Cazelles, "Pentateuque IV: Textes Sacerdotaux," *DBSup* 7 (1966), col. 843, assigns Josh 1:1–5, 11:15–20, and 12:7–24 to P and finds its conclusion at Josh 19:51. I argued for the same terminus in "The Structure of P," *CBQ* 38 (1976) 275–92. In recent decades, however, the view has persisted that P ends with the death of Moses in the final chapter of Deuteronomy; see M. Noth, *A History of Pentateuchal Traditions* (Englewood Cliffs, N.J., 1972 [1948], 9–10, 19; K. Elliger, "Sinn und Ursprung der priesterschriftlichen Geschichtserzählung," *ZTK* 49 (1952) 122; E. Sellin and G. Fohrer, *Introduction to the Old Testament* (Nashville & New York, 1968 [1965]), 179–80; W. Brueggemann, "The Kerygma of the Priestly Writers," *ZAW* 84 (1972) 399; F. M. Cross, Jr., *Canaanite Myth and Hebrew Epic* (Cambridge, Mass., 1973), 320; P. Weimar, "Struktur und Konposition der priesterschriftlichen Geschichtsdarstellung," *BN* 23 (1984) 85–86.

2. H. Cazelles, cols. 833–34 (see Note 1) assigns Ex 19:3b–8b with its allusion to covenant to P, and therefore holds that P does speak of a covenant at Sinai. Israel is a "kingdom of priests" in the sense that Israel enjoys priestly rule in contrast to other nations that have kings. The more common affirmation, however, is that P is

editor rather than author and therefore takes JE for granted as known. But even if we accept this assumption, we would still have to explain why an editor who makes explicit mention of a covenant with Noah and with Abraham is silent when it comes to Sinai. Another problem is that those who hold this view generally deny or ignore the role of a final redactor subsequent to P. On the P ideology as reflected in the Sinai pericope, see K. Koch, "Die Eigenart der priesterschriftlichen Sinaigesetzgebung," *ZTK* 55 (1958) 36–51.

3. R. B. Y. Scott, "A Kingdom of Priests, Ex xix 6," *OTS* 8 (1950) 213–19; W. L. Moran, "A Kingdom of Priests," in J. L. McKenzie (ed.), *The Bible in Current Catholic Thought* (New York, 1962), 7–20.

4. E. W. Nicholson, *God and His People* (Oxford, 1986), 172–78, connects this passage with 19:3b–8; it is earlier than D and describes Israel's priestly consecration.

5. The covenant-treaty analogy suggested an explanation for *two* tablets, for some of the treaties (e.g., between the Hittite king Suppiluliumas and Mattiwaza, ruler of Mitanni on the Upper Euphrates) stipulate that each party must retain a copy and have it read publicly at regular intervals. The analogy does not, however, fit the present context in which Moses receives both tablets. Mekhilta (Baḥodesh 8), the earliest Jewish commentary on Exodus, states that five stipulations were written on one and five on the other; alternatively, the Exodus version was written on one and the Deuteronomy version on the other.

6. In 1 Sam 2:18 the prophet Samuel is also described as *mĕšārēt* and *naᶜar;* cf. 1 Sam 1:24 and 2 Kings 9:4 where *naᶜar* may have this special meaning, with reference, respectively, to Samuel and Gehazi, prophetic acolyte of Elisha.

7. Both Onkelos and the Palestinian Targum to Ex 34:6 transpose the verb *(wayyaᶜabor)* into the causative *(wĕᵓaᶜĕbir):* "YHWH made his Shekinah pass before his face."

8. Pss 24:6; 27:8–9; 42:3; 105:4; 143:7. Cf. the Akkadian expression *amāru pān ili,* "to see the face of the god."

9. The reference is to the Amarna letters from the early fourteenth century B.C. See *ANET* 484, 487.

10. The context, therefore, does not favor the highly speculative conclusion of W. H. Propp *(BR* 4.1 [1988] 30–37) that Moses' face was disfigured by heat generated by the divine presence. Most of the older commentators concentrated on the *masweh,* suggesting comparison with the shawl with which the pre-Islamic *kāhin* covered his face during trance (Wellhausen, Buber), or the cultic masks worn by priests in certain rituals (Gressmann, Jirku). On these and other hypotheses, see F. Dummermuth, "Moses' strahlendes Gesicht," *TZ* 17 (1961) 240–48; M. Haran, "The Shining of Moses' Face: A Case Study in Biblical and Ancient Near Eastern Iconography," in W. Boyd Barrick and J. R. Spencer (eds.), *In the Shelter of Elyon. Essays on Ancient Palestinian Life and Literature in Honor of G. W. Ahlström* (Sheffield, 1984), 159–73.

11. O. Eissfeldt, *The Old Testament. An Introduction,* 213, argues from the use of *dĕbārîm* at 24:3–4, 8 that the *sēper habbĕrît* of 24:7 must be the decalogue; but

his argument requires the excision of "all the ordinances" (v 3) and the transposition of 20:18–20 before the decalogue. One also wonders whether the decalogue, written on tablets *(lûḥôt)*, would be called a *sēper*.

12. Deut 5:5 is problematic since it seems to contradict the previous verse in which YHWH is said to have addressed the people directly ("face to face") during the promulgation of the decalogue. Since *lē'mor* at the end of v 5 would be syntactically feasible only if it followed directly after v 4, v 5 is probably a gloss inspired by the statement that YHWH spoke to the assembly face to face, a mode of communication elsewhere restricted to Moses.

13. Y. Aharoni in M. Avi-Yonah (ed.), *Encyclopedia of Archaeological Excavations in the Holy Land,* Vol. 1 (Englewood Cliffs, N.J., 1975), 86.

14. Reading *gādôl* (great one) for *dāl* (poor person)

15. Assuming an original *lo' taṣdîq rāšā'* for *lo' 'aṣdîq rāšā'*, suggested by McKay, *VT* 21 (1971) 318–19.

16. The only political allusion is the prohibition against cursing a *nāśî'* (22:27 [22:28]), a term used for tribal leadership in the pre-state period and, less commonly, for the monarch (1 Kings 11:34 and Ezekiel *passim)* and the political leadership after the exile (Ezra 1:6).

17. On the goring ox, see S. M. Paul, *Studies in the Book of the Covenant in the Light of Cuneiform and Biblical Law* (Leiden, 1970), 78–85; R. Yaron, "The Goring Ox in Near Eastern Laws," in H. H. Cohn (ed.), *Jewish Law in Ancient and Modern Israel* (Jerusalem, 1971), 50–60; B. S. Jackson, *Essays in Jewish and Comparative Legal History* (London, 1975), 108–52; J. J. Finkelstein, "The Ox that Gored," *Transactions of the American Philosophical Society* 71 (Philadelphia, 1981).

18. One of the most illuminating discussions of the *lex talionis* is that of David Daube, *Studies in Biblical Law* (New York, 1969 [1947]), 102–53.

19. In Ex 34:28 "the ten words" seems to refer to the ordinances immediately preceding, by most documentarians attributed to J and identified as the cultic decalogue. But we have already learned from Ex 34:1 that the new tablets contained the same words as the broken ones, i.e., the decalogue of Ex 20:1–17. Ex 34:28 is therefore very probably a gloss added by the D author, who regarded the decalogue as the essence and summary of the covenant.

20. The enumeration is different in the different religious traditions. In Roman Catholicism and Lutheranism 1 and 2 are joined and 10 is divided. In Judaism the initial divine self-designation counts as the first commandment.

21. This commandment, and the one following, are the only ones formulated positively. It is often maintained that they were originally prohibitions like the others, but if so, it is difficult to see why they would have been reformulated in this way.

22. Exceptions in Deuteronomy 12–18 are 15:1–18; 16:18–20; 17:8–20; 18:15–22. In 19–25 the following belong more to the cultic than the secular sphere: 22:5, 9–12; 23:10–15, 18–19, 22–24 [23:9–14, 17–18, 21–23]; 24:8–9.

23. See especially Jon D. Levenson, "Who inserted the Book of the Torah?," *HTR* 68 (1975) 203–33. Levenson follows Lohfink in accepting the essential unity of Deut 4:1–40 against Mittmann, *Deuteronomium 1,1–6,3 literarkritisch und traditionsgeschichtlich untersucht* (Berlin, 1975) who divides it up among five redactors. The ongoing debate is summarized by A. D. H. Mayes, *Deuteronomy* (Greenwood, S.C., 1979), 30–55.

24. Removing landmarks (Deut 19:14; Micah 2:2); usury and distraining the property and persons of debtors (Deut 24:6, 10–13, 17; Micah 2:8–9a); defense of the poor (Deut 14:28–29; 15:4; Micah 3:1–2; 6:10); maintenance of the judicial system (Deut 16:18–20; Micah 3:9); condemnation of bribery (Deut 16:18–20; Micah 3:11); weights and measures (Deut 25:13–16; Micah 6:10–11).

25. The modern phase of inquiry dates from G. von Rad's *Die Priesterschrift im Hexateuch* (Stuttgart, 1934). B. A. Levine, "Priestly Writers" in *IDBSup* 683–87, provides a more recent guide to bibliography.

26. These symbolic correspondences were recognized by Josephus *(War* 10:55; *Ant* 3:77). See R. E. Clements, *God and Temple* (Philadelphia, 1965), 65–66; Raphael Patai, *Man and Temple in Ancient Jewish Myth and Ritual* (New York, 1967, 2nd ed).

27. E.g., Ezek 20; 46:1–8; Isa 56:1–8; 58:13; 66:23; Neh 13:15–22. Note also the personal name Shabbetai in Ezra 10:15; Neh 8:7; 11:16, and in the Elephantine papyri.

28. E.g., G. von Rad, *Old Testament Theology,* Vol. 1, 259–60. Documented in my "Old Testament Theology and the Jewish-Christian Connection," *JSOT* 28 (1984) 3–15.

29. The designation *hakkohēn hammašiaḥ* (the anointed priest), and the priestly vestments and regalia, including a crown, suggest that the high priest has taken over the ceremonial aspects of the monarchy (Lev 8:7–12; 21:10; cf. Zech 6:9–14, the royal crown made for Jeshua the high priest).

30. *nāśî'* is also used for the ruler in Ezekiel 40–48 and for Sheshbazzar, probably with the meaning "governor," in Ezra 1:8. But since only a goat is here prescribed for the offering, the term probably refers to the head of a *bēt 'ābôt* or phratry.

31. Martin Noth, *The Laws in the Pentateuch and Other Essays* (Edinburgh & London, 1966 [1957]), 85–107.

CHAPTER 7

CONCLUDING REFLECTIONS

"It is not worthwhile to remember that past that cannot become a present."

SØREN KIERKEGAARD

THE FINAL STAGE

The Pentateuch begins with creation and ends with the death of Moses. That it begins with creation is to be expected, but the terminus would seem to call for an explanation. In the original form of the main-line P narrative it seems that the death of Moses was recorded as an event on the way (Num 27:12–23), following on the death of Miriam (20:1) and Aaron (20:22–29), the latter described in similar terms. Moses is told to go up Mount Abarim, view the land, and be gathered to his people, and the obvious implication is that this is to happen at once, as in the account of Aaron's death. The only thing remaining to be done was the commissioning of Joshua as his successor, which is carried out forthwith. But in the narrative as it now stands the death of Moses does not follow, and we may detect in the subsequent narrative in Numbers a note almost of embarrassment that Moses is still alive (e.g., "Avenge what the Midianites have done to the people of Israel; then you will be gathered to your people," Num 31:2). The reason, I believe, is to be found in the amalgamation of Deuteronomy with the Priestly History, which required that the death be

229

postponed until Moses promulgated the Deuteronomic law. This was achieved by the simple expedient of adding a date in the Priestly manner, and therefore reckoned from the exodus (cf. Ex 12:40–41), to the beginning of Deuteronomy (1:3). It was then necessary to transpose the commissioning of Joshua and the death of Moses from their original position in the P narrative to the end of Deuteronomy (32:48–52 + 34:1, 7–9). This revised version, the Priestly character of which has always been acknowledged, was subsequently disturbed by the insertion of the poetic Blessings of Moses (Deuteronomy 33) and minor expansions in the Deuteronomic style (34:2–6).

A synoptic reading of the two versions will, I believe, confirm this interpretation. Both record the command to view the land and die, together with the reason why Moses must die outside the land, and the transposed version goes on to record the death itself. (The expansions in the transposed version are in parentheses).

Num 27:12–14	Deut 32:48–52
YHWH said to Moses: "Go up this Mount Abarim and view the land which I have given to the Israelites. When you have viewed it you will be gathered to your people as Aaron your brother was gathered.	YHWH said to Moses (on that very day): "Go up this Mount Abarim (Mount Nebo, which is in the land of Moab opposite Jericho) and view the land (of Canaan) which I am giving to the Israelites (for a possession). Then die on the mountain which you ascend and be gathered to your people as Aaron your brother (died on Mount Hor and) was gathered to his people.
"For you rebelled against me in the wilderness of Zin during the strife of the assembly, when you were to exhibit my holiness in their sight; these are the waters of Meribath-kadesh in the wilderness of Zin."	For you were unfaithful to me in the midst of the Israelites at the waters of Meribath-kadesh in the wilderness of Zin, in that you did not exhibit my holiness in the midst of the Israelites. (You shall see the land before you but you shall not enter it, the land which I am giving to the Israelites.")

Deut 34:1, 7–9

> Moses went up from the plains of
> Moab to Mount Nebo, the
> summit of Pisgah, which is
> opposite Jericho, and YHWH
> showed him the land . . .
> Moses was a hundred and
> twenty years old when he died;
> his eye was not dimmed nor his
> powers diminished. The
> Israelites wept thirty days for
> Moses in the plains of Moab;
> then the days for weeping and
> mourning for Moses were
> completed.

The earlier version in Numbers records the commissioning of Joshua in considerable detail. Moses makes this final request, he receives instructions how it is to be done, and the commissioning follows (Num 27:15–23). The second P version, obviously based on the first, speaks only of the effects of the act (Deut 34:9):

> Joshua son of Nun was full of the spirit of wisdom, for Moses had laid his hands upon him. So the Israelites obeyed him, and did as YHWH had commanded Moses.

Absent from this revised version is the role of the priest Eleazar, oldest surviving son of Aaron, whose own investiture with the priestly office had been described shortly before (Num 20:25–28). Unlike the situation under the monarchy, when the ruler generally sought guidance from a prophet, it is now the priesthood that exercises spiritual control. We are reminded of the role of the priest vis-à-vis the civic ruler *(naśî')* in Ezekiel 40–48, the relation between Jeshua the high priest and Zerubbabel after the return from exile, and the dominant role of the priesthood in the Second Temple period in general. That Eleazar is not mentioned in the second version may simply mean that Moses is thought to recapitulate in his own person both civic rule and priestly office.

The ritual act of *sĕmîkāh* or the laying on of hands is also featured in both versions, but with a significant difference. In the first Joshua is spirit-endowed before the act, and it is precisely for this reason that he is chosen to succeed Moses. The transfer to him of a part of Moses' authority *(hôd)* is therefore simply a public validation of his charisma in the presence of the entire assembly *('ēdāh)*. In the second version, however, his charisma —enabling him to rule wisely—is not the reason for but the result of the ritual act, which may be taken to exemplify what Max Weber called the routinization of charisma.[1] The difference would seem to emphasize the need for a legitimately established office in the valid line of succession from Moses, and therefore the need for firmly established order in the new epoch about to begin.

This revised version, and the Pentateuch as a whole, is rounded off with a statement which, in effect, denies parity between the mode of revelation proper to Moses ("face to face," cf. Ex 33:11; 34:29–35; Num 12:6–8) and claims staked by prophets throughout the history: "There has never since arisen in Israel a prophet like Moses whom YHWH knew face to face." This final statement is meant to recall the promise of a "prophet like Moses" in Deut 18:15–18, probably as a warning against interpreting it in such a way as to put prophetic mediation on the same level as that of Moses. It represents a resolution of conflicting claims to authority in the religious sphere by defining a certain epoch as normative and, at the same time, relativizing the problematic and ambiguous phenomenon of prophecy.

We should add that canonical stasis has proved difficult if not impossible to maintain; witness the fact that the biblical canon came to include Prophets and Writings and, for Christians, certain of their own writings. The history from the death of Moses to the Babylonian exile (the Former Prophets) was retained by virtue of its close links with Deuteronomy and the Deuteronomic understanding of history and the prophetic function within history which it illustrates. The Deuteronomic prophetic collection continued to be expanded, in the first place with Ezekiel, whose links with the priesthood and the Priestly matter in the Pentateuch are universally acknowledged. Other prophetic writings from the time of the Second Temple were added, and existing prophetic books were expanded as late as the second century B.C. A study of these editorial additions reveals a thrust in the direction of the eschatological world view, a direction quite different from other redefinitions of prophecy during the later period. We find a kind of resolution of this tension between past and future in the final paragraph of Malachi, which inculcates observance of the law of Moses and at the same time anticipates the revival of prophecy with the coming of Elijah on the great and terrible day of YHWH (Mal 3:22–24 [4:4–6]). If, as I believe likely, this was intended as the finale to both Law and Prophets, it goes beyond the coda to the Priestly-Deuteronomic Pentateuch by restoring the tension between institution and charisma, the claims of the past and those of the future.

THE DEUTERONOMIC "CANON"

Before discussing the implications of this restructuring of the narrative of founding events, and the social situation which precipitated it, we need to take another look at its major components, Deuteronomy and the Priestly History. We begin with Deuteronomy since, as Wellhausen put it, "the connecting link between old and new, between Israel and Judaism, is everywhere Deuteronomy" *(Prolegomena,* 362). In several respects this book bears the mark of a canonical document though, as is well known, the language of canonicity is of much later currency. It contains a strict injunction against adding to it or subtracting from it (Deut 4:2; 12:32). It is to be deposited in the sanctuary and read publicly on certain solemn occasions (31:10–13, 26), a ruling which we know to have been followed (e.g., Neh 13:1–3). It is therefore preeminently a public and official document. Deuteronomy is also the first biblical text to speak consistently of "the Torah" or "the book of the Torah", and is presented in the lawgiver's own words as a patrimony to his people, a last will and testament. Its intent is to provide a binding and comprehensive blueprint for the Israelite commonwealth, defining *inter alia* the scope and function of public offices, the operation of the judicial system and the cult, and qualifications for membership.

The character of the Deuteronomic law as a blueprint is especially interesting when we turn to what it has to say about prophecy. By speaking about prophets in the section of the law dealing with the state apparatus—monarchy, priesthood, prophecy, judiciary—it betrays a concern to bring it within the institutional grid of the commonwealth (18:15–22). In doing so it also defines it as "Mosaic," that is, patterned on the ministry of Moses, understood as the fountainhead of prophecy. One consequence is that the principal function of the prophet is now to proclaim the law and warn against the consequences of nonobservance, and the same function is amply illustrated in Dtr (e.g., 2 Kings 17:13). Where Deuteronomy speaks of other aspects of the phenomenon, especially prediction, the tone is unmistakably deterrent. Unauthorized prophets and, a fortiori, those who appeal to deities other than YHWH, are subject to the death penalty (13:1–5; 18:20). Prophets are bracketed with "dreamers of dreams" (13:1), and those whose predictions are falsified automatically lose their prophetic credentials (18:21–22)—a conclusion which did not necessarily follow throughout the history of prophecy (e.g., Amos is reported to have predicted the violent death of Jeroboam II, which does not seem to have been fulfilled, in Amos 7:11).

Whatever one concludes about the origins and authorship of Deuteronomy, a subject of endless and inconclusive debate, its production is

difficult to explain without postulating a class of scribes with responsibility
for the redaction, and presumably also the interpretation, of the laws.
Unfortunately, we know relatively little about scribal schools and scribal
activities in Israel. It is reasonable to assume that the fall of the Northern
Kingdom in the eighth century B.C. would have brought about a more
concentrated effort to preserve the common patrimony, including the legal
patrimony, in writing. Proverbs 25–29 is attributed to "the men of
Hezekiah," and Hezekiah was the first Judean king to reign without a
counterpart in the Northern Kingdom. A rabbinic tradition (b. BB 15a)
has enlarged the activity of these "men" to take in the redaction of Isaiah,
the Song of Songs, and Qoheleth as well. An early draft of Deuteronomy
may have been part of this literary activity, as some scholars have argued,
but the link between the book and the reforms of Josiah a century later is
much more clearly in evidence, however the connection is formulated.
There is also a consensus that further editions of both Deuteronomy and
Dtr were produced some time after the deportations in the sixth century
B.C., either in Judah or somewhere in the diaspora.

This period from Josiah to the deportations also witnessed a crisis
within the ranks of the prophets and in the prophet's relations with his
(less commonly, her) public, a situation which can be deduced from prophetic writings during those years (e.g., Jer 23:9–40; 28–29; Ezek 13). I
would argue that one aspect of that crisis is traceable to a growing tension
between prophet and law scribe. If the point of view of the latter is detectable in what Deuteronomy has to say about prophecy, the prophetic position vis-à-vis the scribes comes to expression in Jeremiah's disparaging
allusion to "handlers of the law" *(tosĕpē hattôrāh),* who are ignorant of
YHWH (Jer 2:8) and his denunciation of scribes who have falsified the law
with their lying pens (8:8–9). The contrast in this last saying between appeal to the (prophetic) word of YHWH and an alleged scribal wisdom
reinforces the suggestion that a "canonical" text like Deuteronomy has
the intent of resolving conflicting claims to authority in a particular society. That such a situation should have arisen is not surprising since, as Max
Weber put it, tension is "characteristic of any stratum of learned men who
are ritually oriented to a law book as against prophetic charismatics."[2]

If the first collection of prophetic writings was put together during the
exilic period by the same school that produced Deuteronomy and Dtr, a
hypothesis which has much to recommend it,[3] the general line of argument
advanced here would be confirmed. The existence of an official corpus of
prophetic writings would not in itself exclude ongoing prophetic activity,
but it would tend inevitably to shift the emphasis from the present to the
past, from the spoken to the written word, and from direct prophetic utter-
ance to the interpretation of written prophecies. This shift in emphasis can
easily be detected in later prophetic books, e.g., in the allusion to the

former prophets in Zech 1:4 and the reinterpretation of earlier prophecies in the later parts of the book of Isaiah.

It is also significant that, in spite of Jeremiah's criticism of scribes and lawyers, his book has received by far the heaviest overlay of Deuteronomic editing. The reason may be that the D editor thought of him as standing at the end of the prophetic succession as Moses the protoprophet stood at the beginning. The parallelism between the call of Jeremiah and that of Moses (Jer 1:4–19; Ex 3:1–4:17) is noted in the commentaries, and the connection is further strengthened by the forty years of prophetic activity editorially allotted to him in the opening verses of the book (Jer 1:2–3, corresponding to 627–587 B.C.). The many prose passages of unmistakably Deuteronomic vintage throughout the book refer often to "his servants the prophets" who, in the course of the history, have urged observance of the laws and threatened disaster as the consequence of non-observance (Jer 7:25; 25:4; 26:5; 29:19; 35:15; 44:4). The same expression occurs often in Dtr (e.g., 1 Kings 14:18; 15:29; 18:36; 2 Kings 9:7, 36; 10:10; 14:25), and this kind of retrospective allusion suggests that prophecy, or at least this kind of prophecy, is understood to be a thing of the past. The hypothesis of a prophetic *diadochē* beginning with Moses and ending with Jeremiah would also explain why the last chapter of the history (2 Kings 24:18–25:30) serves as the conclusion to Jeremiah's prophetic career (Jeremiah 52).

With the publication of the Deuteronomistic corpus in its several parts (law book, history, prophetic collection) we therefore have the following situation: (1) a document claiming immunity from later editorial intrusion containing a law and constitution that may not be altered; (2) a characterization of Moses as prophet (Deut 18:15–18; 34:10; cf. Hos 12:13) and, correspondingly, a redefinition of prophecy as Mosaic; (3) a collection of Mosaic-prophetic books, the exact contents of which are unknown,[4] ending with Jeremiah last of the line; (4) a history of the period subsequent to Moses which depicts it as one of religious infidelity followed by disaster, and therefore a period which in no sense could be regarded as normative. I would submit that we have here the essentials of canonicity, which I take to be the element of closure and the neutralization by redescription and redefinition of claims to new revelation.

One catalyst of the Deuteronomic movement, therefore, was the need to resolve conflicting claims to authority in the religious (and therefore also the political) sphere, which also involved the need to control the potentially disruptive phenomenon of free prophecy. Such claims to divinely warranted authority, to control of "the redemptive media," surface sooner or later in any religiously oriented society which has achieved a certain level of consolidation. We have seen some indications of such tension, involving prophets and scribal specialists in the law, during the last

decades of the Judean monarchy. Appeal to the authority of the past, and
to a great figure in the past like Moses, is of course a standard form of
validation by no means confined to Israel. W. G. Lambert spoke of a
Babylonian concept of canonicity, exemplified in the work of Berossus but
certainly operating much earlier, according to which all revealed knowledge was handed down once and for all to the antediluvian sages.[5] With
respect to Israel, contact with the Mesopotamian intellectual tradition during the Neo-Babylonian period may also have significantly influenced this
appeal to a normative antiquity and the production of a corpus of normative texts. A similar process was at work in the pseudepigraphal writings of
the Hellenistic period, attributed to such ancient worthies as Enoch, Shem,
and even Adam. These too were motivated by concern to validate a particular social world, and the *Weltanschauung* that went with it, over and
against other claims. A similar motivation informed the production of
Deuteronomy which is, after all, an earlier example of the same pseudepigraphal genre.

We recall at this point the arguments advanced in a previous chapter
for a much more extensive D editing of the history from Abraham to
Moses than the classical documentary hypothesis contemplated. We saw
that the focal points of this editorial activity were the promissory covenant
with Abraham in Genesis 15 and the account of the making, breaking and
remaking of the Horeb covenant in Exodus 19–34. We also saw that the
sequence of events in the Exodus passage reflects events in the religious
history of Israel. While the primary allusion is to the establishment of the
separatist cult of the Northern Kingdom recorded in 1 Kings 12, it would
also have been seen to refer to the failure of the Kingdom of Judah to
learn from the disaster of 722 B.C., a point explicitly made in the historian's
reflection on the fall of the Northern Kingdom (2 Kings 17:19–20). From
this history of spiritual failure was born the conviction that a new dispensation, and therefore a new covenant, was needed if Israel was to survive
in any shape or form. It is this conviction that comes to expression in the
announcement of a new covenant inscribed in the heart in a well-known D
passage in Jeremiah (31:31–34). The insistence in Deut 28:69 [29:1] that
the covenant in the land of Moab was quite distinct from the Horeb covenant also indicates the need for a new dispensation following on the experience of apostasy and failure. And in fact, where the compiler of the D
law invites his readers to reflect on this new dispensation, he uses language
reminiscent of the language in Jer 31:31–34:

For this commandment which I command you today is not too hard for
you, neither is it far off. It is not in heaven that you have to ask, who will
go up to heaven and bring it to us, so that we may obey it and put it into

practice? Neither is it beyond the sea that you have to ask, who will cross over the sea and bring it to us, that we may obey it and put it into practice? The word is very close to you; it is in your mouth and *in your heart,* so that you can put it into practice (Deut 30:11–14).

THE PRIESTLY HISTORY

In spite of its claim to finality, Deuteronomy came to form part of a much more extensive complex of narrative and law. The narrative span within Deuteronomy itself takes in only one day, the last day in the life of Moses, and the historical reminiscence which it contains extends the horizon back only as far as the giving of the law at Horeb. The P history, on the other hand, begins with the creation of the world and ends with the setting up of the wilderness sanctuary at Shiloh in Canaan and the distribution of territory to the tribes under the direction of Eleazar the priest and Joshua (Joshua 18–19). This last point about the extent of the P history is often contested, as we have seen, but the P character of the language at the beginning and end of the account of land distribution is, I believe, incontrovertible:

> The entire Israelite assembly *('ădat běnē-yiśrā'ēl)* came together at Shiloh, and there they set up the tent of meeting *('ohel mô'ēd);* the land was subdued *(nikběšāh)* before them (Josh 18:1).

> These are the inheritances *(hanněḥālôt)* which Eleazar the priest, Joshua, son of Nun, and the heads of ancestral houses *('ăbôt)* of the Israelite tribes distributed by lot at Shiloh in the presence of YHWH at the entrance of the tent of meeting. So they completed the distribution of the land (Josh 19:51).

That the ceremony was carried out at the entrance of the tent of meeting, with the Israelite *'ēdāh* in plenary session, arranged according to ancestral houses under the direction of clerical and lay leadership (the priest being mentioned first), is clearly a P construct. We find the same situation in the account of the allotment of land east of the Jordan, in a passage the P character of which has never been challenged (Num 32:1–42). The additional note that the land was subdued before them (see also Num 32:22, 29) recalls the P creation command to subdue the earth—using the same verb and the same substantive (Gen 1:28)—and thus elegantly rounds off the Priestly history.

A determination of the date of the P source requires us to distinguish between the legal material and the narrative, and between the main-line narrative or *Grundschrift* and additions made to it at different points. Advocacy of a pre-exilic date by Kaufmann, Hurwitz, and other Israeli scholars has, I believe, been vitiated by failure to make these necessary distinctions. That much of the ritual law originated in the pre-exilic period and was expanded over a considerable period of time as a deposit of priestly instruction can be accepted without difficulty. But if the primary structure of the narrative is as stated, it would seem to suggest that plans were being elaborated for the restoration of cult and cult community somewhat along the lines of the program in Ezekiel 40–48. This would imply a date somewhere between the destruction of Jerusalem in 587 and the rebuilding of the temple in 515 B.C.

In light of the little that we know of the situation of Jewish communities during this period, it seems most likely that the Priestly *Grundschrift* was composed in the Babylonian diaspora. With the exception of the chief priest of the Jerusalem temple and his deputy, who were executed by the Babylonians (2 Kings 25:18–21), most of the priestly class must have been deported together with others belonging to the higher strata of Judean society. The census list reported twice in Ezra-Nehemiah includes 4,289 priests—and several others whose lineage could not be verified—among those who returned from exile (Ezra 2:40–42, 61–63; Neh 7:39–42, 63–65). Needless to say, the historical value of this list has been questioned. But even if, as has been suggested, it represents the population of the entire province sometime in the fifth century rather than the first wave of immigrants, many of the lineages listed would have been of Babylonian origin. Other cult personnel, including some with expertise in the law, returned with Ezra, himself a priest (Ezra 7:7; 8:15, 24). Before setting out, Ezra was able to recruit several of these from "the place Casiphia," a cultic establishment under the regency of a certain Iddo, presumably a priest (Ezra 8:16–20). This was probably not the only center of worship and learning in the Babylonian diaspora, and it was in all probability at such centers that the work of scholarship and piety we know as P reached its mature formulation.

It is easier to speak of the combination of D and P as literary works than it is to identify the circumstances which precipitated the combination. The extension of the temporal horizon back to creation, taking in the early history of humanity, allowed the compiler to follow the pattern of Mesopotamian mythic thought in grounding institutions like sabbath and the covenant in antecedents of unimpeachable antiquity. It also permitted the introduction of a universalistic perspective of a kind notably absent from

Deuteronomy. Humanity as a whole is now accorded a specifically religious qualification and destiny (Gen 1:26–28), receives the first "torah" in its original and revised form (Gen 1:28–30; 9:1–7), thus adumbrating the sequence of events at Sinai/Horeb, and is the recipient of the first covenant (Gen 9:8–17). As for the conclusion of the narrative structure resulting from the combination, since the temple was now in existence and its cult in operation, the emphasis could be shifted to the Mosaic constitution as a whole, the observance of which both guaranteed the survival of Israel with its own distinctive character and satisfied the requirements of the Iranian overlord. This last point, generally overlooked in biblical scholarship on the Pentateuch, calls for further comment.

THE PENTATEUCH AS A CONSTITUTIONAL DOCUMENT

The combination of the P history with Deuteronomy, resulting in a narrative from creation to the death of Moses, and the concentration of all the legal material within this narrative framework, cannot be explained exclusively in terms of circumstances, exigencies, and events intrinsic to the Jewish community. After the capture of Babylon by Cyrus II in 539 B.C., Jews living in the province of Judah and the Babylonian diaspora came under Iranian rule which lasted for about two centuries, until the conquests of Alexander. During these two centuries the policy of the Achemenids was to respect the very diverse political and social systems obtaining throughout their vast empire, granting semi-autonomous status as long as edicts were obeyed and tribute paid.[6] The same policy held for local cults and cultures; and, in fact, archaeological excavation in provinces as diverse as Bactria, Babylon, Egypt, and Judah itself has revealed very little Persian impact on the material culture of the regions in question.[7]

One aspect of this imperial policy was the insistence on local self-definition inscribed primarily in a codified and standardized corpus of traditional law backed by the central government and its regional representatives. The Persians, it seems, had no uniform legal code of their own. The frequent allusions in the Behistun inscription of Darius I to the law (dāta) refer not to such a code but to the legal order established by that monarch after quelling disturbances throughout the empire during the previous two years (522–520 B.C.). In Babylon, therefore, the Neo-Babylonian laws would have remained in force, and continued interest in the Code of Hammurabi may be deduced from copies made in the sixth and fifth centuries. As for Egypt, the Demotic Chronicle (papyrus 215 of the Bibliothèque Nationale in Paris) informs us that, as an aspect of the reorganization of the empire, Darius I set up a commission of warriors, priests, and scribes to codify the traditional Egyptian laws, the final draft of which was written up in Aramaic and demotic Egyptian.[8] The composition of the commission charged with this task suggests an insistence on a legal system based on consensus. Since internal harmony was essential for the preservation of the *pax Persica* in the many and diverse ethnic groups in the empire, this is no more than we would expect.

The situation in the province of Judah (Yehud) and in the Jewish ethnic minority settled in Lower Mesopotamia, principally the Nippur region, is not so clear. It would nevertheless be reasonable to conclude from the uniformity of Persian policy, the situation of Judah within the same satrapy as Babylon, and its proximity to Egypt that something similar was going on there. Judah would certainly have felt the impact of Darius' reorganization of the empire during the early years of his reign. At that time the rebuilding of the temple destroyed by the Babylonians was completed, and a dominant elite, composed of leading Babylonian lineages and temple personnel, had begun to settle in the homeland with the support of the imperial authorities. While we have no external evidence comparable to the Demotic Chronicle, it is reasonable to suggest that these measures included a first attempt at assembling and codifying the different collections of law then in existence.

According to the biblical record Ezra arrived in the province in the seventh year of Artaxerxes, probably Artaxerxes I and therefore in the year 458 B.C., with a mandate to oversee the administration of "the law of your God and the law of the king," set up appropriate judicial procedures, and enforce penalties for nonobservance (Ezra 7). The law in question was not a new creation since it is assumed that it was known in the province (Ezra 7:25). Explicit references in Ezra-Nehemiah to laws and to practices observed in accordance with laws point unmistakably to Deuteronomy 12–26 supplemented with Priestly legislation, and therefore suggest that Ezra's mission represents a further phase in the consolidation of the legal tradition.[9] In this situation, also, it seems that the impetus came from outside the Jewish community. After the grave problems that faced Artaxerxes I in the early years of his reign, including a major uprising in Egypt supported by the Athenians, one which threatened all of the western provinces including Judah, the need for reorganization and consolidation was urgent. This critical situation provides the most plausible context for the decree addressed to Ezra from the imperial chancellory in Susa and the mission that it mandated.

The traditional view identifying Ezra's law with the legal content of the Pentateuch has been held by many scholars in the modern period, including Wellhausen. But several indications in Ezra-Nehemiah suggest that the final stage of formation came at a somewhat later time. The clearest of these is the observance of a day of repentance and fasting on the twenty-fourth rather than on the tenth of Tishri, as in the Priestly legislation (Neh

9:1; cf. Lev 16:29; 23:27–32; Num 29:7–11). Pointing in the same direction is the temple tax set at a third of a shekel in Neh 10:33–34 [10:32–33] rather than at half a shekel in P (Ex 30:11–16) and for some time thereafter (Mt 17:24; Josephus: *War* 7:218). Our best estimate of the situation, therefore, is that the Pentateuchal law in its final form represents a compromise between different interest groups with their own legal traditions worked out in several stages during the two centuries of Persian rule. As such, it was authorized by the imperial authorities as the law and constitution of the Jewish ethnos, and its implementation was backed by the same authorities. That it was combined with a narrative of founding events resulted from the Jewish community's need for a sense of identity and continuity with the past, though the omission of the conquest narrative was no doubt also dictated by a prudent regard for the political reality of subordination to a foreign power.

A further and final consideration concerns the quantitative preponderance of ritual law and its central position in the Pentateuch. There is ample evidence that Achemenid rulers favored local cult establishments and went to considerable pains to ensure that they operated smoothly. In his propagandistic statement following the fall of Babylon (the much-quoted Cyrus cylinder), Cyrus II took pride in having restored the cult of Marduk and returned other Babylonian deities to their former sanctuaries. In spite of his bad reputation in the classical sources, Cambyses is said to have restored to its former glory the national sanctuary at Sais and to have performed other acts of piety with respect to native Egyptian deities. According to the historian Diodorus, Darius was deified on account of his solicitude for Egyptian religion, and an inscription from Magnesia reports a stern rebuke addressed by him to the local Persian official Gadatas for having interfered with the privileges of the local cult center of Apollo. Also from Asia Minor, probably during the reign of Artaxerxes III, is the trilingual (Lycian, Greek, and Aramaic) Xanthos inscription authorizing the establishment of a sanctuary to the goddess Leto and granting land and tax-exempt status to its clergy. And, to take a final example, we have the letter of Hananiah to Jedoniah, a leader of the Jewish military colony on the island of Elephantine on the Upper Nile, reporting a firman of Darius II mandating the observance of a festival according to accepted Jewish norms.[10]

These examples of a standard Achemenid policy vis-à-vis local cults corroborate the measures reported in Ezra-Nehemiah, no doubt with considerable exaggeration, in favor of the Jerusalem temple, its cult and personnel. The motivation for this policy was not, of course, purely religious, though Achemenid rulers, with the possible exception of Xerxes, seem to have regarded foreign deities as patrons, and we note the insistence that sacrifices and prayers for the royal family be incorporated in the Jerusalem liturgy (Ezra 6:10). The small province of Judah belonged to the category of temple community well attested throughout the Achemenid empire. Political, social, and economic status in this type of organization involved participation in and support of the cult and its numerous dependents. This implied that the maintenance of the cult was seen from the official angle as an essential aspect of imperial control. At this point, therefore, imperial and inner-Jewish interests coincided, especially in the second century of Persian rule with the increasing influence and hegemony of the priesthood —hence the preponderant emphasis on cultic law and the central position in the Pentateuch of dispositions regarding the sanctuary, its personnel, and its operations.

One of the characteristics of a canonical text, by whatever play of circumstances it attained that status, is its capacity to generate commentary. In this respect the Pentateuch has been accorded in both Judaism and Christianity a relative rather than absolute position. In Judaism functional canonicity belongs also to the Mishnah and Gemarah, and perhaps to a lesser degree to the midrash and the work of the great *parshanim* of the Middle Ages; while in Christianity it has been interpreted from the standpoint of a new source of authority, that of the Christ event. But a canonical text is also by definition a text to which one must always return in the unavoidable, ongoing dialectic between tradition and situation. In this process, it is safe to say, no text has played a role comparable to that of the Pentateuch.

NOTES

1. *The Theory of Social and Economic Organization* (New York, 1964 [1922], 363–73.

2. *Ancient Judaism* (New York, 1952 [1917–19], 395.

3. David Noel Freedman, "The Law and the Prophets," *VTSup* 9 (1963) 250–65; "The Canon of the Old Testament," *IDBSup,* 130–36; "The Earliest Bible" in M. P. O'Connor and D. N. Freedman (eds.), *Backgrounds to the Bible* (Winona Lake, Ind., 1987), 29–37.

4. The synchronized reigns of northern and southern rulers in the titles of Hosea and Amos suggest a Deuteronom(ist)ic hand, and Amos 3:7 is certainly a gloss from the same source. Isa 36–39, with the exception of 38:9–20, corresponds to 2 Kings 18:13–20:19 but presents a rather different Isaiah from the author of the sayings in Isa 1–35.

5. W. G. Lambert, "Ancestors, Authors and Canonicity," *JCS* 11 (1957) 1–14; see also Francesca Rochberg-Halton, "Canonicity in Cuneiform Texts," *JCS* 36 (1984) 127–44.

6. See J. L. Myers, "Persia, Greece and Israel," *PEQ* 85 (1953) 13–15; Peter Frei in P. Frei and K. Koch, *Reichsidee und Reichsorganisation im Perserreich* (Freiburg & Göttingen, 1984), 8–11; Pierre Briant, "Pouvoir central et polycentrisme culturel dans l'Empire Achémenide. Quelques réflexions et suggestions," in Heleen Sancisi-Weerdenburg (ed.), *Achaemenid History I. Sources, Structures and Synthesis* (Leiden, 1987), 1–31.

7. For the situation in Judah, see Ephraim Stern, *The Material Culture of the Land of the Bible in the Persian Period (538–332 B.C.E.)* (Warminster, 1982), 336–37.

8. W. Spiegelberg, *Die sogenannte demotische Chronik des Pap. 215 der Bibliothèque Nationale zu Paris* (Leipzig, 1915), esp. 30–32; N. Reich, "The Codification of the Egyptian Laws by Darius and the Origin of the 'Demotic Chronicle,'" *Mizraim* 1 (1933) 178–85; J. Blenkinsopp, "The Mission of Udjahorresnet and Those of Ezra and Nehemiah," *JBL* 106 (1987) 409–21.

9. See J. Blenkinsopp, *Ezra-Nehemiah. A Commentary* (Philadelphia, 1988), 152–57.

10. This important and much-discussed text is No. 21 in A. Cowley, *Aramaic Papyri of the Fifth Century B.C.* (Oxford, 1923). It is discussed by B. Porten, *Archives from Elephantine: The Life of an Ancient Jewish Military Colony* (Berkeley & Los Angeles, 1968), 128–33, 280–82, 311–14 and, with respect to its possible relevance for the formation of the Pentateuch, by P. Grelot, "Études sur le 'Papyrus Pascal' d'Eléphantine," *VT* 4 (1954) 349–84; "Le Papyrus Pascal d'Eléphantine et le Problème du Pentateuque," *VT* 5 (1955) 250–65; "La dernière étape de la rédaction sacerdotale," *VT* 6 (1956) 174–89; "Le Papyrus Pascal d'Eléphantine: Essai de restauration," *VT* 17 (1967) 201–207.

ABBREVIATIONS

AB	*Anchor Bible*
ANET	James B. Pritchard (ed.), *Ancient Near Eastern Texts Relating to the Old Testament* (Princeton, 1950; 3rd ed. with supplement, 1978)
Ant	Josephus, *Jewish Antiquities*
Apion	Josephus, *Against Apion*
b	Babylonian Talmud
BAR	*Biblical Archaeology Review*
BASOR	*Bulletin of the American Schools of Oriental Research*
BB	Tractate Baba Batra
Bib	*Biblica*
BJRL	*Bulletin of the John Rylands Library*
BM	Tractate Baba Mezia
BN	*Biblische Notizen*
BO	*Bibliotheca Orientalis*
BR	*Bible Review*
BZ	*Biblische Zeitschrift*
CBQ	*Catholic Biblical Quarterly*
CJT	*Canadian Journal of Theology*
DBSup	*Dictionnaire de la Bible, Supplément*

DJD	*Discoveries in the Judaean Desert*
Dtr	Deuteronomistic History
EncJud	Roth, C. *et al.* (eds.), *Encyclopaedia Judaica.* 16 vols. New York, 1971–72.
Est Bib	*Estudios Biblicos*
ETL	*Ephemerides theologicae lovanienses*
EvT	*Evangelische Theologie*
HTR	*Harvard Theological Review*
HUCA	*Hebrew Union College Annual*
IDB	Buttrick, G. A., *et al.* (eds.), *The Interpreter's Dictionary of the Bible.* 4 vols. New York, 1962.
IDBSup	Crim, K. *et al.* (eds.), *The Interpreter's Dictionary of the Bible.* Supplementary vol. Nashville, 1976.
Int	*Interpretation*
JAOS	*Journal of the American Oriental Society*
JBL	*Journal of Biblical Literature*
JCS	*Journal of Cuneiform Studies*
JJS	*Journal of Jewish Studies*
JNES	*Journal of Near Eastern Studies*
JNSL	*Journal of Northwest Semitic Languages*
JQR	*Jewish Quarterly Review*
JSOT	*Journal for the Study of the Old Testament*
JSS	*Journal of Semitic Studies*
JTS	*Journal of Theological Studies*
KuD	*Kerygma und Dogma*
LB	*Linguistica Biblica*
LXX	Septuagint
M.	Mishnah
MT	Masoretic text
NRT	*Nouvelle Revue Théologique*
Or	*Orientalia*
OTS	*Oudtestamentische Studiën*
PEQ	*Palestine Exploration Quarterly*
PJB	*Palästinajahrbuch*
RB	*Revue Biblique*
REJ	*Revue des études juives*
RivB	*Rivista Biblica*
RQ	*Revue de Qumran*
RTP	*Revue de théologie et de philosophie*
SBT	*Studies in Biblical Theology*
StTh	*Studia Theologica*
ThRu	*Theologische Rundschau*
ThZ	*Theologische Zeitschrift*

TLZ	*Theologische Literaturzeitung*
TU	*Texte und Untersuchungen*
VT	*Vetus Testamentum*
VTSup	*Vetus Testamentum Supplements*
VuF	*Verkündigung und Forschung*
War	Josephus, *Jewish Wars*
ZAW	*Zeitschrift für die Alttestamentliche Wissenschaft*
ZDPV	*Zeitschrift des Deutschen Palästina-Vereins*
ZTK	*Zeitschrift für Theologie und Kirche*

BIBLIOGRAPHY

The bibliography is, for the most part, limited to works written in this century and to authors named in the text. Where available, an English translation is given, with the date of the original publication in brackets.

Ackroyd, P. R. "Hosea and Jacob," *VT* 13 (1963) 245–59.

Adler, W. "Berossus, Manetho and *1 Enoch* in the World Chronicle of Panodorus," *HTR* 76 (1983) 419–42.

Albright, W. F. "The Babylonian Matter in the Pre-Deuteronomic Privaeval History (JE) in Gen 1–11," *JBL* 58 (1939) 91–103.

———. "The Oracles of Balaam," *JBL* 63 (1944) 207–33.

———. *From the Stone Age to Christianity.* Garden City, N.Y., 1957 [1940].

———. *Yahweh and the Gods of Canaan.* New York, 1962.

———. "Jethro, Hobab and Reuel in Early Hebrew Tradition," *CBQ* 25 (1963) 1–11.

Alonso-Schökel, L. "Motivos sapienciales y de alianza en Gn 2–3," *Bib* 43 (1962) 295–316.

Alt, A. "The God of the Fathers," *Essays on Old Testament History and Religion.* Oxford, 1966 [1929] 3–77.

———. "The Origins of Israelite Law," *Essays on Old Testament History and Religion.* Oxford, 1966 [1934] 79–132.

Alter, R. *The Art of Biblical Narrative.* New York, 1981.

Anbar, M. "Genesis 15: A Conflation of Two Deuteronomic Narratives," *JBL* 101 (1982) 39–55.

Anderson, B. W. "From Analysis to Synthesis: The Interpretation of Genesis 1–11," *JBL* 97 (1978) 23–39.

Anderson, G. A. *Sacrifices and Offerings in Ancient Israel.* Atlanta, 1987.

Auerbach, E. *Moses.* Detroit, 1975 [1953].

Auffret, P. "The Literary Structure of Exodus 6. 2–8," *JSOT* 27 (1983) 46–54.

———. "Essay sur la structure littéraire d'Ex 14," *EstBib* 41 (1983) 53–82.

Auld, G. *Joshua, Moses and the Land. Tetrateuch—Pentateuch—Hexateuch in a Generation since 1938.* Edinburgh, 1980.

Baentsch, B. *Exodus-Leviticus-Numeri.* Göttingen, 1903.

Baltzer, K. *The Covenant Formulary.* Philadelphia, 1971 [1964].

Barr, J. "Philo of Byblos and His 'Phoenician History,' " *BJRL* 57 (1974) 17–68.

Barre, L. M. "The Riddle of the Flood Chronology," *JSOT* 41 (1988) 3–20.

Barthes, R. "The Struggle with the Angel: Textual Analysis of Genesis 32. 23–33," in R. Barthes *et al., Structural Analysis and Biblical Exegesis. Interpretational Essays.* Pittsburgh, 1974 [1971] 21–33.

Begrich, J. "Mabbūl. Eine exegetisch-lexikalische Studie," in Zimmerli, W. (ed.), *Gesammelte Studien zum Alten Testament.* Munich, 1964 [1928] 39–54.

Bentzen, A. *Introduction to the Old Testament.* Copenhagen, 1952 [1948].

Beyerlin, W. *Origins and History of the Oldest Sinaitic Traditions.* Philadelphia, 1965 [1961].

Bimson, J. J. *Redating the Exodus and Conquest.* Sheffield, 1981 (2nd ed).

Blenkinsopp, J. "The Structure of P," *CBQ* 38 (1976) 275–92.

———. *Prophecy and Canon.* Notre Dame, Ind., 1977.

———. "Abraham and the Righteous of Sodom," *JJS* 33 (1982) 119–32.

Bloom, H. and Rosenberg, D. *The Book of J.* New York, 1990.

Blum, E. *Die Komposition der Vätergeschichte.* Neukirchen-Vluyn, 1984.

———. *Studien zur Komposition des Pentateuch.* Berlin, 1990.

Boecker, H. J. *Law and the Administration of Justice in the Old Testament and the Ancient East.* Minneapolis, 1980 [1976].

Bork, F. "Zur Chronologie der biblischen Urgeschichte," *ZAW* 47 (1929) 206–22.

Bousset, D. W. "Das chronologische System der biblischen Geschichtsbücher," *ZAW* 20 (1900) 136–47.

Braülik, G. *Die Mittel deuteronomischer Rhetorik erhoben aus Deuteronomium 4. 1–40.* Rome, 1978.

———. "Die Abfolge der Gesetze in Deuteronomium 12–26 und der Dekalog," in Lohfink, N. (ed.), *Das Deuteronomium: Entstehung, Gestalt und Botschaft.* Louvain, 1985, 252–72.

Brekelmans, C. H. W. "Eléments deutéronomiques dans le Pentateuque," *Récherches Bibliques* 8 (1967) 77–91.

———. "Deuteronomy 5: Its Place and Function," in Lohfink, N. (ed.), *Das Deuteronomium: Entstehung, Gestalt und Botschaft.* Louvain, 1985, 164–73.

Bright, J. *A History of Israel.* Philadelphia, 1980 [1959].

Brueggemann, W. "The Kerygma of the Priestly Writers," *ZAW* 84 (1972) 397–414.

———. *The Vitality of Old Testament Traditions.* Atlanta, 1975.

Bryan, D. T. "A Reevaluation of Gen 4 and 5 in Light of Recent Studies in Genealogical Fluidity," *ZAW* 99 (1987) 180–88.

Buber, M. *Moses: The Revelation and the Covenant.* New York, 1958 [1952].

Budd, P. J. *Numbers.* Waco, Tex., 1984.

Budde, K. "Ellä toledoth," *ZAW* 34 (1914) 241–53.

———. "Noch einmal 'Ellä toledoth,' " *ZAW* 36 (1916) 1–7.

Burstein, S. M. *The Babyloniaka of Berossus.* Malibu, Calif., 1978.

Carmichael, C. M. *The Laws of Deuteronomy.* Ithaca, N.Y., 1974.

———. *Law and Narrative in the Bible: the Evidence of Deuteronomic Laws and the Decalogue.* Ithaca, N.Y., 1985.

Cassuto, U. *The Documentary Hypothesis and the Composition of the Pentateuch.* Jerusalem, 1961 [1941].

———. *A Commentary on the Book of Genesis.* 2 vols., Jerusalem, 1964 [1949].

———. *A Commentary on the Book of Exodus.* Jerusalem, 1983 [1951].

Cazelles, H. *Études sur le code l'alliance.* Paris, 1946.

———. "Les localisations de l'Exode et la critique littéraire," *RB* 62 (1955) 321–54.

———. "Pentateuque. IV. Le nouveau 'status quaestionis,' " *DBSup* 7 (1966), cols. 736–858.

———. *Introduction Critique à l'Ancien Testament.* Paris, 1973.

Childs, B. S. "Deuteronomic Formulae of the Exodus Tradition," *VTSup* 16 (1967) 30–39.

———. "A Traditio-historical Study of the Reed Sea Tradition," *VT* 20 (1970) 406–18.

———. *Exodus. A Commentary.* Philadelphia, 1974.

———. *Introduction to the Old Testament as Scripture.* Philadelphia, 1979.

Clark, W. M. "The Flood and the Structure of the Pre-Patriarchal History," *ZAW* 83 (1971) 184–211.

Clements, R. E. *Abraham and David. Genesis XV and its Meaning for Israelite Tradition.* London, 1967.

———. "Pentateuchal Problems" in Anderson, G. W. (ed.), *Tradition and Interpretation.* Oxford, 1979, 96–124.

Clines, D. J. A. *The Theme of the Pentateuch.* Sheffield, 1978.

———. "The Significance of the 'Sons of God' Episode (Genesis 6:1–4) in the Context of the 'Primaeval History' (Genesis 1–11)," *JSOT* 13 (1979) 33–46.

Coats, G. W. "The Traditio-historical Character of the Reed Sea Motif," *VT* 17 (1967) 253–65.

———. *Rebellion in the Wilderness: The Murmuring Motif in the Wilderness Traditions of the Old Testament.* Nashville, 1968.

———. "The Song of the Sea," *CBQ* 31 (1969) 1–17.

———. "The Wilderness Itinerary," *CBQ* 34 (1972) 135–52.

———. "The Joseph Story and Ancient Wisdom: A Reappraisal," *CBQ* 35 (1973) 285–97.

———. *From Canaan to Egypt.* Washington, D.C., 1976.

———. *Genesis. With an Introduction to Narrative Literature.* Grand Rapids, Mich., 1983.

———. *Moses. Heroic Man, Man of God.* Sheffield, 1988.

Cohn, R. L. "Narrative Structure and Canonical Perspective in Genesis," *JSOT* 25 (1983) 3–16.

Cross, F. M., Jr. "The Priestly Tabernacle," in Sandmel, S. (ed.), *Old Testament Issues,* New York, 1968, 39–67.

———. *Canaanite Myth and Hebrew Epic.* Cambridge, Mass., 1973.

Cross, F. M. and Freedman, D. N. *Studies in Ancient Yahwistic Poetry.* Baltimore, 1950.

Crüsemann, F. "Die Eigenständigkeit der Urgeschichte. Ein Beitrag zur Diskussion um den 'Jahwisten,' " in Jeremias, J. and Perlitt, L. (eds.), *Die Botschaft und die Boten. Festschrift für Hans Walter Wolff zum 70. Geburtstag.* Neukirchen-Vluyn, 1981, 11–29.

Cryer, F. H. "The Interrelationships of Gen. 5, 32; 11, 10–11 and the Chronology of the Flood (Gen. 6–9)," *Bib* 66 (1985) 241–61.

Culley, R. C. "An Approach to the Problem of Oral Tradition," *VT* 13 (1963) 113–25.

———. "Oral Tradition and Historicity," in Wevers, J. W. and Redford, D. B. (eds.), *Studies in the Ancient Palestinian World. Presented to Prof. F. V. Winnett on the occasion of his retirement 1 July 1971.* Toronto, 1972, 102–16.

———. *Studies in the Structure of Hebrew Narrative.* Philadelphia, 1976.

Daube, D. *Studies in Biblical Law.* Cambridge, 1947.

———. *The Exodus Pattern in the Bible.* London, 1963.

Davies, G. I. *The Way of the Wilderness. A Geographical Study of the Wilderness Itineraries in the Old Testament.* Cambridge, 1979.

———. "The Wilderness Itineraries and the Composition of the Pentateuch," *VT* 33 (1983) 1–13.

Donner, H. *Die literarische Gestalt der alttestamentlichen Josephgeschichte.* Heidelberg, 1976.

Douglas, M. *Purity and Danger.* London, 1966.

Drews, R. "The Babylonian Chronicles and Berossus," *Iraq* 37 (1975) 39–55.

Driver, S. R. *An Introduction to the Literature of the Old Testament.* Edinburgh, 1909 (8th ed.) [1897].

———. *The Book of Exodus.* Cambridge, 1911.

Dumermuth, F. "Moses' strahlendes Gesicht," *ThZ* 17 (1961) 240–48.

———. "Josua in Ex. xxxiii, 7–11," *ThZ* 19 (1963) 161–68.

Durham, J. I. *Exodus.* Waco, Tex., 1987.

Eagleton, T. *Criticism and Ideology. A Study in Marxist Literary Theory.* London, 1976.

Eissfeldt, O. "Biblos geneseōs," *Gott und die Götter. Festgabe für Erich Fascher zum 60. Geburtstag.* Tübingen, 1958, 31–40.

———. "Toledot," *TU* 77 (1961) 1–8.

———. *Die Genesis der Genesis.* Tübingen, 1961 [1958].

———. *The Old Testament. An Introduction.* Oxford, 1966 (3rd ed.) [1934].

Elliger, K. "Sinn und Ursprung der priesterschriftlichen Geschichtserzählung," *ZTK* 49 (1952) 121–43.

———. "Das Gesetz Leviticus 18," *ZAW* 67 (1955) 1–25.

Emerton, J. A. "Some False Clues in the Study of Gen. xiv," *VT* 21 (1971) 24–47.

———. "Some Problems in Genesis xxxviii," *VT* 25 (1975) 338–61.

———. "An examination of a recent structuralist interpretation of Genesis xxxviii," *VT* 26 (1976) 79–98.

———. "Judah and Tamar," *VT* 29 (1979) 403–15.

———. "The Origin of the Promise to the Patriarchs in the Older Sources of the Book of Genesis," *VT* 32 (1982) 14–32.

———. "An Examination of Some Attempts to Defend the Unity of the Flood Narrative in Genesis," *VT* 37 (1987) 401–20.

———. "The Priestly Writer in Genesis," *JTS* 39 (1988) 381–400.

Engnell, I. "Methodological Aspects of Old Testament Study," *VTSup* 7 (1960) 13–30.

———. *A Rigid Scrutiny.* Nashville, 1969.

Finkelstein, I. *The Archaeology of the Israelite Settlement.* Jerusalem, 1988.

Finkelstein, J. J. "The Antediluvian Kings: A University of California Tablet," *JCS* 17 (1963) 39–51.

———. "The Genealogy of the Hammurapi Dynasty," *JCS* 20 (1966) 95–118.

———. *The Ox that Gored*. Transactions of the American Philosophical Society, Vol. 71: Philadelphia, 1981.

Fishbane, M. *Text and Texture. Close Readings of Selected Biblical Texts*. New York, 1979.

———. *Biblical Interpretation in Ancient Israel*. Oxford, 1985.

Fohrer, G. *Uberlieferung und Geschichte des Exodus. Eine Analyse von Exodus 1–15*. Berlin, 1964.

———. *Introduction to the Old Testament*. Nashville & New York, 1968 [1965].

Fokkelman, J. P. *Narrative Art in Genesis: Specimens of Stylistic and Structural Analysis*. Amsterdam, 1975.

Frankena, R. "The Vassal Treaties of Esarhaddon and the dating of Deuteronomy," *OTS* 14 (1965) 122–54.

Freedman, D. N. "Archaic Forms in Early Hebrew Poetry," *ZAW* 72 (1960) 101–7.

———. "Pentateuch," *IDB* Vol. 3, New York, 1962, 711–27.

———. "The Law and the Prophets," *VTSup* 9 (1963) 250–65.

———. "Canon of the Old Testament," *IDBSup*. New York & Nashville, 1975, 130–36.

———. "The Earliest Bible," in O'Connor, M. P. and Freedman, D. N. (eds.), *Backgrounds to the Bible*. Winona Lake, Ind., 1987, 29–37.

Friedman, R. E. *The Exile and Biblical Narrative*. Chico, Calif., 1981.

———. "From Egypt to Egypt: Dtr[1] and Dtr[2]," in Halpern, B. and Levenson, J. D. (eds.), *Traditions in Transformation. Turning Points in Biblical Faith*. Winona Lake, Ind., 1981, 167–92.

———. "Sacred History and Theology: The Redaction of Torah," in Friedman, R. E. (ed.), *The Creation of Sacred Literature*. Berkeley, 1981, 25–34.

Fritz, V. *Israel in der Wüste. Traditionsgeschichtliche Untersuchung der Wüstenuberlieferung des Jahwisten*. Marburg, 1970.

Frye, N. *The Great Code. The Bible and Literature*. San Diego, Calif., 1982.

Frymer-Kensky, T. "The Atraḥasis Epic and its Significance for our Understanding of Genesis 1–9," *BA* 40 (1977) 147–55.

Fuller, R. C. *Alexander Geddes, 1737–1802. Pioneer of Biblical Criticism*. Sheffield, 1984.

Fuss, W. *Die deuteronomistische Pentateuchredaktion in Exodus 3–17*. Berlin, 1972.

Galbiati, E. *La Struttura letteraria dell'Esodo*. Milan, 1956.

Galling, K. "Das Gemeindegesetz in Deuteronomium 23," in *Festschrift für Alfred Bertholet*. Tübingen, 1950, 176–91.

Gemser, B. "The Importance of the Motive Clause in Old Testament Law," *VTSup* 1 (1953) 50–66.

Gerstenberger, E. *Wesen und Herkunft des "Apodiktischen Rechts."* Neukirchen-Vluyn, 1965.

Gese, H. "Bemerkungen zur Sinaitradition," *ZAW* 79 (1967) 137–54.

Goldin, J. *The Song at the Sea.* New Haven, 1971.

Gottwald, N. K. *The Tribes of Yahweh. A Sociology of the Religion of Liberated Israel 1250–1050 B.C.E.* New York, 1980.

Greenberg, M. "Another Look at Rachel's Theft of the Teraphim," *JBL* 81 (1962) 239–48.

———. "The Thematic Unity of Exodus III–XI," *Fourth World Congress of Jewish Studies. I.* Jerusalem, 1967, 151–59.

———. *Understanding Exodus.* New York, 1969.

———. "The Redaction of the Plague Narrative in Exodus," in Goedicke, H. (ed.), *The Ancient Near East.* Baltimore, 1971, 243–52.

Grelot, P. "Le Papyrus Pascal d'Eléphantine et le Problème du Pentateuque," *VT* 5 (1955) 250–65.

———. "La dernière étape de la rédaction sacerdotale," *VT* 6 (1956) 174–89.

Gressmann, H. *Mose und seine Zeit. Ein Kommentar zu den Mose-Sagen.* Göttingen, 1913.

Gunkel, H. *Genesis.* Göttingen, 1964 (6th ed) [1901].

Gunneweg, A. H. J. *Leviten und Priester. Hauptlinien der Traditionsbildung und Geschichte des israelitisch-jüdischen Kultpersonals.* Göttingen, 1965.

———. "Anmerkungen und Anfragen zur neueren Pentateuchforschung," *ThRu* 50 (1985) 107–31.

Halbe, J. *Das Privilegrecht Jahwes. Ex 34. 10–26: Gestalt und Wesen, Herkunft und Wirken in vordeuteronomischer Zeit.* Göttingen, 1975.

Hallo, W. W. "Antediluvian Cities," *JCS* 23 (1970) 57–67.

Haran, M. "The Nature of the ''Ohel Mô'edh' in Pentateuchal Sources," *JSS* 5 (1960) 50–65.

———. "Book-Scrolls in Israel in Pre-Exilic Times," *JJS* 33 (1982) 161–73.

———. "Book-Scrolls at the Beginning of the Second Temple Period. The Transition from Papyrus to Skins," *HUCA* 50 (1983) 111–22.

———. "The Shining of Moses' Face: A Case Study in Biblical and Ancient Near Eastern Iconography," in Barrick, W. Boyd and Spencer, J. R. (eds.), *In the Shelter of Elyon. Essays on Ancient Palestinian Life and Literature in Honor of G. W. Ahlström.* Sheffield, 1984, 159–73.

———. *Temples and Temple Service in Ancient Israel.* Winona Lake, Ind., 1985.

Hartman, T. C. "Some Thoughts on the Sumerian King List and Genesis 5 and 11B," *JBL* 91 (1972) 25–32.

Helyer, L. R. "The Separation of Abraham and Lot: Its Significance in the Patriarchal Narratives," *JSOT* 26 (1983) 77–88.

Hendel, R. S. "Of Demigods and the Deluge: Towards an Interpretation of Gen 6:1–4," *JBL* 106 (1987) 13–26.

Henry, M.-L. *Jahwist und Priesterschrift. Zwei Glaubenszeugnisse des Alten Testaments.* Stuttgart, 1960.

Hess, R. S. "The Genealogies of Genesis 1–11 and Comparative Literature," *Bib* 70 (1989) 241–54.

Hoftijzer, J. *Die Verheissungen an die drei Erzväter.* Leiden, 1956.

Hort, G. "The Plagues of Egypt," *ZAW* 69 (1957) 84–103.

Humbert, P. "Die literarische zweiheit des Priester-Codex in der Genesis," *ZAW* 58 (1940/1941) 30–57.

Hurwitz, A. "The Evidence of Language in Dating the Priestly Code," *RB* 81 (1974) 24–56.

Isbell, C. "The Structure of Exodus 1:1–14," in Clines, D. J. A. *et al.* (eds.), *Art and Meaning. Rhetoric in Biblical Literature.* Sheffield, 1982.

Jackson, B. S. *Essays in Jewish and Comparative Legal History.* London, 1975.

Jacob, B. *Das Erste Buch der Torah, Genesis.* Berlin, 1934.

Jacobsen, T. *The Sumerian King List.* Chicago, 1939.

———. "The Eridu Genesis," *JBL* 100 (1981) 513–29.

Jacoby, F. *Die Fragmente der Griechischen Historiker. Erster Teil A: Genealogie und Mythographie.* Leiden, 1957 (2nd ed.) [1923].

Jenkins, A. K. "A Great Name: Genesis 12:2 and the Editing of the Pentateuch," *JSOT* 10 (1978) 41–57.

Jepsen, A. "Zur Chronologie des Priesterkodex," *ZAW* 47 (1929) 251–55.

Johnstone, W. "Reactivating the Chronicles Analogy in Pentateuchal Studies, with special reference to the Sinai pericope in Exodus," *ZAW* 99 (1987) 16–37.

———. "The Decalogue and the Redaction of the Sinai Pericope in Exodus," *ZAW* 100 (1988) 361–85.

Kaufmann, Y. "Der Kalender und das Alter des Priesterkodex," *VT* 4 (1954) 307–13.

———. *The Religion of Israel: From its Beginnings to the Babylonian Exile.* New York, 1960. Translated and abridged by M. Greenberg.

Kellermann, D. *Die Priesterschrift von Numeri 1,1 bis 10,10 literarkritisch und traditionsgeschichtlich untersucht.* Berlin, 1970.

Kikawada, I. M. "The Shape of Genesis 11:1–9," in Jackson, J. J. and Kessler, M. (eds.), *Rhetorical Criticism. Essays in Honor of James Muilenburg.* Pittsburgh, 1974, 19–31.

Kikawada, I. M. and Quinn, A. *Before Abraham Was.* Nashville, 1985.

Kilian, R. *Literarkritische und formgeschichtliche Untersuchung des Heiligkeits-gesetzes.* Bonn, 1963.

———. *Die Vorpriesterlichen Abrahams-Uberlieferungen literarkritisch und tradi-tionsgeschichtlich untersucht.* Bonn, 1966.

Klein, R. W. "Archaic Chronologies and the Textual History of the Old Testa-ment," *HTR* 67 (1974) 255–63.

Knight, D. A. "The Pentateuch," in Knight, D. A. and Tucker, G. M. (eds.), *The Hebrew Bible and its Modern Interpreters.* Chico, Calif., 1985, 263–96.

Koch, K. "Die Eigenart der priesterschriftlichen Sinaigesetzgebung," *ZTK* 55 (1958) 36–51.

———. *Die Priesterschrift von Exodus 25 bis Leviticus 16: Eine überlieferungs-geschichtliche und literarkritische Untersuchung.* Göttingen, 1959.

Kraeling, E. G. "The Significance and Origin of Gen. 6:1–4," *JNES* 6 (1947) 193–208.

Kraus, H.-J. *Geschichte der historisch-kritischen Erforschung des Alten Testaments.* Neukirchen-Vluyn, 1969 [1956].

Külling, S. R. *Zur Datierung der 'Genesis P-Stücke,' namentlich des Kapitels Gene-sis XVII.* Kampen, 1964.

Kutsch, E. *Verheissung und Gesetz.* Berlin, 1973.

Lambert, W. G. "Ancestors, Authors and Canonicity," *JCS* 11 (1957) 1–14.

———. "New Light on the Babylonian Flood," *JSS* 5 (1960) 113–23.

———. "A New Look at the Babylonian Background of Genesis," *JTS* 16 (1965) 287–300.

———. "Berossus and Babylonian Eschatology," *Iraq* 38 (1976) 171–73.

Lambert, W. G. and Millard, A. R. *ATRA-ḤASĪS: The Babylonian Story of the Flood.* Oxford, 1969.

Lambert, W. G. and Walcot, P. "A New Babylonian Theogony and Hesiod," *Kadmos* 4 (1965) 64–72.

Larsson, G. *The Secret System. A Study in the Chronology of the Old Testament.* Leiden, 1973.

———. "The Chronology of the Pentateuch: A Comparison of the MT and LXX," *JBL* 102 (1983) 401–9.

Lehmann, M. R. "Abraham's Purchase of Machpelah and Hittite Law," *BASOR* 129 (1953) 15–18.

Lemche, N. P. "The Chronology in the Story of the Flood," *JSOT* 18 (1980) 52–62.

Levenson, J. D. "Who Inserted the Book of the Torah?", *HTR* 68 (1975) 208–33.

———. "The Theologies of Commandment in Biblical Israel," *HTR* 73 (1980) 17–33.

Levine, B. A. *In the Presence of the Lord. A Study of Cult and Some Cultic Terms in Ancient Israel.* Leiden, 1974.

L'Hour, J. "Une législation criminelle dans le Deutéronome," *Bib* 44 (1963) 1–28.

Lods, A. "Un Précurseur allemand de Jean Astruc: Henning Bernhard Witter," *ZAW* 43 (1925) 134–35.

Loewenstamm, S. E. "The Divine Grants of Land to the Patriarchs," *JAOS* 91 (1971) 509–10.

Lohfink, N. "Darstellung und Theologie in Dtn 1,6–3,29," *Bib* 41 (1960) 105–34.

———. "Der Bundesschluss im Land Moab. Redaktionsgeschichtliches zu Dt. 28,69–32,47," *BZ* 6 (1962) 32–56.

———. *Das Hauptgebot. Eine Untersuchung literarischer Einleitungsfragen zu Dtn 5–11*. Rome, 1963.

———. "Die Bundesurkunde des Königs Josias (2 Kg. 22)," *Bib* 44 (1963) 261–88, 461–98.

———. *Die Landverheissung als Eid. Eine Studie zu Gn 15*. Stuttgart, 1967.

———. "Die These vom 'deuteronomistischen' Dekaloganfang—ein fragwürdiges Ergebnis atomistischer Sprachstatistik," in Braulik, G. (ed.), *Studien zum Pentateuch. Walter Kornfeld zum 60. Geburtstag*. Basle, 1977, 99–109.

———. "Zur deuteronomischen Zentralisationsformel," *Bib* 65 (1984) 297–329.

Long, B. O. "Recent Field Studies in Oral Literature and their Bearing on Old Testament Criticism," *VT* 26 (1976) 187–98.

Lopez, F. G. *Analyse littéraire de Deutéronome V–XI*. Jerusalem, 1978.

McBride, S. D. "Polity of the Covenant People: the Book of Deuteronomy," *Int* 41 (1987) 229–44.

McCarthy, D. J. *Treaty and Covenant*. Rome, 1978 [1963].

———. *Old Testament Covenant. A Survey of Current Opinions*. Oxford, 1972.

McEvenue, S. E. *The Narrative Style of the Priestly Writer*. Rome, 1971.

McKane, W. *Studies in the Patriarchal Narratives*. Edinburgh, 1979.

McKay, J. W. "Exodus XXIII 1–3, 6–8: A Decalogue for the Administration of Justice in the City Gate," *VT* 21 (1971) 311–25.

Magonet, J. "The Korah Rebellion," *JSOT* 24 (1982) 3–25.

———. "The Rhetoric of God: Exodus 6. 2–8," *JSOT* 27 (1983) 56–67, 69–74.

Malamat, A. "King Lists of the Old Babylonian Period and Biblical Genealogies," *JAOS* 88 (1968) 163–73.

Mayes, A. D. H. *Deuteronomy*. Greenwood, S.C., 1979.

———. "Deuteronomy 4 and the Literary Criticism of Deuteronomy," *JBL* 100 (1981) 23–51.

Meinhold, A. "Die Gattung der Josephsgeschichte und des Estherbuches: Diasporanovellen II," *ZAW* 88 (1976) 72–93.

Mendenhall, G. E. *Law and Covenant in Israel and the Ancient Near East*. Pittsburgh, 1955.

———. "The Hebrew Conquest of Palestine," *BA* 25 (1962) 66–87.

————. "The Shady Side of Wisdom: The Date and Purpose of Genesis 3," in Bream, H. N. *et al.* (eds.), *A Light Unto My Path. Studies in Honor of Jacob M. Myers.* Philadelphia, 1974, 319–34.

Merendino, R. P. *Das deuteronomische Gesetz. Eine literarkritische gattungs- und überlieferungsgeschichtliche Untersuchung.* Bonn, 1969.

Meyer, E. *Die Entstehung des Judentums. Eine historische Untersuchung.* Halle, 1896.

————. *Die Israeliten und ihre Nachbarstämme. Alttestamentliche Untersuchungen.* Halle, 1906.

Milgrom, J. *Cult and Conscience. The* Asham *and the Priestly Doctrine of Repentance.* Leiden, 1976.

————. *Studies in Cultic Theology and Terminology.* Leiden, 1983.

Millard, A. R. and Wiseman, D. J. (eds.), *Essays on the Patriarchal Narratives* Leicester, 1980.

Miller, J. M. "The Descendants of Cain: Notes on Genesis 4," *ZAW* 86 (1974) 164–74.

Miller, P. D. *Genesis 1–11: Studies in Structure and Theme.* Sheffield, 1978.

————. " 'Moses my servant': The Deuteronomic Portrait of Moses," *Int* 41 (1987) 245–55.

Mittmann, S. *Deuteronomium 1,1–6,3: literarkritisch und traditionsgeschichtlich untersucht.* Berlin, 1975.

Moberley, R. W. L. *At the Mountain of God.* Sheffield, 1983.

Möhlenbrink, K. "Josua im Pentateuch," *ZAW* 59 (1942/43) 14–58.

Moran, W. L. "A Kingdom of Priests," in McKenzie, J. L. (ed.), *The Bible in Current Catholic Thought.* New York, 1962, 7–20.

Morgenstern, J. "The Mythological Background of Psalm 82," *HUCA* 14 (1939) 93–94.

————. "The Book of the Covenant," *HUCA* 33 (1962) 59–105.

Mowinckel, S. *Le Décalogue.* Paris, 1927.

————. *Tetrateuch-Pentateuch-Hexateuch. Die Berichte über die Landnahme in den drei altisraelitischen Geschichtswerken.* Berlin, 1964.

Muilenburg, J. "The Form and Structure of the Covenantal Formulations," *VT* 9 (1959) 347–65.

Muller, H-P. "Das Motiv für die Sindflut," *ZAW* 97 (1985) 295–316.

Murtonen, A. "On the Chronology of the Old Testament," *StTh* 8 (1955) 133–37.

Nelson, R. D. *The Double Redaction of the Deuteronomistic History.* Sheffield, 1981.

Nicholson, E. W. *Deuteronomy and Tradition.* Philadelphia, 1967.

————. *Exodus, and Sinai in History and Tradition.* Oxford, 1973.

————. "The Decalogue as the Direct Address of God," *VT* 27 (1977) 422–33.

——. "The Covenant Ritual in Exodus xxiv 3–8," *VT* 32 (1982) 74–86.

——. *God and His People. Covenant and Theology in the Old Testament.* Oxford, 1986.

Nielsen, E. *Oral Tradition.* London, 1954.

——. *The Ten Commandments in New Perspective. A traditio-historical approach.* London, 1968 [1965].

North, C. R. "Pentateuchal Criticism," in Rowley, H. H. (ed.), *The Old Testament and Modern Study.* Oxford, 1951, 48–83.

Noth, M. "Der Wallfahrtsweg zum Sinai (Nu 33)," *PJB* 36 (1940) 5–28.

——. "Der Beitrag der Archäologie zur Geschichte Israels," *VTSup* 7 (1960) 262–82.

——. *Exodus. A Commentary.* Philadelphia, 1962 [1959].

——. *Numbers. A Commentary.* Philadelphia, 1968 [1966].

——. *The Laws in the Pentateuch and Other Essays.* New York, 1966 [1957].

——. *A History of Pentateuchal Traditions.* Englewood Cliffs, N.J., 1972 [1948].

——. *The Deuteronomistic History.* Sheffield, 1981 *(=Uberlieferungsgeschichtliche Studien,* 1–110. Tübingen, 1957 [1943]).

Oded, B. "The Table of the Nations (Genesis 10): A Socio-Cultural Approach," *ZAW* 98 (1986) 14–31.

Oden, R. A. "Philo of Byblos and Hellenistic Historiography," *PEQ* 110 (1978) 115–26.

——. "Divine Aspirations in Atrahasis and in Genesis 1–11," *ZAW* 93 (1981) 197–216.

Orlinsky, H. "Whither Biblical Research?", *JBL* 90 (1971) 1–14.

Osswald, E. *Das Bild des Mose.* Berlin, 1962.

Otto, E. "Stehen wir vor einem Umbruch in der Pentateuchkritik?", in Schmidt, W. H. (ed.), *Verkündigung und Forschung. Beiträge zur Evangelischen Theologie.* Munich, 1977, 82–97.

Patai, R. *Man and Temple in Ancient Jewish Myth and Ritual.* New York, 1967 [1947].

Patrick, D. "The Covenant Code Source," *VT* 27 (1977) 145–57.

Paul, S. M. *Studies in the Book of the Covenant in the Light of Cuneiform and Biblical Law.* Leiden, 1970.

Pearson, L. *Early Ionian Historians.* Oxford, 1939.

Peckham, B. *The Composition of the Deuteronomistic History.* Atlanta, 1985.

Pedersen, J. "Passahfest und Passahlegende," *ZAW* 52 (1934) 161–75.

Perlitt, L. *Vatke und Wellhausen.* Berlin, 1965.

——. *Bundestheologie im Alten Testament.* Neukirchen-Vluyn, 1969.

Petersen, D. L. "The Yahwist on the Flood," *VT* 26 (1976) 438–46.

———. "Genesis 6:1–4, Yahweh and the Organization of the Cosmos," *JSOT* 13 (1979) 47–64.

Pettinato, G. "Die Bestrafung des Menschengeschlechts durch die Sindflut," *Or* 47 (1968) 165–200.

Pfeiffer, R. H. "A Non-Israelite Source of the Book of Genesis," *ZAW* 48 (1930) 66–73.

———. *Introduction to the Old Testament.* New York, 1963 [1941].

Phillips, A. *Ancient Israel's Criminal Law. A New Approach to the Decalogue.* Oxford, 1970.

———. "The Decalogue—Ancient Israel's Criminal Law," *JJS* 34 (1983) 1–20.

———. "A Fresh Look at the Sinai Pericope," *VT* 34 (1984) 39–52, 282–94.

Procksch, O. *Das nordhebräische Sagenbuch. Die Elohimquelle.* Leipzig, 1906.

de Pury, A. *Promesse divine et légende cultuelle dans le cycle de Jacob: Genèse 28 et les traditions patriarcales.* Paris, 1975.

von Rad, G. *Die Priesterschrift im Hexateuch literarisch untersucht und theologisch gewertet.* Stuttgart, 1934.

———. *Studies in Deuteronomy.* London, 1953 [1948].

———. *Genesis. A Commentary.* Philadelphia, 1961 [1956].

———. *Old Testament Theology. Vol. I.* New York, 1962 [1957].

———. "The Form-Critical Problem of the Hexateuch," in *The Problem of the Hexateuch and Other Essays.* New York, 1966 [1938], 1–78.

———. "Beobachtungen an der Moseerzählung Exodus 1–14," *EvT* 31 (1971) 579–88.

Radday, Y. T. "Chiasm in Tora," *LB* 19 (1972) 12–23.

Radday Y. T. and Shore, H. *An Authorship Study in Computer-Assisted Linguistics.* Rome, 1985.

Rand, H. "Moses at the Inn: New Light on an Obscure Text," *Dor leDor* 14 (1985) 31–38.

Redford, D. B. *A Study of the Biblical Story of Joseph.* Leiden, 1970.

Renaud, B. "La figure prophetique de Moïse en Exode 3,1–4,17," *RB* 93 (1986) 510–34.

Rendtorff, R. *Die Gesetze in der Priesterschrift. Eine gattungsgeschichtliche Untersuchung.* Göttingen, 1963 [1954].

———. "Genesis 8,21 und die Urgeschichte des Jahwisten," in *Gesammelte Studien zum Alten Testament.* Munich, 1975, 188–97 (=*KuD* 7 [1961] 69–78).

———. *Die überlieferungsgeschichtliche Problem des Pentateuch.* Berlin, 1977.

———. "Pentateuchal Studies on the Move," *JSOT* 3 (1977) 2–10, 43–45 *(=VTSup* 28 [1975] 158–66).

———. *The Old Testament. An Introduction.* London, 1985 [1983].

———. "Between historical criticism and holistic interpretation: new trends in Old Testament exegesis," *VTSup* 40 (1987) 298–303.

———. " 'Covenant' as a Structuring Concept in Genesis and Exodus," *JBL* 108 (1989) 385–93.

Reventlow, H. Graf, *Das Heiligkeitsgesetz formgeschichtlich untersucht.* Neukirchen-Vluyn, 1961.

Robinson, R. B. "Literary Functions of the Genealogies of Genesis," *CBQ* 48 (1986) 595–608.

Rofé, A. "The Covenant in the Land of Moab (Dt 28,69–30,20)," in Lohfink, N. (ed.), *Das Deuteronomium. Entstehung, Gestalt und Botschaft.* Louvain, 1985, 310–20.

Rogerson, J. *Old Testament Criticism in the Nineteenth Century. England and Germany.* London, 1984.

Rose, M. *Deuteronomist und Jahwist: Untersuchungen zu den Berührungspunkten beider Literaturwerke.* Zurich, 1981.

———. "La Croissance du Corpus Historiographique de la Bible—Une Proposition," *RTP* 118 (1986) 217–36.

Rost, L. *Das kleine Credo und andere Studien zum Alten Testament.* Heidelberg, 1965.

Roth, J. "Thèmes majeurs de la tradition sacerdotale dans le Pentateuque," *NRT* 90 (1958) 696–721.

Rowley, H. H. *The Growth of the Old Testament.* London, 1950.

Rudolph, W. *Der 'Elohist' von Exodus bis Joshua.* Berlin, 1938.

Rudolph, W. and Volz, P. *Der Elohist als Erzähler. Ein Irrweg der Pentateuchkritik? an der Genesis erläutert.* Berlin, 1933.

Sandmel, S. "The Haggada within Scripture," *JBL* 80 (1961) 105–22.

Sarna, N. *Understanding Genesis.* New York, 1966.

Sasson, J. M. "The 'Tower of Babel' as a Clue to the Redactional Structuring of the Primeval History [Gen. 1–11:9]," in Rendsburg, G. *et al.* (eds.), *The Bible World. Essays in Honor of Cyrus H. Gordon.* New York, 1980, 211–19.

Scharbert, J. "Der Sinn der Toledot-Formel in der Priesterschrift," in Stoebe, H. J. (ed.), *Wort-Gebot-Glaube. Beiträge zur Theologie des Alten Testaments.* Zurich, 1970, 45–56.

Schmid, H. H. *Der sogenannte Jahwist. Beobachtungen und Fragen zur Pentateuchforschung.* Zurich, 1976.

———. "In search of new approaches to Pentateuchal research," *JSOT* 3 (1977) 33–42.

Schmid, H. *Mose. Uberlieferung und Geschicht.* Berlin, 1968.

Schmidt, L. "Uberlegungen zum Jahwisten," *EvT* 37 (1977) 230–47.

———. *Literarische Studien zur Josephgeschichte.* Berlin, 1986.

Schmidt, W. H. *Die Schöpfungsgeschichte der Priesterschrift.* Neukirchen-Vluyn, 1964.

———. "Uberlieferungsgeschichtliche Erwägungen zur Komposition des Dekalogs," *VTS* 22 (1971) 201–20.

———. "Ein Theologe in salomonischer Zeit? Plädoyer für den Jahwisten," *BZ* 25 (1981) 82–102.

Schmitt, H.-C. *Die nichtpriesterliche Josephgeschichte.* Berlin, 1980.

———. "Redaktion des Pentateuch im Geiste der Prophetie. Beobachtungen zur Bedeutung der 'Glaubens'—Thematik innerhalb der Theologie des Pentateuch," *VT* 32 (1982) 170–89.

Schwarzbaum, H. "The Overcrowded Earth," *Numen* 4 (1957) 59–74.

Seebass, H. "The Joseph Story. Genesis 48 and the Canonical Process," *JSOT* 35 (1986) 29–43.

Segal, M. H. "The Composition of the Pentateuch: A Fresh Examination," *Scripta Hierosolymitana* 8 (1961) 68–114.

Seitz, G. *Redaktionsgeschichtliche Studien zum Deuteronomium.* Stuttgart, 1971.

Simpson, C. A. *The Early Traditions of Israel. A Critical Analysis of the Pre-Deuteronomistic Narrative of the Hexateuch.* Oxford, 1948.

Ska, J. L. *Le passage de la mer: étude de la construction, du style et de la symbolique d'Ex 14, 1–31.* Rome, 1986.

Skinner, J. *A Critical and Exegetical Commentary on Genesis.* Edinburgh, 1930 [1910].

Smend, R. *Die Erzählung des Hexateuch. Auf ihre Quellen untersucht.* Berlin, 1912.

Sonsino, R. *Motive Clauses in Hebrew Law: Biblical Forms and Near Eastern Parallels.* Chico, Calif., 1980.

Speiser, E. A. *Genesis.* Garden City, N.Y., 1964.

Stamm, J. J. and Andrew, M. E. *The Ten Commandments in Recent Research.* London, 1967.

Stenring, K. *The Enclosed Garden.* Stockholm, 1966.

Tengström, S. *Die Hexateucherzählung. Eine literaturgeschichtliche Studie.* Lund, 1976.

———. *Die Toledotformel und die literarische Structur der priesterlichen Erweiterungsschicht im Pentateuch.* Lund, 1981.

Thompson, R. J. *Moses and the Law in a Century of Criticism since Graf.* Leiden, 1970.

Thompson, T. L. *The Historicity of the Patriarchal Narratives.* Berlin, 1974.

———. *The Origin Tradition of Ancient Israel. I. The Literary Formation of Genesis and Exodus 1–23.* Sheffield, 1987.

Tigay, J. "An Empirical Basis for the Documentary Hypothesis," *JBL* 94 (1975) 329–42.

Tucker, G. M. "The Legal Background of Genesis 23," *JBL* 85 (1966) 77–84.

Van Groningen, B. A. *In the Grip of the Past.* Leiden, 1953.

Van Seters, J. "Confessional Reformulation in the Exilic Period," *VT* 22 (1972) 448–59.

———. *Abraham in History and Tradition.* New Haven, 1975.

———. "Recent Studies on the Pentateuch: A Crisis in Method," *JAOS* 99 (1979) 663–67.

———. *In Search of History. Historiography in the Ancient World and the Origins of Biblical History.* New Haven, 1983.

———. "Joshua 24 and the Problem of Tradition in the Old Testament," in Barrick, W. Boyd and Spencer, J. R. (eds.), *In the Shelter of Elyon. Essays on Ancient Palestinian Life and Literature in Honor of G. W. Ahlström.* Sheffield, 1984, 139–58.

———. "The Plagues of Egypt: Ancient Tradition or Literary Invention?", *ZAW* 98 (1986) 31–39.

———. "The Primeval Histories of Greece and Israel Compared," *ZAW* 100 (1988) 1–22.

Vansina, J. *Oral Tradition. A Study in Historical Methodology.* London, 1965 [1961].

de Vaux, R. *La Genèse* (2nd ed. Paris, 1962).

———. *The Bible and the Ancient Near East.* Garden City, N.Y., 1971.

Vawter, B. *On Genesis. A New Reading.* Garden City, N.Y., 1977.

Vink, J. G. *The Date and Origin of the Priestly Code in the Old Testament.* Leiden, 1969.

Vorländer, H. *Die Entstehungszeit des jehowistischen Geschichtswerkes.* Frankfurt, 1978.

Vriezen, T. C. "Exodusstudien, Exodus 1," *VT* 17 (1967) 334–53.

———. "The Exegesis of Exodus xxiv 9–11," *OTS* 17 (1972) 100–33.

Wagner, N. E. "Pentateuchal Criticism: No Clear Future," *CJT* 13 (1967) 225–32.

———. "Abraham and David?" in Wevers, J. W. and Redford, D. B. (eds.), *Studies on the Ancient Palestinian World.* Toronto, 1972, 117–40.

Wagner, V. "Zur Existenz des sogenannten 'Heiligkeitsgesetzes'," *ZAW* 86 (1974) 307–16.

Walcot, P. *Hesiod and the Near East.* Cardiff, 1966.

Warner, S. M. "The Patriarchs and Extra-Biblical Sources," *JSOT* 2 (1977) 50–61.

Weimar, P. "Die Toledot-Formel in der priesterschriftlichen Geschichtsdarstellung," *BZ* 18 (1974) 65–93.

———. *Untersuchungen zur Redaktionsgeschichte des Pentateuch.* Berlin, 1977.

———. "Sinai und Schöpfung. Komposition und Theologie der priesterschriftlichen Sinaigeschichte," *RB* 95 (1988) 337–85.

Weinfeld, M. "The Covenant of Grant in the Old Testament and in the Ancient Near East," *JAOS* 90 (1970) 184–203.

———. *Deuteronomy and the Deuteronomic School.* Oxford, 1972.

———. "The Decalogue: Its Significance, Uniqueness and Place in Israel's Tradition," in Firmage, E. B. *et al.* (eds.), *Religion and Law: Biblical, Judaic and Islamic Perspectives.* Winona Lake, Ind., 1990, 3–47.

Wellhausen, J. *Die Composition des Hexateuchs und der historischen Bücher des Alten Testaments.* Berlin, 1899 (3rd ed.) [1866].

———. *Prolegomena to the History of Israel.* New York, 1957 [1883].

Wenham, G. J. "The Coherence of the Flood Narrative," *VT* 28 (1978) 336–48.

———. *Genesis 1–15.* Waco, Tex., 1987.

———. "Genesis: An Authorship Study and Current Pentateuchal Criticism," *JSOT* 42 (1988) 3–18.

West, M. L. *The Hesiodic Catalogue of Women. Its Nature, Structure and Origins.* Oxford, 1985.

———. *Hesiod. Theogony and Works and Days.* Oxford, 1988.

Westermann, C. *The Promises to the Fathers: Studies on the Patriarchal Narratives.* Philadelphia, 1980.

———. *Genesis. A Commentary.* 3 vols., Minneapolis, 1984–86 [1974, 1981, 1982].

Whybray, R. N. "The Joseph Story and Pentateuchal Criticism," *VT* 18 (1968) 522–28.

———. *The Making of the Pentateuch. A Methodological Study.* Sheffield, 1987.

Wiesenberg, E. "The Jubilee of Jubilees," *RQ* 3 (1961) 3–40.

Wildberger, H. *Jahwes Eigentumsvolk.* Zurich, 1960.

Wilson, R. R. "The Old Testament Genealogies in Recent Research," *JBL* 94 (1975) 169–89.

———. *Genealogy and History in the Biblical World.* New Haven & London, 1977.

———. "Between 'Azel' and 'Azel': Interpreting the Biblical Genealogies," *BA* 42 (1979) 11–22.

Winnett, F. V. *The Mosaic Tradition.* Toronto, 1949.

———. "Re-examining the foundations," *JBL* 84 (1965) 1–19.

Wolff, H. W. "Das Kerygma des deuteronomistischen Geschichtswerks," *ZAW* 73 (1961) 171–86 (= *Gesammelte Studien zum Alten Testament.* Munich, 1964, 308–324).

———. "The Kerygma of the Yahwist," *Int* 20 (1966) 131–58 [1964].

Zenger, E. *Die Sinaitheophanie. Untersuchungen zum jahwistischen und elohistischen Geschichtswerk.* Würzburg, 1971.

———. *Gottes Bogen in den Wolken. Untersuchungen zu Komposition und Theologie der priesterschriftlichen Urgeschichte.* Stuttgart, 1983.

Zevit, Z. "The Priestly Redaction and Interpretation of the Plague Narrative in Exodus," *JQR* 66 (1976) 193–211.

Zimmerli, W. "Sinaibund und Abrahambund. Ein Beitrag zum Verständnis der Priesterschrift," *ThZ* 16 (1960) 266–88.

SUBJECT INDEX

Author Index